Wounded Shepherd

Wounded Shepherd

Pope Francis and His Struggle to Convert the Catholic Church

Austen Ivereigh

HENRY HOLT AND COMPANY   NEW YORK

Henry Holt and Company
Publishers since 1866
120 Broadway
New York, NY 10271
www.henryholt.com

Henry Holt® and 𝕞® are registered trademarks of Macmillan Publishing Group, LLC.

Library of Congress Cataloging-in-Publication Data

Names: Ivereigh, Austen, author.
Title: Wounded shepherd : Pope Francis and his struggle to convert the
    Catholic Church / Austen Ivereigh.
Description: First edition. | New York : Henry Holt and Company, 2019. |
    Includes bibliographical references and index.
Identifiers: LCCN 2019015365 | ISBN 9781250119384 (hardcover)
Subjects: LCSH: Francis, Pope, 1936–
Classification: LCC BX1378.7 .I945 2019 | DDC 282.092 [B]—dc23
LC record available at https://lccn.loc.gov/2019015365

Our books may be purchased in bulk for promotional, educational, or business
use. Please contact your local bookseller or the Macmillan Corporate and
Premium Sales Department at (800) 221-7945, extension 5442, or by email at
MacmillanSpecialMarkets@macmillan.com.

First Edition 2019

Designed by Meryl Sussman Levavi

Printed in the United States of America

10 9 8 7 6 5 4 3 2 1

To J, his sentinel

Contents

Wounded Shepherd

Prologue

In June 2018, I was under an umbrella at the *porticone* to the left of St. Peter's trying to tell the Swiss Guard over the din of the downpour that I had a meeting with Pope Francis. I wasn't on their list—his private meetings seldom are—so they had to call up to what is likely the world's most famous guesthouse to make sure.

After the nod and the salute, and a ten-minute walk through the cobbled courtyards, I was at the Casa Santa Marta, an unremarkable building that from the outside could be a bank or an office. I had last met its long-term guest in November 2014, when, after Mass, I had presented him with a copy of my biography, *The Great Reformer: Francis and the Making of a Radical Pope.*

This time, I had a recorder in my pocket, but wasn't sure if I would use it. The book in your hands, an account of church reform over the past six years, 2013 to 2019, was already substantially written, and I bubbled with questions. But it was the pope who, via an intermediary, had asked for the meeting, in the gentlest way possible: could I perhaps find the time, when I was next in Rome?

I was shown into the visitor's room on the ground floor, from where I imagined I would be taken to his three-room suite. But it was Francis himself who came in, closing the door behind him, as I stumbled awkwardly to my feet. There was no courtier to say, "The Holy Father will see you now," just the pastor-in-chief taking my hand and thanking me for my kindness in taking the trouble to come and see him. His graciousness is as legendary as his serenity, simplicity, and humility, but no less surprising when you experience it for yourself.

No, no, thank *you*, I spluttered, and he laughed that I spoke Spanish like a *porteño*, someone from his home city of Buenos Aires. Then we sat down opposite each other. There was a pause, as he looked at me tenderly. "I've read a number of things you've written about me," he said, "and I just have one criticism." I braced myself. After a pause, he said, smiling: "You're too kind to me." The word in Spanish was *benévolo*, something like "indulgent." Relieved and charmed, I assured him I would be more critical in the future, and we both laughed. The pope is fun.

He was also serious. He went on to explain, as he often has to others, that no one had thought this "change of diocese" was a possibility, that in March 2013 he had a small suitcase and expected to be back in Buenos Aires for Easter, how he didn't come with some great plan but had been managing the best he could with what he had.

I never did get my recorder out, and didn't need to: the following forty-five minutes were unforgettable, and have invigorated what follows in these pages. But afterward it was that first exchange that stayed with me. I realized that—for my own good, and for the sake of truth—he was warning me against the "great man" myth beloved of Hollywood and a certain kind of history, in which an anointed, otherworldly figure rises up to defeat overwhelming challenges with superhuman prowess.

I realize now that *The Great Reformer* contributed to that myth: written in the dizzying first months of his pontificate, the parallels with his life—how he appeared at moments of crisis in the Church—offered an irresistible narrative: cometh the hour, cometh the man. I cringe now that I even likened him to a gaucho riding out at first light.

Six years on, the time for such projections is over. We know too much about the limits of reform: paths blocked, resistance mobilized, mistakes made. No longer the great reformer of myth, he is the wounded shepherd: to be chosen by the Holy Spirit is not to be spared the trials of history. Spending time with him, I found him to be smaller, older, more vulnerable, more ordinary than in my mind's eye. I was meeting the person, not the personality.

Yet here's the thing. I also met his holiness. I saw it in the pauses, when he was listening to his heart, to those prompts of the Spirit that guide him. I saw it in his serenity, his peaceful freedom. It is a paradoxical quality: self-effacing, yet powerful; something you have, but also give away (it left me feeling loved, and free). I met the pope, in short, in all his ordinary humanity, yet at the same time was captivated by the extraordinary quality of what he was open to, of what he puts at the center of his existence. And I got the point he wanted me to understand. The real center of the Church, he told journalists shortly after his election, was not the pope, but Jesus Christ.

What follows is the story of Francis's attempt to put Christ at the Church's center. Even though it ranges widely and deeply to explain the change that Francis seeks to bring about, *Wounded Shepherd* is not systematic, episodic, or chronological. There are big gaps on topics such as diplomacy and ecumenism, which an official account would need to cover. Its focus, rather, is on the conversion that Francis has sought: where it comes from, what it is, and why it has triggered such turbulence. It is the story as much of his opening of the Church to the possibility of conversion as it is of the changes he has sought to bring about.

A metaphor to capture this came in a moment of inspiration to one of my Latin American interviewees as we sat talking in his house. I was with the archbishop of Arequipa in southern Peru in April 2016, the day after the release of Francis's document on marriage and family, *Amoris Laetitia* (The Joy of Love).

As Archbishop Javier del Río Alba explained his understanding of the "pastoral conversion" to which the pope is calling the Church, I looked beyond his shoulder through the window to the spectacular snowcapped volcano of El Misti. Following my gaze he suddenly said: "What the Pope is doing is like an earthquake, a tremor, which is moving and shaking things up. And in that shaking up what will fall is what has to fall, and what will rise up is a new era in the history of the Church."

A Sinner's Mission

The pope was at lunch with boisterous relatives in the archbishop's residence in Turin. "Eat, Giorgio!" the old lady told him. "No, no, I have to watch myself," he protested, refusing a second helping as the six cousins and their families, more than thirty people in all, roared with laughter. It was June 2015. Even before his election two years earlier, Francis had lost the lanky, tall figure he had had for decades in Buenos Aires, and now, at seventy-eight, with the sciatica pills and the pasta, and no longer being able to *callejear*—to walk the streets as he used to—he had filled out. But not for Signora Carla. "But what do you live off?" she remonstrated. "You eat nothing!"

He is a pope of the people, for the people; but most of all, he is a pope *with* the people. It is what everyone, admirers and enemies alike, notices about Francis: his natural affinity with the human race, the way he turns people you wouldn't look at twice into subjects and protagonists. Some say he is a populist in an age of populists, but that is to misunderstand populism. He is not using his at-oneness with the people to create power, for he rejects that kind of power; he does not offer boundaries to protect people from perceived threats, but doors and bridges to expand their possibilities. He is captivating and energetic, but humble. He makes mistakes, and asks forgiveness. His mission is to take the Church to the people, in order to not just save the people but to save the Church.

The people, he likes to say, are infallible "in their believing." They may not be able to tell you why they believe in God, but they know God. People like old Carla, whom he knew from regular visits over the years after he was made archbishop of Buenos Aires in 1998, when he began to fly at least once a year to Rome for meetings—usually in February, his Lenten penance—and would sometimes add on some days around Turin. From there it was two hours into the hills around Asti, the fons et origo of the Bergoglio clan, where he enjoyed cookouts with cousins in the village of San Carlo in the region of Tigliole.

So now, on his first visit to Turin since he was made pope, there is no shortage of locals who can say what he is like. One is San Carlo's parish priest, Don Angelo Franco, who describes for local TV the pope's excellent Piedmontese dialect and his enthusiasm for the local dishes, the ravioli and the bagna cauda. He may be pope and he may be Argentine, Don Angelo declared on television during the papal visit of June 2015, but you could see he was still a humble *astigiano* like his father and grandparents, "full of humanity."[1]

This was time out for Francis. Like Jesus stopping in Bethany with his old friends before leaving for Jerusalem to turn the temple tables, Francis came to his grandparents' city not long before his visit to the United States, where his most ferocious critics had their bunker. Among the ordinary faithful, his popularity and prestige were at their zenith. The media still painted him as the reformer pope who had set the Church on a bold new Gospel path, facing resistance from a corrupt old guard, a simplistic narrative that had so far held. And while the tide of angry opposition was already visible, its force had not yet been felt in petitions and accusations of heresy. His Vatican reforms were battling institutional sclerosis, but had not yet stalled; nor had bishops' mishandling of abuse in past decades yet erupted into the public eye with devastating force, as it would three years later. There was even a feeling—partly because of hints that Francis himself had strategically dropped—that his would not be a long pontificate and some of the old guard in the Vatican had been persuaded that they just had to batten down the hatches and wait for the Argentine storm to pass. In fact, it was just building its strength.

The Turin visit took place at the tense midpoint between two turbulent synods, on the eve of the release of his explosive ecology encyclical, just a short time before the most ambitious trips yet of his papacy: to South

America, to Cuba and the United States, and then, in November, to Africa, to inaugurate the Jubilee Year of Mercy in a war zone.

This was one of three Italian visits in 2015: he had been to Naples in March, and would give a blockbuster address in Florence in November. As on all his apostolic visits, he came to Turin to comfort and to edify, to invigorate and to inspire, to shore up the local Church and throw ropes across the ravines of prejudice and misunderstanding. But he had another, personal goal that made this, the sixteenth trip of his pontificate, different from all the others: to touch that European piece of his soul that his father and grandparents had left behind when, seven years before the future pope was born in 1936, they had boarded a boat to Argentina.

In the profile of Jorge Mario Bergoglio, tall, thickset, with a square head and a piercing gaze, you could catch the outline of his grandfather Giovanni. They say an Argentine is an Italian who lives in South America and speaks Spanish, and it is true: Piedmont runs in the pope's veins. The Alpine land that Giovanni and his wife, Rosa, abandoned for the pampas had imprinted upon their grandson something of its *rassa nostrana libera e testarda,* "our free and headstrong local race," as the local poet Nino Costa painted the folk who lived at the foot of the Alps: straight-talking, stubborn types who speak little but say much; who walk slowly but go far; who work hard but know how to enjoy their wine. Jorge Mario had learned the poem "Rassa nostrana" by heart as a child from Rosa in Buenos Aires. Now, in Turin, he recited part of it in dialect halfway through his homily in the Piazza Vittorio, at one point choking with emotion, maybe thinking of Rosa. The crowd teared up with him, erupting in applause.

As ever, Francis came to announce the closeness of God, the mercy lede that somehow Catholics had managed to bury in the lower paragraphs of the Christian Good News story. He was in Turin to affirm the periphery-focused, joyful Church-that-goes-out, to show that Jesus could still be found beyond the introverted, clericalist institution that squatted on its neo-Christendom laurels while the pews drained. But this time he had an extra purpose: to honor his saintly stubborn forebears whose peasant piety was as solid and fertile as Piedmont's hazelnut-tree hills.

In February 2001, in the days before he would be made a cardinal in the square of St. Peter's by Pope John Paul II, Archbishop Bergoglio made a visit to Asti with his Jesuit nephew, Father José Luis Narvaja. They went with two of the Bergoglio cousins to the hamlet of Portacomaro Stazione, fifteen minutes outside the town, where their forefathers were raised in a farmhouse. Its current owner showed them the stunning view over the bottle-green valley of Monteferrato, as well as the defunct winepress and vast oak barrels he still kept in the cool cellar in the back, which Bergoglio's great-grandfather—called Francesco, the name he would one day take as pope—used to age his *vino rosso*.

There is a photo, which Father Narvaja says could be from that trip, or maybe another (there were many). On either side of the two priests under a terra-cotta-roofed porch stands the pair of ruddy cousins beaming in rolled-up shirts and hats. The sixty-five-year-old cardinal-elect, at that point still lanky, has gray hair thinning on his bald patch and a weak smile. (He always hated posing and even today almost always looks like a sourpuss in protocol shots.) His grandfather Giovanni often spoke to him of the farmhouse, called Bricco Marmorito, with its twenty acres of vineyard and woods. The old man loved to recall the verdant hilly beauty of the region, so that by the time his grandson made it there, it had lived long in his imagining.

Giuseppe Bergoglio and his two brothers bought Bricco Marmorito in the early 1800s. Giuseppe's son Francesco had four children, among them the future pope's grandfather Giovanni, born in 1884. Giovanni's brothers, Lorenzo, Eugenio, and Vittorio, later lined up with the tens of thousands who left for Argentina after the First World War, but Giovanni didn't join them until 1929. By then he was in his mid-forties, and had his wife, Rosa, and his only son, the twenty-year-old Mario, the future pope's father, in tow.

Between abandoning Bricco Marmorito for Turin at age twenty-two and leaving Italy for Argentina at age forty-five, Giovanni worked in the city making the bitter wine enriched with herbs and spices known as *vermut*, for which, along with its hazelnut chocolate, the city was renowned. Soon after arriving in Turin, in 1907, he met and married Rosa Margherita Vassallo, from Piana Crixia, some fifteen miles north of Savona on Piedmont's southern border. Rosa had lived in the city since the age of eight, when her mother had sent her to live with her aunt on the advice of her parish priest. The pastor had seen the girl's intelligence and thought that with an education she could rise out of her peasant surroundings.

In her teens Rosa became a *sartina*, one of Turin's four-thousand-odd dressmakers supplying the city's burgeoning fashion trade. Most of the seamstresses scissored and sewed not in sweatshops but from home, organized by Catholic labor activists inspired by Pope Leo XIII's great 1891 encyclical, *Rerum Novarum*, and its call for just wages and worker dignity. The Turin seamstresses' guild, born to combat the double exploitation of women and the poor, organized the city's first ever strike and was the crucible of Italy's suffragette movement. Out of this ferment came Rosa's passion for social justice, her ready identification with the struggling classes, and her vocation as a lay leader, which would later be forged in Asti's Catholic Action.

In 2018, when Francis published a teaching document called *Gaudete et Exsultate* (Rejoice and Be Glad), he described how the Holy Spirit bestowed holiness in abundance among God's holy, faithful people, and he painted what that looked like: the patience of parents who struggled to raise their children, for example, or the sick and elderly who never lost their smile. Citing what he called "the particular genius" of female holiness, he contemplated a woman out shopping who resisted the temptation to indulge in the latest gossip but came back to listen patiently to a child share her hopes and dreams. Francis's imagined saint-next-door felt a surge of anxiety but prayed her Rosary with faith, and later stopped to speak kindly to a poor person in the street. These outwardly ordinary actions, Francis wrote, were about filling ordinary moments with love, modeled on Christ. Every saint like this is "a mission, planned by the Father to reflect and embody, at a specific moment in history, a certain aspect of the Gospel." That was how real change happened, for "the most decisive turning points in world history are substantially co-determined by souls whom no history book ever mentions."

No one would ever have given her a second thought had her grandson not become pope, yet she was a mission planned by the Father. Rosa was one of those "unknown and forgotten women who, each in her own way, sustained and transformed families and communities by the power of their witness," as her grandson would describe them. She was passionate, hardworking, and resourceful. She had a canny political mind and a melting smile; she was prayerful and compassionate; she had a deep trust in Jesus Christ and a love of His people. Hers was the kind of faith that Francis needed to draw on to convert the Church.[2]

Francis likes to point out that Jesus always took time to stop and listen to the people. At the 2018 synod he called it "the apostolate of the ear:

listening before speaking" and asked forgiveness of the young people there "if often we have not listened to you, if instead of opening our hearts, we have filled your ears." He once encouraged taxi drivers in Buenos Aires—many of whom are out-of-work psychoanalysts—to exercise this "apostolate of the ear" because when they heard confessions with their hands on the wheel they opened "doors of hope."[3]

That's why he hates to turn up like a politician on a campaign, to give a speech and leave. He likes first to hear from those whom he addresses, and to dialogue. He is the pope of proximity. *Vicinanza*, the Italian word for "closeness," is a key word for Francis now, just as the word in Spanish, *cercanía*, was in Buenos Aires. How could he preach the closeness of God in Turin's Piazzetta Reale if he didn't get to know them a little? The Kingdom of God isn't an idea, but a happening, a relationship: God has come near to His people, and to the extent that His people grasp this, history turns. God's love is not the possession of good people, nor a reward for the righteous. You have to show, not tell: because it is not an idea, a doctrine, a rule, a norm, or a law, a scholar and a bishop have no more access to it than the out-of-work Turin car workers and cleaners who share their stories with the pope now.

What Francis wants to communicate is that God, when you turn to Him, changes your horizon, as Benedict XVI once put it in a quote Francis likes to repeat. You don't have to be strong or rich or clever, and power and wealth and learning can make the Good News harder to receive. God is mercy, and mercy is close and concrete; mercy never stands outside, giving lectures or rolling eyes, but enters right in with rolled-up sleeves. But to receive it, you have to be humble. That's what lets love in.

What did the Kingdom of God mean right now for the *Torinese* workers who struggled to get to the end of the month alongside Romanians and Macedonians willing to work for half the wages? Across the Western world, capital was in flight and workers were being cast off the production lines by blinking boxes and robots. A populist would rub salt on their anger, promise to protect them by sacrificing the foreigners. But Francis focuses on the suffering of both, the change both need for their basic human flourishing. He urges solidarity: migrants, too, "are victims of inequity, of this throwaway economy and of war," he tells them in the Piazzetta Reale. He adds that women workers bear the greatest burden in taking care of the home yet "are still discriminated against, even in the workplace." Maybe as he spoke, he was thinking of Rosa, who back in the 1920s in Asti used to give talks on Catholic social teaching until the fascists shut her down.[4]

Francis wants the workers to organize for change, to band together against the new harsh winds of the global economy: "only by joining forces can we say 'no' to the unfairness which generates violence," he tells them. The following month in Bolivia he would give his second rousing speech to the "popular movements," mobilizing them in favor of another kind of globalized modernity, one that didn't make shareholder profit the main criterion of economic organization, but the right of all to land, labor, and lodging. When Francis spoke like this he was called Marxist, but it was an old call, repeated by popes across the twentieth century, for the markets to work for the many, not the few, the kind of thing President Juan D. Perón tried to create in Francis's childhood Argentina, or Franklin D. Roosevelt in the United States. Work, Francis told the workers in Turin, was key to human and social flourishing. Society had to be organized to produce jobs for all.

When Leo XIII said this in 1891, during that first era of globalization, the European Catholic bourgeois of the time had said the pope was crazy. What did the old man in Rome know of the scientific wonders of the market? Why not stick to faith and morals and leave business to the businessmen? Now, 124 years later, the Catholic conservative business folk in the United States and the colleges and institutes they funded were saying the same about Francis's teaching document on the environment, *Laudato Si'*, before it was even out. The pope hadn't any authority to speak on the science of climate change, so why listen to him when he tells us to conserve energy and cut consumption?

It was easy for rich people to believe their good fortune. In their world, hardworking, upstanding people were rewarded; the iron law of the market, the logic of the world, the law of "real life" in which the strong swim ahead because they deserve to—it all made sense to them. That made it hard for the rich to receive the Good News, said Francis at the canonization of Pope Paul VI and Óscar Romero in October 2018, not because God was harsh but because "our having too much, our wanting too much suffocates our hearts and makes us incapable of loving." Because the logic of the system worked for the poor in the opposite way—they had toiled their whole lives yet others reaped the reward; they did their best for their families, but remained poor—it was easier for them to grasp the logic of the Gospel. The real strength was not theirs but God's. And because they could grasp this, they could more easily become channels of God's power as He worked through history to create a new people. That was the Good News.[5]

Returning to Turin in 1918 after two years' fighting in the Great War, the pope's grandfather Giovanni found a restless city boiling with tension. Jobless young men were clashing in rival political mobs and piling onto boats bound for America. His brothers were on one to Buenos Aires, but he and Rosa, then in their early thirties, moved instead into the hills of Asti, where he had relatives in the villages around the town. There was work there, and their only son, Mario (Rosa's other five children were stillborn), could go to school in peace. In Asti, Giovanni worked in a café, and eventually he opened his own. Rosa never stopped sewing but also became a leader in a church movement created by the bishops to mobilize ordinary Catholics.[6]

Catholic Action was divided into four groups: men, women, boys, and girls. They had grown rapidly in Asti to around 7,000 members in 1930, of which the women's branch was the largest: 2,398 organized in 53 parish groups. It was a formidable network of cooperatives, savings and loan schemes, and guilds of peasants and workers. Together they formed the backbone of an early Christian-democrat movement, Father Luigi Sturzo's Italian People's Party. But the sudden growth of both Catholic Action and the Popolari alarmed Benito Mussolini's Blackshirts. Their offensive against the Catholics in the early 1920s was felt especially in Asti, where both Popolari and fascists were strong. After Mussolini's March on Rome, the new pope, Pius XI, dialed back the tension, committing Catholic Action to political neutrality and distancing himself from Sturzo's movement, while remaining resolute in defending the Church's freedom to organize. But the standoff remained tense. "Catholics could meet to hear Mass and pray the Rosary, but little else," recalls the historian Vittorio Rapetti.[7]

In an effort to resist this attempt to deny the Church's growing public presence, Catholic Action formed bold leaders, especially women, who were given special training to give talks in public—a scandalous idea to the petit bourgeois fascists of the time. Rosa became one of the outstanding leaders of the women's branch. She appears various times in the town's only newspaper, the diocesan weekly *Gazzetta d'Asti*, where she is described as AC's moral action counselor (*consigliera d'azione morale*), as well as the social action secretary of its women's branch. Twice a week she gave marriage preparation classes to women in the San Martino church, and wrote popular pamphlets. Her oratory and courage made her well known in the parishes in and around the city, which in turn made her a target for the fascists, who did not like women imitating men. They heckled and cajoled her, one time shutting down the hall where she was due to speak. Unable to gain entry, she instead made her speech in the street, standing on a table. Rosa had cojones.

Her son became active in the youth branch. The *Gazzetta d'Asti* described Mario as a student of accountancy (*studente in ragioneria*) who at the age of seventeen in 1925 spoke "with passion and strength." His favorite topic was revealed three years later, when the *Gazzetta* recorded the father of the future pope giving "a very fine illustrative speech on the papacy, culminating in a hymn of praise and admiration to Pope Pius XI, the Pope of Catholic Action."

Giovanni and Rosa couldn't manage the fees of his local technical college, but Mario got a rare scholarship for bright poor students. After graduating in 1926, he went to work at the local Banca d'Italia branch in Asti, where his last appraisal, highlighting his competence and skills, was in October 1928. A few months earlier, Mario was in the *Gazzetta* again, as a judge in a catechists' competition. By this time he was a trained bank clerk, and at close to six feet, was tall for his time and place. But although he was active in the local sports club he was turned down for military service at nineteen because of "serious constitutional weakness," according to the town's registry.

By then the Blackshirts had gained a decisive hold; it was a matter of time before Rosa would be forced to drink castor oil. Giovanni decided finally to leave with his family to join his brothers in Argentina. In early 1929, Mario, then twenty-two, was on the *Giulio Cesare* with his parents bound for Buenos Aires, carrying a letter from the Salesian priests in Turin.[8]

Francis began his June 21, 2015, address to the Salesians of Turin in their vast basilica, Our Lady Help of Christians, by ditching his prepared text as too formal. This settling in for a fireside chat was straight out of the Francis playbook. Speaking *a braccio* (off the cuff), as the Italians say, creates closeness. It was a politician's skill he had seen in General Perón, who created the sense of speaking as one of the people, rather than at them; but it was also his imitation of Jesus.

The Salesians, a religious order founded in Turin by St. John "Don" Bosco in the late nineteenth century, educated the young Jorge Mario Bergoglio, he told them, in beauty and work; and they opened his heart to Don Bosco's "three white loves": Our Lady, the Church, and the Eucharist. They had cultivated in him "affectivity," and taught him how to be a missionary who could respond, practically, to the needs of the poor.

"I think of the early days of Patagonia," Francis mused, "when the sisters went around in their habits—how did they ride the horses?—evangelizing Patagonia. And the Salesian martyrs of Patagonia . . ." He described how his grandparents and father had lodged with the Salesians in Buenos Aires after arriving in 1929, and again in 1932, following the failure of his great uncles' business in Paraná. How the priests had arranged a loan that enabled the family to start again, and how, through the Salesian basilica in Almagro, known locally as the "Italian church," his father, Mario, met his wife, Regina, whom he married in 1935. And he described the key role played by the family priest at the Italian church, Father Enrico Pozzoli, who was also Piedmontese. Don Enrico baptized most of the children there, and he continued to help the Bergoglio family in countless ways—arranging schooling for the eldest for a year when Regina fell ill, for example.

But there were stories Francis didn't tell about Don Enrico. How the priest tried to mediate, often without success, in the furious rows and feuds on Regina's side of the family, for example. Or the time in December 1955 when the atmosphere in the Bergoglio household turned toxic because Regina was furious when Jorge Mario revealed that he was going to be a priest rather than a doctor. Don Enrico had celebrated a private Mass for the family on Mario and Regina's twentieth wedding anniversary, and afterward he took them to a Flores café for breakfast, where he softened Regina's heart with stories of various vocations, including his own. Or how Jorge Mario, after a year in seminary, had to leave on a stretcher, on the verge of death from complications from tuberculosis that required the removal of the upper lobe of a lung; and how, in that winter of 1957, Don Enrico had helped him choose a new vocation, as a missionary in the Jesuits rather than to the diocesan priesthood.[9]

The story Francis wanted to tell in the basilica in Turin was not really about his own family but the bigger family: how Don Bosco's men and women helped to form a people. Forty years earlier, in 1975, in a lecture the then Jesuit provincial in Argentina had given, he had described how Don Bosco's early collaborators had accompanied the great Piedmontese transatlantic migration of those years—over two million went to Argentina alone—acting as agents of integration, forming hundreds of thousands of displaced newcomers into a people under the wings of the Church and its networks of charities and schools. He singled out the Salesians' role as missionaries among the native Indians in the harsh wilderness of Patagonia, how they stood up against the racism that was then part of the official nation-building ideology, and how in Argentina they had founded "oratories" to give migrant families food, schooling, and dignity. The Salesians even created a football team, San Lorenzo, to which the pope's father, Mario, remained devoted for the rest of his life.[10]

When, as Jesuit provincial, Bergoglio created night schools for the jobless and popular kitchens for the hungry in the parish he founded from the Colegio Máximo in the early 1980s, he was accused of trying to "Salesianize" his order. And when, as cardinal, he was criticized for creating networks of practical schools in the slums of Buenos Aires, he defended himself by citing the example of Don Bosco. For Francis, the Salesians represented Christ's closeness to the people. "The Salesian is concrete," Francis said in Turin. "He sees the problem, thinks about it, then takes it in hand."[11]

Speaking now in the basilica of Turin, he noted how many things were far better since Don Bosco's time, yet some problems had come back again, like youth unemployment. Nearly half of Italian young people under the age of twenty-five neither worked nor studied, and too many died young from addictions or suicide. Francis urged the Salesians to respond as Don Bosco did, by pioneering networks of small, local schools that taught technical trades and crafts to help young people into jobs. "Let's give them whatever can be a source of work, even basic work, even if it's just work for today and not tomorrow," he urged. That evening, he told young people in the Piazza Vittorio how he hated to see them "retire at 20." "When a young person loves, lives, grows, he does not retire; he grows, grows, grows and gives." He quoted Saint Ignatius of Loyola: love was known "more in deeds than in words."[12]

Francis rode to Turin's cathedral by popemobile through cheering crowds to pray before a world-famous thirteen-foot length of herringbone linen that has been housed there since the end of the Middle Ages. After sitting motionless before the Shroud of Turin, he made a sign of the cross, and moved forward to touch the case that preserves the cloth in gas. Maybe he imagined Rosa doing the same back in 1898. A teenager in Turin at the time, she was almost certainly among the 800,000 who flocked to venerate the cloth when it was put on display that year and photographed for the first time.

The negative from that photo caused astonishment. It seemed to prove what had been long claimed: that this holy relic, passed between French knights and finding its way to the Savoy family at the end of the Middle Ages, had once wrapped Jesus's crucified body. Now, on the eve of the twentieth century, the negative showed a bearded man's shadow on the rough cloth, his wounds of torture precisely matching the Gospel account. The image was as close as anyone had come in the modern era to physical evidence of the crucifixion, and it triggered a century of squabbles over science versus religion. Either it was the very cloth in which the crucified, scourged Christ (or someone who shared precisely the same fate at the time) was wrapped, or it was the most astonishingly creative, pious medieval forgery.

But the deeper truth of the shroud was what it revealed about humanity.

Shroud Man is a very different symbol from Leonardo da Vinci's abstract Vitruvian Man, geometrically perfect, free from all blemish and suffering. Shroud Man was all wounds and shame. Which was more human? Which was love?

"The Shroud attracts people to the face and tortured body of Jesus and, at the same time, urges us on toward every person who is suffering and unjustly persecuted," Francis said during the Angelus in the Piazza Vittorio. This, the suffering face of Christ, was the authentic image of man, but it was also the humility of God, his *synktakábasis*, his coming down to the people, his becoming weak with the weak.[13]

At the end of the afternoon, in between meeting the sick and the young people, Francis made an unscheduled stop at a little eighteenth-century pink-marbled church in the old quarter. The Carmelite priests who ran the parish of St. Teresa of Ávila had been told to keep his coming quiet, for security reasons, and there were just a few friars to welcome him and his entourage. After bending to kiss the baptismal font, he made his way to the center of the church in front of the altar where he set a vase of flowers. He asked to pray there, so they brought out a chair on which he sat silently, slightly hunched forward, with the friars behind him on the pews.

Before leaving, he asked for the guest book. "I thank the Lord for the gift of my family in this church of Santa Teresa where my grandparents were married and my father baptized," he wrote in his round, spidery handwriting, adding: "I prayed especially for the forthcoming Synod on the Family."

The Bergoglios struggled at first in Argentina. The collapse of Giovanni's brothers' pavement business in Paraná in 1932, a victim of the global recession, led to a second uprooting, this time to Buenos Aires. With a loan arranged by Father Pozzoli, the family set up a corner grocery shop in Flores, a neighborhood of Italian immigrants. Giovanni and Rosa sold a little of everything—sugar, beans, rice, oil, and wine—and their good cheer and kindness soon built a clientele. Mario, unable to work in banking because his accountant's qualification wasn't recognized, made grocery deliveries from his bicycle.

At the Salesian basilica in Almagro, Mario continued the Catholic Action formation he had begun back home. The basilica was his hub, the place he met friends and his future wife, Regina Sívori. Don Enrico married them on December 12, 1935, and baptized their firstborn, Jorge Mario, on Christmas Day the following year. Four other children followed in quick succession: Oscar Adrián, Marta Regina, Alberto Horacio, and María Elena, Francis's only surviving sibling. As bookkeeping work began to come in, Mario was able to feed his growing family. He rented a house in Flores, a simple one-floor *casa chorizo*, named after a sausage because each room led off the other. Jorge Mario would later recall his father poring over the fat ledgers of local companies while Italian operas crackled from the state radio station. It left him, he joked, with a horror of finances.

When Marta was born, Jorgito was dispatched each day to his grandparents' house just a few blocks away. Giovanni and Rosa were the anchor of his early, carefree years: his first memories are of going each day back and forth between the houses. While his parents were keen to move ahead and fit into their new country, speaking only Spanish and putting Turin behind them, Giovanni and Rosa were only too happy to teach their grandson everything they loved, happily mixing Italian, Spanish, and Piedmontese. They gave him a backstory.

It was an austere but happy lower-middle-class family life. But while there was peace in the Bergoglio households, among the Sívori, on his mother's side of the family, it was a different story. At their house in the Almagro neighborhood of Buenos Aires, on Quintino Bocayuvá Street, a long-standing feud between Regina's brothers often broke out in violent tempests that Don Enrico tried helplessly to mediate. "In my family there was a long history of disagreements: uncles, cousins—quarrels and bust-ups," Francis confided in a 2013 letter to a Brazilian priest, Father Alexandre Awi, who had acted as his interpreter on his first visit to Rio de Janeiro. "As a child, I cried a great deal in secret when these fights were talked about or when we could see a new one coming. Sometimes I offered a sacrifice or a penance to try to prevent them occurring. I was very much affected."

Jorge Mario was a sensitive, bighearted child whose primary experience was one of warmth and protection, above all from his grandmother. The trauma of the fights and breakups became the source of what would become one of his life's defining missions: to reconcile and depolarize. How can people live with tension and disagreement, and see in these not a reason to fall apart but a more fruitful way to live together? Over time he came to call this a "culture of encounter," a means by which differences could be contained and made fruitful in what he called a "reconciled diversity."[14]

It was his intellectual passion as a Jesuit in the 1960s, when he read widely in the French new theology, drawn to a form of Catholic dialectical thinking that developed in critical response to Hegel. Drawing on the great nineteenth-century Tübingen scholar Adam Möhler, the Jesuits Gaston Fessard, Erich Przywara, and Henri de Lubac saw the Church as a *complexio oppositorum*, a system that synthesized elements that ordinarily pull in opposite directions, creating—through the power of the Holy Spirit—a unity out of diversity that respected difference. Later, in the 1980s, by then in his fifties and with direct experience of leading a divided body at a time of polarization in Church and society, Bergoglio began doctoral research to develop Romano Guardini's theory of polar contrasts, applying four principles of discernment, which later appeared in *Evangelii Gaudium*, and which have long guided his governance: means of bringing about peace within the tension of difference. It can all be rooted back to his childhood family experience, one that "created in my heart a desire for people not to fight, to stay united," he told Father Awi. "Or if they do fight, to remain friends."[15]

The rows made him a serious, self-contained, thoughtful child. He loved music and dance and could laugh and josh; but all who knew him as a teenager stressed his qualities as a leader and protector, one who saw himself as strength for others. He had a robust inner life, reinforced by being sent away at age eleven to board when his mother had health problems after the birth of his youngest sister. The year he spent at the Colegio Wilfrid Barón de los Santos Angeles in 1949 immersed Jorge Mario in a boys' world of sports, learning, and a muscular religious diet of daily Mass and Rosary, weekly confession, and devotion to the Virgin. The Salesian boarding school toughened him further for secondary school, which he attended starting at the age of thirteen while working part-time in a food chemistry laboratory.

At that time he was seldom at home, spending mornings at the factory from seven until one, returning only for lunch before attending classes until eight at night. His chemistry school classmates describe him as fiercely smart, excelling especially in literature and religion. But they also stressed a side of him that was unusual: he seemed concerned less with his own goals than with helping others achieve theirs. "Even as a teenager, he devoted himself to his fellow man," recalls his classmate Horacio Crespo.[16]

He was intrigued by politics: not just the power of ideas, but the idea of power, how it is built and used. When he had free time, he loved to hang out in political clubs and meeting rooms where socialists, radicals, and Peronists met and argued. He remains, to this day, *Homo politicus*, committed to what he calls "big politics," the construction of the *polis*. As a Jesuit, Bergoglio later identified with the popular nationalism of his mother's family, and especially with Peronism in its original late-1940s phase, when it made Catholic social teaching its governing ideology. But during Perón's second term (1952–1955) Jorge was drawn, like so many at that time in Latin America, to Marxist analyses, which he devoured from books lent to him by a Paraguayan communist woman he worked with. Unconvinced by its materialist theories, he nevertheless related to Marxism's rage at injustice, and he would always be convinced that communism had thrived because Western Christianity had neglected the Gospel's call to put the poor first.[17]

Faith and social justice were his two abiding passions. But he was also wrestling with a third.

Francis reads his spiritual journey through chapter 16 of Ezekiel, the story of Israel's vexed "marriage" with God, the drama of a spoiled wife who became a forgiven whore.

It is a heady brew of shame and grace that begins with a girl born unloved and left to die who is rescued by God. He nurtures her until she is of marriageable age and adorns her in the finest jewels. Clothed in divine splendor, she is dazzling in her beauty. But later, self-infatuated and proud, she prostitutes herself, squanders her gifts, and sacrifices her children. Furious, God pledges violent justice: she will be stripped naked before a crowd who will stone her and stab her to death. But the flash of anger soon gives way to a pledge of mercy. "I am going to renew my covenant with you," God tells Ezekiel/Israel, "and you will learn that I am the Lord, and so remember and be covered with shame, and in your confusion be reduced to silence, when I have pardoned you for all you have done."

When Francis reads those pages, he told Andrea Tornielli, "everything here seems written just for me. Jesus looked at me with mercy, he took me, he put me on the street. . . . And he has given me an important grace: the grace of shame." Jorge Mario encountered that grace—God's favor—late in his adolescence, just at the point when he was developing into a tough, self-reliant leader. The experience of shame and grace, of being forgiven, taken in and sent out, has been the template of his teaching: how the experience of mercy leads into mission. It has been the lens through which he has read, for example, the Church's sex abuse crisis.[18]

At sixteen, going on seventeen, Jorge was in the full flowering of what psychologists call "ego formation." His mother had already mapped out a future for him in which her eldest would be a doctor and lead the family into bourgeois respectability. But like the camel-borne magi after Bethlehem, he found himself on another road. He has often spoken of what happened in the Basilica of Flores on September 21, 1954, each time adding extra details. But until he spoke about it with Tornielli during the Jubilee of Mercy, he had never given away the depth of raw emotion the experience involved.

He was drawn into the basilica, the family church in Flores, while on his way to meet up with friends, among them the girl to whom he was planning to open his heart. The basilica was the center of his adolescent religious life. He was there not just for Mass on Sundays with his family, but for weekly evening meetings of the young men's branch of Catholic Action.

It was a time of change; new winds were blowing. His Catholic Action group was devouring, for example, the American monk Thomas Merton's memoir *The Seven Storey Mountain*, recently published in Buenos Aires.

Merton's extraordinary story of mercy and redemption "opened new horizons" for them, Francis later recalled. It was the same phrase he would use in speaking of Merton while addressing the U.S. Congress in September 2015.[19]

The teenage Jorge Mario was observant rather than prayerful. He had had no particular experiences of God's mercy as a young child. While at the Salesian school he had pondered the priesthood, but as an idea rather than as a result of prayer, and the desire soon vanished. His real passion was politics. When he wasn't thinking about politics, he was thinking about girls, and especially the one girl whom he had begun to think of as his girlfriend, to whom, on that day, he was about to profess his love.

For one who trusted his intellect rather than his heart, what he was poised to do was terrifying. Yet not to do it was weakness. He was in turmoil. Crying out inside for strength and peace, he suddenly found himself at the door of the basilica he knew so well, and plunged in, obscurely hoping to find there some relief and sense of direction. As his eyes adjusted to the cool gloom, he saw, at the far left-hand corner, the open door of a confessional, and entered it, drawn as if by a twitch upon an invisible thread. He later described his confession as a "fluke," unexpected, like, he said, being thrown from a horse.

It was the feast day of Saint Matthew, the money changer turned disciple whom Jesus recruited from his tax collector's booth. "Without me being even at the customs post, like the saint of the day, the Lord was waiting for me, '*miserando et eligendo*,'" Bergoglio told the Argentine Salesian provincial Don Bruno, in 1990. "After that I had no doubt that I would be a priest." The Latin phrase *miserando et eligendo*—"looking at him with the gaze of mercy, he chose him"—was taken from the Venerable Bede's description of that moment in which Jesus captivated Matthew. It would be Bergoglio's motto as bishop and now as pope, and his template for evangelization.

Jorge opened more than the door of the confessional that day. Whether or not he shared some burden of serious guilt or simply poured out his confusion and shame, what he accused himself of is not important. What mattered was that his shame, and act of self-accusation, threw him in trust on God's mercy, and swung wide the door of grace. What he saw and felt on the other side is hard to capture in metaphors—an eagle soaring? a sudden burst of sun from a mountain?—but real. What is awakened at such moments is a consciousness of the awesome totality of everything yet, at the same time, the particular love of the Creator for a person, just as they are. And with that experience comes a new horizon: that the universe is not, after all, a cold, empty place of grim survival but a warm womb of possibility, created by and in love. A man can find that out as a teenager and spend his life trying to communicate it.

"A personal encounter, which has touched my heart and given direction and new meaning to my existence" is how Francis described it to his atheist friend Eugenio Scalfari. The Italian journalist and editor, like many modern skeptics, had questioned the need for the institutional church: why not believe without belonging? Francis told his story to show that the "personal encounter" that changed his life had been made possible by "the community of faith in which I have lived . . . Believe me, without the Church I would not have been able to encounter Jesus—even though I am aware that the immense gift that is faith is kept in the fragile earthen vessels of our humanity."[20]

The Church supplied not only the place of that encounter, but a guide through the thickets of decision-making that followed. His confessor, Father Carlos Duarte Ibarra, was a humble pastor from the poor province of Corrientes then living in the clergy house in Flores while receiving treatment for leukemia. "On confessing myself to him, I felt welcomed by the mercy of God," the pope told Tornielli. Over the following year, as Jorge went to him for spiritual direction, Father Ibarra helped the young man become aware of the "motions" in his soul, the way God's gentle call can be made out through the storms of our desires and confusions. That call might have been to marriage and medicine, but Jorge discovered that it was to priesthood and mission, and specifically to offer what he experienced with Father Ibarra: the tenderness of God in guided spiritual discernment. As pope over sixty years later, he has worked to ensure the Church offers that experience to every young person.

A year after Jorge's encounter with God's mercy, the cancer that had been devouring his confessor finally claimed him. The young man was devastated. "I cried a lot that night, really a lot, and hid in my room. . . . I had lost a person who helped me feel the mercy of God."

By then he was on a path. The following year he finished his chemistry studies and announced to his shocked mother that he was to be a doctor of souls rather than bodies. While waiting to enter the seminary, he went to pray in the Salesian basilica in Almagro, the church where he had been baptized, to struggle in the tension between the One who gently calls and the self that tries to cling to what he has.

On a day's visit to Genoa on May 27, 2017, Francis began as he had in Turin, with a question-and-answer meeting with the workers in a struggling steel plant. He told them how moved he was at being so close to the port where his father and grandparents had departed for Buenos Aires in the midwinter of 1929. "As a child of migrants," he told them, "I thank you for your welcome."

Then he began a day of evangelizing, teaching the closeness of God to the people of God. From the steel plant he went to meet with clergy and religious in the city's cathedral, after which he held an encounter with young people gathered at a Marian shrine overlooking the city and the sea. Afterward he lunched with 120 refugees, migrants, and homeless people, before visiting a pediatric hospital. Then he celebrated Mass near the port with some 80,000 people.

To the workers and businesspeople, he didn't just spell out the ethical principles of a justly ordered economy, but pondered the difference between an entrepreneur and a speculator. The good entrepreneur knows his workers, invests in them, creates opportunities for them, and is deeply pained at having to lay them off, whereas a speculator has no love for workers, seeing them as dispensable means of securing his own profit. He drew the larger lesson. "When the economy loses contact with the faces of the people, it becomes faceless and therefore ruthless."[21]

With the pastors he used the same idea, contrasting the good-shepherd priest with the businessman-priest. Look at how Jesus spent his day, Francis told them: plenty of time in solitary prayer, then on the road with a crowd, "close to people and to their problems. He never hid." Always on the move, he was never, as it were, looking at his watch, saying, "I have to do this, this, this," but always open to people, especially the needy. Don't be afraid of being pulled this way and that, Francis told them: "let yourself be tired out by people." Be afraid, rather, of stasis and excessive organization, of wanting everything perfectly organized. "I would say that kind of life, so structured, is not a Christian life," he told them, smiling. "Maybe that parish priest is a good businessman, but I wonder, is he a Christian?"

Asked about vocations—the calling to priesthood, religious life, and marriage—he said people could only ever choose what is attractive, and what attracts is joy. "We have to give a witness that shows we are happy and that we will end our lives happy that Jesus chose us," he told them. But joy wasn't the same as having fun, he told the young people at the Sanctuary of Our Lady of the Watch. Joy was born in the heart and couldn't be taken away, and it happened when people went out among others, not as tourists but on mission, as fellow children of God. It meant being part of the people, listening carefully and looking at others with "the eyes of the heart." It meant compassion. "Love is being able to take a hand that is dirty and the ability to look in the eyes of those who are in distress and say, 'For me, you are Jesus.' This is the beginning of every mission, this love with which I must go out and speak."

Then he told the young people how he had visited a prison once in Buenos Aires and met a man who had murdered more than fifty people. "And I thought: *but you are Jesus,* because He said, if you come and see me in prison, I'm there, in that man."

To be missionaries, he said, means that kind of craziness.

"I go on mission," he said, "to bring great love."[22]

two

If the Dogs
Are Barking

It wasn't the aftershocks from the earthquakes in central Italy in January 2017 that so disturbed the peace of the grand master of the Order of Malta, but another kind of tremor under the ancient foundations of its Rome headquarters. What he could hear was the rumble of reform.

"Whilst I was trying to enjoy a peaceful Advent and Christmastide, I have barely been able to concentrate on anything else," Matthew Festing wrote wearily to the thousands of knights from his desk at the Magistral Palace. "It has been most tiring."

Even by the stiff-upper-lip standards of the English landed classes, this was an understated description of the toe-to-toe confrontation with Pope Francis into which the grand master had plunged the order. What the *New York Times* called "a full-scale proxy war between Pope Francis and the Vatican traditionalists who oppose him" was the Order of Malta's greatest crisis in the modern era, yet Fra' Festing ("Fra" is short for *frate* [brother]) wrote as if the servants were all down with the flu.[1]

The Knights of Malta versus Pope Francis? It was catnip to news desks. Ever since the papal bull *Pie Postulatio Voluntatis* of February 15, 1113, which placed the order under the aegis of the Holy See, loyalty to the papacy had been as much part of the knights' colorful history as their tales of military derring-do and care for the sick.

Founded at the time of the Crusades as a religious order of men to defend and tend to pilgrims en route to the Holy Land, the Knights Hospitaller, as they were first known, helped defeat the Turks at the Battle of Lepanto and for five centuries ran the two Mediterranean islands of Rhodes and Malta, until they were ousted by Napoleon at the end of the eighteenth century. Now they faced a new kind of challenge: a dispute over the direction of the order that had spun out of control after a traditionalist American cardinal tried to use the pope's authority in a Vatican power play worthy of the days of the Borgias.

These days landless, yet with a claim to sovereignty for humanitarian purposes, since the nineteenth century the order has run its worldwide charitable activities from 68 Via dei Condotti, Rome's ultra-high-end shopping street. Like a dowager countess on a supermodel catwalk, its seventeenth-century musty palazzo sits incongruously wedged between the gleaming storefronts of Hermès and Jimmy Choo. Inside the Magistral Palace lurks a world of good breeding and ancient wealth. Flunkeys with silver trays pad through salons of ornately gilded furniture, muffled by silk-lined walls hung with Old Masters. The corridors are heavy with display cases of ornate swords once used to disentrail Ottoman invaders. There is even a chapel by Piranesi.

The order long ago dismantled its military wing to focus its efforts on caring for the sick. The hospital for the needy downstairs is part of the order's $1-billion-a-year worldwide medical-humanitarian mission in 120 countries involving 13,500 "knights" and "dames," 25,000 employees, and 120,000 volunteers. Parked outside is a fleet of black Mercedes bearing the order's diplomatic flag and license plates, a reminder that the order has sovereign relations with over a hundred states, including the Holy See, the European Union, and the United Nations, the last of which recognizes the order as a non-state actor, like the Red Cross.

Yet the Order of Malta is not simply an NGO. It is a lay religious order, with a few dozen celibate men under vows—the so-called first-class knights—at its core, who with thousands of "ordinary" knights, mostly married laypeople, are dedicated to "the promotion of the glory of God through the sanctification of its members, service to the Faith and to the Holy Father [the pope], and assistance to one's neighbor," as its charter puts it. To oversee the order's spiritual purpose and especially its first-class knights, the pope names a cardinal *patronus*, or chaplain, to represent him. In November 2014, Francis appointed his most prominent critic, the

American cardinal Raymond Burke, cheerleader of the Church's vociferous traditionalist wing.

A star of the American and Italian conservative lecture circuit, Burke was infamous in the Church for the exuberance of his high-camp liturgical dress, typically processing in vast velvet gloves and trailing a silk scarlet cappa magna carried by altar boys coughing under a mushroom cloud of incense. In a book about homosexuality at the Vatican, Frédéric Martel noted how Burke "can stroll about in full sail, in his cappa magna, in an unthinkably long robe, in a forest of white lace or dressed in a long coat shaped like a dressing gown, while at the same time, in the course of an interview, denouncing in the name of tradition 'a Church that has become too feminized.'"[2]

Burke was extravagantly traditionalist, but no fossil. His fear-filled, mournful lectures and dark pessimism about the state of the world and of the Church were combined with a childlike trust in the merits of Donald Trump and an openness to the media that was rare among cardinals. When not traveling he could easily be found in his 4,500-square-foot apartment just off the Via della Conciliazione, where his biretta sits in a glass case, like a relic. There he received a constant stream of rich right-wing Americans who knelt to kiss the gold ring on his finger.[3]

Burke was a canon lawyer, and until Francis named him as the order's *patronus* the cardinal had been the Vatican's leading judge in the Supreme Tribunal of the Apostolic Signatura, the equivalent of a final appellate court. His supporters had painted Burke's removal from the Signatura as Francis's punishment for the toxic interviews the cardinal gave during the family synod of October 2014, when he told a Spanish weekly that the Church under Francis was "like a ship without a rudder" in which the faithful felt "seasick because the Church's ship has lost its way."

But the pope's collaborators say Burke was removed from the Signatura because of his opposition to a key policy change mandated by the bishops—to make the process of marriage annulments swifter and cheaper. The pope and Burke agreed to the move before the synod but they did not announce it until afterward, to allow the cardinal to take part. Nor did the pope have any intention of silencing his fiercest cardinal critic. When Burke told Francis that the only way he could serve him was by "speaking the truth in the best and clearest way possible," the pope told him: "That's what I want." Far from muzzling or punishing Burke, Francis's appointment set him free to air his views as never before, and the cardinal soon exploited that opportunity.[4]

Francis had his reasons for naming Burke as chaplain to the order. At a meeting on September 9, 2014, Francis told his new *patronus* to carry out "the necessary cleansing of a secular spirit and, specifically, of Freemasonry from the Order of Malta," for which task he needed a younger cardinal and an American. Burke asked him if he had concrete information he could act on. Francis said only that he was certain that there were Freemasons who were also knights.[5]

He knew this from Argentina. The Order of Malta there was better known for its power-brokering and business activities than for its charitable ones, and Francis knew of knights who were also wealthy members of Masonic lodges. The local branch of the order had exerted an outsize influence in the Argentine Church owing to its close links with Saint John Paul II's secretary of state, Cardinal Angelo Sodano, and Sodano's number two, the Argentine cardinal Leonardo Sandri. Both were prominent knights of Malta with strong links to the Argentine businessman Esteban "Cacho" Caselli, who as religious affairs minister in the deeply corrupt 1990s government of Carlos Menem wove a web of ideological and financial ties with the order. Caselli, famously linked to a powerful Italian Masonic lodge called P2, ensured a constant stream of Argentine taxpayers' funding of Vatican projects. Sodano and Sandri, despite Caselli's Masonic ties, opened the doors to make him a knight. Later, Caselli's son Antonio was named the order's ambassador to Buenos Aires.[6]

When he was made archbishop in 1998, Bergoglio famously resisted the elder Caselli's bid to suborn him, following which Cacho sought to block him at every turn. Relations were, as a result, tense between Bergoglio and the Argentine knights, whose members included two ultraconservative bishops. One, the archbishop of La Plata, Héctor Aguer, was Bergoglio's main opponent in the bishops' conference between 1998 and 2013. Another was Oscar Sarlinga, a knight who was named bishop of Zárate-Campana after Sodano and Caselli persuaded Benedict XVI in 2006 to appoint him against the wishes of Bergoglio and the bishops' conference. Sarlinga, who was the knights' chaplain, was later at the center of a plot in 2008 to remove Bergoglio as archbishop of Buenos Aires.[7]

These shenanigans were what Francis meant when he spoke of the "worldly spirit" of the order: the use of the Church and its organizations for power plays and favor trading. But Burke was hardly the man to counter such schemes; he planned to use his Malta sinecure to advance his own traditionalist movement. Specifically, he wanted to secure funding from the order for the society of traditionalist priests he patronized, the Institute of Christ the King Sovereign Priest (ICKSP), whose members deny that the Second Vatican Council carries doctrinal authority.

Burke's long-term goal was to integrate his institute into the order, and to seek more influence and power than his arm's-length position entitled him to. For this, he needed to make himself indispensable to Festing and the other first-class knights, who were at that moment fending off a bid by German reformers and modernizers in the order. Unlike Fra' Festing and his first-class knights, the Germans were mainstream Catholics who were happy with the Second Vatican Council and the papacy of Francis. A clash was inevitable.[8]

Burke's arrival at the Magistral Palace stoked a fire that had been lit earlier that year by elections within the order, which had brought into the open a struggle between two groups. On the one hand was the small, traditionalist clique of the few dozen first-class knights around Fra' Festing; on the other were the thousands of "second-class" knights and dames, mostly married laypeople. Among the latter the wealthy German Association—which runs Malteser International, the order's humanitarian aid organization—was particularly strong. In 2014, Festing lost control of the government of the order after the second-class knights secured over half of the seats on the order's governing body, the eleven-member Sovereign Council, hitherto dominated by the first-class. Dealings between Fra' Festing and his council, and between the professed and the second-class knights, became increasingly tense. The grand master had a particular loathing of the de facto leader of the German group, Baron Albrecht von Boeselager, who as a result of the election was now grand chancellor, a role that combined prime minister and foreign minister. Boeselager, representing the wider order, wanted reform.

Ironically, the traditionalist Festing, who could barely bring himself to mention Francis, was grateful for the new *patronus*, whereas the German Association, who were supportive of Francis, was horrified by the pope's choice. What galled them were Burke's astonishingly vociferous hard-right views on immigration and Islam, which cut across Malteser International's advocacy of migrants as well as its relations with the Muslim countries where it operated relief efforts. To forestall a crisis in the event of push-back from the Middle East, the order's communications officer agreed with Burke on a press statement to make clear that the cardinal's views were his own, and not the order's.[9]

As grand master—a lifelong appointment—the sixty-seven-year-old Fra' Festing was a bluff, jovial, portly figure who could often be found in Rome serving pasta to the homeless at night. But he had struggled in his governing role. Easily led by others (as he would be by Cardinal Burke) yet prickly in defense of his authority, he was especially resentful of attempts by Boeselager, the aristocratic grandson of an acclaimed anti-Nazi resistance leader, to hold him accountable for his decisions.

Boeselager was a revered figure within the order with long experience of managing its humanitarian arm, Malteser International. He was highly critical of Festing's governance, which he believed ignored the transparency and accountability demanded by the order's constitution, and especially of a number of episodes that brought the knights into disrepute, such as his poor handling of a traditionalist member of the order in England who was convicted of sex offenses against young boys. Festing was increasingly irritated by his German critic, and the two men clashed repeatedly.[10]

Now, with Burke's help, Festing could see a way of removing Boeselager. The plan involved condoms.

As head of Malteser International, Boeselager, then the grand hospitaller, had discovered in 2013 that some of the agencies the organization funded were advocating or even distributing contraceptives as part of their attempt to combat AIDS in South Sudan, Kenya, and Myanmar. He at once withdrew funding from two of the projects, but for a time he continued to allow the third to operate in a desperately poor part of northern Myanmar where forced prostitution was behind the rapid spread of AIDS and condoms were effective in reducing it.

He sought advice at the time from Malteser International's ethics committee, who supported Boeselager's choice of action. Eventually, funding was withdrawn from the third agency, too. But the issue was ethically complex, and Boeselager tasked a working group under Malteser's spiritual adviser, Bishop Marc Stenger of Troyes in France, to draw up guidelines in line with those of other Catholic development charities. The order agreed and revised the guidelines in 2014, around the time that Boeselager was elected grand chancellor.

The legitimacy of the use of condoms to prevent the transmission of diseases (as opposed to their use as a means of contraception within marriage, which had been forbidden by the 1968 encyclical *Humanae Vitae*) had been for many years warmly discussed by Catholic ethicists and argued between cardinals, most of whom invoked the doctrine of double effect. If the primary intention of prophylactic use was to prevent death and disease rather than to avoid pregnancy, it was not contraception; and in cases where sexual abstinence (the most effective means of preventing AIDS) was not possible or reasonable, it could be licit or justified.

Most Catholic development agencies, however, refused to distribute condoms and instead promoted abstinence and fidelity, which were anyway the most effective solutions to AIDS. But they recognized a gray area in high-risk groups such as prostitutes who sold their bodies to feed their children, or serodiscordant married couples (in which one partner had AIDS but the other did not). Many ethicists, including in the Vatican's Congregation for the Doctrine of the Faith (CDF), argued that, especially in the case of the serodiscordant couple, such prophylactic use could be legitimate, and therefore their use could at least be recommended by agencies. But a small group of hard-liners who then dominated the Pontifical Academy for Life argued against that position; they said the use of condoms was always and intrinsically wrong because condoms led to "nonmarital" acts. Even when they were used for prophylactic purposes, their use amounted to "cooperation in evil."

Conscious of the heartbreaking situations faced by development agencies on the ground and the lack of consensus among ethicists, Benedict XVI was careful not to come down on either side. But in 2010 he gently took a stand against the hard-liners when he observed in a book interview that the decision to use a prophylactic by a male prostitute to prevent AIDS could be the beginning of a moral awakening. The rigorists, among whom were Academy of Life members and professors John Haas and Luke Gormally, were livid, and witheringly suggested that the pope lacked competence in moral theology.

When Festing in October 2014 learned of the new guidelines adopted by Malteser International, with Burke's backing he commissioned a report from Haas and Gormally. Their hopelessly one-sided findings of January

2016 slammed Malteser's ethics committee as "inadequate" and "incompetent" and claimed decisions made by Boeselager were "erroneous." Their criteria for reaching that verdict rested on assumptions about what the Church taught that went well beyond magisterial teaching and were out of step even with CDF positions. But the report suited Burke and Festing, who could use it against Boeselager.[11]

In June 2016, Francis received the grand master and other high officers, including Boeselager, but without Burke present. The pope asked them whether Burke had made progress in purging the order of Freemasons, but it was the first they had heard about the pope's mandate; Burke had told them nothing.

The following November, Burke met Francis for the first time in two years. Six weeks earlier the cardinal had begun his crusade against the pope's exhortation on the family, *Amoris Laetitia*, which had emerged from a consensus in two turbulent synods that people who had divorced and remarried without an annulment could in some instances be admitted to the Eucharist. Together with three retired cardinals, Burke had written to the pope to accuse him—by means of a series of yes/no questions, crafted as doubts, or *dubia*—of rejecting church teaching. Francis ignored the letter when they met. A few days later, the cardinal made it public in a theatrical display of sorrow and grief.[12]

At their meeting, Francis asked what progress Burke had made in the mission he had given him two years earlier. The answer was none. But the cardinal claimed to have uncovered another kind of "worldliness" in the order. Triumphantly pulling out the rigorists' report damning Boeselager and his ethics committee, Burke handed it to the pope, giving him a verbal summary of its findings. Like the *dubia* letter, it was a wily lawyer's trap. If the pope failed to react to the report's findings, Burke could use it to claim Francis was failing to defend church teaching; if he responded positively, Burke and Festing could use it to oust Boeselager.

Francis promised that he would send Burke a formal letter with instructions on reforming the order. When it came, dated December 1, the pope's missive was emphatic that Burke should carry out his duty of "promoting the spiritual interests of the Order and its members, and relations between the Holy See and the Order." In particular, Francis stressed, Burke should ensure that the knights avoid "associations, movements and associations of a relativist nature" and that any knights who were members of such organizations "be asked to remove themselves from the Order." It was an unambiguous mandate, in writing, that Burke should now do what the pope had asked him to do two years earlier.

Francis then carefully responded to the report Burke had given him, saying he would be disappointed "if—as you told me—some of the high Officers were aware of practices such as the distribution of any type of contraceptives and have not yet intervened to end such things." In this case, he went on, "I have no doubt that by following the principle of Paul and 'speaking the truth in love' (Ephesians 4:15), the matter can be discussed with these Officers and the necessary rectification obtained." Boeselager, of course, had been aware and had acted to end any complicity with distribution three years previously.

Burke, however, thought he had what he needed to get rid of Boeselager for Festing. He triumphantly presented the papal missive to the grand master on December 6 with a cover letter that summed up Francis's mandate as "the purification of a mundane spirit and of the use of methods and means contrary to the moral law" in the order. But he failed to mention Freemasonry, implying that the pope's mandate was in reference to the condoms issue. "Given the seriousness of the matter," Burke told Festing in some excitement, "I ask your fullest cooperation, lest the Holy Father find it necessary to address directly his concerns through a visitation of the Order."[13]

The same afternoon, Festing met with Boeselager in the presence of Burke and the order's grand commander, Ludwig Hoffmann von Rumerstein. Festing accused Boeselager of being a "liberal Catholic" and demanded he resign, telling him it was "the express wish of the Holy See, as communicated to him by the Cardinal Patron." If he did not resign, Festing warned, there was the risk of an "apostolic visitation." "Is that a threat?" asked Boeselager. "No," said Burke coldly. "It's a fact." Boeselager refused to resign.[14]

The following day Festing asked the Sovereign Council to vote to remove Boeselager with a two-thirds majority, but the council refused. Meanwhile, Boeselager sought and received confirmation from the Secretariat of State that Burke's claim was quite untrue: it was not the "will of the Holy See" that he stand down. In the evening, Festing met Burke, who now took control. The cardinal told him that the following day "one of three things will happen": either Boeselager would agree to resign, Festing would remove him on grounds of disobedience, or "the Cardinal Patron will recommend to Pope Francis to initiate a visitation of the Order."

On December 8, Festing found a way of bypassing the council, issuing a "Magistral Decree" suspending Boeselager as grand chancellor on grounds of disobedience. The grand master then wrote to more than two hundred high-ranking officials in the order to inform them of the decision, threatening to suspend anyone who disagreed. Alarmed, some wrote to the secretary of state, Cardinal Pietro Parolin, to ask if it was really true that the pope wished Boeselager to resign.[15]

The press then got wind of the story, and suddenly this discreet aristocratic order found itself in the eye of a storm.

Francis is often described, with some awe, as a master strategist, an astute leader who can steer through a conflict by always seeing many steps ahead. It is true: he has a native cunning that is not always typical of highly intelligent people. It is rooted in his capacity to "read" people and situations, the fruit, in large part, of his experience as a master of the Spiritual Exercises. But some of it, at least, comes from the influence of Peronism.

In the early 1970s, the young Jesuit Father Jorge Mario Bergoglio was involved, tangentially, with the curiously named "Iron Guard," a grassroots Peronist organization that was active among the lower-middle classes of Argentine cities like Buenos Aires and Rosario. Bergoglio had gotten to know the Guard through the Jesuit parish in San Miguel, where he had served as a priest, as well as in Buenos Aires, where they had a strong presence in the Jesuits' Salvador University.

Bergoglio was not a member of the Guard. But he had a natural affinity with the movement inspired by General Juan Domingo Perón's two presidencies (1946–1955). Perón widened the electorate to include the urban working class and women, benefiting from a wartime boom in manufacturing of goods that had formerly been imported. His rhetoric closely identified with social teaching of the popes, and his government legislated for what the Church had long urged: just wages, unions, housing, welfare, and votes for women.

But Péron's second term was a different story. The movement lost its roots, became ideological and authoritarian, embattled and aggressive. Perón was removed in a military coup in 1955 after a clash with the Church over the regime's descent into a quasi-religious personality cult. But the repression of Peronism in the following years by the military establishment served only to cement the attachment of ordinary people to the movement.

In the late 1960s, as Argentina endured another dictatorship, the call for Perón to return from his exile in Madrid and take part in elections grew ever more insistent. Between 1969 and his return in 1973, Argentina was roiled by strikes, protests, and guerrilla campaigns of bombing and kidnapping.

These were the years of Bergoglio's rapid ascent within the Society of Jesus. Ordained in 1969 just prior to his thirty-third birthday, he returned to San Miguel, after spending some months in Spain, and received his degrees in February 1971. He was given major roles: vice-rector of the Colegio Máximo, novice master, and professor of pastoral theology. He became a "consultor," a member of the provincial's council of advisers, and in April 1973, he took his final vows of poverty, chastity, and obedience, together with the fourth vow of obedience to the pope for missions. The following July he was named provincial, at the age of just thirty-six, in the midst of a leadership crisis in the Jesuit Province of Argentina and divisions in both Church and society.

The Guard was one of many organizations—including armed groups on both the right and left—that were agitating for Perón's return, but it was the only one that was authentically, doctrinally Peronist and obedient to the leader's orders. Unlike the Montoneros and other armed groups, it rejected violence, and it closely identified with Peronism's national-popular and Catholic roots. Without being a party affiliate, Bergoglio identified closely with the Guard's political culture, as well as its vision of Latin American continental unity, *la patria grande*. He was "a priest who happened to be a Peronist, rather than a Peronist priest," in the words of the politician and former *guardián* Julio Bárbaro. In the young Jesuit, the Guard found a priest who could be close to them during its short but intense existence between 1969 and 1974, when it was dissolved following Perón's return as president and his death a year later. The Guard in that time mushroomed to ten thousand members and shaped a generation of future Peronist politicians and activists, many of whom would meet Bergoglio again when he was cardinal and they were government ministers or trade unionists.

Francis is the first pope to suggest that visitors record on their smartphones short video messages of encouragement from him to take back to their communities. In the early 1970s Guardia leaders would travel to Spain to meet the exiled leader and bring back recordings of Perón's messages for the people. The *guardianes* would go from door to door, playing the tapes in the poor barrios of Buenos Aires and Rosario. Hearing the voice of *el líder* and his messages of encouragement provoked powerful reactions and helped shape their consciousness. "This is what formed us," recalls the jurist and Peronist intellectual Humberto Podetti. "The idea was to learn in the dialogue between Perón and the people."[16]

Experience in the barrios was complemented by a formidable reading list; among the books were practical tomes on military strategy and political theory. But mainly it was about studying Perón's thinking and tactics. Two texts above all stood out: his 1949 vision of organization, *La Comunidad Organizada*, and *Conducción Política*, a collection of talks the general gave on strategy and leadership in 1952. Both would be formative for Bergoglio, for they contained practical lessons that complemented the insights on leadership he drew from the Spiritual Exercises and the Jesuit Constitutions.

Conducción Política translates as "political leadership," but in Perón's vocabulary the *conductor* is less like a politician and more like the director of an orchestra. *Conducción* involves craft and technique, tactics and strategy, but above all, a visceral, emotional connection. A *conductor* inspires and encourages. He models optimism, clear objectives, courage, and virtue; he is willing to sacrifice everything for his people. He organizes, educates, and forms his followers into a body capable of action. He is able to exert discipline because he is respected and because he attains goals on the people's behalf. "A good leader," says Perón, "never has to give an order, because he is able to direct."

That capacity to direct depends on his ability to persuade and convince. "Bosses cannot always do what they want," Francis told Reuters in the summer of 2018. "They have to convince. There is a verb, a word, which helps me very much in governing: 'to persuade.' It is persuasion, slowly persuading, if you can manage to do it." In *Conducción Política* Perón shows how to persuade: both clever framing of messages—thus, Perón's slogan of "political sovereignty, economic independence and social justice" for Argentina forced his opponents either to agree with those aims or to oppose them—but also, crucially, following through with concrete acts that demonstrate the leader's commitment to the message he advocates.[17]

The leader brings in changes decisively but patiently, working "from the periphery in," says Perón, to give time for people to adjust: too much change at the center produces a defensive reaction. Meanwhile, the leader needs to stay above the fray in disputes, and without taking sides he encourages different factions to enter into relationship. He doesn't let events lead him off course: unexpected outcomes are inevitable, but they can be accommodated if the leader is resolute in pursuing his overall plan, just as tactical losses are not fatal if overall the strategy is successful. The same will be true of a leader's popularity, which will wax and wane week by week, but a leader can endure unpopularity as long as his credibility and prestige steadily increase.

A good leader, according to Perón, is never rigid. He needs to adapt and be flexible and must only ever be intransigent when core principles are involved. In order for a leader to get others to do half of what he wants them to do, he must allow them to do half of what they want to do, while making sure his half is key to his overall objectives. A leader should never rely on single or secondhand sources of information but should personally verify from original sources wherever possible: his leadership is only as good as the information to which he has access. He should be inscrutable, playing his cards close to his vest, and use surprise as a secret weapon. A sudden, unanticipated action that disarms opponents is one of a leader's most effective tools. Success, taught Perón, "is obtained at a decisive moment and with a decisive strike." That means patiently putting up with attacks over time, while identifying the "center of gravity" where the action will take place. Then, at the right time, the leader should hit hard, "when it hurts, where it hurts."

"No one doubts in Argentina that the pope is a 'pure Peronist,' an admirer of Perón who is fascinated by politics," notes the political commentator Carlos Cué. But modern Peronism is far from pure. The last time Bergoglio expressed any support for the party was in 1983, when Argentina held its first elections after the Falklands/Malvinas War had put an end to military dictatorship. The then rector of the Colegio Máximo and his circle were conspicuously pro-Peronist in an election in which most Argentines voted for the victor in that election, the Radical Civic Union human rights lawyer Raúl Alfonsín. But thereafter, Peronism degenerated into left-right factions that were indistinguishable from other political ideologies; as bishop in the 1990s and cardinal archbishop in the 2000s, Bergoglio kept a cool distance from the presidencies of Carlos Menem and Néstor Kirchner.[18]

Yet old-style Peronists from the Guardia generation see Francis in action and smile at the similarities in style and governance, not least the way he reaches out to all yet ties himself to no one, or how he identifies with the "people" against the "elites." "To lead a people," Perón wrote in *Conducción Política*, "the first requirement is to have come out of the people, to think and feel like the people—that is, to be 'as' the people." The general made much of his mestizo origins—he was said to be Tehuelche Indian as well as the usual Argentine mix of Italian and Spanish—and was proud of them, never aspiring to be part of Argentina's landowning classes, just as Francis resists being identified with aristocracies of any sort. Perón was a master communicator, with an ability to express big ideas in simple codes, using homespun metaphors and gaucho expressions, insisting that his followers also be "of the people," speaking and acting in ways that kept them close to ordinary folk. It is hard not to see parallels in Francis's insisting that pastors belong to the people of God, or the way he uses the folksy language of a pastor rather than the lofty tones of a theologian, quoting his *nonna* Rosa that shrouds have no pockets, or quipping that you never see a moving van behind a hearse.

This isn't just political savvy. In both Francis's and Perón's rhetoric, there is an iconoclastic, anti-aristocratic element, one that performs a shift: that power is being taken from elites and handed to the people, but in an organized, controlled fashion, with the *conductor* firmly in charge. And in both cases there is a radical, plebeian element that can often sound like a suspicion of academics and social privilege. Francis likes to recall Perón's closeness to a bishop, Nicolás de Carlo, whom he would consult to check that his speeches were in line with Catholic social teaching, and how on bestowing an award on de Carlo in 1948, Perón told the bishops that Christianity was a "religion of the poor, of those who hunger and thirst for justice." It is this biblical energy of early Peronism that old Peronists in Argentina have spotted in Francis. They see him rescuing the spiritual insight at its core and reformulating it for a future generation, just as, when Francis speaks in Rome, they are reminded of *el líder* in his Madrid exile, providing guidance and orientation for the militias back home.[19]

The old *guardianes* see in Francis too the same native gift for governing: the secretive style that keeps everyone guessing, the same ability to juggle different groups, keeping them in tension, the way he seems to know everyone and everything. Those who try to thwart Francis with schemes and power plays are usually undone in the process. Afterward they grumble without irony that one who understands the use of power so well can hardly be a holy and humble Christian. Yet it was Jesus who urged Christians to have the hearts of lambs yet the cunning of serpents. As the pope told the Jesuits in Lithuania in 2018, they had "to discern both in the field of God and in that of the devil . . . We need to ask to know both the intentions of the Lord and those of the enemy of human nature, and his deceptions."[20]

In mid-December 2016, Francis's secretary of state, Cardinal Parolin, wrote Festing to clarify that the pope had been explicit that dialogue should be used to solve problems and that there was no "will of the Holy See" that Boeselager be removed. Parolin asked that the grand chancellor be reinstated. Festing refused, declaring—on what Order of Malta sources say was Burke's advice— that his was an "act of internal governmental administration of the Sovereign Order of Malta and consequently falls solely within its competence." For a Catholic organization to speak to the pope's representative in this way was breathtaking. What Festing said was also untrue. As Parolin pointed out in his reply, the Holy See was entitled to intervene because the Order of Malta professed obedience to the successor of Saint Peter.

Francis named a commission of five heavyweights headed by a Vatican diplomat, Archbishop Silvano Tomasi, with a brief to report swiftly, before the end of January 2017. Festing airily declared the commission a "judicial irrelevance," and in a letter to the knights across the world he told them not to collaborate. If they did give evidence, he said, they were compelled to agree with Festing's decision to oust Boeselager.

Burke's followers now took to articles and blogposts in which they accused the pope of an "autocratic" purge. The UK weekly the *Catholic Herald* headlined its story "The Knights Who Won't Retreat" and claimed that the Vatican's intervention was tantamount to the invasion of one country by another. But this was to confuse the order's dual nature. Its autonomy pertained to its dealings with other states as a humanitarian body, a sovereignty it could only claim because it was under the protection of the Holy See. Insofar as it was a religious body, the order was under the direct jurisdiction of the pope.[21]

Donations began to plummet. "People decided not to help us anymore because they thought we were fighting against the pope," the current grand hospitaller, Dominique Prince de La Rochefoucauld-Montbel, later ruefully recalled. Worldwide, the knights rose up not against the pope but against the grand master, ignoring his threats of retribution if they gave evidence of his leadership failures. When Tomasi's report was handed to the Holy See on January 23, 2017, it included over a hundred written testimonies of Festing's mismanagement.

The writing was now on the wall. In hasty meetings arranged between the order's Sovereign Council and the Secretariat of State, the rebellious knights—reduced to a tiny circle of die-hards around Festing and Burke—raised a white flag. As the society magazine *Tatler* headlined its story, Festing's knights were now "the toffs who took on the Pope (and lost)."[22]

Around that time, Francis gave an Argentine priest who was visiting him a detailed summary of the different factions and the tensions within the Order of Malta's governing body. "You never know what he's thinking until he's got it all worked out," the priest, who had worked for years alongside Bergoglio in Buenos Aires, told me over dinner in Rome that night. "When he suddenly tells you, it's because he's about to act." The next day, sure enough, Festing was summoned to meet with the pope and asked to resign.

Also at our table that night were two close collaborators of the pope's who work in the Vatican, as well as a second Argentine priest and theologian who knows the pope well. They agreed that Francis excels in this kind of tension, not just in the sense that he knows how to manage it but because he sees it as fruitful. "It's not that he *enjoys* conflict, exactly," one of them observed. "But he sees in it the opportunity for change. That's what's happening here."

"He will sometimes do or say something to provoke, so that people show themselves," confirmed Father Antonio Spadaro, SJ, at the headquarters of the famous journal he edits, *La Civiltà Cattolica*, which, by a glorious coincidence is called Villa Malta. "Then he's happy, back in charge." Francis told Spadaro in an interview that "opposition opens up paths," and that "in general, I can say I love opposition." Tension stirs things up, opens new horizons. It is a sign of life. When everything is quiet, on the other hand, Francis begins to be concerned. He needs to see all the pieces in play. In the exotic tussle over the Order of Malta, Francis had seen the opportunity for a reform to liberate and confirm the order's unique mission. Burke's machinations had created chaos but also the chance for change. Once it is brought out into the open, opposition can be used to fulfill God's purposes. Another close collaborator of the pope's says he likes to quote an apocryphal phrase attributed to Cervantes's Don Quixote: "If the dogs are barking, Sancho, it shows we're advancing."[23]

After Festing met with the pope the next day, January 25, 2017, and was shown a long list of complaints about his leadership, he said the pope was kind, telling him he was a good man and a faithful Catholic. Francis had insisted that it would be easier to reform the order without him, and Festing had agreed, relieved to return to his house in Northumberland, England. Burke meanwhile tried without success to persuade the Englishman to withdraw his resignation, claiming that Francis had no right to ask for it. In a press conference in early February, Boeselager would only say, with aristocratic discretion, that the grand master had been "ill advised."[24]

The Sovereign Council met to ratify Festing's resignation and to implement the moves demanded by Vatican Secretary of State Parolin—to reinstate Boeselager and nullify all of Festing's decisions following his sacking of the grand chancellor. A communiqué said the Holy Father's decisions were "carefully taken with regard to and respect for the order, with a determination to strengthen its sovereignty." Boeselager later told journalists that the knights' sovereignty had never been in question, and that the pope had only intervened because his authority had been invoked.

Francis now gently steered a process of reform, naming a top official in the Secretariat of State, Archbishop (now Cardinal) Angelo Becciu, to take charge of the spiritual and moral renewal of the order, and especially of its professed members, in line with the order's own purpose: "to promote the glory of God through the sanctification of its members, the service of faith and of the Holy Father, and helping their neighbors." Burke nominally retained his title but, as Francis made clear in his letter to his delegate, was in practice supplanted by Becciu. But the pope did not punish Burke. Later he gave him the task of investigating sex abuse in Guam, and even reappointed him to the Signatura as a judge.[25]

The pope's letter to the order was paternal but left no room for doubt: the order's sovereignty was *for a purpose*. The knights' unique character as simultaneously a religious organization and a sovereign entity in international law was the basis "for a more effective service according to its ancient yet ever relevant charism." The charism was in its motto, *tuitio fidei et obsequium pauperum*: safeguarding the faith and assistance to the poor. They were mutual; one had to inform the other.

Becciu called for the knights to consider how they could be tied more closely to the Church, and how "greater impetus can be given to charitable service to the most needy, both on a spiritual and a material level." Gradually a clearer mission emerged. As Boeselager would define it: "We cannot go to the poor without Christ, but we cannot follow Christ without going to the poor."[26]

That new understanding came out of a discernment meeting on April 25, 2017, when Francis met fifteen senior knights for an hour in the Casa Santa Marta. He was there "in a double capacity," he told them at the start of the meeting. "I am your superior as far as you are a religious order and your First Class is concerned, and I have to carry out my duty as superior. For the rest of you, I am your pastor and your pope and I will do what I can to further your mission and I will not interfere with your sovereignty but will defend it because I have understood how important it is."[27]

It was an open exchange led by an old Jesuit spiritual master. He told them that the crisis had come about because God was involved, and that meant the devil was also, but that all such moments of temptation, especially when followed by failure, are a golden chance for renewal, for a renewed dependence on Christ.

A theme emerged: the role of the Order of Malta in the Church's mission to the margins. The knights had a mission to two frontiers, both of which were in need of salvation: to the world's poor and marginalized on the one hand, and to the rich and noble on the other. The order was called to live in the spiritual tension between these poles, to hold together in discomfort what the world saw as being in contradiction, for it was in just such spaces that the Holy Spirit could act.

Francis didn't want to suppress the rich and noble "pole." He didn't want the knights to dispense with their épeés and epaulets, their capes and their berets. Uniformed flunkeys would continue to slide through silk-lined corridors. This was an aristocratic order that was attractive to wealthy nobles; it had a tradition, and a culture. But it also had a mission to the other margin, the world of those who were suffering and in need, and by holding these two poles together conversion became possible. "When you bring these [privileged] people into contact with the poor, that is the moment when the Holy Spirit can start working," Francis told them.

The order began to reform. Two members resigned as knights after it was discovered they were Freemasons, and the order "remains vigilant," its spokesman told me. The first-class knights "now have periods of community life, to strengthen their spirituality," he said, adding that new sets of rules aimed at "a more transparent administration and financial compliance" had been introduced. Women members, known as dames, were given greater roles in the governance of the order. The recruitment process for the professed knights, which had become alarmingly lax under Festing, was tightened, and formation of all the knights was improved. In June 2019, the order even banned the use of the old rite Mass from its official celebrations, citing the need for unity. The move closed off any future attempts by Festing's allies "to make the Tridentine rite and traditionalism the central ideology of the order," as one source in the order put it.[28]

There had been a conversion in Francis, too. The pope had come to see past aspects of the order that had so appalled him in Argentina. He had seen into the mission at the heart of the knights' ventures, how their members could grow close to God through service of the poor. "A Church that is not close to people is not a Church," Francis had told *El País* in January 2017, in the midst of the standoff.

> It's a good NGO. Or a pious organization made up of good people who meet for tea and charity work. The hallmark of the Church is its *proximity*. We are all the Church. Therefore, the problem we should avoid is breaking that closeness. Being close is touching, touching Christ in the flesh and blood through your neighbor. When Jesus tells us how we are going to be judged, in Matthew chapter 25, he always talks about reaching out to your neighbor: I was hungry, I was in prison, I was sick. . . . Always being close to the needs of your neighbor. Which is not just charity. It is much more.[29]

Although for most it was a relief, Festing's resignation came as a shock for some knights, who told Reuters it was akin to the resignation of Benedict XVI. The weekend following the grand master's removal, dozens of posters appeared around the Vatican picturing a grim-faced Pope Francis over words written in Romanesco street dialect accusing him of "decapitating" the Order of Malta. The use of Romanesco was designed to suggest that this was somehow the voice of the "people" rather than a wealthy lobby of traditionalists.

Francis didn't refer to the posters until a few weeks later, when he told *Die Zeit* in early March that while he didn't consider Cardinal Burke an enemy—"he's an excellent lawyer"—fundamentalist Catholics put him in mind of the certainty of the apostle Peter just before he betrayed Christ. Asked about the posters, he said the Romanesco dialect was "beautiful," clearly the work of a "very cultured person."

"Someone from here?" the journalist asked, meaning the Vatican.

"No: a cultured person!" Francis replied, roaring with laughter.

It was a joke with echoes of St. John XXIII, who was asked how many people worked in the Vatican and replied: "About half."

When Cardinal Bergoglio had a frugal broth lunch (it was Lent) with two Spanish cardinals during the pre-conclave General Congregations in early March 2013, they agreed that the next pope should be a "Saint Francis of Assisi" type of person, with a love of the poor and a religious outlook that rejects an us-and-them mentality. And, as proof of his humility, he should also have a sense of humor.

To have a sense of humor is a "grace," a "fruit of the consolation of the Holy Spirit," Francis told the Irish Jesuits in 2018 when they asked him how he kept his "heart happy" with all that happened to him. "It seems as if the Lord has given it to me," he told them.

Prayer helps him to receive it. Every day for forty years, after saying the psalms and prayers from the Church's Morning Prayer, Francis has recited one written by Saint Thomas More that ends: "Grant me, O Lord, a sense of good humor. Allow me the grace to be able to take a joke and to discover in life a bit of joy, and to be able to share it with others."

He would need that good humor more than ever in tackling Vatican finances.[30]

three

Mediators, Not Middlemen

During the 2016 "Vatileaks" trial of two of Francis's financial reformers, one of the accused regularly visited a confessional in a church just across the Tiber from the Vatican. Francesca Chaouqui went into St. Louis the French not, however, to be absolved of her sins but to feel inside a ripped cushion for the notes that had been left for her by a friendly official in the Secretariat of State, who wanted to keep her spirits up.

From one of these notes, Chaouqui discovered that Francis had been assured that her trial would be over by the opening of the Jubilee of Mercy in December 2015, and he was irritated that it was dragging on. From another she learned that her co-defendant, Monsignor Lucio Vallejo Balda, had tried to commit suicide in his Vatican cell.[1]

The choice of San Luigi dei Francesi was ironic, given the church's long connection with the theme of money: it was founded to cater to French notaries, bankers, and merchants who came to Rome to do business with the Papal States. In the far left-hand corner of the chapel hung Caravaggio's famous cycle of paintings on the life of Saint Matthew, whose career before meeting Jesus was in accountancy. The first of the cycle, *The Calling of St. Matthew*, was a long-standing favorite of Francis's. During his annual visits to Rome as a cardinal, when he stayed in the nearby clergy guesthouse on the Via della Scrofa, he would pop in to contemplate the painting, and these days he keeps a copy close by in his room in the Casa Santa Marta.

Caravaggio's Jesus bursts into a dimly lit, seedy backroom. Men are huddled around a table with coins that one of them is counting. Christ points toward the bearded man, who looks befuddled, as if asking, "Who, *me*?" while another bearded man, presumably Peter, is trying to dissuade Jesus, as if to say, "Not *him*, surely?"

Francis sees in Caravaggio's picture a dramatic telling of his own conversion story in the basilica of Flores in 1953. "That finger of Jesus, pointing like that at Matthew. That's me, how I feel. Like Matthew," he told Father Antonio Spadaro in 2013. "He clings to his money, as if saying, 'No! Not me! No, this money is mine!' That's what I am: a sinner on whom the Lord's gaze has fallen."

He said something similar to young Filipinos in Manila in January 2015: that Matthew had betrayed his Jewish countrymen by collecting money from them on behalf of the occupying Romans, but then he was suddenly, unexpectedly, chosen by Jesus. "Those who were with him are saying, 'What, *him*? That good-for-nothing traitor?' and he grabs the money and doesn't want to let go. But the amazement of being loved overcomes him and he follows Jesus, . . . who had surprised him with something more important than all the money he had."[2]

This struggle within two obstinate forces, God's mercy versus human stinginess, is the subject of Bergoglio's first published article, in 1968, on the drama of a vocation. Heavily influenced at the time by Gaston Fessard's groundbreaking 1956 book on the "dialectic" of the Spiritual Exercises, Bergoglio posited the "election" in terms of the irony of freedom: that a person can only be truly free by overcoming self-affirmation and allowing himself to be overcome by God, something he cannot do alone but through the mediation of the Creator, a mediation that is in turn only possible by means of the believer's freely given assent. In the tense, dynamic interplay of wooer and wooed, whose freedom God chooses to respect yet whose good His love can never stop seeking, is the story of God's interaction with humanity. Why do people resist? Because—as Bergoglio explained—of the human illusion that what we have, we have earned; and because what we think we deserve to keep, we fear to lose. Yet all we are and have is pure gift, to which the only reasonable response must be a joyful surrender in gratitude, expressed in service to others, in obedience to the source of our good.[3]

It is a lifelong process. Even after nine years as a Jesuit, Bergoglio, in a "personal credo" penned in a moment of great intensity prior to his ordination in 1969, spoke of God's loving gaze on him doing battle with "the stinginess of my soul, which seeks to take without giving." When he described the effect of Saint Matthew's conversion at a homily in Holguín, Cuba, in September 2015, he was surely speaking out of his own experience:

> After the Lord looked upon him with mercy, he said to Matthew: "Follow me." Matthew got up and followed him. After the look, a word; after love, the mission. Matthew is no longer the same; he is changed inside. The encounter with Jesus and his loving mercy has transformed him. His table, his money, his remaining outside—all these were left behind. Before, he had sat waiting to collect his taxes, to take from others; now, with Jesus, he must get up and give, give himself to others. Jesus looks at him and Matthew encounters the joy of service. For Matthew and for all who have felt the gaze of Jesus, other people are no longer to be "lived off," used and abused. The gaze of Jesus gives rise to missionary activity, service, self-giving. Other people are those whom Jesus serves.[4]

In his note at the end of the Second Week "on the amendment and reform of one's personal life and state," Saint Ignatius in the Spiritual Exercises observes how a person "will make progress in things of the spirit to the degree to which they divest themselves of self-love, self-will and self-interest." Clinging to wealth or influence, which Saint Ignatius calls *honra*, is a way of resisting self-giving love. Thus, simplicity of life—not pauperism, which rejects the good of material things, but sobriety, which treats them as gifts—is a hallmark of those who have centered their lives on Christ. "Each one must live as the Lord asks him to live," Francis told journalists on the plane from Rio de Janeiro in July 2013. "But austerity, a general austerity, I think is necessary for all of us who work in the service of the Church."[5]

Both Lucio Vallejo Balda and Francesca Chaouqui were passionate and dedicated reformers, members of the financial audit team Francis created in 2013, known as the Commission for Reference on the Organization of the Economic-Administrative Structure of the Holy See (COSEA). But they also had ambitions: he to lead Francis's new finance ministry, the Secretariat for the Economy (SPE), she to have the Vatican as a client of her communications consultancy. Within them, as within most human beings, the call to serve jostled with a clinging to *honra*.

When Francis appointed Cardinal Pell to run the SPE in early 2014,

Vallejo Balda suffered the sudden deflation of rejection. After spending more and more time at parties with Chaouqui and her friends, he fell out with her. At the trial he accused her of seducing him. She accused him of being gay. He claimed that she pressured him to leak information to journalist Gianluigi Nuzzi; she that he did so out of revenge.

"I wasn't in my right mind," Vallejo Balda confessed to the judges in March 2016. "I was convinced there was no way out." Nuzzi and another journalist, Emiliano Fittipaldi, had published their books six months earlier, in November 2015, days after Vallejo and Chaouqui—dubbed "Baldy and Chooky" in Vatican cafés—were led off in handcuffs for questioning. Chooky, by that time pregnant, was released after questioning, but the gendarmes put Baldy, the man in day-to-day charge of COSEA, in the police cell behind Vatican walls. It was the same cell that had been occupied four years earlier by Benedict XVI's butler, Paolo Gabriele, after he was convicted of leaking Vatican papers to the same journalist. There was a collective media groan: had nothing changed in the Vatican?[6]

Yet this wasn't the same movie. Nuzzi's 2012 Vatileaks exposé, *His Holiness*, painted Benedict as a remote and ineffectual leader sitting atop a Curia run amok with infighting and corruption, while his 2015 *Merchants in the Temple* showed Francis as a can-do sheriff leading a vigorous reform that was getting blocked at every turn. Neither narrative was quite accurate. Far from being passive, Benedict had commissioned reports into Vatican lobbies and corruption and made key personnel changes on the eve of his resignation. Equally, the changes Francis had begun to put in place at the end of 2013 and in early 2014 were already bearing fruit by the time *Merchants in the Temple* was published in November 2015.

By then a rash of reforms—new laws and procedures, watchdog mechanisms, makeovers, investigations and prosecutions—had begun to take effect that transformed the Vatican's financial management and clamped down on wrongdoing. Yet the story of that makeover, initiated by Benedict XVI and carried through resolutely by Francis, has barely been told, in part because the media narrative of a reformer pope being resisted by a corrupt old guard has proved so durable.

Chooky ended up with a ten-month suspended sentence after her worn-out lawyer claimed she should not go to prison merely for being "unpleasant, insufferable, arrogant, and presumptuous." Baldy was given eighteen months' detention in a religious house but served less than half of that time before Francis freed him to return to Spain for Christmas.

"Scandals will come," Francis told reporters on his way back from the Holy Land in May 2014. "The issue is how to prevent more of them happening." There had to be transparency and honesty in Vatican finances, and new structures and regulations were vital to implement them. But that was never going to be the end of the story. "There will be inconsistencies," he warned. "They will always be there because we are human, and so the reform has to be ongoing."

The call to serve would always jostle with the urge to take.[7]

Cardinals in conclave don't campaign, nor are they elected on mandates. But no pope chosen in March 2013 would have been in doubt about what was expected of him. The need to clean up and radically reorganize Vatican finances was a major topic of discussion in the pre-conclave cardinals' discussions, uniting senior churchmen who on many other matters of doctrine and theology would struggle to agree. The consensus among the 115 or so voting cardinals was that the new pope needed to "bring about a radical reform of the Roman curia and Vatican finances and examine whether the Vatican really needs a bank," as the Vatican spokesman, Father Federico Lombardi, summarized their discussion. Cardinal Wilfrid Fox Napier, the archbishop of Durban, South Africa, spoke for many when he called for getting rid once and for all of "this cloud that was hanging over the Church."[8]

After reading the report Benedict had commissioned, Francis felt free, finally, to place on a modern pope's lips the "C"-word his predecessors had studiously avoided. Corruption was "a daily temptation," Francis said in a 2014 weekday homily, to which "a political, a businessman, a prelate" can all fall. Later he said it more directly: "There is corruption not just in politics but in every institution—even the Vatican." Wherever there was corruption, it was the same: the intermediaries always profited from those who had the least. Corruption, Francis wrote in his 2016 letter on mercy, "shatters the plans of the weak and tramples upon the poorest of the poor."[9]

Bergoglio's famous pre-conclave speech—the one that led so many cardinals to think of electing him—pointed, like Jesus's finger in the Caravaggio picture, to the self-referential, spiritually worldly Church that lived from its own light. Overspending, cronyism, and a lack of transparency were symptomatic of a Vatican turned in on itself, with its back to the world, imperious and self-seeking. That's what had to be reversed. As the former Jesuit superior general Adolfo Nicolás put it, the financial reform for the pope was about the Church's evangelizing credibility, one that "touched a missionary nerve that for him is extremely important."

In using the "C"-word, Francis was shattering the bella figura culture of denial, of always presenting the best face to the outside world, of heaping the blame on rotten apples while defending the barrel. To counter the bella figura with a *brutta figura*, the pope had to speak directly and fearlessly, and to appoint as his finance chief a man who delighted in telling the emperor he had no clothes. Nothing signaled an end to circumlocution and cronyism so much as his choice of the then archbishop of Sydney, Cardinal Pell, as prefect of the new SPE (pronounced *SPAY*, the Italian acronym for the Secretariat for the Economy), in February 2014.[10]

"The Church was robbed," Pell told me bluntly when we sat down three years later in the SPE's splendid office a short walk up from the Sant'Anna gate. It is hard not to feel, in his presence, as if you are being corrected for something you haven't yet done or said. Like a kindly if overbearing professor, Pell gave me a lengthy rundown on the financial reform: what had changed, where the holdouts were. But what he was really keen for me to grasp was how bad things had been before Francis's reforms began.

It was like this, he said, moving his little white china cup of espresso to the edge of a round table and explaining that the tabletop represented international criminal networks. This—he pointed at his espresso—was the Vatican, a little circle at the edge of the big circle. At that intersection, he explained, crimes were committed, both outside and within the Vatican. There was theft of the Church's money. But mostly it was of other people's money. The issue was the fact that the Vatican was exploited—with the cooperation of curial middlemen—by networks of patronage and favor-trading that tied Vatican officials to Italy's business and finance circles, linking the Holy See to some very unholy characters: mobsters, tax evaders, and money launderers.

Taking a sip from his visual aid, which seemed tiny in his meaty hands, Pell described how the Vatican had been doubly vulnerable to this exploitation as a sovereign state within a corrupt Italy. If Vatican sovereignty gave the Church freedom to serve the common good of humanity, it would be safe; but if it was a license for criminality and impunity for criminals, it was built on sand. It was hard not to think of a parallel with the row over the Order of

Malta's sovereignty: no one questioned it as long as it served humanity, but if it was used to further the interests of cliques it was impossible to justify.

At stake in this reform was more than just the restoration of good housekeeping. This was—whisper it—about the very future of the Catholic Church as a global body at the service of humanity with a sovereign state at its core. Put differently, only by opening up and internationalizing the city-state, freeing it from the favor-trading networks known as *le lobby*, could the Vatican guarantee the sovereignty that was essential to its global mission. That also meant disentangling the Vatican from Italian interests, introducing sound regulations, and turning it outward, in service of the papal mission and the wider Church.

That meant a radical overhaul of personnel and culture, and new structures of accountability and oversight. This was the task of a generation, not a single papacy. Francis could not sack everyone and start again. Even if it were feasible legally or financially, the disruption would not get him more quickly to where he needed to go. He had little choice but to keep the people he had, losing them naturally when they reached the age of retirement, and promoting new ones from below. But he could move quickly on two fronts that would open the path to far-reaching, long-term change. The first was to create new regulations and structures of oversight. The second was to challenge the culture of kickbacks and intermediaries and focus the Curia outward, on Christ and on mission. For the first, he would need help, from people like Pell; the second he could take charge of himself. It was what, after all, he had been doing for decades.

In his account of Jesus driving out "all who sold and bought in the temple," Saint Matthew's Gospel records two responses. On the one hand there was the fury of the chief priests and scribes, who plotted to kill Jesus; on the other there was the delight of the poor, who flocked to Jesus to be healed. What Francis did after his election to destroy the Vatican's financial culture was decisive and unprecedented. And it triggered a ferocious reaction from many curial officials.

It is a bank that you cannot borrow from. It is in the Vatican yet does not manage its money. Its sole shareholder is the pope, and its acronym in Italian sounds like "Eeyore," the depressed donkey in the Winnie-the-Pooh stories.

The answer to the riddle is the IOR, or, to give it its full, unbankerly name, the Institute for the Works of Religion. Created during World War II to move money to missions in both Axis and Allied countries, it occupies a library-quiet former dungeon with thick curved walls next to the Apostolic Palace. The funds it manages belong to dioceses, religious orders, and charities that use the IOR to channel funds around the globe, through local partner banks. The bank invests its roughly $8 billion in assets, pays out interest, and generates income for the Vatican. In 2016, for example, the IOR earned the Holy See $53 million; in 2018, $19.8 million.

Although it is known colloquially as "the Vatican Bank," the IOR is not to be confused with the Administration of the Patrimony of the Apostolic See, known by the Italian acronym APSA, which is the Vatican's true financial center, a kind of general accounting office that pays the salaries of Vatican employees and acts as a purchasing office and human resources department. APSA administers the so-called patrimony, a portfolio of real estate and stocks bought with the endowment Mussolini paid in 1929 in compensation for Italy's earlier takeover of the Papal States. The patrimony was valued by COSEA in 2014 at around $800 million, mostly held in property and land—APSA manages, for example, 102 million square feet of housing in Rome as well as hundreds of properties elsewhere in Europe—which make up the nonliquid assets the pope has at his disposal. Despite suspicions that its accounts have been used in the past for money laundering and insider trading, APSA has mostly resisted efforts to make it transparent and accountable and has led a quiet life in comparison to the scandal-prone IOR.[11]

When the cardinals in the 2013 pre-conclave meetings said, "No more Calvis," they meant the bad old days of the 1970s and 1980s, when IOR's cigar-smoking American head, Archbishop Paul Marcinkus, entwined the Vatican's investment portfolio with two shady business magnates. This was what Pell meant when he spoke of mobsters and Freemasons. The wealthy Sicilian financier Michele Sindona and Roberto Calvi, head of the Milan-based Banco Ambrosiano, were both members of the immensely powerful Propaganda Due (P2) Masonic lodge that funneled millions in cash through "black" IOR accounts.

When Marcinkus switched his loyalty to Calvi following the collapse of Sindona's business empire, the IOR became ipso facto the underwriter of Calvi's elaborate maze of offshore banks and holding companies. Then the Ambrosiano failed in 1980, and the house of cards collapsed. Calvi vanished in a blizzard of fraud charges until he was seen a year later hanging by a rope under London's Blackfriars Bridge with bricks in the pockets of his tailored suit. The Vatican paid out a humiliating $406 million as a "voluntary contribution" in recognition of its "moral involvement" in the bank's collapse, a loss that was in addition to the tens of millions of dollars of now worthless investments in Calvi's shell companies. But a greater loss than both was the trust of ordinary Catholics. After Sindona's 1983 murder in jail, a steady stream of conspiracy books on the Vatican's links with mafiosi and Masons led Catholics across the world to withhold Peter's Pence, the worldwide voluntary contribution to support the pope's intentions.[12]

The faithful eventually began donating again, but the United Nations in 2000 still had the Vatican on its list of the world's most attractive financial laundromats, ahead even of Liechtenstein and the Bahamas. Real reform only began in 2009, after the European Union demanded that Italy's central bank tighten its anti-money-laundering controls over the Vatican, and Italian authorities froze $30 million of IOR bank money until they could be persuaded that the Vatican was sincere about change. In December 2010 Benedict XVI approved the Vatican's first anti-money-laundering law and created a watchdog to implement it, the Vatican Financial Information Authority, known by the Italians as the AIF. But the AIF was defanged by Benedict's secretary of state, Cardinal Tarcisio Bertone, and by April 2012 the Council of Europe's financial transparency watchdog Moneyval declared that the Vatican had, if anything, gone backward. In January 2013, shortly before Benedict announced his resignation and the cardinals gathered to elect his successor, Italy's central bank suspended credit and debit card transactions in the Vatican in protest at the city-state's failure to abide by European money-laundering norms.

This was the paralysis that underpinned the Vatileaks scandal: Nuzzi's *His Holiness* laid bare the internal power struggles unleashed by Benedict's efforts to achieve financial transparency. By the time the book came out in late 2012, the German pope had already made his secret decision to stand down the following February, after asking three cardinals to investigate *le lobby*, the favor-trading networks that blighted the Vatican bureaucracy. The cardinals' three-hundred-page report was what Benedict handed Francis in a white box after the election. It was said to detail various "lobbies" that promote and protect the interests of those who belonged to them. They are usually the source of the leaks and damaging news stories that swirl around the Vatican, aimed these days often at Francis.

Benedict also made two key appointments that would bear fruit under

Francis. In response to Moneyval's damning report on the IOR in July 2012, which complained that it was impossible to track the money passing through the bank's thirty-three thousand accounts, Benedict appointed René Brülhart, a respected Swiss regulator with a record of cleaning up Liechtenstein, as head of the AIF. Then, right after his shocking resignation announcement on February 11, 2013, the outgoing pope appointed Ernst von Freyberg, a German Knight of Malta, as the new director of the IOR. "It seemed right, for many reasons, not to put another Italian at the helm of the bank," the pope emeritus wryly recalled.[13]

The Vatican faced bankruptcy, that much was clear. Costs were spiraling and income falling. But when Pope Francis received a handwritten note from the foreign auditors two months after his election, he realized why no one could explain precisely where the losses were coming from.

The five auditors—outsiders who counseled the Vatican's finance oversight body, the Prefecture for the Economic Affairs of the Holy See—had for many years pointed Benedict XVI to a crisis coming down the tracks, warning him in 2011 that "decisive leadership" was called for. Now, meeting Francis, they believed that leadership had arrived.

They attended the pope's seven a.m. Mass in the Santa Marta guesthouse in May 2013 and spoke to him afterward. Later they wrote to him with their mobile numbers to warn of "a complete absence of transparency" in the affairs of the two financial entities of the Vatican, both the "Holy See" (that is, the government of the global Catholic Church, including its departments, or "dicasteries," in Rome, as well as its worldwide network of nunciatures, or embassies) and the "Governorate" (which runs the city-state, receiving funds from its museums and shops to pay for its gardens and gendarmes). The source of the fug, the advisers told Francis, was the Vatican's culture. There was a self-absorption and unreality among curial officials, who were convinced that the ordinary rules of the world didn't apply to them.[14]

Francis spoke to the "Council of 15," the body of cardinals that for years had overseen Vatican finances, the following week. "Our books are not in order, we have to clean them up," he told them, before going on to list a catalogue of woes: millions of euros paid out for improper work executed without oversight and with padded invoices, disastrous investments that yielded virtually no interest, crony employment practices, as well as the hopeless lack of transparency and protocols for competitive bidding.

He then announced something quite unprecedented in the history of the city-state. He had named, he told them, a commission of outside investigators, chaired by one of the foreign auditors, Maltese banker Joseph Zahra, to comb through the accounts of the entire Vatican. COSEA would get a true snapshot of the finances and would design a new structure capable of transparent, efficient, scandal-free governance. The commission would be run day-to-day by its secretary, Spanish monsignor Lucio Vallejo Balda, who brought in his friend Francesca Chaouqui, a PR expert with Ernst & Young in Italy. On its board were Jean-Baptiste de Franssu, ex-chief of the asset-management giant Invesco in Europe, as well as Jochen Messemer, a top German executive at the insurer ERGO, and George Yeo, former foreign minister of Singapore.

At his first meeting with the COSEA team at the Santa Marta guesthouse, they listened, open-mouthed, as Francis denounced with fearless directness the very culture the foreign auditors had warned him about: the way inept and scandal-ridden practices had inhibited giving and caused distrust, and how unpredictable, unaccountable spending had bloated the bureaucracy. They were astonished at how, within months of his election, he had grasped the nature of the problem. Francis criticized what he called a "nouveau riche" mentality, a culture of self-entitlement and carelessness about costs that gobbled up revenue from Peter's Pence, which was supposed to be used for the pope to assist the needy, not to plug budget deficits. For the Church's evangelizing message to be credible, the Vatican's finances had to be, too. "Let us make money to go to the poor," Francis told them, adding: "You are the experts and I trust you. I want solutions to these problems, and I want them as soon as possible."

Meeting the pope for the first time, Chaouqui was unprepared for the steel behind Francis's warm, humble exterior. She was surprised, too, by the ferocity of the intelligence behind the pope's kind gaze. He was a "warrior," she decided, and they were his "sword ready to be unsheathed."[15]

What the pope sought, above all, were structures to support culture change. The existing system—a toothless Prefecture and an oversight council of cardinals who had little choice but to accept the figures they were given—was not fit for the purpose. There had to be a proper segregation of powers, systems of checks and balances, accountability and transparency. Strict protocols had to be designed to end the cycle of scandals. Sound financial management must now replace haphazard autonomous budgets so that a leaner, self-sustaining administration could balance the Vatican's books and free up funds, ending an annual deficit of over €30 million that was running down the patrimony and swallowing more than half of Peter's Pence. The pope was in a hurry. He needed to know why the Vatican's budgets were out of control and he needed outline proposals for new structures to present to his new council of cardinal advisers, the C9. And he needed it all by an apparently impossible deadline: the following February 2014.[16]

COSEA met regularly over the next ten months, operating around the clock with some secrecy out of Room 127 in the Casa Santa Marta. Its base in the papal guesthouse underlined both its authority and its independence: the commissioners had a mandate directly from Francis to penetrate the penumbra of curial obfuscation and identify the obstacles to change. Given sweeping powers to inspect the books, Zahra's team recruited global accountancy firms to assist them. KPMG, Deloitte, PricewaterhouseCoopers, Ernst & Young, and Promontory sent in experts with clipboards and spreadsheets who fanned across the Vatican asking awkward—and often ignorant—questions. It was a major external shock to an insular, courtly culture that had long been accountable only to itself.

Francis made clear to Zahra that there were two important extra principles involved in the makeover: the Vatican's universality, and the presence of qualified laypeople. The two principles were related: the leading posts in finances were almost all occupied by Italian clergy, and to throw off the Italian patronage networks, the Vatican needed a global, professional workforce. But how could that happen when Francis had set as a nonnegotiable principle that nobody would lose their jobs, while at the same time demanding that costs be cut? The makeover had to take into account that Francis would be mostly stuck with the existing Vatican workforce, while at the same time preparing for it to evolve over time into a more lay, professional, international body. What mattered, therefore, was to change the culture and introduce new structures and regulations to support that change.

Francis's backing for the reforms was essential, Pell told me in 2017. "I honestly don't know if there would have been many others who would have been able or game to disturb the status quo in such a way."[17]

In 2002, during Argentina's financial meltdown, the country's then nuncio, Spanish cardinal Santos Abril y Castelló, was approached by two businessmen in Buenos Aires. They offered to "transit" $2 million through an IOR account, leaving a sizable sum "for the Church" as a charitable donation. Abril y Castelló refused and informed Cardinal Bergoglio. Thirteen years later, Abril y Castelló was in charge of the Basilica of St. Mary Major in Rome. He was the obvious person for Francis to ask to advise on whether to close the IOR.

In principle, Francis hated the idea of the Church owning an offshore bank. Saint Peter, he enjoyed pointing out, seemed to have gotten by without one. But he also knew that the IOR served an important missionary function, and he was willing to hear the case for keeping it—as long as it could be made as pure as virgin snow. So while Abril y Castelló's commission on the reform of the IOR, known as CRIOR, mulled the bank's fate, Francis urged Benedict's eve-of-resignation appointee Ernst von Freyberg to press ahead with the bank's cleanup.[18]

Von Freyberg brought in U.S.-based Promontory Financial Group, which stationed twenty inspectors inside the IOR to pore through the accounts of 13,700 individuals and 5,200 institutions to truffle out dubious account holders and suspicious transactions. Thousands of accounts—around a third of the total—would eventually be closed. IOR was able to publish externally audited accounts for the first time in its 125-year history and brought in a communications expert to open up the fortress to a suspicious press. The cleanup cost of that first year was around €7 million, a long-delayed funeral parlor bill for burying Marcinkus and Calvi. On CRIOR's advice, Francis in the end concluded, on balance, that a regulated, transparent, cleaned-up IOR was better news for the world's poor than no IOR at all.[19]

The cleanup led to a series of arrests. First to fall was Polish monsignor Bronisław Morawiec, who held the purse strings of the Basilica of St. Mary Major. His four-year prison sentence for embezzling €230,000 was the first sign that criminality would no longer be tolerated. But far more spectacular was the arrest in June 2013 of a senior accountant at APSA as he stepped off a light airplane packed with bags of €500 notes. Monsignor Nunzio Scarano later faced trials in two cases: conspiracy to smuggle €20 million in cash into Italy from Switzerland to help friends avoid taxes, and money laundering through his account at the IOR. Although he was later acquitted, the backstories of his lavish living and high-powered connections provided rich pickings for the press, and made him the symbol of the culture Francis was taking on.

In the old days the Vatican would have invoked its sovereignty to deal—or usually not—with the matter internally. The Scarano case showed how different it was now. This time the Vatican's different bodies worked with each other and with the Italian authorities in a common front. The arrest followed a tip-off from within the Vatican to its watchdog, Brülhart's Financial Information Authority (AIF), which sent its first ever rogatory letter (requesting mutual legal assistance) on financial crimes to the Italian authorities. Meanwhile, von Freyberg handed the AIF a 110-page summary and executive report on all of Scarano's transactions, which Brülhart handed on to the Italian police. The Scarano arrest in turn triggered the resignations of the IOR's managing director and deputy, Paolo Cipriani and Massimo Tulli, who would be fined by a Rome court in February 2017 for breaking money-laundering laws, as well as convicted in a civil Vatican case brought by the IOR of mismanaging investments.[20]

Francis's Scarano memo could not have been clearer: there was no hiding criminality now behind the Leonine walls.

Suddenly exposed, *le lobby* pushed back, leaking stories of the supposedly outrageous costs of international auditors and other external consultants. But the stories seldom took wing or backfired. The most spectacular was an early attempt to bring down the IOR chaplain Francis had named to be his eyes and ears at the bank, Monsignor Battista Ricca. The leaked claim that while assigned to the nunciature in Montevideo years earlier, Ricca had frequented gay bars, led to Francis uttering his famous phrase, "Who am I to judge?" in response to a journalist's question during his first airborne press conference. What got missed in the brouhaha over the phrase was that this most iconic of Francis's off-the-cuff replies neatly deprived *le lobby* of their weapon of choice: blackmail.[21]

The AIF's head, Brülhart, was a discreet reformer who understood the need to move patiently and quietly. For months the Swiss regulator lay low, listening and building consensus for reform, until he was ready to present a plan to Francis in September 2013. The object of his proposed regulatory framework was to bring the Vatican into line with contemporary European oversight mechanisms without sacrificing its uniqueness as a global religious institution. He worked to three core principles: sound governance, transparency (accountability), and internationalism (de-Italianization) and moved ahead on two fronts: a cleanup to assure Catholics their money was well managed, and bolstering Vatican sovereignty by aligning its financial oversight mechanisms with the best in Europe. All the reforms had the objective of reducing the Vatican's vulnerability to Italian political and financial influence, which had reached new lows in the Benedict-Bertone era.

Francis backed the Brülhart plan and issued new laws to shift the Vatican from an anarchic, self-regulating environment to one in which state-of-the-art financial rules enforced across Europe were applied with equal rigor. After the laws were promulgated in November 2013, Francis elevated the AIF from a financial intelligence unit to a proper regulator, and, at Brülhart's urging, brought in lay experts from Singapore, France, Germany, and the United States to replace the Italians on the board. The number of instances in which the AIF shared information with regulators in other countries grew from a dozen cases in 2012 to fifteen hundred by the end of 2016, while suspicious activity reports—flagging transactions that could be connected to criminals or terrorists—soared from just one in 2012 to more than a thousand in 2016. In that year, for example, a former Benedict abbot on the run from British police over abuse allegations tried to transfer funds from his IOR account to Kosovo, triggering an alert from the Vatican to the UK's Financial Intelligence Unit that led to Laurence Soper being arrested by Kosovo police.[22]

Brülhart was eventually able to bring the Holy See into the Egmont Group, the global network of financial intelligence units that coordinates the policing of transparency regulations. By then it was clear, at least, that when it came to the monitoring and supervision of financial transactions, the Vatican was no longer as Pell had portrayed it: Italy's pocket wild west. The point was made, inadvertently and colorfully, by a prominent Milan politician who was convicted of taking bribes. "There is no longer any protection in the Vatican," Gianstefano Frigerio lamented to an accomplice in a cell phone call that was wiretapped by Italian police. "The new pope . . . couldn't give a crap about the Italian world, and then among the cardinals there is no one who can offer protection anymore."[23]

For Francis, the policies and structures were only ever a part of the response. What mattered most to him was to get at the spiritual sickness that lay at the root of the problem: the nest-feathering mentality that was the very opposite of the mind-set of service presented in the Gospel. He had experience from Buenos Aires of priests who took state handouts for projects in exchange for kickbacks, bishops who accepted personal donations for favors, and diocesan bureaucrats who, for a fee, would look the other way. He had spent over a decade challenging that mind-set.

In Buenos Aires he had invited his clergy to choose between being a *mediator*, one who serves another's needs and intercedes for them, and an *intermediary* or middleman, who profits from others. The problem of the latter was at the core of what the Jesuit theologian Henri de Lubac called "spiritual worldliness," a sickness that Francis believed was the worst temptation that could befall the Church, along with its close relative, clericalism. Both led to the Church closing in on itself, living for itself; living *off* people, rather than *for* them. Spiritual worldliness was the use of the goods of the people of God for self-enrichment. The mediator, Bergoglio told Buenos Aires priests in 1999, built up others at the cost of himself, while the intermediary or middleman built up himself at the cost of others. One interceded; the other exploited. Which were they, he asked: "pastors of the people" or "state clerics"?[24]

Now, in his Santa Marta daily homilies at the end of 2013 and in early 2014, Francis polarized the choices facing clergy in the same way, mocking the "peacock-priest" and the "priest entrepreneur" as pitiful figures, "devotees of the god Narcissus." He also made fun of clergy who went down to the Euroclero vestments shop in Rome to try on elaborate cassocks and vestments; self-focus was a downward spiral, at the bottom of which was corruption. "We might start with a small bribe, but it's like a drug," Francis warned in November 2013, going on to pray "that the Lord may change the hearts of those who worship the kickback god." Like an Old Testament prophet or medieval monk-reformer, he poured scorn on those who thought of themselves as good Catholics but cared only for money, telling benefactors to take back their checks if the money came from profits made through unfair wages. "The people of God—that is, the Church—don't need dirty money," he said, but "hearts that are open to God's mercy."[25]

His harangues made the news. Accustomed to popes chastising laypeople about sex rather than clergy about corruption, reporters could now file stories on a "pope at odds with his workforce," with an inevitable quote from a disgruntled unnamed monsignor complaining that Francis never seemed to have a good word to say about his priests. Why was the pope of mercy, ran the regular complaint, so "merciless" with his clergy?

The answer was in Bergoglio's 1991 essay discerning the difference between sin and corruption.

As long as a person was a sinner, there was hope, because the sinner accepted the truth of who she really was and how far she had fallen short; once she was ready to turn to God in shame and repentance, she could be forgiven and change. The Church's task with the sinner, as Jesus showed, was to be compassionate and merciful, always offering a space for her conversion.

With the corrupt, on the other hand, mercy could not yet reach them, because they had no shame. The corrupt denied the truth about themselves and refused to admit they were falling short; they turned not to God in shame, but away from God and out to others, whom they made complicit in their webs of deceit and self-justification. (This was particularly serious in the case of clergy, said Bergoglio, because *corruptio optimi pessima*—the corruption of the best is the worst: the self-righteousness of the corrupt religious made them the most resistant of all to conversion.) The corrupt could be turned around only by a major external shock, some great tribulation such as prison, bankruptcy, grave illness, or a humiliating scandal. In the absence of these, a public dressing-down by the pope was a mundane cleric's best hope.[26]

Because Francis had a decades-long reputation, as both a Jesuit and a bishop, for austerity and frugality, he could castigate the corrupt and profligate with credibility. This was the pope who famously kept his old black shoes and silver-plated pectoral cross along with his last-century plastic watch, who after his election as pope had gone back to the clergy house on the Via della Scrofa—where the cleaners say he was the only priest who ever made his own bed—to pay his bill; and who in countless gestures, big and small, had issued a firm "no" to the Constantinian imperial frippery of ermine-trimmed crimson capes and scarlet footwear.

Esquire had even toasted him as 2013's best-dressed man, claiming the simplicity of the pope's couture "signaled a new era." Austerity was "in": stories abounded of Francis's frugal style suddenly being imitated by clerics formerly known for their flamboyance. But not everyone in Rome was impressed. Raniero Mancinelli, papal tailor for many decades down on the Borgo Pio, said cardinals as a result were ordering from him "things that are much lighter, simpler and more sober . . . and consequently"—he mourned to Claire Giangravè of *Crux*—"less expensive." Francis's own simple white vestment was old, vulnerable to wear and tear from so much contact with people, Mancinelli sighed, adding sadly that he imagined that "in the evening [the pope] just puts it to wash, and wears it again the next morning."[27]

Perhaps recalling how an Argentine bishop in the late 1960s famously deplored how bishops went out to meet the poor "in a car of the latest model or a first-class railway carriage," Bergoglio in Buenos Aires avoided cars whenever possible, preferring to be with the people on the bus or the *subte* (subway). It broke his heart, Francis told seminarians in the summer of 2013, to see a priest or a nun behind the wheel of the latest automobile. As pope he could not get around Rome as he did in Buenos Aires, but he could at least opt for the car an ordinary Italian family might use. It took a pope from the developing world, one who had spent years of his life immersed in the lives of struggling people, to put the shoes of the fisherman in a Ford Focus.[28]

The Casa Santa Marta, the marble-and-wood-paneled guesthouse built by John Paul II where Francis had opted to live, is simple, though hardly (as some in the media persisted in portraying it) humble. Inside, his Room 201—a modest space with a bedroom, sitting area, and study—is in striking contrast to the princely spaciousness of many cardinals' apartments in Rome. Benedict XVI's secretary of state, Cardinal Tarcisio Bertone, for example, has a 4,305-square-foot top-floor bachelor pad on the edge of the Vatican Gardens with fabulous views of St. Peter's Basilica, which became public knowledge as the result of a scandal over the use of Bambino Gesù hospital funds for a $500,000 renovation.

Yet Francis wasn't criticizing opulence by living in the Santa Marta—the Apostolic Palace was hardly luxurious. What he didn't like was that the palazzo was lonely. Francis had spent almost all of his Jesuit existence in the enormous Colegio Máximo in San Miguel, an hour from Buenos Aires, in a hundred-room study house, as well as many years in the forty-room Colegio del Salvador in the city center. During nearly fifteen years as archbishop, he lived in a flat in the multistory curial offices on the Plaza de Mayo in Buenos Aires after turning the archbishop's palace he had inherited into a home for old priests. In all three cases—the Colegio Máximo, the Buenos Aires Curia, and now the Santa Marta—he dwelled in the crossroads of human traffic, with the buzz of pastors' conversations, in buildings where there were communal chapels, dining rooms, and common rooms. "It's not just about wealth," he told students. "For me it's a question of personality. I need to live among people and if I lived alone, perhaps rather isolated, it wouldn't be good for me . . . I can't live alone, do you understand?"[29]

But that wasn't the whole story. Living in the Santa Marta was also a blow against the papal court. Nothing turned Vatican officials into intermediaries like the Apostolic Palace, with its chain of interlinked rooms and sentinels who isolated the pope and traded on his authority. Francis believed (as he told me in June 2018) that the court was the main reason that Benedict XVI had failed to tackle the problems he so clearly saw: he had less authority in practice over the Vatican than a bishop has over his diocese.

In the Santa Marta, on the other hand, it was clear who was in charge. Francis's secretaries were mediators, not intermediaries. The pope managed his own diary, made his own calls, organized his day, received guests directly, and sat with them in the simple waiting room at the bottom of the stairs by the reception, or upstairs in Room 201. Most days he could be found at his table in the dining room or saying Mass at seven a.m. in the Santa Marta chapel. Those at the Mass were there for a good reason— because his secretary or another mediator believed they should be, not because of a donation traded by an intermediary. In this way Francis destroyed the patronage networks that had metastasized under John Paul II and Benedict XVI. A healthy sign was that archbishops were soon complaining that being unable to offer a papal baciamano had left them little to give back to wealthy donors.[30]

At its first meeting in early October 2013, the pope's new cabinet of cardinal advisers, later known as C9, approved COSEA's proposal of a powerful finance ministry headed by a czar with overall responsibility for setting Vatican budgets. Zahra's commission had concluded that only a Vatican authority that was independent and had real teeth would be capable of confronting the nouveau riche, intermediary culture. Francis announced the move at the February 2014 gathering of cardinals, known as a consistory.

The new body had a two-tier structure: a Council for the Economy to set the overall direction and policies of Vatican finances, overseeing the audits and signing off on the accounts; and the SPE (Secretariat for the Economy), to take charge of the day-to-day management of the Vatican's money and to implement the council's policies. The statute, "Faithful and Prudent Administrator," said the Church must see its possessions and financial assets in the "light of its mission to evangelize, with particular concern for the most needy."

Also at COSEA's urging, Francis created a new, powerful office of auditor-general with the responsibility of carrying out audits of the Holy See and Vatican City State. In early 2019, Francis strengthened the auditor general's office further by making it an "Anti-Corruption Authority" with unlimited authority to access any administrative or financial documents relevant to its audit.

There was a close link between the C9—so called because it had nine cardinal members from all continents, plus the secretary of state, Pietro Parolin—and the new structures. The Council for the Economy was chaired by C9 German cardinal Reinhard Marx, with Zahra as vice-chair; while Pell, who was also on the C9, moved from Sydney to run SPE full-time. The SPE's oversight body offered a glimpse of the changes to come: it had an unprecedented equal balance of senior churchmen and expert laypeople from across the world with equal say and vote.

Pell soon announced a raft of new financial appointments. Of the seventeen he named—including French economist Jean-Baptiste de Franssu as head of the IOR—almost all were laypeople and only two were Italians. In June 2014, Libero Milone, a Dutch-born chairman of Deloitte Italy, was made the Vatican's first auditor-general.

By the end of 2014, Pell was in a position to announce that "the primary structural reforms" were now in place and that the Vatican was no longer "incompetent, extravagant and easy pickings for thieves." In February 2015, he gave to the cardinals the first comprehensive rundown of Vatican finances, unprecedented in its detail. After uncovering slush funds that had been siloed in the different departments, Pell announced with satisfaction that total assets were close to twice what had been believed: nearer to $3.2 billion. *Bloomberg* was amazed that the presentations included lay experts, not just clergy, and that some of them spoke "English, the language of commerce." Clearly, said its reporter, "Pope Francis is not your father's Holy Father."[31]

Over the next two years, Pell moved decisively to change the internal financial culture of the Vatican, introducing professional accounting standards, as well as timely and dependable budgets. Costs gradually began to fall, although when we spoke in March 2017, he was frustrated that there was still too little control of expenditures, and that the portion of Peter's Pence being used to subsidize the deficit was still too high. The target of his ire was the "Vatican old guard," who were tenaciously clinging to their autonomies, reluctant to hand over control, and who were hitting back by leaking documents that claimed to show Pell's profligacy.[32]

Francis had warned colleagues after appointing him that Pell's manner was brusque, but that he was sure the Australian was the right man to challenge the culture of prevarication and evasion. As time went on, however, Pell's brutta figura began to be a liability. There were widespread complaints of his arrogant, offhand manner and his tendency to regard any kind of objection or hesitation as betrayal. Unlike Brülhart and Zahra, who advanced prudently and carefully, listening and building consensus, Pell charged ahead with bovine impatience, seeing conspiracies everywhere, gradually squandering the goodwill his competence, courage, and determination had at first created. Resistance was especially strong at the Secretariat of State, still the Vatican's eight-hundred-pound gorilla.

It was one thing to be close to pro-market and pro-business, as Pell clearly was; it was another to treat the Church like a corporation of which he was CEO. When Pell commissioned an audit of Vatican departments from PricewaterhouseCoopers and signed the contract "The Manager of the Holy See," the Secretariat of State balked. The number two, Cardinal Angelo Becciu, stepped in to cancel the audit four months into its task, saying that its brief and scope needed to conform to Vatican law. "There was the risk that [people] that came from abroad," Becciu later explained, referring rather obviously to Pell, "could confuse the Holy See for a company, applying the principles of a company to the Holy See. . . . I felt the need to tell someone who spoke of 'companies' that the Vatican is not a company, it is a church, in which money is required to advance the mission of the Pope."

Pell, furious, saw a re-circling of the wagons by the old guard wanting to protect their turf or even conceal wrongdoing. But Becciu was hardly "old guard," and he was sincere about wanting to preserve the Church's independence and sovereignty. Auditing accounts was the task of the new auditor-general's office. But while the auditor-general got up to speed, the reformers believed a Big Four external audit would demonstrate to the world that the Vatican could now be trusted and was transparent. Yet to the Secretariat of State, auditing the Vatican as if it were a corporation would undermine its status as a spiritual sovereign entity under international law.[33]

These tensions—turf wars that reflected clashing priorities and values—considerably lessened after July 2017, when at a hastily arranged press conference a shattered but determined Pell announced his return to Australia to face child molestation charges. It was hard to find anyone in the Vatican—friend or foe—who thought the charges credible; nor did anyone seem to believe he would get a fair trial. Francis was careful to leave Pell's post vacant, yet few believed the SPE prefect would be back.

Days earlier, Pell's ally and appointee, the Vatican's auditor-general, Libero Milone, had stepped down just two years into his five-year contract, accused of recruiting an outside firm to spy on Vatican officials. The auditor-general's story of being blocked from seeing Francis after April 2016, and being increasingly isolated and impeded in his work, fitted the popular narrative that the financial reform had been finally put to bed by the "old guard." The pope had gone soft and given up the fight, the critics said, and everything had slipped backward.

It wasn't true. The idea that reform was contingent on Pell and Milone was disproved by the pace of change after their departure. In mid-2018, a Council for the Economy official, Monsignor Brian Ferme, reported "a gradual change of mentality in respect of transparency and accountability" and far greater cooperation than hitherto with the financial reforms, while the official in charge of the SPE similarly recorded that there was now much more cooperation and far less resistance to the Secretariat's control and vigilance. Monsignor Luigi Mistò, Pell's deputy who was SPE's prefect in all but name after Pell's departure, also remarked on a widespread "budget culture" of transparency and accountability in the Vatican that had been largely absent in 2013, as well as agreed universal "contract codes" covering all agreements with suppliers. Overall, despite bumps in the road, the financial process was "steadily going ahead," said Mistò.[34]

Similarly, in June 2018, the auditor-general's office under its interim head completed the first ever Vatican-wide audit carried out to international accounting standards or IPSAS, which was signed off by the Council for the Economy's board of heavyweight outsiders. (Although the 2017 accounts weren't made public, it is hoped the 2018 ones will be.) The transformation in Vatican money management was increasingly recognized by outside bodies. In April 2017, Italy put the Vatican on its "white list" of states with cooperative financial institutions, and the following month, Moneyval praised the "basically sound legal structure that has been put in place." In November 2018 the European Union, which had pressed so hard for reforms ten years earlier, made clear its approval by accepting the

Vatican into the Single Euro Payments Area. That meant that, for the first time, the Vatican had its own International Bank Account Number (IBAN) for international money transfers, a further sign both of its probity and its emancipation from Italy.

There was progress, too, in AIF's fifth annual report, which showed a marked reduction in suspicious financial transactions as a result of new reporting measures. In five years, Brülhart's team had put a total of fifty-six cases for investigation on the desk of the Vatican's chief prosecutor, Gian Piero Milano; twenty-two were from 2016 alone. They generally involved tax evasion, financial misappropriation, and corruption of the usual "kickback" sort that is common in Italy; almost all the accused were Italian citizens whose misdemeanors involved Vatican institutions. A handful were Vatican officials.

Francis was determined to secure convictions, even if only to pass them on to Italian courts, to show that the Holy See was no longer a soft touch. But financial crimes are not simple to investigate, and the Vatican gendarmerie struggled. By May 2017, Moneyval lamented, there had been only two indictments and no prosecutions. That changed a few months later, when former officials of the Bambino Gesù hospital went on trial for the misuse of funds in the upgrade of Cardinal Bertone's apartment, which led to a year's detention and fines for one of them. In February 2018, two former IOR officials who had stepped down in 2013 were found guilty of mismanagement and ordered to pay damages. In May 2018, Angelo Caloia, IOR's chief between 1999 and 2009, went on trial for embezzling millions of euros in a property scam.

In an interview with Reuters in June 2018, Francis said he was mostly happy about the Vatican financial reforms. The IOR "now works well," he said. But he was concerned about the lack of transparency at APSA, and he said that he would be accepting Cardinal Domenico Calcagno's retirement on grounds of age. "The mentality has to be renewed," he said. Shortly afterward Francis named Bishop Nunzio Galantino, then the secretary general of the Italian bishops' conference, to replace Calcagno. He was the "really fresh air" APSA had been waiting for, a senior official in Vatican finance told me.

Like Bergoglio had in Buenos Aires, Galantino had dispensed with the driver, secretary, and palatial residence when he was made bishop of Cassano all' Jonio. In a book on the Church's renewal, inspired by *Evangelii*

Gaudium, he said the Church shouldn't just set an example of probity, but that the option for the poor should determine its management of material goods.

Interviewed by *Corriere della Sera*, Galantino said he had received the pope's call while opening an orphanage in Lebanon, and he hadn't yet got his head around APSA's figures. But what he could say was that clarity and transparency would benefit everyone, and that the Church's patrimony was for the sake of its mission, which meant acting on behalf of the poorest. For this reason, he added, "the pope is inviting us to live and act in ever greater sobriety."[35]

As a summary of Francis's financial reform, that wasn't bad.

four

A Time to Serve

A North American Jesuit who has worked in Rome since Benedict XVI's time vividly recalls the dismay among Vatican officials when the light in the pope's study failed to come back on. For as long as anyone could remember, the solitary window glowing late at night high up on the great façade of the Apostolic Palace on the right side of St. Peter's Square had sent out a sweet message, that the remote yet vigilant monarch was overseeing his people from the solitude of his palace desk. But then Benedict resigned in February 2013. The light went off, as it always did during the *sede vacante*, that strange between-popes interregnum that ends with a conclave. Only this time it never came back on.

Francis went to live not in the Apostolic Palace, but in the Casa Santa Marta guesthouse because he didn't think of himself as Rome's emperor, but the Church's pastor-in-chief. He believed the Vatican should not be a court of intermediaries, ruling over the local churches, but a mediator, to facilitate their mission. "Either there is a pyramidal church, in which what Peter says is done, or there is a synodal church," he told the Belgian magazine *Tertio*. He defined this "synodal church" as a kind of inverted pyramid, "in which Peter is Peter but he accompanies the Church, he lets her grow, he listens to her, he learns from this reality and goes about harmonizing it, discerning what comes from the Church and restoring it to her."[1]

The attempt to create a synodal Church has triggered an existential crisis among those who were invested in the imperial model, as the fury of those who worked in my Jesuit friend's department showed. Many *curiali*, as Vatican officials are called, saw the pope's decision to use the Apostolic Palace only for head-of-state protocol meetings and other formal gatherings as a downgrading of the papal office. They said it was a loss of his dignity, but they meant theirs. Most had never actually met the pope and didn't expect to. But belonging to the papal court had made them feel special, privileged, tied to the ancient power of a sacred office. If the light never came on in the pope's study, if the emperor was no longer an emperor, who were they? Their anger was visible from the start of the Francis pontificate. "They criticize me, first, because I don't speak like a pope, and second, because I don't act like a king," Francis told the then Jesuit superior general, Father Adolfo Nicolás.[2]

Most *curiali* are dutiful, loyal, hardworking, some holy, even. Yet dismantling the courtly mind-set that is common among them has been slow and painful. The offices of the Curia have been the means by which popes have exercised control over the teaching, worship, and many other aspects of the Church's life, and the people who work in them have long arrogated the pope's authority to assert that control. Before Francis's time, it was common for bishops to complain that they were summoned to Rome to be scolded or given orders by officials who treated them as branch managers of a global corporation. Many *curiali* are laypeople who are committed to the institution, if not always to the faith ("I think you'd be lucky to find many more than half of them at Mass on Sunday," a senior Vatican official told me), yet for whom the prestige of the papacy is sacrosanct.

In naming himself after Saint Francis of Assisi, by living in the Santa Marta, by riding out in his dark-colored Ford Focus without an escort of motorcyclists and with his window wound down, by his warm approachability and his easy way with the world, Francis has gently blown apart this system of courtly networks, while triggering in some who depended on it for their own sense of self a major existential displacement.

The sense of being demoted and put in their place is real. When the pope abolished the honorific title of "monsignor," C9 president Cardinal Óscar Rodríguez de Maradiaga told me, it "created not a little friction, and I must say, barely concealed opposition." Yet the idea of the pope as a distant monarch bestowing honors belongs to another era, to when "spiritual power naturally took on a spirit of jurisdiction," as Father Yves Congar,

OP, author of a famous 1950 book on church reform, put it. The Second Vatican Council renounced that idea of a monarch and priestly class ruling over *subditi*, or subjects, and recovered an earlier understanding of the Church as first the "people of God," in which the pope governs in collaboration with the bishops in the service of the faithful and of humanity. In taking seriously that idea and seeking to make real that understanding, Francis has been doing nothing that postconciliar popes have not talked of doing, and which was specifically mandated by the cardinals before the conclave. But he has done it with an energy and decisiveness that makes the reform appear sudden and shocking.[3]

His target is the mind-set of clericalism, a Catholic form of enlightened absolutism that belongs more to the eighteenth century than the twenty-first. When Jesus commanded his followers not to "lord it over" others as the Romans did (Mark 10:42–44), he was asking them to avoid *potestas*—power *over*, in the sense of ownership of rights over others, as a company boss or landlord or king has—in favor of *ministerium*: God's sovereignty, delegated for the purpose of caring for others and creation, a power to nurture and guide. "Let us never forget that authentic power is service," Francis said at his inauguration Mass, citing as a model Saint Joseph, "who is able to hear God's voice and be guided by his will; and for this reason he is all the more sensitive to the persons entrusted to his safekeeping." To instill that notion of service has been the primary aim of Francis's reform.[4]

He modeled this power-as-service at the start of the Easter liturgies that first year as Jesus had at the Last Supper: by washing feet. Popes traditionally performed the Holy Thursday ritual in a basilica in Rome, with clergy standing in for the apostles. But as he had done for years in Buenos Aires, when as cardinal he took Jesus's love out to "places of pain" as he called hospitals and prisons, Francis in 2013 chose the Casal del Marmo, a young offenders' institution in Rome. He told the inmates that "the person who is most high among us must be at the service of the others," and that "we have to help one another, each one." Among the twelve whose feet he washed were two women, one of them a Muslim. She said later it was the first time in her life she felt loved.

The startling shot of the pope kneeling over a washbasin kissing a Muslim woman prisoner's foot fast became the most iconic of early Francis pictures, astonishing and delighting a world accustomed to popes seeming distant and imperious. But it equally scandalized those whose first concern was the defense of boundaries, of various kinds. The newly insurgent right-wing nationalists, admirers of Vladimir Putin and Steve Bannon, hated it, because they feared Christian culture was being liquidated by Muslim immigration; so, too, did the Vatican's self-appointed lace police, who angrily insisted that the pope had the right to make liturgical rules but not break them.

Was he breaking them? Most of the world's bishops—as the Americans had in 1987—had made clear that the *viri selecti* specified in the 1955 rubrics could mean either men or women, but the Bishop of Rome never had. So for the avoidance of doubt, Francis asked Cardinal Robert Sarah, head of the Congregation for Divine Worship, to clarify that "from now on the pastors of the Church should be able to choose the participants in the rite from all the members of the people of God," which would mean Muslims and Jews and atheists, both genders, short and tall: Jesus's act, said Francis, expressed his "limitless love for all." Sarah, a traditionalist prone to bouts of pessimism, dragged his feet, taking over a year to sign the decree, in January 2016, and conspicuously leaving it to his deputy to explain the measure. It was an early signal of the truculent resistance Francis would face from parts of his own Curia.[5]

The foot-washing ritual—which he has done every year as pope in different Roman prisons—was an act of evangelization, one that showed God humbly entering into the life of the people. When the Church was close in this way—*ministerium*—it was a channel of the Holy Spirit, a vehicle of grace, a source of empowerment, or *potentia*. But when the Church resorted to *potestas*, lording it over the people, it excluded grace and inflicted damage. The *potestas* mind-set was not confined to the clergy. "You do not have to be a priest to be clericalist," Francis told Father Fernando Prado. "Clericalism is an aristocracy."[6]

To counter it, Francis declared that this was the hour of the people of God. "I believe the Lord wants a change in the Church," he told the Jesuits in the Baltic states. "I have said many times that a perversion of the Church today is clericalism. But fifty years ago the Second Vatican Council said this clearly: *the Church is the People of God*." It was time to make good on that promise. Christ had visited His people, yet the institution seemed to be looking the other way, at itself. What were the Vatican scandals and the clerical abuse crisis but the death rattles of this self-serving, self-referential aristocracy? "Laypeople are part of the faithful Holy People of God and thus are the protagonists of the Church and of the world," Francis told Cardinal Marc Ouellet in a 2016 letter. "We are called to serve them, not to be served by them." Clericalism must now be cast aside, for it "extinguishes the prophetic flame to which the entire Church is called to bear witness in the heart of her peoples."[7]

The title of my biography of Francis, *The Great Reformer*, is problematic, for it suggests a superman or revolutionary sweeping in to overturn an institution according to some predetermined agenda. Yet that "superman" myth is one he continually seeks to puncture.

"I'm not a visionary [*iluminado*]," the pope insisted to *La Vanguardia* in 2014. He said the same to *Die Zeit* in 2017, that he didn't feel like an "exceptional man," that he was a fallible sinner who made mistakes, and that when people idealized him it felt like an act of aggression because he wasn't allowed to be who he was. As cardinal archbishop he criticized the "myth of efficiency," the illusion one person can do everything, and checked himself often for "playing Tarzan." "In some ways I was saying to myself, 'Look how good I am, how great I am, how many things I can do,'" he told Sergio Rubín and Francesca Ambrogetti. "Pride affected my attitude."[8]

When we met in June 2018, he stressed to me what he has often told others: that he came without a plan and with only a small suitcase, hadn't thought he would be elected, and had no inkling of the meetings before the conclave where some cardinals had been active in promoting him. Even when the votes were piling up for him in the conclave, he still didn't think he would be pope, that they would after a time switch to another candidate. When they didn't, he was at peace, and the peace has never left him. He is in God's hands and does what he can. "I just want to put Christ ever more at the center of the Church," he told Father Spadaro in 2013. "Then He will do the necessary reforms."[9]

Yet this re-centering of the Church on Christ and de-centering out to humanity is no small thing. It is to subject the Church, as Spadaro tells me, to "a gentle, subtle, but constant earthquake, a Gospel tremor, to allow what should fall to fall and what should remain to remain." This is a *religious* reform, one centered on conversion, not simply a structural makeover. Reform "is not an end in itself," Francis told the cardinals in February 2015, "but a means of bearing a powerful Christian witness." The aim is not profit or efficiency but the transformation of church structures for the purpose of better communicating God's saving, merciful love. The fruits of that reorientation can be known in greater transparency, accountability, humility, sobriety, zeal for the Gospel, and concern for the poor. These are the signs that the re-centering is happening. The witness is the *forma Christi*, and it will be apparent when people come to Rome and see the Gospel rather than a stuffy Renaissance court. The Vatican will look more like what it proclaims, and can better fulfill the end for which it exists: a means of evangelizing, not an obstacle to it.[10]

Early on, Francis handed to the C9 the task of devising new structures to support and facilitate that conversion. The C9 has taken that to mean reorganizing the Curia as a facilitator rather than a filter, encouraging whatever helps the Vatican be of service to the local Church, rather than a bureaucracy controlling it. "Before, the idea was you help the local Churches by helping the Holy Father," says C9 member Cardinal Oswald Gracias of Mumbai, India. "Now the idea is you help the Holy Father by helping the local Churches."[11]

Until the fall of 2018, when its membership was renewed, the C9 was made up of archbishops or former archbishops of Santiago de Chile, Mumbai, Munich, Sydney, Kinshasa, Boston, and Tegucigalpa who met every two months in Rome over five years. Apart from Pell, who in 2014 transferred to Rome to be finance prefect, and the secretary of state, Cardinal Parolin, these men were all archbishops who continued to live in their dioceses, and who flew in to Rome every two months for their two- or three-day meetings with Francis. The creation of the C9 has been the single most decisive step in the modern Church toward allowing "the various episcopates of the world to express themselves in the very government of the Church," as Francis put it to journalists in July 2013. It was a move toward "a Church with an organization that is not just top-down but also horizontal."[12]

Again, this was a mandate of the cardinals, who saw the way Benedict had struggled with the task of governing the universal Church. "Peter will make his task easier to the extent that he shares it with the other apostles," Cardinal Prosper Grech said in his address to the cardinal electors in 2013. Because the Vatican reform has been designed by the C9 acting with the pope, rather than by papal diktat, the process has performed the change it is seeking. The C9 represents the College of Cardinals, among whom around 120 will elect the pope at the next conclave, at the meetings that follow Francis's death or resignation. When that happens, it will not be the pope's reforms the cardinals discuss, but their own.

The C9 has been the pope's sounding board, his kitchen cabinet whom he consults before making nearly all his big decisions. In between the three-day gatherings in the Santa Marta guesthouse six times a year, the C9 members communicate with each other via a dedicated iPad. When they meet, votes are taken and action agreed only if there is unanimity or very close to unanimity; if not, the question will be revisited. It is a "collegial body [where] no one dominates, and everybody has a chance to speak," according to Cardinal Gracias. He says the pope mostly listens, raising his hand when he wishes to say something, and encourages them to speak if they disagree. Francis has never vetoed a proposal and can be persuaded to change his mind.[13]

In the process of curial reform Francis's own role is less that of a "great reformer" than a spiritual director leading a group on a retreat, creating time and space for change while setting boundaries and clearing blockages. There is a paradox: the reform that has seemed so sweeping and dramatic has been, in reality, gradual and gentle. For Francis, it has been an exercise in "traveling in patience," as he calls it, accepting limits, which means, above all, working with the people he has. In six years, he has replaced very few, denying himself the most effective means available to a new boss for transforming an institution. He has baked graduality into the very process of institutional change.

Rather than sacking officials, he has sought to renew them, which is a much longer process. But it is also smart. Curial officials close to Francis explain his thinking: replacing too many people, too soon, without changing the culture, creates disruption for no purpose, and may even slow change; better to change the culture over time and to support the transformation with the gradual introduction of new structures and new people. Rather than "cut off heads," Francis likes to say, he waits for people to reach the age of their natural retirement, and promotes new people from below. After five years, he had appointed only eight heads of the thirty-six significant Vatican departments, compared to John Paul II changing eighteen and Benedict XVI sixteen in their first quinquennium. Despite the howls of protest, there has been no mass clearing out of the "old guard," just a gradual chipping away around them. Only in one exceptional case— Cardinal Gerhard Müller, whom Francis replaced in June 2017 as prefect of the Congregation for the Doctrine of the Faith—it was at the end of his five-year term; in seven other cases, resignations were accepted after they reached seventy-five, the Church's age of retirement for bishops.

Appointed by Benedict a year before Francis's election, Müller had spent four years trying to correct Francis and those around him, claiming that it was his job to give a "theological" structure to a "pastoral" papacy—a wholly novel role for a CDF prefect. He embodied the old "command-and-control" Curia, but Francis had no intention of allowing him to tell the Church what to think or to correct its theologians, leaving Müller to act out the role he had cast for himself on conservative Catholic TV shows. Francis meanwhile worked in practice with his number two, Archbishop (now Cardinal) Luis Ladaria Ferrer, whom he then appointed as prefect.

He has done the same in the Congregation for Divine Worship, largely ignoring Sarah in favor of his British deputy, Archbishop Arthur Roche. Like Burke, Sarah has used his position to promote an obviously traditionalist agenda at odds with the Second Vatican Council. On one occasion he urged that altars be turned to enable priests to celebrate Mass with their backs to the congregation, and on another claimed that those who take Communion in the hand—a normal practice in the early Church that returned with the Second Vatican Council—could be tools in the hands of Satan. Francis has been forced each time to publicly correct him, yet, remarkably, has kept him on.[14]

Francis has made clear to heads of dicasteries that they cannot expect to remain in their post beyond the age of seventy-five yet must be open to staying if asked. "Whoever is preparing to present their resignation has to prepare adequately before God, stripping themselves of desire for power and of the pretension of being indispensable," he wrote in an edict of February 2018, "Learning to Say Farewell." If they are asked to remain in their post, this was not a personal triumph or proof of the esteem in which they are held, but "an act of governance" by the pope, who has considered what is best for the Church. At the same time, he has made clear that in the future five-year terms for Vatican officials will increasingly be the norm, with clergy returning afterward to their dioceses. This will not only ensure greater circulation and diversity, and act to curb ambition—"please, shun ecclesial careerism," he told seminarians studying in Rome, "it is a plague"—but should also improve the quality of the officials involved, because bishops will be less reluctant to part with their competent priests if they know they will be back after a few years.[15]

The need to build up consensus and ensure maximum flexibility in implementation has made the makeover slow and laborious, "like cleaning the Sphinx of Egypt with a toothbrush," Francis joked in his Christmas 2017 address. But while slow, it has been decisive. After the financial reforms of 2014 came a top-down overhaul of communications in 2015, and the creation of two new "super-dicasteries" that merged eight pontifical councils in 2016. Both are outward facing, concerned with issues of broad human concern. The first deals with laity, family, and life, the other with integral human development. In 2017 a new "third section" was created within the Vatican's Secretariat of State to provide better spiritual and professional formation and pastoral care for Rome's diplomats. Finally, in 2018, the C9 drew up its draft new constitution for the Curia, the first of its kind in thirty years, to codify the reform, which is expected to be approved in 2019.

Yet arguably the greater transformation has occurred beneath the surface in the culture and mind-set of the Curia. When Francis told Vatican officials in his Christmas 2017 speech how happy he was that bishops reported being "received well and listened to by all the dicasteries," it was a signal moment. For decades, the bishops visiting Rome, Bergoglio among them, had complained of their treatment by high-handed officials, and those who remember how it used to be are astonished at the change. The archbishop of Quebec, Cardinal Gérald Lacroix, described in amazement how the Canadian bishops' *ad limina* in May 2017 (an *ad limina* is when the entire bishops' conference of a country spends a few days in Rome, usually every five or six years) began with officials telling them: "The Holy Father wants us to listen to you and your experiences. So why don't we start with that?"

Where before they were given presentations by the different departments, and sometimes admonished by them like errant altar boys rather than the successors of the apostles, now they were asked, "What do you want to share with us? How can we help?" Looking back on his previous experience in 2011, the Archbishop of Melbourne, Peter Comensoli, saw a complete turnaround. "There's none of this 'we're the schoolmaster, and you are the pupil'—all that seems to have gone," he told *The Tablet* during the Australian *ad limina* in June 2019.

Both archbishops were bowled over by the meeting with Francis. Gone was the stiff informality and the pre-prepared address of the Benedict XVI years. "It was: 'Welcome brothers. I am here as your brother, and let us converse together,'" recalled Comensoli. "He asked us to be honest, say what we wanted to say, ask what we wanted to ask, and to know that it was private and would stay in the room, including if we had complaints about him or the Curia. For me, it was spiritually intense." Lacroix described a three-hour free-flowing exchange, with Francis listening carefully and responding at the end with pearls of wisdom. "It's not just words," Lacroix told Gerard O'Connell of *America*. "We're discerning together. We're listening to each other, to discover what the other one is living. Francis is making that happen."[16]

When Cardinal Bergoglio spoke to Rubin and Ambrogetti of "traveling in patience," he told them the phrase had come to him after pondering a book of theology that "shows how Jesus entered into patience." What he didn't say was that he had read Father John G. Navone's *The Triumph of Failure* during the spiritual desolation of his "desert" period in the late 1980s and early 1990s, a time of purgation that led finally to an eighteen-month internal "exile" in the Argentine city of Córdoba. He was in his early fifties, and his world had crumbled. Somewhere in the wreckage that followed, an at times impatient, authoritarian leader was broken, and a patient pastor was born.

Astute and energetic, compelling and charismatic, as provincial and rector Bergoglio was by far the most dominant figure among the Argentine Jesuits of his day. Having steered his province through the guerrilla violence and the brutal military crackdown of the 1970s without losing one of them to a violent death, in the 1980s he attracted and kept dozens of vocations at a time when they were in freefall elsewhere, both in Latin America and above all in Europe. At the Jesuit Curia in Rome, they scratched their heads: what was Bergoglio doing right that other Jesuits had missed?

But there was resentment and jealousy, too, and anxiety about what he was creating that seemed so at variance with Jesuit formation in Europe and elsewhere in Latin America. Foreign visitors were struck by the rigor, vigor, and prayerful austerity of the regime in the Colegio Máximo but concerned by its intensity and personalism. In Argentina, the "Peronist" version of liberation theology practiced by Bergoglio and his circle was hostile to what they perceived as foreign Enlightenment ideologies of the right and left. His "Salesian" focus on pastoral work among the poor of San Miguel meanwhile alienated many of the upper-class Jesuits in the province.

Bergoglio was like the nineteenth-century Argentine rural strongmen, the *caudillos*, who were adored by the common folk but abhorred by the doctors and merchants. Divisions arose: between a new *bergogliano* generation, and an older, "liberal" one; between more upper-class, radical-supporting, cosmopolitan Jesuits, and the *pueblo* Jesuits with their natural Peronist sympathies. There were fears of the province splitting as it polarized around two competing notions of what it meant to be a Jesuit. Eventually, the new worldwide superior general of the Society of Jesus was persuaded to intervene. Father Peter Hans Kolvenbach changed the provincial leadership and scattered Bergoglio and his followers abroad. But the new regime provoked anger and nostalgia for the exiled *caudillo*, and the splits continued for many years.

Bergoglio was increasingly blamed by Kolvenbach's appointees for causing divisions until, in 1990, he was sent to Córdoba without a mission. There he suffered, often depressed and sick, appalled by the destruction of so much of what he had built up. He did as Saint Ignatius advises in long periods of desolation: he spent more time in prayer and dedicated himself to others, to care of the elderly in the Jesuit community, and to hearing confessions. He read widely and deeply—including a multivolume history of the papacy—and wrote some of his most powerful reflections, full of insights he draws on today. Some close to Francis say that his pontificate is in so many ways the fruit of that desert.[17]

Before he died in December 2016, Navone recalled that there was "a blessed juncture between my theology and [Bergoglio's] crisis," which was "a kind of light in the darkness to him." Originally published in the 1970s in Italian as *Teologia del Fallimento* (*A Theology of Failure*), the Gregorian University professor offered a startling account of how God saved by means of human limitations and realities. Navone showed how God saved humanity through the incarnation but why He chose the way of powerlessness and failure. The book helped Bergoglio see that his soul-death was not the end of the story—not *his* story, nor history itself—but the ground of future possibility.[18]

What Navone nailed was the holiness of *patientia*, the faithful willingness to suffer in the hope of unseen future change. It was how the prayerful poor lived. It was how Jesus had lived. Lasting change came from fidelity to the divine will, not the slavish pursuit of present success. To allow God to act meant, in fact, to accept failure. The world judged Jesus a loser: He did not convert Israel, left intact the oppressive structures of politics and religion, and died the death of a criminal, abandoned even by His disciples. Nothing in this outcome suggested success, and His disciples were paralyzed by desolation following the crucifixion. But in the resurrection, God overturned that judgment, transforming Jesus's followers' understanding of what God's reign really involved: freedom, nonviolence, and what the world saw as weakness and failure. The drama of the Christian proclamation bursts forth from that central paradox that reveals the true power operating in history.

Navone enabled Bergoglio to reread his own failure, and to learn from it. Had he moved too far, too fast, giving into the despair and sterility of impatience when what was needed were patience and constancy? His powers— his extraordinary intelligence and astuteness in governance, his ability to read hearts and discern spirits, the power to inspire and mobilize—had brought, at times, a temptation "to bring forward the triumph without passing through the Cross," as Bergoglio put it in his searing 1990 essay, "Silencio y Palabra" ("Silence and Word"). This "spiritual boyscoutism" was a kind of "we're happy, we're fine, we're on the road to victory" attitude, in love with statistics and progress, but it ended in the attitude of the Pharisee standing apart mentioned by Jesus in Luke 18:11, whose prayer was: "I thank you, God, that I am not like those others."

Navone's theology shed light on so much that Bergoglio had already written as a Jesuit on leadership, distinguishing, for example, between *fortaleza* (strength, constancy, determination) and *fuerza* (force or might). There was a good strength and a bad strength, a way to lead in tune with the Gospel as opposed to the world's way. The temptation of any religious body that brought people together and inspired them to act was to become a vehicle for human power, not God's, and to develop a mind-set that justified that power. He had lived through an era in Argentina when idealistic Catholic guerrillas were ready to kill and die for a Cuban-style kingdom of God, and Mass-going Catholic military men were willing to torture them to preserve Western Christian values. Even among those who rejected violence, like the Jesuits, there were laboratory utopians wanting revolutionary changes and arch traditionalists pining for incense and mothballs. Yet in preferring their own elite schemes—to restore a lost golden age, or engender a utopia—they ignored Argentina's broken, wounded people, who trusted in God's mercy, not some theologian's great insight.

Why did Jesus, a Jewish man of tradition who respected institutions, enter into conflict with His people's guardians, the religious elites of His day, the Pharisees, Sadducees, and Zealots? After examining the attitudes of each group, Bergoglio concluded that those groups shared the same elitist attitude that claimed to think on behalf of others, denying them freedom and agency. In arrogating God's glory and power to act, they also denied their brothers the capacity to decide, the right to form a body; they were like the restorationists and utopians of the modern era who preferred their own schemes to God's action in the body of the people, and so fractured it. Jesus, on the other hand, operated peacefully and patiently, within the body of the people, accepting limits and failure.

Christ did not run ahead of the people to save the people, but acted in and out of the people, through the ordinary and everyday, attentive to the concrete needs of the poor, teaching and healing and serving the people. The people, Bergoglio wrote, embraced "the deep privilege of time, of unity, of the whole, and of reality."[19]

Renewing the culture and outlook so the Curia could belong to the people of God rather than ruling over them meant a hearts-and-minds conversion. The weeklong retreats for cardinals and archbishops who head dicasteries used to consist of edifying talks within the Vatican, in between which many of the officials could return to their desks during the coffee breaks. But under Francis, around eighty prefects and their deputies leave Rome with Francis in a coach during Lent for a five-day silent retreat in a religious house in the Alban Hills. "You'll be sitting in chapel, or at a table at mealtimes, and you'll find the pope popping down next to you," a senior official who has been on retreat each year told me. "He's one of us. It does wonders for a spirit of unity and togetherness."

Outside the Lenten retreats, the main vehicle for the conversion has been his annual Christmas speech to the same leading officials. Previous popes had used those late-December addresses in the Sala Clementina to review the year, sharing thoughts on issues facing the world with an eye to the media. But Francis used them as a spur to change, modeled on Saint

Ignatius's Spiritual Exercises. Taken together, his Christmas speeches make up something like an Ignatian manual of institutional conversion.

Just as the "Principle and Foundation" begins the Exercises with a reminder of the source and purpose of life itself ("The human person is created to praise, reverence and serve God our Lord, and by so doing save his or her soul"), Francis's first address in 2013 reminded officials that the Curia's purpose was service: both to the pope *and* to the bishops, to both the universal Church *and* to the dioceses of the world. When it betrayed its call to "discreet and faithful pastoral service, zealously carried out in direct contact with God's people," the Curia became a "ponderous, bureaucratic customshouse, controlling and inquisitorial, hindering the work of the Holy Spirit and the growth of God's people."

Having set up a typically Jesuit choice (or "election") between two paths, the following Christmas, in 2014, Francis moved into the First Week of the Exercises, in order to encourage his readers to—in Saint Ignatius's words—feel "inner knowledge of [their] sins and an abhorrence for them." Only when sin is engaged emotionally and honestly does a person see its damage and feel shame; and only then, usually, does a person look to God's mercy, realizing with joy that she has been spared what her sin deserves.[20]

Francis's catalogue of "curial illnesses" that "weaken our service to the Lord" was a savagely acute diagnosis of what had rotted in Rome. Using the Ignatian insight that the devil has a triple entry point to the soul through the doorways of riches, honors, and pride, and by means of this seduction produces "division and confusion" in the Christian body, he linked rivalries and rows in the Vatican to the pursuit of wealth and obsession with appearances. Launching a frontal assault on the clericalist culture of arrogance and self-regard, he warned above all against "the disease of thinking we are 'immortal,' 'immune' or downright 'indispensable.'"

Every dicastery prefect sooner or later encountered the objection: "But we've always done it this way!" Six of the illnesses outlined in the 2014 address reflected the grim bureaucratic culture of self-sufficiency and pride that produced the mind-set of a rigid functionary with "static, unchanged positions." At its extreme this mind-set of workaholism, hiding in paperwork, and functionalism degenerated into "spiritual Alzheimer's," that is, "a state of absolute dependence on one's imaginary points of view."

The nadir was the eighth illness, the "existential schizophrenia" of those who "abandon pastoral service and restrict themselves to bureaucratic matters, thus losing contact with reality, with concrete people." This last reflected his concern about the Vatican's mid-level officials, priests who arrived in Rome young and lived in clerical residences or apartments with no pastoral contact with laypeople. Many of them "create their own parallel world" and "begin to live a hidden and often dissolute life."

The remaining four illnesses described the divisions that resulted from a court bureaucracy. One was a lack of coordination, when the body's parts stopped working together and became simply "an orchestra that produces noise"; another was "the terrorism of gossip" and rumor-mongering that curial factions used in power games. In an obvious reference to *le lobby*, he also cited "the disease of closed circles, where belonging to a clique becomes more powerful than belonging to the Body and even to Christ himself," and over time this tendency "enslaves its members and becomes a cancer which threatens the harmony of the Body and causes immense evil." He also deplored the way *le lobby* fed the media damaging material to trash their rivals, "often in the name of justice and transparency."

To anyone who knew the Vatican's recent history in the final years of John Paul II and under Benedict XVI, the pope's X-ray pinpointed with amazing accuracy the dark shadows on the curial body, yet without naming names or pointing fingers. When it came out in February 2019, the French journalist Frédéric Martel's exposé of homosexuality and hypocrisy in the Vatican graphically supported that picture of a vicious culture in which rumors peddled about the homosexuality of a prelate "are often leaked by homosexuals, themselves closeted, attacking their liberal opponents."[21]

Splashed across the front pages, the speech was inevitably reported not as a spiritual master guiding his leaders on a retreat but as the pope as CEO giving a tongue-lashing to his "squirming" employees. Pundits lined up to warn the pope to go easy on the Curia, that he risked alienating the very people whose goodwill he needed. Yet many of those who worked at senior levels in the Curia saw it differently—as a hard-hitting wake-up call to renew their vocations. "Listening to him, I thought, after more than one of the diseases, 'yes, that's me,'" one senior curial official who was present that day told me. "Of course it's challenging, but conversion always is. Where I felt shame, I knew that's what I had to work on."[22]

The pope's December 2015 speech a year later made clear that the institutional ills he had identified had revealed themselves in the course of the year, "causing no small pain to the entire body and harming many souls, even by scandal." He knew there were plenty of *curiali* who were waiting for his pontificate to pass in order to resume (in some cases literally) business as usual. So he made clear that reform was "irreversible," that he would press on "with determination, clarity and firm resolve." *Ecclesia semper reformanda est,* he reminded them. The Church was in a constant process of seeking to conform itself to Christ, and obstacles and setbacks were a chance to redouble efforts and "return to what is essential."

This time he handed out what he called "curial antibiotics" to prevent and treat the diseases he had diagnosed. They brought to mind the "Two Standards" meditation of the second week of the Exercises, when Saint Ignatius imagines two opposing armies: that of Lucifer, summoning demons to lay traps and chains for people through riches, honor, and pride, and that of Christ, asking His followers to be ready to embrace poverty, humiliation, and service. In inviting the Curia to adopt twelve pairs of virtues and values—"openness and maturity," "respectfulness and humility," "accountability and sobriety," and so on—Francis was imagining the call of the Good King to the Vatican. Quoting Saint Ignatius's discernment rule for "people who are making serious progress in the purification of their sins," he noted how the bad spirit sought to "harass, sadden, and obstruct, and to disturb with false reasoning," while the good spirit sought "to give courage and strength, consolations, tears, inspirations and quiet" in order to make it easier to do good.[23]

In December 2016, Francis expounded upon the principles underlying the curial reform itself, again referencing the Exercises, but referring this time explicitly to the resistance to the reform. When he said it was a sign of "the devil's ugly odor," it was assumed he was reacting angrily to criticism, not least from those who, seduced by Cardinal Burke's crusade to rescue Catholicism from the pope, were lashing out at *Amoris Laetitia.* But it wasn't to specific criticisms he was reacting, but to the spirits involved in the mounting accusations. Where there was "open" resistance from people of goodwill who sincerely disagreed with his changes, it was a sign of life, and their criticisms should be welcomed and respectfully listened to, whether justified or not. "Hidden" resistance, on the other hand, came from fearful or stonyhearted people who were outwardly supportive of the changes but inwardly determined that everything should stay exactly the same. Then there was a third, "malicious" kind of resistance—exemplified, many assumed, by Cardinals Burke, Müller, and Sarah—which brazenly denounced and accused others as a way of avoiding their own need for conversion, while dressing themselves in the mantle of "tradition" or "orthodoxy." It was this last kind that Francis saw as not of "God's good perfume" but of "the devil's ugly odor."

Francis was offering criteria for the people of God to do their own discernment faced with the accusations against him. Critics in the Church always appealed to the good and claimed noble motives, but what in fact drove them? Did they act out of freedom and desire for the good, or out of malice and vengeance? Opposition was a sign that the reform was of God—why else would the devil bother to resist it?—but not all opposition was of the devil; God also spoke through loving, constructive criticism. Discernment was needed. If criticism were from God, it would be patient and persistent, a gentle light that lasted and finally won through; whereas the devil's resistance was like the blinding flash of a noisy firework that dazzles but soon fades.

Like a battlefield general scanning the horizon, carefully observing the enemy's tactics and wiles, Francis knew he had to advance cautiously, warning in his 2016 speech that the path of reform called for courage, discernment, humble listening—and above all plenty of prayer. In his Christmas 2017 address, Francis seemed to suggest he was now in the fourth week (*conformata confirmare*, to strengthen what has been conformed) because he was returning to the refocusing with which he had begun five years before, stressing service. The Roman Curia was *ex natura ad extra*, he said: intrinsically outward focused, yet pulled back into itself by "the intrigues of little groups" and officials tempted by "ambition or vainglory." This time he had harsh words for those who, after being removed from their posts, muttered about a "pope kept in the dark" by advisers "rather than reciting a *mea culpa*," and he warned that others in the Curia had been given time to change, "with the hope that they find in the Church's patience an occasion to convert and not to take advantage." It was hard not to think of Cardinal Müller, who after being relieved as prefect of the Congregation for the Doctrine of the Faith in June 2017 had done an endless round of interviews blaming a magic circle of advisers around Francis and complaining indignantly of his unjust treatment.

Yet Francis was careful to praise the "commitment, fidelity, competence, dedication, and great holiness" of the great majority of those who worked in the Vatican, who were like antennae broadcasting the pope's mission to the world and relaying to him the joys and pains of the worldwide Church. They represented all that was great about Rome: patient, gracious, prayerful people who built bridges, promoted peace, served the local churches, worked for reconciliation, and helped shield humanity from the destructive effects of egotism; a global servant Church that knew how to wash the feet of others, able to fulfill its purpose because it was "free of any mundane or material interest." Then he gave them a Christmas gift of an early-seventeenth-century text by the fifth Jesuit Superior General, Father Claudio Acquaviva, titled *Tips to Cure the Ills of the Soul*. Among the ills listed were lack of obedience, love of honors, lack of transparency, courtly flattery, obstinacy, rigidity of judgment, and sowing discord. "I think it could help," Francis smilingly told them.[24]

The opposite of clericalism is *synodality*, meaning a method and process of discussion and participation in which the whole people of God can listen to the Holy Spirit and take part in the life and mission of the Church. The Second Vatican Council had called for mechanisms for consultation and participation, but early experiments in assemblies and diocesan synods had run aground after the 1980s, in part because of Vatican suspicion of any local initiatives that could foster "dissent." Francis's challenge was to give new life to such mechanisms, yet in ways that reflected authentic church traditions.

It was the challenge of the age: how to move from representation to participation. Across the Western world, institutions were suffering a loss of credibility among voters and citizens who saw them as distant and uncaring. Two years before Brexit and Trump, Francis warned the European parliament in Strasbourg of "growing mistrust on the part of citizens towards institutions considered to be aloof, engaged in laying down rules perceived as insensitive to individual peoples, if not downright harmful." But the answer was not to put faith in populist strongmen. "In times of crisis we lack judgment," he told *El País* on the day that Trump was inaugurated in January 2017, warning that people who were unsure of their identity at such times were taken in by saviors who promised to protect them with walls. The answer, instead, was to learn to debate and disagree in good faith; that was how true unity and identity were created. In his determination to breathe new life into ancient church traditions of participation, Francis was acting not just for the sake of the Church but for the world.[25]

The theologian Massimo Faggioli believes that the decisive "baby steps" Francis has taken in the direction of a "synodal Church" constitute the most important institutional reform of his pontificate. Synodality is in many ways the heart of Francis's reform.

It began with his overhaul of the synod itself. The modern Synod of Bishops, inspired by the councils of the early Church, was created by Pope Paul VI in 1965 to make it easier for the pope and the Curia to listen to the local Churches and engage the faithful. But under the long pontificate of John Paul II the traffic was mostly in the other direction: the synod became simply another means used by Rome for making sure the bishops listened to the Vatican. Having been a delegate at various synods, one of which he chaired in 2001, Bergoglio was convinced that, as it was then constituted, the synod could never be a means of discerning how to respond to doctrinal and pastoral challenges by the light of the Holy Spirit. Reflecting a view common among bishops who took part in them, he believed that the system was "not dynamic" and needed an overhaul.[26]

He was speaking not just from his negative experience of synods in Rome, but from his very different experience in Latin America, the only area of the world where the Church had decades of lived synodality to draw on. There had been five continent-wide, general conferences since the 1950s organized by its episcopal council, CELAM. The hundreds of local meetings across Latin America to prepare for the most recent, the general conference of Aparecida in May 2007, were without precedent in the Catholic Church. The mutual listening, consultation, and discernment of the run-up to Aparecida gave the people of God the opportunity to speak freely about the obstacles and opportunities the Church's proclamation faced. It was an example of the shift that Aparecida itself would call for: from a clericalist, introspective Church concerned above all with catechesis, to an evangelizing Church involving the body of ordinary faithful. The involvement of the people of God was crucial to the bishops coming up with a genuinely groundbreaking pastoral response.[27]

The experience of Aparecida led Francis to confidently tell the bishops in the 2015 synod in Rome that "it is precisely this path of synodality that God expects of the Church of the third millennium." His speech marking the fiftieth anniversary of Paul VI's refounding of the synod, during the final session of the Second Vatican Council, was the boldest treatment of the issue yet by a pope. There could be no clear distinction between the "teaching" Church (*Ecclesia docens*) and the "learning" Church (*Ecclesia discens*), he told them. To teach meant to listen. And hearing what the Holy Spirit had to say to the Church could only happen through a deep, mutual interaction among the people of God at all levels.

The people's participation, he said, was a right, according to the ancient Church principle that *quod omnes tangit ab omnibus tractari debet*—what affects all should be discussed by all. But synodality was also key to fostering the kind of adult Christian culture required by an evangelizing Church. It was vital not just for revitalizing Catholicism, but for Christian unity. It was also a sign in a world that too often "consigns the fate of entire peoples to the grasp of small but powerful groups." A Church that was a model of mutual listening and reconciled diversity can "help civil society to be built up in justice and fraternity, and thus bring about a more beautiful and humane world for coming generations."[28]

While the synod remained consultative, not deliberative, Francis wanted to reform it so that it could be more like Aparecida, using a method and process that made it a mechanism of ecclesial discernment that could have a real impact on future pastoral policy. The synods on the family of 2014 and 2015 road-tested the new methodology, often in a spirit of what is known in Latin America as "constructive disorganization." Part of the energy and shock of the synods came from the bishops discovering that they were genuinely free to speak and that they had sincere, sometimes deep-seated disagreements; yet they also saw how the Holy Spirit could somehow work through their disagreements to create new thinking that reconciled those differences. The experience has inspired, as Francis hoped it would, bishops to do the same in their local Churches. One of those bowled over by both the synod and the pope's speech was the archbishop of Brisbane, Mark Coleridge, who is currently helping to organize the first "plenary council" in eighty years involving the whole Church in Australia, to conclude in 2020.[29]

After approving in early 2018 the results of a three-year reflection by theologians on "synodality in the life of the Church"—in itself an extraordinary development—Francis set down his overhaul of the synod in a detailed formal document called *Episcopalis Communio*. It made clear that while only bishop delegates would vote, there were many different ways the assembly could be "a suitable instrument for giving voice to the entire people of God." Consultations of the faithful as well as the active participation—giving speeches, attending small groups—of plenty of non-voting members would bring the voice of the wider Church into the synod hall, along with invited experts and delegates from other Churches. At the October 2018 synod on youth and vocation, the point was illustrated by thirty young adults attending the assembly, and at the pope's urging clapping or staying silent in response to what they heard. Many delegates understood what Francis meant in *Episcopalis Communio*, that the bishop was a disciple, one who "listens to the voice of Christ speaking through the entire people of God."[30]

Episcopalis Communio made clear that, if the pope approved it, the synod's final document would be part of the Church's teaching, to be adopted and adapted locally. He would approve it if a consensus had emerged that was the fruit of "the workings of the Spirit," reflected in a vote of more than two-thirds on each paragraph of the final report, as happened in 2015. Not only was the synod now a permanent central body, separated from the Roman Curia and subject directly to the bishops and the pope, but it was recognized as having the authority to teach and steer the universal Church under the guidance of the Holy Spirit.

For anyone who is familiar with the modern Church, this was an astonishing development. Rather than waiting for a Roman dicastery to close off discussion, the synod in Rome was a means of opening it. It meant that the synod could finally be, as Francis put it in his 2015 speech, "an expression of episcopal collegiality within an entirely synodal Church." That made it powerful, because "power is something that is shared," he told *El País*, adding: "Power exists when we make decisions that have been meditated, talked about, and prayed over."

Although it was often used in connection with synodality, and was obviously a part of it, "episcopal collegiality" had a particular meaning that was defined at the Second Vatican Council: not only were bishops responsible for their dioceses, but as a body they were also co-responsible for the governance of the universal Church. The College of Bishops governed the universal Church *sub et cum Petro*, that is, under and with the pope, and never without him. The idea was expressed at the Second Vatican Council in the Dogmatic Constitution on the Church, *Lumen Gentium*, but Paul VI tamped it down under pressure from the Curia, and under John Paul II the idea was gradually reduced to mean that bishops were in communion with Rome and each other.

Francis signaled he was serious about "effective" rather than simply "affective" collegiality on the very night of his election, when on the balcony of St. Peter's he used a famous formula from Christianity's first centuries to describe his new diocese as "the Church of Rome that presides in charity over all the Churches." Presiding in *caritas* meant that as a pastor, in concert with his fellow bishops, he would respect the life of the local churches, listening and dialoguing with them.

Collegiality meant the pope remained the supreme legislator, the final arbiter, the focus of unity, but that didn't mean he should usurp "the place of local bishops in the discernment of every issue which arises in their territory," as Francis made clear in *Evangelii Gaudium*. His 2013 exhortation called for a "healthy decentralization" and he was as good as his word. Bishops had drowned for decades in a flood of documents and directives from Rome; Francis reduced them to a trickle.

He also pledged to restore the teaching and pastoral latitude that a bishops' conference was given by the Second Vatican Council yet which had been largely squashed by Rome in the 1980s. It was regrettable, he said in *Evangelii Gaudium*, that "the juridical status of episcopal conferences which would see them as subjects of specific attributions, including genuine doctrinal authority, has not yet been sufficiently elaborated." In his 2016 document on marriage and family, *Amoris Laetitia*, he made clear that "not all discussions of doctrinal, moral or pastoral issues need to be settled by interventions of the magisterium." What the Church believed and taught was not up for grabs, but it was for the local Church to seek "solutions better suited to its culture and sensitive to its traditions and local needs."

Inculturation was a corollary of the incarnation. For the Church to "enter into the people, it must be with the people, and cause the people and their culture to grow," Francis told Dominique Wolton. "The people must be able to do the liturgy in this or that way. . . . That's the great contribution of Vatican II: inculturation." Hence the call, in the 2019 synod on Amazonia, for the Church to have an "indigenous and Amazonian face," recognizing native spiritualities as "a source of riches for the Christian experience," for ways of teaching and preaching that use narrative and storytelling, and for practicing liturgies with languages and clothing "in communion with nature and the community."

Because of this core principle, few episodes in the Church's recent past had caused more anti-Vatican resentment among bishops than Rome's takeover of the process of liturgical translation in John Paul II's final years, above all in the English-speaking world. Because the liturgical translation saga was a microcosm of the fate of synodality and collegiality after Vatican II, Francis's move to reverse the centralism of the John Paul II years was his clearest sign of the Church's new direction.[31]

The Council gave local churches the task of organizing translations from the Latin of the Church's universal prayers. In the English-speaking world this was carried out by a joint commission of eleven Anglophone bishops' conferences, known as the International Commission on English in the Liturgy, or ICEL. The first translation, in the early 1970s, was by common consent rushed and in need of revision, and ICEL's translators in the 1980s began work on a new translation of all the liturgical texts. It was a monumental task that took until 1998 but was worth the wait. More accurate and faithful to the Latin, the new translation also managed to be elegant English prose.

After it was approved by all its eleven member bishops' conferences, ICEL sent the 1998 translation to Rome for what should have been a mere rubber stamp of approval. But the Congregation for Divine Worship rejected it on the grounds that it did not adhere to a new set of translation criteria that it was planning to introduce. In 2001 the Congregation's prefect, Chilean cardinal Jorge Medina Estévez, issued the new criteria, substituting the long-standing principle of "dynamic equivalence" for the idea of a "sacred vernacular." A word-for-word equivalence with Latin, he decreed, must now take preference over a meaning-for-meaning translation. If this resulted in obscure, Latinate, hieratic language, so be it: priests were on hand to use the bewilderment of their congregations as teaching opportunities.

When ICEL insisted on its own translation, Medina sacked its staff and convened a Rome-based body to supervise a new English translation according to the new principles. As a result, the lyrical, prayerful 1998 English translation never saw the light of day. Over a decade later, a Vatican-engineered replacement landed with a thud on the English-speaking Catholic world. It was stodgy, archaic, and unloved, using "a language that falls halfway between Latin and English," as Father Gerald O'Collins, SJ, puts it, in which words like "compunction," "laud," and "supplication" replaced "repentance," "praise," and "prayer."[32]

Vatican arrogance, the absence of effective collegiality, and the harm to inculturation of the Gospel were all vividly illustrated in the saga. So when Francis returned to local bishops the right to judge the best way of rendering into local languages the Church's base book of liturgical prayers, the decision had a resonance well beyond the arcane world of liturgical translation.

Magnum Principium, the title of Francis's edict of September 2017 overturning Medina's centralist coup, was taken from a speech in which Saint Paul VI reminded translators of the "great principle" of making faith accessible to ordinary people. After he made clear that this was a task entrusted to the bishops, not the Holy See, Francis said translators should follow guidelines where these proved "useful" but made clear his preference for dynamic equivalence in calling for translators to render "fully and faithfully the meaning of the original text." Pointedly referring to the "difficulties" that had arisen "between the bishops' conferences and the Apostolic See," Francis called for "collaboration marked by mutual trust" in the future.

It was a little earthquake. Rome still had a right of veto over translations into the eighty-seven global languages recognized by the Vatican, but the Congregation for Divine Worship could no longer act unilaterally, imposing its will; approval could only be withheld if some serious anomaly were at stake. The president of the German bishops' conference, Cardinal Reinhard Marx, expressed his "great relief." "Rome is responsible for dogmatic interpretations but not for matters of style," he said. "Now the bishops' conferences have far greater freedom."[33]

They needed greater freedom also to apply teaching and doctrine, not—as conservatives feared—in order to opt out of or dilute universal teachings, but in order to better incarnate them in local circumstances. This meant quietly reversing Saint John Paul II's 1998 edict *Ad Apostolos Suos*, which required unanimous decisions when bishops' conferences were voting on doctrinal matters, failing which the teaching had to be referred to the Holy See for approval or disapproval. Because unanimity is almost always impossible in practice, especially in large conferences of bishops, the result of John Paul II's edict had been in practice to undermine the local Church: it sent the message that Rome always knew best.

Francis now made clear that bishops' conferences had a special duty to seek consensus but did not need unanimity in order to explore the possibility of changes in pastoral practice. Hence, while making clear that the priesthood would remain celibate, he has made clear that he is open to the ordination of married men in remote areas such as Amazonia and the

Pacific Islands in order that people can receive the sacraments. But rather than simply allow it, he has asked for bishops to first reach agreement on proposals, which can then be put to the synod.[34]

The lack of a consensus led Francis to turn down a German bid in February 2018 to make it easier for Protestants married to Catholics to receive the Eucharist in a Catholic Church. Three-quarters of the sixty-seven German bishops backed draft guidelines on the criteria for allowing intercommunion in "mixed marriages," but thirteen opposed it, a number of whom appealed to the Vatican. Francis made clear that the proposal needed to mature, and that the bishops should try "to come to an agreement as unanimous as possible in the spirit of ecclesial communion." The answer this time was no, but his reasoning implied something quite new: that where bishops did reach a peaceful consensus following a period of authentic discernment, Rome was now likely to respect their decision.[35]

Francis wanted a less bloated, more agile and humble Roman Curia, with a more global—that is, less Italian—staff that included more laypeople, especially women, in senior roles. But there were limits: only clergy, for example, could run departments with jurisdiction over ordained ministers or sensitive doctrinal matters, which were around a quarter of the total. With the four new Vatican bodies he created between 2014 and 2016, however, Francis was less constrained. The economy secretariat, the dicastery for communications, as well as the two new super-dicasteries concerned with laypeople and justice matters were either concerned with technical issues not proper to clergy or were outward-facing, "apostolic" bodies. That meant that laypeople and religious—especially including laywomen and women religious—would be able to occupy senior roles.[36]

In principle, Francis has made clear, there is no obstacle to a woman heading a Vatican department that does not have jurisdiction over clergy. Whatever a layman or religious brother can do, in other words, a laywoman or religious sister can do. Pledging in *Evangelii Gaudium* to create "still broader opportunities for a more incisive female presence in the Church," he brought seven mostly laywomen into senior roles: Barbara Jatta as the first director of the Vatican Museums; Paloma García Ovejero as the first vice-director of the press office, later replaced by Christiane Murray; and at the Dicastery for the Laity, Family and Life, Gabriella Gambino and Linda

Ghisoni as undersecretaries (department heads), and Marta Rodríguez as head of women's issues. In 2018, Francis named three women as consultants to the Congregation for the Doctrine of the Faith, the first time laypeople have had that role, while his revamping of the Pontifical Commission for the Protection of Minors that year led to an equal number of women and men being on it. The following year, Francis named six women religious as the first full members of the Vatican congregation overseeing religious life. Rumors in 2019 that Cardinal Pell's replacement as the Vatican's finance minister would be Secretariat for the Economy official Claudia Coccia also pointed to a new openness to women in executive positions.

Francis told Dominique Wolton that it wasn't misogyny that kept women out of senior roles at the Vatican but clericalism: "when [the *curiali*] see how much better women are at doing things, there's no problem," he said; rather, it was "a problem of power." The point is underscored by Barbara Jatta, who, as director of the Vatican Museums, says she has never felt a conflict between her roles as wife, mother, and accomplished art historian, and a career spent for the most part in and around the Vatican. But she credits Francis with increasing the presence of women in leadership roles, saying he "has in some way perceived [the changes] in our society and in our times."[37]

Sister Carmen Sammut, at that time president of the International Union of Superiors General (UISG)—which represents in Rome the leaders of around 450,000 women religious around the world—says "doors have been slowly opening" in Vatican dicasteries under Francis. UISG vice-president Sister Sally Hodgdon agrees that "things have changed radically" in this respect. "It seems each year they listen a little more and follow through more on our ideas," she told reporters in May 2019, speaking of the dicasteries and the synod. "Under Francis, there's a lot more movement, a lot more talk about women," agrees Tracey McLure, a laywoman working at Vatican Radio who runs a new association to represent women who work in the Curia. She created the association in response to the pope's critique that women in the Church have too often occupied a place of "servitude rather than true service."

Francis insists that the task is not just a functional matter of filling decision-making posts with women but a question, again, of conversion of mentalities: it is time to take seriously the femaleness of the Church itself. Speaking after Ghisoni's address to the world's bishops at the global abuse summit in February 2019, Francis observed that "to invite a woman to speak about the wounds of the Church is to invite the Church to speak about herself, about the wounds she has." It was about "integrating the woman as the figure of the Church into our thinking," he said. Afterward, Gambino agreed with this need "to think of the Church also in the categories of a woman."[38]

In 2015, Francis announced that for the first time in its history, five out of the thirty theologians in the Vatican-appointed International Theological Commission were women, but in a phrase that was immediately misinterpreted as patronizing, criticized the number as too few: "They are the strawberries on the cake," he said, "but there is need for more." The odd metaphor aside (he was speaking Italian but probably thinking in Spanish, where the phrase means not that the women were decorative, but the pièce de resistance), his point was clear: it was not about bringing in a few more women here and there but integrating the female into the heart of the Church's thinking. "Francis is saying it is not enough to 'concede' minor positions to women that previously belonged exclusively to men; women must be valued in their own right," observes Rita Ferrone. "And, finally, when they are valued in their own right, and at their true worth, their value in the life of the church surpasses that of the male hierarchy."

Ferrone, a U.S. liturgical expert who is a sharp observer of women's roles in the Church, believes that although Francis continues to use the language of complementarity of the sexes—men and women are different, a difference that reflects the male-female duality reflected in Creation itself—he does it in a way that does not draw straight lines from biological difference to social roles. In this he differs from, say, Saint John Paul II, whose theology of the sexes seemed often to imply that decision-making and leadership roles went against the "maternal" nature of women. "When we speak of complementarity between man and woman," Francis told the Humanum conference in 2014, "let us not confuse that term with the simplistic idea that all the roles and relations of the two sexes are fixed in a single, static pattern." Ferrone points to statements like this to argue that Francis sees male-female complementarity "as an evolving reality," one that "takes a great variety of forms and grows in freedom through the gifts of the Spirit."[39]

It is typical of Francis to throw out an intuition and leave it to others to wrestle with it conceptually. But he came closest to explaining his insight in a homily at a Mass on the first celebration of the Blessed Virgin Mary,

Mother of the Church, in May 2018, a feast that he had introduced into the liturgical calendar two months earlier. In his homily he explained that the word "church" (at least in Latin languages) is a woman, which means that it is called to have the outlook of a wife and mother. To forget this is to be "a Church of bachelors, who live isolated and incapable of love, incapable of bearing fruit." To be a female Church was to communicate God: "gentle, tender, smiling, full of love."[40]

Francis's boldest gesture in relation to women has been to raise expectations of their admission to the clergy, not as priests, for which there is no tradition in the Catholic Church, but as deacons, for which there is a long precedent in its first millennium. The idea came from a UISG plenary meeting with 850 women leading religious orders in 2016, when the sisters challenged him to appoint a commission to explore whether the women identified as deacons in the New Testament were actually ordained or simply "blessed" in some way for service. The pope accepted the challenge, appointing twelve scholars (six women and six men) under Cardinal Ladaria of the Congregation for the Doctrine of the Faith who carried out a two-year study of ancient manuscripts in the Vatican and other libraries. Although they reached agreement in many areas, there was no consensus on the key question of whether the female diaconate was a sacramental ordination, Francis told journalists flying back from north Macedonia, adding that there was a need for more study.[41]

The women deacons commission was not asked to recommend if the female diaconate should be restored, though it raised expectations about new ministries for women that could be recognized by the Church. But it wasn't clear if expanding the clergy to include women deacons would help dismantle clericalism, or the reverse. For Francis, it was important that such debates did not confuse being ordained with having the spiritual gifts and power to evangelize, which belongs to all the baptized. "When we speak of sacramental power, 'we are in the realm of function, not that of dignity or holiness,'" Francis said in *Evangelii Gaudium*, quoting Saint John Paul II. The power to minister, to serve, to heal, preach, and teach are all gifts of the Spirit with which the people of God are anointed. Yet only a tiny percentage of churchgoers saw themselves as subjects rather than objects of the Church's mission. For all the talk in the Church after Vatican II of "the hour of the laity," Francis caustically observed in his 2016 letter to Cardinal Ouellet, it appeared that "the clock had stopped."

Francis charged the new super-dicastery for the Laity, Family and Life with starting it ticking again. He told its prefect, American cardinal Kevin Farrell, that his was the most important department in the Curia because almost all Catholics in the world were laypeople. Its statute pledges the dicastery to reflect on "the relationship between men and women in their respective specificity, reciprocity, complementarity and equal dignity," and on "the identity and mission of women in the Church and in society, promoting their participation." It also commits the dicastery to promoting "laypeople who are formed well, animated by a clear and sincere faith, whose lives have been touched by a personal and merciful encounter with the love of Jesus Christ." It is a definition that could profitably be extended to clergy too.[42]

In creating the dicastery, Francis decided to place the Pontifical Academy for Life under it, and to overhaul the academy's membership and approach. Created under Saint John Paul II, it had become under Benedict XVI a refuge for die-hards who set ever stricter purity tests for each other on bioethical issues, as the Order of Malta row revealed. The makeover was a chance to renew the members and recast the pro-life message in terms of what its new president, Archbishop Vincenzo Paglia, called "an authentic 'human ecology' that helps recover the original balance of creation between the human person and the entire universe."[43]

The anti-abortion witness from the Vatican would now be part of a consistent global humanitarian ethic of life that includes other issues such as concern for migrants dying in the Mediterranean or the deserts of the Mexican border as well as capital punishment, gun control, and infant malnutrition. The message was clear: Catholics could no longer claim that issues such as abortion were "nonnegotiable" while others such as the death penalty or immigration were "prudential issues" on which they could legitimately disagree. "Values are values, and that is it," Francis told *Corriere della Sera*. "I can't say that, of the fingers of a hand, there is one less useful than the rest. So I don't see in what sense there can be 'negotiable' values."[44]

In August 2018, Francis made clear that the death penalty was inadmissible under all circumstances, "no matter how serious the crime that has been committed," because it is "an attack on the inviolability and the dignity of the person." Saint John Paul II had vigorously opposed capital punishment, making it for the first time a pro-life issue, and said cases requiring the execution of the offender "are very rare, if not practically nonexistent."

But he left open the hypothesis that such situations could exist, which was used by Catholics in the United States to justify the death penalty, since they could argue that the Church was not actually against its use for egregious kinds of murder (and what murders aren't egregious?). Francis's alteration now closed that door for good. The death penalty contradicted the Gospel, was nowadays unnecessary, and its use in the past was "a consequence of a mentality of the time—more legalistic than Christian—that sanctified the value of laws lacking in humanity and mercy." There were howls of protest from right-wing Catholics in the United States, who served up a toxic mix of theological justifications for vengeance and traditionalist objections against any changes in doctrine. The protests revealed, again, how isolated from mainstream Catholic values were large parts of the American Church. When the U.S. bishops voted to incorporate the revision of the *Catechism* into their own teaching documents, eleven of them opposed or abstained.[45]

Francis's updating of the *Catechism* wasn't just aimed at opposing the death penalty; it also committed the Church to work for its abolition worldwide. It was one of the tasks Francis entrusted to his other new super-dicastery, which began operations in 2017 on the fiftieth anniversary of Paul VI's great development encyclical, *Populorum Progressio*. The Dicastery for Promoting Integral Human Development—the phrase used in *Populorum Progressio*—absorbed the work previously done by four pontifical councils: for justice and peace, migrants and itinerant peoples, health workers (which oversees the work of around six thousand Catholic hospitals and eighteen thousand clinics across the world), as well as the Vatican's charitable arm, Cor Unum. Francis's statutes said the new dicastery "will be competent particularly in issues regarding migrants, those in need, the sick, the excluded and marginalized, the imprisoned and the unemployed, as well as victims of armed conflict, natural disasters, and all forms of slavery and torture." He named as its prefect the Ghanaian cardinal who headed the former Pontifical Council for Justice and Peace, Peter Turkson, but in an unprecedented move, he reserved leadership of the migration section of the office for himself.

The messages from the two new dicasteries were clear: The Vatican was no longer "self-referential." Their concerns were not just focused on the needs of the institution, but on the service of humanity and the promotion of all that was authentically human. Their purpose was to assist the bishops' conferences around the world to do the same.[46]

This is the shift that the new constitution for the Curia, which the C9 has been working on since 2014, aims to capture. The key element of *Praedicate Evangelium* (Preach the Gospel) which replaces Saint John Paul II's 1989 constitution, *Pastor Bonus* (Good Shepherd), said C9 president Cardinal Rodríguez de Maradiaga, was its "spirit." Before, you thought in terms of a pyramid, with the pope at the top, the Curia in the middle, and the bishops' conferences at the bottom. But in the new vision "the Curia isn't an organism of power but of service." It was not going to be a mere "cosmetic change but will promote the change in mentality that has already started," Cardinal Rodríguez said. "The Roman Curia will never again be the same."[47]

five

A Church of Wounds

Early in his papacy, when the world was fascinated with him and he seemed to walk on water, Francis wondered to one of his close collaborators what his "cross" would be. He knew God was preparing something. No disciple, least of all Saint Peter's successor, could follow Christ without some share in His suffering and failure. Patiently bearing trials, crucified by the world yet trusting in the new life beyond, came with the white cassock and the fisherman's ring.

Many assumed he already had his cross in the form of the change-phobic Vatican. But while grumbling resistance to reform could be a trial, it was hardly a *Via Dolorosa*, a time when strategies fail, the body polarizes, and confusion and misunderstanding reign. Francis's dark night of ferocity and tribulation, it turned out, was the long-simmering clerical sex abuse crisis.

The annus horribilis of 2018 seemed to come out of nowhere, a tide of revelations that punctured the present by shattering open new layers of a shameful past. First out of the gate was Australia's Royal Commission, which ran the conclusions of its four-year probe into institutional mishandling of sex abuse in December 2017. The biggest ever study of its kind, it revealed that close to 2,500 survivors over sixty years had suffered sex abuse in Catholic institutions, mostly at the hands of clergy. Then came the report by the German bishops made public in September 2018 that identified 3,700 cases of alleged sexual abuse of minors by Catholic priests, deacons, and clergy over a sixty-eight-year period. Yet in terms of sheer shock value, nothing quite compared to the August 2018 inquiry by the Pennsylvania grand jury into the alleged abuse of some one thousand identified minors by three hundred priests in six dioceses over many decades. It wasn't just the scale but the graphic nature of the pain and suffering depicted there—the nature of the evil involved—that triggered a tsunami of shame and anger. How could these priests have gotten away with it? How could the bishops have been so indifferent? After reading the report, Andrew Sullivan captured the reaction of many Catholics: "We may still believe in Jesus," he wrote in *New York* magazine. "But precisely because of that, we can no longer believe in the Church."[1]

Looking at the figures alone, the reports added little to previous findings. It was already known that there had been astonishingly high levels of abuse—anywhere between 4 and 8 percent of clergy were accused—prior to the 1980s, when bishops, first in the Anglo-Saxon world, began to wake up to the scale and hidden nature of the challenge. At the turn of the new millennium, the Church in Ireland, Australia, the United States, and the UK introduced "zero-tolerance" measures, pithily summed up in Saint John Paul II telling the American bishops that "there is no place in the priesthood and religious life for those who would harm the young." Files over decades were combed through in search of abusive priests being shuffled between therapy centers and parishes. It was the U.S. Church's own investigations in 2004 and 2011 that first revealed that 4,392 priests, between 4 and 5 percent of the Catholic clergy, had been responsible for more than eleven thousand cases of sexual abuse of minors between 1950 and 2000. Determined to ensure it could not happen again, the U.S. bishops passed a raft of measures in the so-called Dallas Charter in 2002, backing it with self-policing measures. Allegations in the Catholic Church dropped off sharply, to little more than a trickle. The Pennsylvania report proved the charter's effectiveness: only two of the three-hundred-plus priests in the report had abused in the previous decade, and both had been reported by their dioceses.

The new thing in that 1,300-page grand jury account was the bishops' mishandling. What was shocking was the grotesque contrast—milked for more than it was worth by the report's authors—between the horrific suffering of the victims and the inept, inadequate response of bishops, who too often preferred the excuses of their priests to addressing the suffering of the victims. Theirs wasn't a conspiracy of silence, or even, for the most part, a deliberate cover-up; the bishops tried, often ineptly, to come to terms with the problem. Yet it was hard to miss the picture of detachment, of indifference, of managerial types living in a self-enclosed clerical bubble, with their backs to the people, yet parasitic on them. Even after dioceses paid billions of dollars in settlements and introduced prevention programs that were far ahead of those at other institutions, the Church's sexual abuse crisis was not only not over, but it had entered a vivid new stage. It was no longer just the abuser priest who stood indicted, but clericalism.[2]

Clericalism is the perverse idea that clerics of any sort—bishops, priests, consecrated persons—are superior to non-clerics, who are treated as inferiors, or children, whose task is to pray, pay, and obey, and not to question the cleric. It is a perversion because ordination gives powers to administer sacraments, and to teach and govern, but it does not confer superiority— morally, spiritually, or intellectually—over the non-ordained. To believe that it does is against the Church's own teaching at the Second Vatican Council, and insisting on this lordship is the refuge of spiritually empty people with fragile egos.

Nothing could be better designed to bring about the death of clericalism than the revelation of extreme suffering inflicted by clerics on the vulnerable and voiceless, and the failure to stop it. And nothing better illustrated it than the scandal that exploded around the archbishop emeritus of Washington just weeks before Pennsylvania. On June 20, the Holy See suddenly removed eighty-seven-year-old Theodore McCarrick from ministry, subjecting him to a prayer-and-penance sanction following the revelation of a forty-seven-year-old allegation that he had abused a minor during his days as a priest in New York. Although the news itself was shocking, there was at least a silver lining: the Church's processes had worked well. The victim had stepped forward because of a compensation program created by New York's archbishop, Cardinal Timothy Dolan. The archdiocese was given permission by Rome to investigate. The claim was deemed credible, and McCarrick was removed from ministry. The crime was too old to be dealt with under civil law, but the Church had acted swiftly and decisively.[3]

The silver lining soon vanished, however, when the *New York Times* a

few weeks later revealed McCarrick's long history as a homosexual predator. Especially in the late 1980s and early 1990s, as archbishop of Newark,
"Uncle Ted" had been notorious for inviting seminarians to weekends at
his beach house on the Jersey Shore, making sure that one of them shared
his bed. It had been an open secret, the kind of thing joked about know-
ingly over gossipy clerical dinners. As the stories tumbled out—the Newark diocese revealed that it had settled with two of the ex-seminarians in
the late 1990s—it appeared that nothing could have stopped McCarrick's
ascent, until Francis took action at the end of July following the New York
archdiocesan probe. He ordered McCarrick to resign from the College of
Cardinals, the first time a pope had demoted a prince of the Church since
1927, and the first time in history for sex abuse. McCarrick would live a
hidden life of "prayer and penance" while investigations were made that
would lead to his dismissal from the priesthood in February 2019.

But nothing could stop the flow of indignant questions in the meantime. How, when there was widespread knowledge of McCarrick's past,
could Saint John Paul II have named him to the leading post of archbishop
of Washington in 2000? Was it the result of his smooth charm, his closeness to the Polish pope's inner circle, above all Archbishop Stanisław
Dziwisz? Was it linked to the millions his Papal Foundation funneled to the
Vatican for the Polish resistance movement? The image of a self-serving,
corrupt, and morally degenerate episcopate made it much easier to believe
the exaggerated claim by the Pennsylvania grand jury that in response to
the exploitation by priests of innocent young people, bishops "not only did
nothing; they hid it all. For decades."[4]

The past was now knocking on the doors of the present, demanding answers and action. Catholics in the United States were in a punitive
frame of mind. As indignation spread in the summer of 2018, the idea
that a bishop could have made a mistake in the 1990s and learned from it
was greeted with derision. Cardinal Donald Wuerl of Washington, D.C.,
mentioned fifteen times in the Pennsylvania report, eventually resigned
in October 2018 over the reaction to claims that he had mishandled cases
back in the 1990s in Pittsburgh, despite his later having formulated new
procedures that would have made such mishandling all but impossible. In
a letter, Francis made clear that Wuerl made, rather than covered up, some
mistakes. "However your nobility has led you not to choose this way of
defense. Of this, I am proud and thank you."[5]

The pope, too, had had his own steep learning curve. His misreading of the situation in Chile had come to a head while he was visiting the country in January 2018. But he had seen where he had gone wrong, begged forgiveness, and acted radically in the light of new knowledge. Yet rather than applaud the greatness of a pope who had the humility to see his mistakes and act on them, his critics in the United States seized the moment to claim that the pope's fallibility in Chile was proof he could not be trusted on the issue. By the end of the summer, halfway through Francis's visit to Dublin, the organized opposition—the same group of wealthy conservatives who hated him for his critiques of free-market idolatry and his embrace of the divorced—launched their most aggressive strike yet, in the form of a former Vatican official's claims that Francis had covered up for McCarrick and should resign.

In the fast-paced events and hysteria of 2018, most missed what was arguably one of the biggest stories of the Francis pontificate: the way that the Chile episode of the first quarter of the year revolutionized the pope's discernment of the abuse crisis, which would in turn shape his guidance of the Church through its time of distress.

What Francis described to me, when we met in June 2018, as "the lowest moment" of his pontificate, came five months earlier on his last day in Chile. On January 18 he was in Iquique, in the country's desert north, about to board the popemobile that would take him to the final Mass of his visit. Some local radio journalists called to him through a chain-link fence. They asked him for a few words; he praised the warmth of the Chilean people before signing a blessing. But as he moved toward the popemobile, one of them asked him about the bishop he had appointed in 2015, Juan Barros. Francis stopped and turned, his face darkening. Visibly frustrated at what he saw as the hounding of an innocent man, he told the reporters that the allegations against Barros were "all a calumny" and that "when they bring me proof, we can talk."

He had spent three years obdurately standing by Barros, a mild-mannered bishop accused of covering up for the notorious abuser he had once looked to as a spiritual father, Fernando Karadima, priest of the famous upper-class Santiago parish of El Bosque. The 2010 revelations of Karadima's abuse in the 1990s had rocked Chile, and Barros had become a symbol of the Church's pain and shame. The criticism of the pope for taking Barros under his wing had come from all sides—Karadima's victims, the media, Chile's bishops—and there had been many painful moments along the way. But this was the worst. Some in Chile would soon be comparing his "Iquique moment" to that fatal scene thirty years earlier, when John Paul II appeared on the balcony of the presidential palace in Santiago alongside the dictator General Augusto Pinochet. But while the pope's defenders could insist at that time that John Paul II had been maneuvered, no one doubted this time that Francis's defense of Barros was sincere and steadfast, an obstinate stand based on his reading of the facts: *Franciscus contra mundum*.[6]

At first there were two rival pope stories vying to lead the news. On the way to the Iquique Mass, Francis had stopped to help a policewoman who had fallen from a horse that shied as the popemobile came up from behind. Then, on the short flight to Peru, he had interrupted the onboard service to marry a LATAM Airlines steward and stewardess, telling them not to keep their rings too tight, but not so loose that they fall off. But as local television news cut between the papal plane story and a press conference hastily called by Karadima's three celebrity victims in the Chilean capital, it was clear which news would take wing. James Hamilton, Andrés Murillo, and Juan Carlos Cruz insisted that they had provided testimony but had not been believed, and they now regarded the pope's apology over abuse at Santiago's presidential palace two days earlier as empty.

On the flight back to Rome three days later, Francis explained to reporters that he had seen no convincing evidence, and that people had to be considered innocent unless proven guilty. But Hamilton, Murillo, and Cruz insisted they had long before sent that evidence; why, if their testimony had been good enough for the Vatican in 2011 to convict their abuser, wasn't it good enough to persuade Francis that Barros had covered up for Karadima? Wasn't this the Church again standing by a cover-up bishop while victims were ignored and disbelieved?

Two months later, when the fifth anniversary of his election came around, it was a commentariat cliché that Francis was somehow "tone-deaf" on the abuse issue, that he lacked reforming zeal in responding to the greatest challenge to Catholicism since the Reformation.

It wasn't that he lacked sensitivity or empathy toward victims, with whom he had met regularly in the Casa Santa Marta, sometimes various times a month, usually on Fridays, in meetings of the strictest confidentiality. (Baroness Sheila Hollins, the leading British psychiatrist who sat on the pope's anti-abuse expert commission, says Francis has always showed an "extraordinary empathy" for victims, often moved to tears by their stories.) Nor had he failed, over and over, to condemn the sexual abuse of minors by priests in piercingly prophetic language, nor to warn that bishops who failed to act against abusers would be held accountable. Yet to critics, his reforms seemed slow and hesitant. He had created a commission of anti-abuse experts, yet he seemed not to want to deal with the resistance to it. But it was above all his defense of Barros that became, for many, the symbol of the pope just not "getting it."[7]

Few knew, however, that inside the Casa Santa Marta that Easter of 2018, the pope was radically changing course. Disturbed and perplexed by what he had encountered in Chile, he had commissioned a report whose findings had shattered his viewpoint. Archbishop Charles Scicluna's report wasn't just about the abuser-priest Karadima; it also covered religious orders and dioceses across Chile that had been covering up abuse and predation, in spite of the norms and protocols that were in place. Reading it, Francis realized that he had experienced in Chile nothing less than an institutional cover-up: a *modus operandi et cogitandi* based on primitive mechanisms of denial and suppression. Worst of all, he saw that he himself had been entrapped in those mechanisms and had been incapable of proper discernment.

The knowledge was devastating, but also liberating. Now that he knew the truth, he could act.

Two things became clear to Francis that would, after Easter 2018, shape his response to the unfolding crisis. The first realization was that it was no longer enough for him to hold in balance different policy priorities. In order to eradicate both abuse and its cover-up at their systemic roots, he had to confront not just sin but corruption. The second was that the endless scandals and revelations now buffeting the Church and apparently destroying its credibility were a sign of God acting in history. In the vindicating of the victims and the indicting of the institution, a great unveiling was taking place. At the heart of both abuse and cover-up was a perversion of power, diabolical in its nature, the defeat of which required far more than judicial mechanisms, for what was at stake was the heart of faith itself.

It was the same diabolic perversion that had existed since the beginning of time and could be found everywhere today in the degrading treatment of the vulnerable; but it had taken root in the Church via clericalism, the sense of entitlement and superiority that turned self-denying service into self-gratifying, predatory exploitation. Legal and institutional reform was necessary but inadequate. Only prayer and fasting, and a process of conversion, could purify the Church.

The task was not to batten down the hatches and wait for the storm to pass. The storm would not pass, not for a long time, not until it had achieved the purification that each scandal called forth. His role was to lead the Church on a retreat, a journey of conversion; to guide it and hold it to that path; to encourage it to open up in humility to Christ and His grace. And because whenever there is an opening to grace, there is always a temptation to avoid it, Francis's task was to identify those temptations and mechanisms of denial.

That meant not retreating defensively but boldly facing the Church's sin and failure. In the fall of 2018, Francis told French priests in Rome that "the barque of the Church faces violent headwinds as a result of the serious failings of some of its members," and that in this context its priests were "called to witness to the strength of the Resurrection in the wounds of this world." Do not fear, he told them, to look on the wounds of the Church, not to lament them, but to be led to where Christ is.

There could be no hiding now, no subterfuge, no more denial. The Church would be flayed in endless inquiries, its failures paraded before an accusing world. Cardinals would be jailed, and the Church would appear to the world to be synonymous with depravity and failure. The pope would no longer walk on water, but be crucified. But it was as God wanted: only as the wounded shepherd could he guide his wounded Church to where Christ was calling it.[8]

Prior to Chile, Francis's primary concern was to hold in balance five policy priorities he had inherited from his predecessor that were essential to combating the scourge of abuse.

The first was to ensure that victims were listened to and accompanied, for God spoke through their experience. The second was to make sure that the Church across the world put in place robust safeguarding protocols, best practices that flowed from an awareness of the seriousness of this issue, above all in parts of the developing world where often that awareness was severely lacking. The third was to ensure the smooth functioning of judicial procedures to bring offenders to justice, not just cooperating with civil authorities but also speeding the canonical processes coordinated by Rome. The fourth was to create mechanisms of accountability for bishops who failed to act properly to defend the flock against predators. Finally, it was important to uphold the principle of *in dubio pro reo*; although most allegations of abuse were true, a significant number were not, and everyone had a right to the presumption of innocence until the facts were clear.

But often the facts weren't clear, and when they weren't it wasn't always easy to hold these principles in balance. The so-called Romanones case showed why.

Daniel (not his real name) was a twenty-five-year-old university lecturer, a married member of Opus Dei living in Pamplona, Spain, when in 2014 he wrote Francis a harrowing five-page account of his three-year-long sexual abuse at the hands of a group of priests a decade earlier in his home city of Granada in the south. He had been an altar boy and catechist until the priests persuaded him to live with them in their parish to explore his vocation. He claimed he was repeatedly abused between the ages of thirteen and seventeen, when he fled the parish. Years later, by then married and working, he suffered from anxiety attacks. He wanted the pope to know what he had been through, so it wouldn't happen to others.

Daniel was on the street when he took the call on his cell phone and couldn't at first believe it was the pope. Clearly shaken, Francis was calling to express his deep shame on behalf of the Church, to ask Daniel's forgiveness, and to assure him that action would be taken. Granada's archbishop was alerted, and the police informed. Three priests and a layman were arrested in October 2014, all members of a "conservative spiritualist" group called Los Romanones, led by sixty-one-year-old Father Román Martínez. The Vatican suspended the priests from ministry, as church law demands as soon as a credible allegation, however old, is brought forward. In the media, the pope's action was hailed as a turning point, "a prime example of the more open and assertive approach to the issue of clergy sexual abuse that Pope Francis has taken," as the *New York Times* put it.[9]

For months, as the police probe was under way, Spanish media exploded with eye-popping details of orgies, rape, and the torment of a teenager persuaded to live with a ring of gay priests who went round the house naked. Due in part to Spain's statute of limitations and the lack of corroborating evidence, however, most of the molestation charges were eventually dropped, and only Father Martínez was tried for rape, for which the prosecutor sought a nine-year jail sentence. But at trial in March 2017, the case collapsed. Daniel's testimony was deemed inconsistent and flawed, and Father Martínez was freed. The judge was harsh with Daniel, imputing bad faith, and ordered him to pay court costs. But Spain's Supreme Court later walked back that ruling, saying lack of sufficient proof did not imply the accusations were false.

In November 2017, after its own investigations, the Vatican lifted the three priests' suspensions. The following summer, in July 2018, the pope received them in the Casa Santa Marta to ask their forgiveness. It pained him that they had spent years being pilloried and shunned, unable to exercise their priesthood. On the flight from Dublin a month later, he told the story as a lesson to journalists not to assume guilt when they reported such cases. Perhaps because he was still moved by what the priests had gone through, he described Daniel as a "fantasist." Hurt, Daniel wrote Francis that the Supreme Court had made clear that being unable to prove the charge of sexual abuse with penetration did not mean that the facts of the case were untrue. "I feel rage and pain," he wrote, "to see how you receive, embrace and support those priests . . . who have destroyed my life."[10]

Where did the truth lie? What was the appropriate papal response in these circumstances? Was it right for Francis to have gotten so directly involved?

Those questions had already been asked in the Barros case.

Francis's decision to name Barros to head the southern Chilean diocese of Osorno in early 2015 was a mistake on many fronts. The progressive German missionaries who were highly regarded in the city were appalled at being given a bishop who—as the military ordinary at the time—had presided at the 2006 funeral of the dictator General Augusto Pinochet. But mostly it was a mistake because Barros had become a lightning rod for the indignation over the Karadima scandal.

Yet the Vatican and Francis himself had reviewed the files prior to naming Barros to Osorno, and they could find no reason, legally speaking, not to appoint him. Barros and the other four bishops who had come out of El Bosque were adamant that they had never known at the time of Karadima's sexual abuse, as Barros confirmed to me in Santiago the day before the pope arrived. No civil or Vatican inquiry had established that he was lying, and the Vatican's Congregation for Bishops had found no "objective" reasons against the appointment. "There was nothing consistent in the information they had in the Vatican," Francis told Philip Pullella of Reuters.

Cruz, Hamilton, and Murillo claimed that Barros was "a man we know and have accused of witnessing abuse, our abuse, and therefore encouraging the perverse dynamics of power." But Chile's two cardinals, the current and former archbishops of Santiago, Ricardo Ezzati and Francisco Errázuriz, had assured the Vatican that the three victims were out to inflict maximum damage on the Church and were after money, in the form of a $450,000 civil case against the archdiocese for failing to act (the court eventually found in favor of the victims in March 2019). But Ezzati and Errázuriz did not want Francis to give Barros a diocese. Ezzati even spent over an hour at the October 2014 synod trying to persuade the pope not to appoint him, as did a number of other Chilean bishops. They wanted to put as much distance as possible between the Church and Karadima, and they saw Barros as an obstacle to that strategy.[11]

Meanwhile, Francis's concern was for Barros, whom he saw as a scapegoat for national anger over Pinochet and Karadima. Not only did he see Barros as a vulnerable figure in need of protection; he also trusted the judgment of a Spanish Jesuit spiritual guide, Father Germán Arana, SJ, who had helped Barros in 2014 after the Chilean had been removed as bishop to the armed forces. Arana believed Barros had been wrongly accused. Given the information he had, therefore, the choice for Francis was straightforward: all the indications were that Barros had every right to lead a diocese, and not to appoint him would constitute an injustice. To say he should be sacrificed for the sake of the institution was the logic of Caiphas in condemning Jesus. As pope, he had a duty to defend the innocent.

Francis's blindness to the wider Chilean context stemmed also from a failure to grasp the gravity of the Karadima scandal. From Buenos Aires, the wealthy central Santiago parish of El Bosque had looked as it did to many Chilean Catholics: a hive of pastoral and missionary activity that produced record numbers of vocations, especially in the 1990s. When the Karadima abuse allegations exploded in 2010, it was a profound shock, and the first reaction of many churchmen—Bergoglio possibly among them—was simply not to believe it, not least because it was used as a stick that political enemies used to beat the Church. Although Karadima was tried and removed from ministry by Rome a year later, his canonist advocates did a good job of minimizing or disputing many of the central allegations. The advocates were Argentine canonists at the Catholic University of Buenos Aires said to be close to Bergoglio. One of them, Monsignor Alejandro

Bunge, was called to Rome by Francis after his election to work in the Vatican's appellate tribunal, the Roman Rota.[12]

"Had the pope realized who Karadima was," a source close to Francis told me, "he would never have appointed Barros to Osorno."

El Bosque and Karadima were everything Francis was not: a clericalist corruption of money, power, right-wing politics, and homoerotic subculture. The parish, frequented by General Pinochet's men, was just a few blocks from the nunciature, where the Holy See's representative from 1977 to 1988, Angelo Sodano—later John Paul II's all-powerful secretary of state—was firmly pro-Pinochet and close to Karadima as well as Pinochet's minister for religious affairs. Close to fifty "prize" priestly vocations from Santiago's professional classes later sprang from El Bosque. Four of them, including Barros, were promoted by Karadima and Sodano to key posts in the Church in Chile and would become bishops.

Together with fellow *karadimista* bishop Horacio Valenzuela, Barros described to me in January 2018 how they had increasingly been alienated from El Bosque as Karadima became increasingly paranoid and authoritarian, obsessed with money, and cruel. Both bishops were emphatic that they never saw sexual abuse, let alone covered it up, and when the allegations were made public in 2010 they were as shocked as anyone else. Yet it was clear that few believed them. Barros carried around with him a folder of cuttings from social media sites that vilified him, and he complained of the left-wing forces behind them.

Francis's decision to appoint Barros to Osorno caused outrage when it was made public in January 2015. To prepare, Barros did the monthlong Spiritual Exercises in Madrid under Father Arana's guidance, flying afterward to Rome to see Francis in the Santa Marta. Barros offered, in light of the fury in Chile at the appointment, not to take up his diocese, but Francis refused, telling him that the accusations were "self-evidently inconsistent." Barros was installed at Mass in Osorno's St. Matthew's Cathedral on March 21.[13]

It was pure chaos. Dozens of police outside fought to hold back three thousand demonstrators, while inside protesters holding black balloons heckled and shoved the new bishop, knocking off his mitre, and drowning out his homily with cries of "Judas!" A handful of other bishops and the nuncio were present, along with Arana, but the country's most senior bishops boycotted the Mass, something virtually unheard of in the Catholic world. At the center of the maelstrom was Barros himself, bewildered and stammering as he carried out what he insisted was the pope's will.

Francis's obduracy over Barros was one of the causes of tension inside the Pontifical Commission for the Protection of Minors, created in early 2014 at the urging of C9 cardinals Reinhard Marx and Seán O'Malley. Their idea was to create a commission of expert outsiders to advise the pope on best practices, and to help promote a front line safeguarding culture across the Church. It would have an office and staff within the Vatican, and the standing that came with being a "papal commission," but the commissioners themselves would fly in for meetings, thus retaining the credibility of a certain independence. It would turn out to be a near-impossible tension.

The first set of commissioners included people long involved in assisting the Vatican with the issue, including Baroness Sheila Hollins, the British psychiatric expert, and Marie Collins, the Irish abuse victim and expert. It also included Hanna Suchocka, a former Polish prime minister. The commission was chaired by Cardinal O'Malley, and run from day to day in Rome by its secretary, Monsignor Robert Oliver, a Boston priest and former Congregation for the Doctrine of the Faith "promoter of justice," the Vatican equivalent of a district attorney. The Pontifical Commission for the Protection of Minors (PCM) also included the vice-rector of the Gregorian University and head of its psychology institute, Father Hans Zollner, SJ, whose presence was a guarantee that the pope was serious. No one in the Vatican understood the issue of abuse better or was so dedicated to converting the Church to be a world leader in safeguarding the vulnerable than the German Jesuit, whose Center for Child Protection, based at the Gregorian, was a leader in the field.

The PCM was tasked with developing policies in the realm of safeguarding and prevention, above all with spreading to Africa and Asia lessons learned in the Church's battle against abuse in the Anglophone world. In this focus on prevention, it was clearly distinct from the Congregation for the Doctrine of the Faith's discipline section, which dealt with priests who had been accused of abuse. There was also no comparison between the status of the two bodies. The CDF was a heavyweight dicastery, listed first in John Paul II's curial constitution, whereas the PCM wasn't a dicastery at all. In the status-conscious world of the Curia, that meant that the

PCM had no right to hold dicasteries like the CDF accountable, and it had no right to speak or act on behalf of the Holy See.

Yet Collins in particular acted as if she had a papal mandate to hold the CDF accountable, and she painted any resistance from it as a betrayal of the pope's wishes. Her approach created considerable resentment from the get-go, and relations quickly broke down, forcing all communications in 2015 to be in writing. A CDF representative didn't attend a commission meeting until September 2016. In her impatience to see change and her readiness to see resistance as betrayal, there was an ironic parallel between Collins and the financial reformer she criticized for mishandling abuse cases back in Australia, Cardinal George Pell.

Although there were a number of other issues, her main complaint against the CDF was that it was blocking what she saw as the pope's desire for a new CDF tribunal to try bishops who had "covered up" abuse, meaning those who had failed to act on allegations against priest abusers.[14]

The existing CDF tribunal had been devised under the congregation's then prefect, Cardinal Joseph Ratzinger, in the last years of John Paul II. After a number of reforms, it had been revised a number of times since. It was working well, but struggling to keep pace with the number of cases. In the decade between 2004 and 2014, a tidal wave of 3,400 cases, mostly dating from the 1960s to the 1990s in the Anglophone world, had been referred to Rome after victims stepped forward and dioceses and orders reviewed their files. However old an abuse allegation, the bishop had to look into it at once, and if it was credible, he had to inform the civil authorities (police and social services), as well as the CDF, whose discipline section monitored the case to ensure it was properly handled. The priest was immediately removed from ministry while police gathered evidence; if the case fell within the country's statute of limitations it could proceed to trial and result in a prison sentence in that country. But whether or not the priest was indicted in civil law, the CDF carried out its twin-track investigation and imposed penalties on those who were found guilty, in most cases delegating the trial to a local tribunal.

The sentence was usually either loss of the clerical state, otherwise known as "laicization," or a less severe removal from priestly ministry, sometimes known as a "prayer-and-penance sanction." In the first case, the offender ceased to be a priest and was no longer the responsibility of his diocese or religious order. But most often, especially if the priest was by then elderly and infirm, removal from priestly ministry and retirement under supervision was the preferred sentence, not just for humanitarian reasons but for practical ones: laicization was a complex, lengthy procedure, and as long as the offender was still a priest his diocese or order could keep an eye on him.[15]

At the time of Francis's election in 2013, the CDF was laicizing around a hundred priests a year, half against their will, the other half after the accused admitted their crimes, and removing from ministry around twice that number. The number of cases referred to the discipline section of the CDF remained close to what it had been, but the countries had changed: cases from Poland and Germany gradually replaced those from Ireland and the United States.

The processing was slow, and there was concern over the backlog of cases that had not been concluded; too many accused and victims died before a definitive decision could be made in their cases. Francis managed eventually to increase discipline section staff from ten to seventeen—no mean feat given the paucity of canonists specializing and willing to work in this area—which meant that by 2019 the backlogs were subsiding. The increase in staff, along with improved organization and tracking, meant that most cases may conclude within a year or two. Meanwhile, to speed up "appeals"—recourse in administrative penal processes—Francis created a college of jurists under Archbishop Scicluna, who from 2002 to 2012 had been Benedict XVI's promoter of justice. Scicluna heard around three recourses each month, refusing most. Meanwhile, between 2013 and 2018, Francis told journalists, he had directly received around twenty-five requests for clemency in abuse cases and refused them all.[16]

Nevertheless, the process crucially depended on the bishop taking action at the start, and even now—notably in the developing world—many failed to do so. At the time of Francis's election, reformers such as Zollner pointed to this as the next area needing attention in the Church's battle against abuse: a better way of holding bishops accountable. "The Catholic people could understand that a priest can be a sicko, but they can't understand a bishop who puts children in harm's way by keeping such a man in ministry," Cardinal O'Malley told me in 2017.

Only the pope had the authority to ask a bishop to stand down, and a number of bishops had tendered their resignations after being asked to do so by Benedict XVI. But the official reason given by Vatican statements was vague—if not for reasons of age, a bishop always retired early due to "ill health or some other grave cause"—and after September 2016, no reasons at all were given, even though Francis was known to have stood down a number of bishops for mishandling abuse. Victims, and the people of God, deserved better. Meeting in 2014, the PCM commissioners asked for a process that was transparent and effective. Collins in particular believed that only when bishops were publicly punished for their failures to act against abusers could the culture of cover-up give way to a culture of accountability that put victims first.[17]

At the PCM's suggestion, Francis wrote in February 2015 to the world's bishops asking them to cooperate with the commission, warning that "priority must not be given to any other kind of concern, whatever its nature, such as the desire to avoid scandal, since there is absolutely no place in ministry for those who abuse minors." After meeting five clerical sexual abuse victims in Philadelphia in September 2015, Francis was emphatic on the flight home that it was "a very ugly thing" for a bishop to fail to act against an abusive priest in order to avoid scandal, and that if he had done so, he should resign.

At about this time the PCM floated the idea of expanding the CDF tribunal to try bishops for a new crime of "abuse of office," requiring proof of criminal intent or culpable negligence. But the CDF lawyers pushed back. Bishops failed to act over abuse for a broad variety of reasons, often—especially in the developing world—out of ignorance, cultural blindness, or naïveté rather than an intent to conceal a crime. Then there was the jurisprudential challenge that in some countries abuse of minors wasn't a crime at all. What national or cultural standard of action in response to allegations could the CDF take as its norm? In countries that had no laws protecting minors, what obligations rested on a bishop to alert the police? The Church could demand universal and internally consistent procedures for bishops to follow in relation to canon law, but even then, there was too much cultural and legal variation in the way different parts of the world responded to sexual abuse to make it easy to establish that there was a "delict" or crime involved in failing to report or act on an abuse complaint.

In the midst of these discussions in June 2015, the Holy See Press Office suddenly briefed journalists that following deliberation in the C9, the pope had declared that the various congregations in charge of bishops were competent to receive and investigate complaints of "episcopal abuse of office." The briefing also appeared to announce the new tribunal, giving the CDF the authority to "judge bishops with regard to crimes of the abuse of office when connected to the abuse of minors," for which a "new judicial section" in the CDF would be necessary. Collins was delighted, hailing it as a victory for abuse victims everywhere and a big success for the commission in particular. But the champagne turned out to be premature. No one could explain where the announcement had come from. Not even O'Malley had any idea it was coming, while in the CDF, the Rota, and elsewhere in the Vatican, people were completely taken aback. The announcement remains a mystery, but could well have been made at the request of a pope who was impatient to see some action.[18]

If his object was to put salt on the CDF's tail, it worked. What followed was a year of intense discussion among canonists about how to hold bishops accountable using existing jurisprudence. What they eventually came up with was a mechanism that applied the same principles of canon law that give bishops the power to remove parish priests who, for whatever reason, are unable to pastor properly. Rather than punishing a bishop for a crime, under the new proposal, the relevant Vatican dicastery could investigate a bishop for incompetence (non-criminal negligence) and recommend he stand down for the good of the community. Because there was no need to prove malice or culpability, the system required only objective incapacity or inability, so the cultural context was irrelevant. Action could be taken swiftly and simply. After investigation, the Congregation for Bishops or one of the three other relevant bodies overseeing bishops could report to the pope that a bishop had acted negligently in response to an abuse case. The bishop would be asked to stand down, and if he refused, the pope could call together a commission of jurors to force him.

Francis opted for this *tertium quid*, issuing the relevant law in June 2016. Although it covered negligence in general, *Come Una Madre Amorevole* (Like a Loving Mother) made clear that it applied "in particular to sexual abuse inflicted on minors and vulnerable adults." It had the advantage of being immediately workable, used existing law, and required no new staff or section, while at the same time it sent a clear message to the world's bishops that failure to properly handle abuse cases would lead to their immediate retirement. The PCM's secretary, Monsignor Oliver, was delighted, declaring that Francis had given the Church "authoritative means" for dismissing bishops who were negligent over abuse. Archbishop Scicluna, too, was pleased, seeing the process as much broader and more flexible in scope than the tribunal proposal. Not only did it fit better with existing jurisprudence but it also reflected more realistically the reasons why bishops failed to act properly in abuse cases.[19]

Collins, however, saw the edict as a betrayal. After her resignation she said she had been "totally disgusted" by the CDF's refusal to implement a recommendation of the commission that had been approved by the pope. Even though the PCM "had always known that the Holy Father might come up with another way of doing this," Cardinal O'Malley recalled, some of the commissioners "felt that once the announcement was made this was the path we were going on, so that a change seemed like a retreat."[20]

By this time the commission had settled down to focus on its primary objectives and had expanded to a group of eighteen commissioners who were impatient to go on with what they saw as the PCM's core mission. The commission announced working groups on pastoral care for survivors, guidelines, formation in priesthood and religious life, as well as what it called "ecclesial and civil norms governing allegations of abuse." They also agreed not to speak publicly about particular cases, but to stick to safeguarding policy questions. But that decision proved hard to accept for a second survivor and campaigner who was one of the new intake. A British man who had joined the PCM in February 2015 after meeting Francis the previous July, Peter Saunders saw himself as first accountable to victims' groups. Although he was convinced of the pope's sincerity in tackling abuse, throughout his time on the PCM he suffered enormous pressure to persuade the groups he wasn't "selling out" by serving as a papal adviser.[21]

The agreement not to comment on particular cases stretched Saunders to a breaking point over the Barros installation the following month. Later in the year, the pope was recorded telling Chilean pilgrims in St. Peter's Square that the protesters in Osorno were "judging a bishop without proof" and that if the diocese was suffering it was because "it does not open its heart to what God says, and instead gets carried away by all this foolishness." Having been assured by Barros and others that left-wing opponents of the Church in Chile were behind the Osorno protests, Francis also blamed the *zurdos*, a word used by Pinochet's regime to describe the left, triggering a firestorm of criticism. (*Ni Zurdos Ni Tontos*—"Neither Leftist Nor Dumb"—would be one of the protest banners during the papal visit to Chile two years later.)

The pope was recorded making the remarks in May 2015, but the video didn't come to light until the following September, to a storm of criticism. Collins said she was "discouraged and saddened" by the pope's remarks, while Saunders threatened to resign unless he received an explanation (he didn't, and stayed). But when Saunders launched a ferocious public attack on Cardinal Pell, at that point still the Vatican's finance czar, on a major Australian television program, describing him as a "serious obstacle" to Francis's child protection policies, the commissioners had had enough. The PCM "is not competent to investigate or to pronounce specific judgements on individual cases," they said in a testy statement. In October, the PCM again made clear that it had no oversight or decision-making functions, before going on to list the workshops, conferences, and seminars it was organizing worldwide as a resource for local Churches.[22]

But when emails from Chile's two cardinals referring to Karadima victim Juan Carlos Cruz as a "liar" and a "serpent" who was out to destroy the Church were leaked and made public at the end of 2015, Saunders came to the next commission meeting the following February angrily telling journalists that Francis should sack Barros. Telling the pope what he should do via the media was a step too far, and the commission now suspended Saunders, regretting that he was unable to work within its mandate. Collins stayed until March 2017 when she, too, resigned, complaining that although Francis had been "100 percent" behind the commission and its proposals, he had been thwarted by a stonewalling Curia. In August 2018, Francis said on his flight from Dublin that Collins had been "fixated" on the idea of a tribunal and was unable to see that the same end had been achieved by other means that allowed for different cultures.[23]

Yet, although "Like a Loving Mother" appeared to be working well—following its promulgation a number of bishops were indeed stood down over failures to deal properly with abuse—it was impossible for anyone to know. The Vatican continued not to give reasons for a bishop resigning, mostly out of concern not to damage his good name (being incompetent was not a crime), and the lack of transparency remained a source of frustration for the reformers.

The commission meanwhile made progress on its core activities in education and awareness raising among dioceses, religious orders, and the 113 bishops' conferences across the world. By the end of its three-year mandate in December 2017, it could point to solid achievements, including more than two hundred seminars of two to five days each in dioceses across the developing world. The PCM was increasingly regarded as a resource by the dicasteries for clergy and bishops in Rome, incorporating safeguarding into the syllabuses for trainee priests, recently appointed bishops, and the Holy See's diplomats. But the real driver remained Zollner. After leading more than six hundred workshops in four years and instituting a new degree course in Rome for dozens of religious and priests from the developing world, the Jesuit said he could see the tide turning. "I think of all those countries where I get invitations now, that didn't talk about this publicly even a year or two ago," he told *Crux*.[24]

The PCM had new energy when it was reconstituted in February 2018 with a number of old members reappointed and nine new experts added, from Australia, Brazil, Ethiopia, India, the Netherlands, and Tonga. Some had direct experience of sexual abuse, but none were linked to survivors' groups. They were committed to what was now a firm priority of the Francis pontificate: to make the Church a global leader in promoting a culture of safety and protection for young and vulnerable people from abusive relationships of whatever sort.

But Zollner insisted that, however good the protocols, the Church needed to tackle the underlying clericalist culture that allowed perpetrators to abuse and led bishops to cover up their offenses. It was that culture that, through his Chilean dark night, Francis also came to see.

The government blamed militants linked to the native Mapuche in Chile's south for the mysterious firebombs and anonymous threatening pamphlets in Santiago's churches prior to the pope's arrival on January 16, 2018. But it wasn't just the Mapuche who were angry with the Church. Every survey told the same story of falling Mass attendance, vocations at an all-time low, the Church's massive loss of credibility (down to around 30 percent), and young people increasingly drawn to evangelicals. Chile was now—with the exception of Uruguay—the Latin American country with the fewest practicing Catholics. It also had the least favorable view of the pope—and not just because he was an Argentine.

What had gone wrong? One answer was technology and modernity. Stretching in a sliver down South America's Pacific coast, wedged between the mountains and the sea, Chile was the Switzerland of Latin America: stable, prosperous, middle-class, and, like secular Europe, socially mobile, with more shopping malls per capita than anywhere in the world outside the United States and Canada. In their reports and homilies Chile's bishops lamented the morally corrosive effect of consumerism, relativism, and individualism that went with the country's rapid social and economic growth, blaming the culture for the Church's unpopularity.

But six hundred miles south of Santiago in Osorno, where Catholics living under the volcano of that name had been mobilized by the Barros saga, there was a rather different explanation. On the eve of the papal visit, the young, articulate spokesman of the diocese's protesters, Juan Carlos Claret, published an excoriating three-part essay on the Spanish-language website *Religión Digital*, in which he documented abuse allegations and cover-ups in dioceses across the country, along with gay-clergy sex rings (including one diocese with unusually high HIV rates among priests), concealed behind a Sicilian-like culture of *omertà*. "To be aware of this ecclesial misery," Claret wrote, "forces us to experience a pain and shame that should open the way to humility and to live in a true and permanent attitude of pastoral contrition."

Claret charged the bishops with authoritarianism and clericalism, of being obsessed with culture-war issues such as abortion and marriage at the expense of other pressing issues such as poverty and climate change, and of being, in general, a dysfunctional, inward-looking, haughty institution in which abuse cover-up was the symptom of a much deeper malaise. He claimed that Chile's bishops had rejected the pastoral, missionary conversion called for by the Church of Latin America at Aparecida in 2007, instead scapegoating external agents or blaming the amorphous idea of social change for the Church's decline. The people of God, far from becoming the missionary disciples called for at Aparecida, had been marginalized and alienated by a clerical caste. Claret concluded, devastatingly:

> This is not a crisis of faith, nor a loss of meaning. What is behind this is an institutional crisis that has overwhelmed a clergy unable to adapt to changes. The result is an abyss of incomprehension between laity and hierarchy. The Church that the pope will receive is in crisis, a crisis triggered by a lack of love and spirit of service. When society looks at the Church it sees an institution that fails to witness, beset by deep divisions, disconnected from reality, incapable of understanding the different conditions and situations of human life, and attached to money and power.[25]

Nothing had better symbolized this attachment to money and power than El Bosque parish in the upper-class district of Providencia in Santiago, whose abuse scandal in 2010 had set off the explosion that was still being felt eight years later. In the 1980s and early 1990s the leading families of Santiago had regarded El Bosque's unctuous, impeccably dressed parish priest as a saint and had gladly entrusted their children to him. Like a good pastor, Karadima was adept at spotting vulnerability and need, especially in young men who lacked father figures in their lives. He separated them from their families, winning their loyalty to the parish, then abused them. Rumors and accusations against Karadima swirled at the time, yet Pinochet and Sodano continued to protect him.

Years after their abuse, Cruz, Hamilton, and Murillo denounced Karadima in a series of approaches to church authorities between 2003 and 2006. Although initially disbelieving, Cardinal Errázuriz, Santiago's archbishop, eventually retired Karadima when the priest turned seventy-five, and referred the case to the Vatican. By then the story had exploded in a TV documentary, *The Sins of Father Karadima*, triggering a flood of further revelations. A civil court found the victims' evidence credible, but Chile's statute of limitations prevented a trial and prosecution of Karadima. The Vatican in 2011 sentenced Karadima to a life of prayer and penance in a convent outside Santiago.

As with so many Catholic Church abuse scandals, the issue wasn't only about the abuse itself but the powerful culture that overlooked and tolerated it, that failed to spot it, or was complicit. How could an institution that once stood prophetically for the poor, whose human rights advocacy had once been the inspiration of the Latin American Church, have fallen so far?

The bishops wanted to use the pope's visit of January 2018 to move out from under the cloud of Karadima. Speaking alongside President Michelle Bachelet at the presidential palace of La Moneda, Francis obliged, expressing "pain and shame" for "the irreparable damage caused to children by some ministers of the Church," and with his brother bishops he pledged to support victims and learn from the mistakes that had been made. Later that day, he had a private meeting with victims, and in the cathedral that afternoon he spoke of this "serious and painful evil" and of "the harm and sufferings of the victims and their families, who saw the trust they had placed in the Church's ministers betrayed." But when Barros turned up to concelebrate the papal Mass for 400,000 people at O'Higgins Park along with the other bishops, cameras and microphones remorselessly focused on him, creating what Cardinal Errázuriz would later airily dismiss as "an undesirable and parallel focus to the Holy Father's visit."[26]

Critics saw in Francis's pointedly affectionate greeting of Barros at the cathedral that afternoon a circling of the Church's wagons. But that was to misread the internal dynamics. Francis knew that the bishops had opposed Barros's nomination; by publicly including him, the pope sought to rehabilitate him—and not just among the bishops. Judging by the obsessive focus on Barros by Chile's media, as well as by church commentators, the scapegoat mechanism was in full play, and Francis wanted to resist it by publicly embracing an innocent man on whom the past sins of others, in his view, were being unfairly heaped.

At the cathedral, Francis gave one of the most important addresses of his pontificate, charting for the Church in Chile a route out of the desolation brought on by institutional failure and the loss of social and cultural prestige. In it he quoted a little-known prologue he had written in 1987 to a series of historic letters by Jesuit superiors general, which contained, as he later explained, "criteria of discernment, criteria of action so as not to allow ourselves to be dragged down by institutional desolation." They showed a path to follow in times of persecutions and tribulations by avoiding the temptations characteristic of desolation: debating ideas, becoming fixated with enemies, developing an exaggerated sense of victimhood, and "dwelling on our own desolations." These were temptations that came from not trusting God and thereby missing the grace that was always offered in times of distress.[27]

Using the same criteria, Francis warned the religious and clergy in Santiago's cathedral of two temptations in particular, in an era of change and anxiety: "of becoming closed, isolating ourselves and defending our ways of seeing things, which then turn out as nothing more than fine monologues," and "[thinking] that everything is wrong, and in place of 'good news,' the only thing we profess is apathy and disappointment." Francis pointed to Saint Peter, who having betrayed Christ at His passion allowed himself to be forgiven by the risen Jesus. Facing his weakness, Peter was saved by God's mercy; the failed sinner became a joyful, grateful apostle, sent out to serve. Following that same path, the Church was called to be the sign of a "transfigured" community, wounded and humble, but capable of evangelizing because it embodied the Good News that it proclaimed.

"A wounded Church does not make herself the center of things, does not believe that she is perfect, but puts at the center the one who can heal those wounds, whose name is Jesus Christ," was how Francis summed up the conversion, adding: "To know both Peter disheartened and Peter transfigured is an invitation to pass from being a Church of the unhappy and disheartened to a Church that serves all those people who are unhappy and disheartened in our midst."

This was, in a nutshell, the discernment that would guide his leadership of the Church through the rough seas ahead. He later returned to it in all his communications with the Church in Chile over the next months, inviting the bishops to see that the failures and wounds of the Church were not a reason for recoiling from the world but an invitation to serve it in humility. The pastoral conversion that this called for would enable the Church to deal with the root cause of sexual abuse and its cover-up, namely the mind-set of clericalism.

Yet while Francis's discernment was impeccable, he hadn't yet made the connection between the Church's desolation and the corruption and collusion in the Chilean hierarchy, of which he was still largely unaware. He had framed abuse in his cathedral speech, quoting Cardinal Ezzati, as "weeds of evil and their aftermath of scandal and desertion"—the failure of individuals that the Church's detractors had exploited, creating an atmosphere of hysterical scapegoating that claimed innocent victims like Barros. Francis was still, essentially, seeing individuals as guilty but defending the innocence of the institution—including Barros—from the mob carrying pitchforks.

The Iquique moment reflected that framing. When he told the reporters in Iquique that "there isn't a single proof against [Barros], it's all calumny," Francis was using a word that had a powerful Gospel resonance for him. *Calumnia*—as he has made clear elsewhere—was how the devil sought to undermine what was good and of God, first by subtle temptation and distraction, and when that failed, by outright attack through defamation. Because the outrage it provoked eventually led the pope to question this reading of Chile, the "Iquique moment" turned out to be providential. But at the time, it was hard to see it as anything but a disaster. You could almost hear the groans across the Catholic world, and see the newspaper editors shaking their heads in disbelief. In implying that Karadima's victims were liars, Francis unwittingly placed himself with Ezzati and Errázuriz in putting the institution at the center, the very thing Francis had identified as the bishops' failing. It was "an astonishing end to a visit meant to help heal the wounds of a sex abuse scandal that has cost the Catholic Church its credibility in the country," as the Associated Press put it.

No one had anything good to say. Cardinal O'Malley, one of Francis's closest allies, even caught a plane to Peru to rebuke him. "Words that convey the message 'if you cannot prove your claims then you will not be believed' . . . relegate survivors to discredited exile," he told journalists. The archbishop of Boston said Francis knew all about the Church's failures and the impact of abuse on victims, and he could not understand "why the Holy Father chose the particular words he used at that time." What mattered to O'Malley was putting clear blue water between himself and the pope, and reassuring victims that they had an ally in him. In five years, Francis had never been so alone.[28]

"I realized something was wrong and I needed to find out what," the pope told me in June 2018. He knew he had misjudged the situation but could not explain why—he had a gut feeling that things were amiss. Long before Iquique, he had felt a strange coldness from the bishops and the Chilean Church in general. The level of division, scapegoating, and mutual recrimination, as well as arrogance and defensiveness, in the episcopate pointed to something far more serious than "weeds of evil and their aftermath of scandal and desertion."[29]

In the angry victimhood and desire for control that he had found in Chile, Francis saw the domination of the bad spirit. His 1984 essay "On Self-Accusation" was concerned with the way that the Spirit of the Lord is undermined at every turn by the bad spirit operating against it, through accusation and suspicion. At the root of a bad-spirit domination is often failure or guilt that people are projecting onto each other rather than facing. In such cases of general or institutional desolation, it is impossible to know what is true and what is false. What if Karadima were not just a rotten apple, and the barrel itself were putrid? There seemed to be an inordinate number of abuse cases in Chile. What was going on?[30]

Two weeks after returning to Rome from Peru, Francis sent Maltese archbishop Charles Scicluna, together with a sharp Spanish CDF official, Father Jordi Bertomeu, to investigate. Such "apostolic visitations" were among the pope's most potent weapons. As far as the local Church was concerned, it was as if the pope himself were coming to ask questions.

No one was better qualified to investigate than "the Eliot Ness of the Vatican." Fearless in truffling out the truth, Scicluna was, with Zollner, the Vatican's lead reformer on abuse. As the first promoter of justice in the new tribunal set up by Cardinal Ratzinger in 2001, over the following decade he processed more than three thousand priest abuse cases. None came close in notoriety to that of the Mexican founder of the Legion of Christ, Marcial Maciel, who had been untouchable under John Paul II's secretary of state, Cardinal Sodano, but who was swiftly placed under sanction once Benedict was elected and put Scicluna on the case. At the groundbreaking 2012 Gregorian University conference he had organized with Zollner, Scicluna had bluntly warned bishops against "a deadly culture of silence, or *omertà*" in relation to abuse; it was the first time anyone of that level in the Vatican had used the analogy of a mafia code of silence.[31]

Francis sent Scicluna to Chile not expecting him to question his judgment of the Barros case, but with a brief to uncover the broader picture. Scicluna stopped off in New York en route to meet Juan Carlos Cruz, who said afterward that it was the first time he had felt listened to by the Church. In Santiago, Scicluna and Bertomeu held dozens of meetings in a designated office in the capital, away from the bishops' conference, a place to which anyone could come with information. Among those who gave their testimony were clergy and lay delegates from Osorno, who said afterward they were confident that the investigators now had a clear picture of what was happening in the diocese. The visitors had to extend their stay by five days because Scicluna needed emergency gallbladder surgery. While the Maltese archbishop recovered in the hospital, his Spanish assistant recorded yet more witnesses' stories. "People took the opportunity to talk about all these other cases, which we weren't expecting," Scicluna recalled.[32]

In the end, the investigators returned with sixty-four testimonies collated in a devastating 2,300-page report. Scicluna did what he did best: provide raw data and testimony as well as his reaction to the witnesses to allow a third party to evaluate them. Back in Rome, he spent many hours discussing the findings with Francis, who at once saw how wrong he had been. He would later tell Chile's bishops in a leaked letter that the report had revealed nothing less than a systemic cover-up, how abuse had been ignored or minimized, priests shuffled between parishes, incriminating documents destroyed, claimants belittled and pressured, safeguarding procedures casually and carelessly applied, and whole educational institutions entrusted to active homosexuals. Running through it all was an ecclesial culture of denial and mutual recrimination, collusion, and corruption. Taken in toto, his summary of the report vindicated the devastating picture painted by the Osorno activist Claret.[33]

Francis took the report into his Easter. He saw, first of all, that he had badly misread the entire Karadima-Barros situation. It wasn't the Church that had been scapegoated by its rivals and opponents, but the other way around. Lacking proper information, he had failed to discern, and thus allowed himself to fall into the trap that the ancient Greeks called a *skandalon*. But the truth had set him free, now, to confess it, and to act. On April 8, he wrote an open letter to Chile's bishops to describe "the pain of so many victims of grave abuses of conscience and power, and in particular, of acts of sexual abuse of minors committed by many different religious in your country," as well as "many crucified lives" that "[cause] me pain and shame." He called them to Rome, he said, to help them discern, as a body, the way forward—by which he meant to help them convert.

He also made a moving apology. He said he took responsibility for his own "serious mistakes in the assessment and perception of the situation, especially because of the lack of truthful and balanced information" he had been given. Begging forgiveness "from all those I offended," he promised to do so in person with the victims. The papal apology, unprecedented in the depth of its personal contrition, led the news: the media could now add a declaration of papal fallibility to the list of what they never expected to hear from a pope.

Because it was not clear from that first letter what Scicluna had uncovered, most headlines claimed the pope was sorry for getting Barros wrong. But that was to miss the forest for the trees. He was sorry for his misreading of the situation as a whole, for failing to understand the depths of Karadima's depravity, and for being blind to the level of corruption in the Church that went well beyond the Karadima case, which his defense of Barros had unwittingly helped to conceal. In concentrating on the legal innocence of Barros and ignoring that corruption, the pope had been complicit in the attempt of the Church in Chile to divert attention from its wrongdoing. While defending Barros from the logic of Caiaphas, he had ended up in a Caiaphas-like defense of the interests of the temple against the vulnerable. It was for this devastating realization that he now wept bitter tears.

But the shock and shame of this realization also forced the pope to see the abuse and its cover-up in a radical new light, as the symptom of something much more profound—and diabolical. It was the corruption of power linked to benefaction, the twisting of power for service into power to exploit, a perversion of the very mission entrusted to the Church by Christ—to defend the vulnerable from the wolves. Precisely because it was so evil, clerical sex abuse of minors would always seek aggressively to conceal itself, through primitive mechanisms of denial, suppression, and silence in the body itself. This was, to use his old distinction, more about corruption than sin, and the networks of collusion could only be expunged by the external shock of scandal and revelation. Thus, the victims who made allegations and the journalists who wrote exposés did the work of the Holy Spirit, like the prophet Nathan confronting arrogant King David about the murder he had committed and later covered up in order to obtain Bathsheba.

His second realization was that this was not an issue that could be resolved simply by sacking bishops or putting in new laws, necessary though these might be. What was needed was conversion: a restoring of Christ to the center. And for this, the weapons were those of old: squarely facing the truth, the confession of sins, fasting and prayer, hope in God's mercy, and trust in redemption.

In "On Self-Accusation," Bergoglio had discussed the desert monk Dorotheus's insight that to counter the enemy spirit of accusation, it is vital not to be ensnared by it, but to expose it by confessing your sin. "Whoever accuses himself makes space for God's mercy," Bergoglio had summed up Dorotheus. Therein lies the power to defeat the enemy. By accusing yourself—not in a generalized way, but by specifically naming your failure—you show yourself weak so you can be "defended by the Paraclete." Accusing yourself before others, confident of God's mercy, unmasks those who accuse others to conceal their sin.

While heartfelt, therefore, the pope's self-accusation wasn't just a personal expiation. He was also showing what now had to be done at an institutional level. By accusing himself and hoping that the bishops would do the same, he sought to unite the Church and break the mimetic cycle of recrimination and self-justification that was holding everyone back.

This was what gave his first letter to Chile's bishops, despite the gravity of its content, a joyful quality. The pope had seen the conversion being offered. He was asking the bishops to recognize Jesus at their door, waiting to free them from the iron cage of institutional self-centeredness and denial. It was at times like this, he wrote poetically, when we are "weak, frightened and armor-plated in our comfortable winter palaces," that "God's love comes out to meet us to purify our intentions, that we might love as free, mature and critical people."

Scicluna's report was the earthquake that would move the Church in Chile out of its winter palaces of self-justification, accusation, and denial, into the desert of humiliation, self-accusation, and conversion. The brutal truth about the Church's failure, carefully documented by Scicluna and Bertomeu and made public by Francis in his apology, brought down the full weight of lawyers and journalists on the Church in Chile. A time of tribulation was upon them. But in its humble response to that failure, its trust in God's mercy rather than in its members' own powers, which Francis had modeled, the Church could at last face the truth, confess its sin, and be united and conformed to Christ. Embraced in faith, Chile's abuse meltdown could be a royal road to pastoral conversion.[34]

While Chile's bishops reacted in different ways to his letter—some were rather too busy saving their own skins to put on sackcloth and ashes—Francis made his next move. He had promised to apologize in person to Karadima's victims, Hamilton, Cruz, and Murillo, but in the end he went much further, asking them to stay with him at the Casa Santa Marta, before the bishops arrived. The trio whom Chile's cardinals had painted as serpents out to destroy the Church became, at the end of April, the pope's honored guests at the Vatican. Francis took personal charge of the arrangements, ensuring they were received with the utmost graciousness and respect. He met each of them individually for as long as was needed, two or three hours at a time, before speaking with all three together. In total, they spent seven hours in meetings with him in addition to other times eating and praying with him. "We were treated like kings, the bishops like children," Cruz told *El País*.

"I was part of the problem! I caused this. I am very sorry, and I ask your forgiveness," the pope confessed to each of them at the start of their individual meetings. Cruz said he had never in his life witnessed such depth of contrition. Francis deferred to their wisdom and experience, asking for advice on how to put the Church in Chile back on track. The stones that the builders had rejected were now the cornerstones of its renewal. The victims afterward spoke of the affection, respect, and closeness the pope had showed them, the depth and honesty of their discussions with him, and their hope, now, for a new future. Murillo, who works with abused young people in Chile, was struck by the pope's depth of understanding of the issue. When, deploying his famous distinction, Francis told him that sexual abuse wasn't just about sin but more profoundly about corruption, Murillo later told journalists, "I felt he understood and will do something important."

For Cruz, the meetings were personally healing. "We spoke of everything: my life, what happened to me, the bishops' inaction, how they tried to make us feel guilty," Cruz later reported. "He told me: 'Juan Carlos, it doesn't matter that you're gay. God made you that way, and I'm fine with it. The Pope loves you as you are, you have to be happy with who you are.'" Cruz warned him that some of Chile's bishops were "a real mafia, they put a lid on everything, minimize it . . . The pope was amazed." He also told Francis he could have a "spectacular papacy" if he took the bull by the horns and dealt with the abuse issue once and for all. "He answered me: 'Help me so that the Spirit guides me so I can see clearly what I have to do.'"

They forged a bond. Cruz returned to see Francis at the Santa Marta many times afterward. "I came to Rome, I talked to him, and from there we struck up a true friendship that for me has been healing and saving" is how he summarizes it.[35]

A fortnight after the three victims left the Santa Marta, Chile's thirty-two bishops—virtually the entire conference, including auxiliaries and retired bishops—arrived in Rome for their three-day "synodal process" with the pope on May 15–18. It wasn't the first time a pope had called church leaders to Rome over abuse: in April 2002, some U.S. cardinals met Pope John Paul II, and eight years later, twenty-four Irish bishops came to see Benedict XVI, on both occasions in response to abuse revelations. But this was the first time an entire nation's body of bishops had been summoned. To their surprise, the pope had prepared a ten-page letter that he read out to them before giving it to them to go off and pray over. It showed that Francis had, indeed, listened carefully to the victims.

The letter was written like points a spiritual director might offer during a Jesuit retreat. It began by recalling God's original favor and mercy, asked the bishops to recognize where God had been rejected in favor of idols, and invited them to come home. The Church in Chile had once been prophetic, outward focused, courageous, and holy. Because it put Christ at its center, it evangelized; because it was close to the people and humble enough to confess its sins, it was joyful; because it defended the poor, it generated holiness. But then it went astray. It turned in on itself, becoming clericalist, elitist, authoritarian, and internally divided. In trying to save itself, the institutional Church had usurped the consciences of the faithful, recoiling from God's holy, patient, and faithful people, "the Church's immune system." In denying and concealing its sin to maintain its bella figura, paradoxically, its sin became all anybody would see.

Francis made no mention of what the Sodano-Karadima-Pinochet network had done to the Church in Chile, but he invited the bishops to ask themselves how it had come about, urging them to "go more deeply to discover the dynamics that made such attitudes and evils possible." He asked them to be honest and contrite, and to take responsibility rather than blaming and scapegoating. The only way forward was to assume the task synodally, as a body, walking together. Then he added: "Brothers, we discuss ideas, but discern situations. We are gathered to discern, not to discuss."[36]

He had said the same in his Santiago cathedral speech, quoting his 1987 prologue to the "tribulation letters." What did he mean? In times of distress, it was vital for people to ask what God was asking of them, to find the grace of conversion in the midst of the confusion, and not be distracted by intellectual analysis. To discuss was to analyze, to give answers, to offer solutions, to argue about who or what was to blame; it was to keep *us* in charge. But by focusing instead on the spiritual confusion the attacks provoked, and by working to discern God's will for them in the midst of it, they could avoid being seduced into the devil's dynamic, in which they would see themselves as innocent victims and their attackers as evil. A discerning stance was to grasp that both in "us" and in "them" there were always good *and* bad spirits at work.

Cruz, Murillo, and Hamilton had been derided as enemies of the Church yet were vehicles of justice and truth. Conversely, many vigorous defenders of Catholic orthodoxy and the institutional Church had blamed everyone but themselves, had concealed or minimized abuse, and had failed to recognize their own complicity with corruption. So who, in this scenario, were the good Catholics? In the confusing tribulation that now beset the Church in Chile, the call was to discern the good and bad spirits, not to argue about who was right and wrong; and the sign that they had discerned well would be the true peace that was the fruit of seeking God's will, not the false tranquility that came of falsely dividing the world into goodies and baddies.[37]

At the end of the three-day meeting, the bishops offered their resignations for Francis to accept when he saw fit. They pledged action and change, a radical revision of abuse procedures, as well as a "new culture of being Church": listening, humble, discerning. Having abandoned their winter palaces, the bishops went home to face the earthquakes. Within days of returning from Rome, the bishop of Rancagua, north of Santiago, suspended fourteen of his priests—around a fifth of the clergy of his diocese—after a TV station revealed a clerical abuse ring known as "the Family," in which priests exchanged pornographic images of minors. The bishop, Alejando Goić, then resigned as head of the local Church's abuse prevention commission after it was revealed that he had first learned of the allegations two years earlier. As the stories came tumbling forth, each more outrageous than the previous, it was still possible to be shocked: the Santiago archdiocese admitted that Father Óscar Muñoz Toledo, who had been in charge of handling clergy sex abuse complaints for the diocese, had been himself sexually abusing youths at the very time when he ignored Hamilton, Cruz, and Murillo's original allegations against Karadima. Because his alleged abuses continued to the present, as did the failure to report them, Muñoz illustrated that "protocols are only as valuable as the will to apply them," as one seasoned commentator put it.[38]

At the end of May, Francis wrote a third Chile "tribulation letter," this time an eight-page missive addressed to the people of God in which he showed that the institution's distance from the people of God "casts us into desolation and the perversion of the Church's nature." Clericalism could not be defeated by clericalism. Hence his call on the whole Church in Chile, "anointed by the Holy Spirit," to be bold, critical protagonists of reform, helping to restore Christ to its center. Replacing a few bishops would not be enough; renewal had to involve the whole people of God.

In this Francis was going a long way beyond Benedict XVI's classic 2010 letter to Irish Catholics, in which he criticized "a misplaced concern for the reputation of the Church and the avoidance of scandal" as factors behind the crisis. In essence, Francis was linking abuse and its cover-up to an internal ecclesiastical culture in which discussion and disagreement were silenced and deafness to victims was a symptom of a broader author-itarian, clericalist mentality. What was needed now, he said, was a new "culture of care" that would permeate "our way of relating, of praying, of thinking, of exercising authority, as well as our customs and language and our relationship to power and money." He said he had prayerfully consid-ered what God's purpose was in allowing all this to come out now, and he saw that the Holy Spirit was calling forth "a Church that is every day more synodal, prophetic and hopeful; less abusive, because it puts Jesus at its center in the shape of the hungry, the imprisoned, the migrants and the abused." It was the first time he had stated so explicitly how he believed God was acting through the abuse crisis, and the pastoral conversion at the end of it.[39]

In early June, Francis received a group of Karadima's victims, accompa-nied, the Vatican said, by "two lay people involved in the suffering" related to the case. One of them was Fernando Karadima's younger brother, Oscar. Francis gave him a photo, on the back of which he had written a blessing for the Karadima family and an expression of sympathy for what they had suffered. "In the name of Fernando, dumb and incapable of realizing what he has done, I ask forgiveness," he wrote. In the history of papal apologies, it was another first: he was offering his own contrition in the place of a predator priest's.

Days later, Francis accepted the resignations of the bishops of Puerto Montt and Valparaíso, who were under a cloud for protecting gay clergy rings and ignoring sex abuse claims. At the same time he stood down Bar-ros, while assuring him privately of his affection and concern. Barros was no longer a scapegoat; the whole body of bishops had assumed collective responsibility. But he had been a part of the Karadima culture and Osorno needed a fresh start. Soon he accepted the resignation of another of the Karadima bishops, Horacio Valenzuela of Talca, at the same time as stand-ing down Goić. Others would follow over the next months as more cases came to light. At the end of August 2018, the Chilean authorities said they were investigating 119 cases involving 178 victims, and 167 alleged per-petrators, including 7 bishops and 96 priests. A series of laicizations were announced from Rome, including Karadima, along with two retired Chil-ean bishops who had abused minors. Francis also accepted Ezzati's resig-nation as Archbishop of Santiago on grounds of age, replacing him with a Franciscan friar who insisted that Catholics now had to live in the truth.

"The Church doesn't keep its good name by putting a lid on its wounds, but by recognizing them and curing them," said Bishop Celestino Aós.

Archbishop Scicluna and Father Bertomeu—the pope's sheriffs—returned to a hero's welcome in Chile to set up a dedicated "listening service" to encourage victims to step forward. The allegations would be funneled straight to the Vatican. Down south, Scicluna presided at a Mass in Osorno's cathedral to welcome Barros's replacement, an apostolic administrator (finding bishops untainted by scandals was no small task). At Francis's request, Scicluna offered a heartfelt apology to the people of the diocese on the pope's behalf. The Mass was joyful and peaceful, without a black balloon in sight. Among the congregation was Juan Carlos Claret, the young prophet whose barely noticed j'accuse on the eve of the papal visit now read like the pope's own diagnosis.

Claret was pleased but cautious. A lot of healing had to happen. And listening. But just maybe, he reckoned, the process that had begun in Chile could be an example for the world. Pope Francis, he said, had diagnosed a culture of abuse, cover-up, and an elitist mind-set, "and we must now work to secure a real change so that the same error is not repeated."[40]

Chile was a turning point for Francis. He had been deeply, personally involved, relying primarily—for good and ill—on his own discernment and judgment in the management of a Church he knew well from Latin America. Latin American bishops were traditionally Roman; whoever the pope was, they were loyal. But it was a different story in the United States, to where the crisis shifted in the summer of 2018, where a sizable bloc of the episcopate was suspicious and even hostile. In the United States he would rely heavily on cardinals he trusted such as Blase Cupich of Chicago and Joe Tobin of Newark but above all on his nuncio, the French archbishop Christophe Pierre, an ally whom he had appointed to Washington, D.C., in March 2016 after the nuncio had spent nine years in Mexico.

The discernment he had developed in Chile would remain the template for the pope's handling of the U.S. crisis. But there was a big difference between the two situations. The United States had already been through the fire in 2001, with the Boston crisis that led to the Dallas Charter. The stories that came to light in June and August 2018—bookended by McCarrick and Pennsylvania—long predated Dallas. Yet they were read now through a new lens, one that was finely tuned to the moral depravity of the eroticized power relations within the institution and which was focused on the institutional dynamics that allowed it, failed to prevent it, and even normalized it. The American situation was in many ways more serious because it involved a deeper kind of corruption, one that to some extent applied to the Church as a whole.

It was a media myth that the Catholic priesthood was a "haven of abusers," or that celibacy or homosexuality per se had anything to do with abuse. This was the finding of not only the Church's own experts, but secular ones, too. The institutions placed under the spotlight by the four-year Australian Royal Commission—the largest ever inquiry into historical abuse—concluded that "the sexual abuse of children has occurred in almost every type of institution where children reside or attend for educational, recreational, sporting, religious, or cultural activities," and that "people in religious ministry and teachers" were the most common perpetrators. Each case involved the misuse of authority and power, whether secular or religious.

Yet in abuse by Catholic priests and religious there was a particular feature: that those in orders were distinguished from the ordinary believer not by function but by being holy and special. As the Australian Royal Commission put it: "Clericalism is linked to a sense of entitlement, superiority, and exclusion, and abuse of power." Clericalism also created a bunker mentality that has led naturally to cover-ups. "Clericalism nurtured ideas that the Catholic Church was autonomous and self-sufficient, and promoted the idea that child sexual abuse by clergy and religious was a matter to be dealt with internally and in secret," the commission concluded.

This finding chimed with Father Zollner's research. As the German Jesuit put it in *La Civiltà Cattolica* in January 2018: "Whoever in infancy or youth or as a candidate for priesthood learned that a priest is always blameless can easily develop the mindset that he does not need to justify himself to anyone. Anyone endowed with sacred powers can take anything he wants for himself." Hence the startling characteristic of clerical sexual abuse, he wrote, is that the perpetrator often experiences no guilt, while the victim must deal for years with the crippling dilemma "of perceiving oneself as the victim of an irrepressible act of violence and the enormous weight of having to attribute this cruelty to a priest."

Once clerical sex abuse came under the spotlight, it was clear that a perversion of the priesthood was at the heart of it. There were priests, Zollner wrote, who saw themselves as belonging to a kind of profession and that, "as soon as the workday is done they do in private things that are not reconcilable with their priestly life." Such priests "are yearning for the privileges, power, and beauty of that state in life but they are not ready to pay the price specified in the Gospel—poverty, chastity, and obedience—and essentially to give up their lives for Jesus."[41]

For Zollner, Francis's chief adviser on abuse, the crisis would never be over until this mind-set changed; laws and protocols were not enough to heal the systemic root of the problem. On the other side of the scandals was the hope for the Church of the Second Vatican Council, of Aparecida, and of *Evangelii Gaudium*: a Church of missionary disciples, equal before God, anointed by the Holy Spirit, and a priesthood not set apart and sacralized, but at one with the people, not abusing them but serving them.[42]

The challenge was not to run from the shock and shame but to discern and embrace the grace of conversion being offered. The problem was that many in the Church in the United States were in no mood for a process of collective self-purification by the Holy Spirit. They wanted to find the guilty and inept and kick them out. When the Vatican expressed "shame and sorrow" in response to Pennsylvania and said the pope was learning from victims "how to root out this tragic horror that destroys the lives of the innocent," to many he sounded passive and ineffectual. The loss of trust in bishops had created a power vacuum, which the internal civil war in the U.S. Church rushed to fill, thickening the air with accusation. Conservatives seized their moment to denounce liberals, homosexuals, Vatican II, and modern theology. There had been too much "openness to the world," declared Bishop Robert Morlino of Madison, Wisconsin: "what the Church needs now is more hatred." On social media people demanded purges and protocols.[43]

This was precisely the temptation Francis had warned the Chileans against that, if indulged, would prevent conversion. On August 20, just five days before he was due to arrive in Dublin, Ireland, to close the World Meeting of Families, he issued a two-thousand-word "Letter to the People of God," which developed and summarized his key messages to Chile in ways that could help the Church in the United States in particular to accept the grace it was being offered in its time of trial. He named two temptations that would block this receptivity. One was to focus on norms and protocols, which risked making the institution and its survival an end in itself and so perpetuating the problem. The other was the desire to denounce, blame, and scapegoat, to call up a restorationist reform and crusades of purification against "enemies within" and avoid the hard task of self-accusation.

Francis wanted people to trust God and to embrace the *kairos*. The past was rupturing the present so that the pain from the wounds of victims could be heard. He offered a reading of the previous decades in which the pained, courageous voice of victims eventually defeated the bid to silence them: "the Lord heard that cry and once again showed us on which side he stands." God had vindicated the victims and had indicted the institution. Now there needed to be a "personal and communal conversion that makes us see things as the Lord does," together with a way forward based on solidarity.

All had suffered as a result of the crisis; now all were called to take on responsibility for conversion, to "take on the pain of our brothers and sisters wounded in their flesh and in their spirit." Concretely, Francis invited all in the Church to "a penitential exercise of prayer and fasting," aimed at awakening consciences and arousing solidarity because "the only way that we have to respond to this evil that has darkened so many lives is to experience it as a task regarding all of us as the People of God." Assuming that task penitentially and prayerfully was not meant to exclude new actions and policies, but to ensure they were "attuned to the Gospel." New measures needed to be born of and support institutional conversion, lest they risk becoming a way of avoiding that conversion. Without an "active participation of all members of the Church," he warned, the necessary changes could not take place.[44]

The letter went down poorly among conservatives in the United States, where many asked indignantly why *they* should do penance for the sins of errant clergy and corrupt bishops. Others complained about the lack of "concrete measures" in the pope's response. For their part, the U.S. bishops were remarkably silent about it. Their best-known communicator, YouTube star Bishop Robert Barron, recorded two widely viewed videos on the abuse scandals a few days after it was released, without once mentioning the letter.[45]

As Francis arrived in Ireland the air there, too, was thick with accusations that the pope and bishops had failed to atone for the past's long shadows and must now do so in the form of bold new measures. Ireland had been still an observant Catholic nation in 1979, when most of the population had turned out for Pope John Paul II; but these days there were more demonstrators than pilgrims, and it was a different Ireland. Two-thirds of the population had voted to legalize abortion, and the Taoiseach (prime minister), Leo Varadkar, was openly gay. Francis came in humility, telling Varadkar in Dublin Castle that the failure to adequately address the "repugnant crimes" of abuse has "rightly given rise to outrage" and that he shared the pain and shame of the Catholic community.

That evening he met eight abuse survivors, including Marie Collins, at the papal embassy. They briefed him on the mother and baby homes scandal that had been the subject of a recent government inquiry following the discovery of mass graves: how tens of thousands of mothers in the 1940s and 1950s had been forcibly separated from their children by nuns and told that it was a mortal sin to contact them. Deeply moved, Francis agreed to speak of it the next day, and he began to draft with them the remarks he would make at the start of Mass in Dublin's Phoenix Park on August 26, during the so-called Penitential Rite.

Speaking in Spanish, he referred to his meeting the night before and said he wanted to "place before the mercy of the Lord these crimes, and ask forgiveness for them." His atonement for the sins of the Church in Ireland was comprehensive and detailed. It included the exploitation of minors in manual work and the separation of mothers from their children. It was not a mortal sin for the mothers to look for their children, he made clear, but obedience to the Fourth Commandment (to honor parents). He ended with a prayer to "sustain and increase this state of shame and repentance and give us the strength to commit ourselves so that these things may never happen again and justice may be done."

The retreat was under way, and Ireland was a beautiful example of it. But then, out of nowhere, came the sabotage.

Abuse victims often talk about the paralysis that freezes them when their assailant moves on them with sudden, overwhelming force. Catholics had something akin to that feeling on the morning of August 26, 2018, as they absorbed a ferocious attack on the pope by a retired Vatican official and diplomat named Carlo Maria Viganò.

The former nuncio to the United States, who had been retired by Francis in March 2016 after he had clumsily attempted to manipulate the papal visit the previous September, claimed he was breaking a "conspiracy of silence" over former Cardinal McCarrick that "reached to the very top of the Church's hierarchy." At the conclusion of his seven-thousand-word, eleven-page "testimony" Viganò dramatically called on Pope Francis to resign, claiming he had covered up for McCarrick and given comfort to a "homosexual current" of bishops.

His allegations carried weight because of the posts he had held in the Secretariat of State before Benedict XVI named him nuncio in 2012. He confirmed what the *New York Times* report on McCarrick's past had strongly suggested: that in 2000 McCarrick had been made archbishop of Washington by Saint John Paul II despite the fact that the Vatican knew of his earlier predatory homosexual behavior as a bishop in New Jersey. But what few knew was that further reports had reached the recently elected Benedict XVI in 2006, and some years later—around 2009–2010, Viganò estimated—the pope imposed on McCarrick "sanctions similar to those now imposed on him by Francis," namely prayer-and-penance penalties that removed him from the active priesthood, and which meant he could no longer give talks or travel. Viganò then claimed that, despite knowing about McCarrick's past, Francis had, after his election in 2013, "lifted" the sanctions imposed by Benedict, made use of McCarrick as an adviser on bishop appointments in the United States, and sent him on missions. Thus Francis had "covered up" for McCarrick and should resign.

The attack came out of the same wealthy, conservative, and neo-traditionalist American circles as Team Burke's putsch had two years earlier. Viganò was closely tied to those circles and had appeared alongside Burke to publicly oppose *Amoris Laetitia*. In case there was any doubt, the document was released at dawn in a coordinated effort involving various anti-Francis media: crafted by traditionalist journalists in Italy, translated by the Rome reporter for the Canadian alt-right LifeSite News, and released through Cardinal Burke's in-house scribe, the Rome correspondent for the *National Catholic Register*.

The timing was a giveaway. Released to inflict maximum embarrassment on the pope during his in-flight press conference on the flight back from Dublin, it marked a shocking new low in the tactics of the increasingly sophisticated anti-Francis operation. His enemies had seen the pope's mistakes and apology over Chile as a weakness they could exploit, and the abuse crisis as a heaven-sent opportunity to scatter sparks over the dry brushwood of anger toward the bishops.

It was effective. Viganò's theatrical confidence in his own righteousness allowed him to spin his betrayal of his sacred oath of confidentiality as the courageous act of a conscience-driven whistle-blower. America's indignant faithful were crying out to be seduced by a masked crusader with a simple narrative explanation for the Church's woes, and Viganò delivered in style, offering extravagantly "to free the Church from the fetid swamp into which she has fallen." But the swamp, in his view, was not really abuse but homosexuality, the former nuncio's idée fixe (the word appears sixteen times in eleven pages). Indeed, his real targets were what he claimed to be members of the "homosexual current," a bizarre list of more than forty senior prelates that mixed together abusers and active homosexuals with cardinals and bishops who had been, in his view, too friendly toward gay people.

Viganò encapsulated the very temptations that the pope had warned against in his letters to Chilean bishops and the people of God, in at least four ways. First, rather than discern spirits, Viganò had latched onto simple, reductive ideas: that the abuse crisis was a result of a lack of adherence to "truth" and the prevalence of homosexuality. Second, rather than embrace a collective conversion in humility, Viganò sought scapegoats, ranting—against the findings of all the expert studies—that gay priests were more likely to abuse, and those who blamed clericalism were deflecting attention from the "real problem." Third: for the ex-nuncio, there was no role for God's grace or mercy; when he spoke of conversion he meant a Pelagian effort by the Church to "amend and renew itself" by means of a moral crusade of purification, orthodoxy, and expulsion. Finally, where Francis had insisted on the need for a synodal response to the abuse scandals—only by the active involvement of the "people of God" could the Church rid itself of clericalism—for Viganò, a clericalist *pur et dur*, their only role was to be cannon fodder in his anti-papal crusade, passive followers he could whip into a rage.[46]

Francis learned of Operation Viganò as he left Dublin by helicopter Sunday morning for the sanctuary of Knock in County Mayo. Arriving in the soft rain, he was at peace but solemn in the shrine as he sat for four minutes in silent prayer before representations of Mary, Joseph, and John the Evangelist. When the three appeared to a village girl in 1879, the Virgin was silent; the only words in the scene before Francis were in the book John the Evangelist held open: "And the Lamb will be victorious." With the pope that morning and aware of the Viganò missile, the Irish archbishop Eamon Martin felt the intensity of the moment. Francis, he said later, was "placing it all at the feet of Our Lady, the Queen of Ireland and asking for her protection and her intercession."[47]

Our Lady's silence would be the pope's response to Viganò. Asked on the plane by Anna Matranga of CBS News to respond to the claim that he had known about McCarrick in 2013, Francis told her: "I will not say a single word about this. I believe the statement speaks for itself. And you have the journalistic capacity to draw your own conclusions. It's an act of faith. When some time passes and you have drawn your conclusions, I may speak."

The words came to him in that moment as a movement of the heart, without premeditation, he later told a close collaborator. Yet many Argentine Jesuits were struck by parallels with the early 1980s when, after the end of the Argentine military dictatorship, Bergoglio had been accused by left-wing Catholics, including some Jesuits, of collaborating with the military junta's tortures and disappearances. Then, as now, there was evidence from an apparently credible source, a respected Catholic human rights activist; then, too, the atmosphere was febrile, as Catholics absorbed with anger and shame revelations of bishops' failures to protect their flocks.

Bergoglio discerned then that it was not right to try to defend himself, and he never spoke about it publicly until he had to give testimony to a state inquiry in 2010. By that time the accusations had long since broken down under scrutiny. The questions circulated briefly again after his election as pope, but the answers soon came back that not only was he innocent of the charges but that he had at great personal risk helped people who were fleeing the dictatorship.[48]

Some Argentine Jesuits also recalled his powerful essay of 1990 called "Silencio y Palabra" (Silence and Word), which begins: "Sometimes it happens that silence is not a virtuous act but is the only option, one imposed by circumstances." Meditating on the Passion in the Third Week of the Spiritual Exercises where Saint Ignatius describes how God "goes into hiding" when faced with the forces determined on his death, Bergoglio asked why Jesus, after the "trial" at the Sanhedrin, falls mute. Not only is direct response futile when an accuser is determined on your destruction, he concludes, but it risks sucking you into the contagion of vengeance. But most important, silence allows the different spirits to be revealed. In a time of tribulation, that is never easy: in the electric storm of claims and counterclaims, truth and lies get fused, and everyone claims noble motives. Jesus shows how to force the devil to reveal himself. "There is only one way to make space for God, and this has been taught by Jesus himself:

humiliation, *kenosis* (Phil 2:5–11)," Bergoglio wrote. "Be silent, pray, and humble yourself."

What happens next is an increase in the ferocity of the attack, as the devil mistakes silence for weakness and redoubles his assault. Gradually, the rage focuses on a single person, and what is false and malicious suddenly comes into view. "The meekness of silence will show us to be even weaker, and so it will be the devil who, emboldened, comes into the light, and shows us his true intentions, no longer disguised as an angel but unmasked." In adopting Christ's strategy of silence in response to Viganò, while inviting the journalists to dig around, Francis was rejecting the mimetic contagion of accusation while putting his faith in the triumph of truth.[49]

Sure enough, it took just four days for Viganò's narrative to collapse. It was true that Benedict had issued "instructions" to McCarrick (in 2007, not 2009), but the restrictions he asked for were voluntary, and McCarrick, by then long retired, ignored them. Benedict never chose to make them public, meaning that they could not be imposed. Francis had not lifted any sanctions because there were no sanctions for him to lift. The point was proven by the actions of Viganò himself, who surfaced in an embarrassing 2012 video fulsomely welcoming McCarrick at a gala reception at which the nuncio gave him an award and showered him with praise.

The "testimony" was rich in untruths. McCarrick had not influenced Francis's U.S. bishop choices. He had played no part in his election. Not only was he not a papal ally, but in Buenos Aires Bergoglio had been at odds with McCarrick, who had been sent more than once by Cardinal Sodano to Argentina to carry out ordinations in a traditionalist order that was banned by the Argentine bishops. Nor was it because of any link to McCarrick that Francis in 2013 had failed to do what neither John Paul nor Benedict had done, namely, impose public sanctions on an eighty-three-year-old retired archbishop for noncriminal (i.e., adult sexual) misconduct twenty-five years earlier that seemingly everyone knew about but few had wanted to air. As Francis would later make clear in an interview with Valentina Alazraki, he had had "no idea" about the earlier allegations. Yet as soon as McCarrick was credibly accused of abuse of minors in June 2018, Francis did what no pope had been prepared to do before then. He issued public sanctions, removed McCarrick's red hat, and began a canonical process that led to the former archbishop of Washington's laicization in February 2019.

Meanwhile, information surfaced about Viganò and his motives: his turbulent past in the Vatican, including his central role in Vatileaks, and the background to Francis's retiring him at age seventy-five in March 2016. Among his many grievances was being passed up for the red hat he craved and having to move, in early 2018, out of his lavish apartment inside the walls of the Vatican to a Rome palazzo housing other former nuncios (a cardinal heard him vow that "all hell would break loose" if Francis insisted on the move). Whatever else was driving him, it was clear that loathing of the pope was paramount, and there was little love lost on the other side: Francis had been furious at Viganò for ambushing him at the end of his September 2015 visit to the United States in an embarrassing episode that dragged him into the culture wars.[50]

Yet despite the collapse of Viganò's credibility, the conservative and far-right groups remained inflamed, egged on by Cardinal Burke, who claimed that "the corruption and the filth that have entered the Church must be purified at their roots." Even more shocking, two dozen U.S. bishops—many of whom owed their nominations to Viganò—sided publicly with the ex-nuncio, rushing out statements painting him as credible and honorable, and calling for his claims to be investigated. Almost all the *viganista* bishops made no mention of his call for the pope to resign, while many criticized Francis for his silence. The contrast with the European and Latin American bishops who rushed to deplore Viganò's attack and to stand by Francis could not have been starker. These were signs of a latent U.S. schism, in which a substantial minority of bishops no longer accepted the pope's legitimacy while presenting their conservative American ethical and political ideology as orthodox Catholicism.[51]

In early October 2018, a "Viganò's army" of 250 well-heeled conservative Catholics gathered in Washington, D.C., for a conference in response to the abuse scandals. The Napa Institute's Timothy Busch, an EWTN board member and multimillionaire patron of Catholic University of America's Busch School of Business (home of the "theology of capitalism"), was a long-standing Viganò ally who was part of the operation to release his testimony. At his "Authentic Reform" gathering he rallied his troops: "We're going to bring them to justice, move them out and restore our church to holiness," he promised, without specifying whom he meant. "Viganò has given us an agenda," he added.

Busch spoke as if the Church were a corporation ready for a shareholder takeover. Elsewhere, the *viganisti* treated the Church as a political arena: the Red Hat Report announced a plan to spend $1 million publicly to link cardinals deemed corrupt or homosexual to abuse scandals. "Had we had the Red Hat Report, we may not have had Pope Francis," announced its director, a recent convert from Islam who believed in "traditional values." Whether or not they knew it, the very idea of a papal election voting guide violated the rules governing the conclave, which banned "all possible forms of interference, opposition and suggestion whereby secular authorities of whatever order and degree, or any individual or group, might attempt to exercise influence on the election of the Pope."[52]

On the return trip from Ireland the pope had said he might speak once the journalists had done their work. In his morning homilies from the Santa Marta in September, he did, but indirectly, offering discernment guidance to the people of God. "The truth is meek. The truth is silent. The truth is not noisy," he said at his first Mass after the summer break, going on to warn that "the father of lies, the accuser, the devil, acts to destroy the unity of a family, of a people," but "with his silence Jesus wins against the devil who sows lies in the heart." He spoke of the importance of self-accusation, warning that there were "people who go through life talking about others, accusing others, and never thinking of their own sins," adding that "a sign that . . . a Christian does not know how to accuse himself is when he is accustomed to accusing others." A few days later he said it seemed as if "the 'Great Accuser' has been unchained and is attacking bishops," pointing to their sins in order to scandalize people. "And when I enter into this logic of accusing, cursing, and looking to do evil to others, I enter into the logic of the 'Great Accuser' who is a 'Destroyer,' who doesn't know the word 'mercy,'" the pope said.

Viganò took it personally. "He has compared his silence to that of Jesus in Nazareth and before Pilate, and compared me to the Great Accuser, Satan, who sows scandal and division in the Church—though without ever uttering my name," he complained in a new missive. He was wrong: the pope would never compare himself with Jesus, nor any human being with Satan; but it was a basic tenet of spiritual discernment that people are tools or channels of the spirits. The task was to discern which spirits were of God and which of the *diabolos*. The voice of the frenzied pitchfork mob calling for expulsions and purges in language soaked in anger and self-justification was unlikely to be of divine origin, while those who trusted the power of God to convert hearts and showed a spirit of humility and mercy were unlikely to be doing the devil's work.

Viganò's wounded victimhood—he claimed, absurdly, to be in hiding from those who might want to harm him—was a new tactic. He no longer called for the pope to resign and seemed happy to accept he had been wrong about the public sanctions. But rather than repent and return to the fold, as Cardinal Ouellet called on him to do in an excoriating public letter, Viganò doubled down, claiming his actions were justified because the pope was "negligent in exercising his principal mission, which is to confirm the brothers in the faith and in sound moral doctrine." It was for this reason, he said, that he had spoken out.[53]

It was a remarkable admission that was lost on most commentators. Viganò was admitting that McCarrick had been the excuse, sex abuse the opportunity. The crusade of purification, the ranting at gays in the Vatican, were all just a veneer; his real target was Francis, whom he blamed for infidelity to doctrine. Operation Viganò turned out to be the same *dubia* corpse, reinflated to make it look alive.

Just before leaving for the Baltic states, Francis called the French Jesuit in charge of the pope's Worldwide Prayer Network and asked him to urge the faithful throughout the world to pray the Rosary and invoke the protection of Saint Michael the Archangel "to protect the Church from the devil, who always seeks to divide us from God and to cause divisions among ourselves." It was an unprecedented request in the modern Church. It was clear from his conversation with Francis, Father Frédéric Fornos, SJ, said, that the pope believed the Church was under severe attack, and that when the Church is "faced with this devil that seeks to divide us, the only thing that works is prayer."[54]

Determined to hold the Church on the path he had set in his August letter to the people of God, Francis in mid-September announced he was calling a global summit of church leaders in February 2019 organized by, among others, his two anti-abuse pioneers, Father Zollner and Archbishop Scicluna. Attending would be the presidents of bishops' conferences, heads of religious orders, as well as prefects of Vatican congregations, around 190 in all.

In the United States, the summit was interpreted as a bid to "change the narrative" around McCarrick and Pennsylvania, but the United States wasn't Francis's primary concern. He wanted to end the culture of denial and cover-up, especially in poorer parts of the world, and to ensure that all the bishops were at the forefront of combating abuse in their flocks. It was a global version of the Chilean bishops' gathering, but organized as a synodal experience, with plenty of prayer, input from outsiders, and victims' testimonies front and center—an unprecedented bid to secure the conversion of hearts and minds, which was key to overthrowing the clerical culture.

The leadership of the U.S. bishops' conference, however, remained focused on cleaning the outside of the cup, appeasing Viganò's mobs and the media by "concrete actions." At a meeting of the executive of the U.S. bishops with Francis the day after his summit announcement, the USCCB president, Cardinal Daniel DiNardo, archbishop of Galveston-Houston, told the pope the bishops lacked all credibility, and he listed the juridical measures they wanted to take to restore it. They saw only a tide rising on all sides. DiNardo was under fire for mishandling a sex abuse case in 2010, while on the day of their meeting the Vatican announced that the bishop of Wheeling-Charleston, West Virginia—the cousin of USCCB general secretary Monsignor Brian Bransfield, who was also at the meeting with Francis that day—had resigned following allegations that he had sexually harassed adults. (Bishop Michael Bransfield was later banned from ministry following multiple allegations of sexual harassment of adults and financial improprieties.)

Francis saw it differently. "You lack credibility because you are divided," he told them. Dismissing their request for a Scicluna-style, Vatican-led investigation of McCarrick in the United States, the pope urged them to cancel their November meeting and have all the bishops spend a week together in retreat instead. That way, he said, the Catholic people would see them placing themselves in God's hands and would trust them again. DiNardo balked at the idea, but later agreed to a retreat in January 2019, to which the pope promised to send the preacher to the papal household, Father Raniero Cantalamessa. In early October, the Vatican also announced that it would begin an investigation into McCarrick, promising to go wherever the truth led.

The U.S. bishops' executive meanwhile pressed ahead with their own mechanisms for holding bishops accountable. Bransfield and his predecessor as general secretary, Monsignor Ronny Jenkins, dean of canon law at the Catholic University of America, spent much of October drawing up a code of conduct for bishops and a proposed lay-led commission to receive and act on complaints against them. The idea was for DiNardo to announce the changes with a flourish at the November USCCB meeting and get them approved by the bishops in a dramatic show of their determination to respond to criticism.

The proposals drawn up by Bransfield and Jenkins—a couple so inseparable that even in the Vatican they were referred to by a single nickname, "Bronny"—involved spelling out "standards of episcopal conduct" and creating an independent commission of laypeople to receive complaints, investigate bishops, and report their findings to Rome. But the methodology flew in the face of the law and tradition of the Church, one embedded in the Second Vatican Council as well as canon law, that only the pope has the right to judge bishops and open investigations into bishops. Any probe, in other words, had to be approved and delegated by the Holy See, as had happened, for example, in the McCarrick case, when the New York archdiocese sought the pope's permission to look into the allegation.

The Bronny proposal denied the pope this agency, while ominously placing in the hands of unaccountable laypeople the power to name and shame bishops, even before their names had reached Rome. It was poor law, drawn up in haste for public relations purposes, and more reflective of a punitive American juridical and corporate culture than a Catholic one.

Even more shocking, the Bronny strategy was to deliberately exclude Rome from the design of the proposal. DiNardo would present the plans at the November 2018 meeting in Baltimore and ask the bishops to vote on them before Rome had a chance to see them first. The Vatican would be given the documents after the fact. "Their strategy was to confront the pope with a fait accompli," a well-informed source told me. "They were thinking, 'If this passes, what's Rome going to do? Reject it?' Their concern was to look as if they had done something, and if Rome objected, that would make Rome look bad."

Just over a week before the opening of the Fall General Assembly, the Vatican got wind of what Bronny and DiNardo were up to. In a November 6 letter, the prefect of the Congregation of Bishops, Cardinal Ouellet, demanded to see the proposals and asked that the bishops not vote or make any decisions on them in Baltimore. The plans were sent over on November 8, just four days before the meeting opened. Vatican Secretary of State Parolin was appalled. Ouellet wrote again, on November 11, to confirm that the U.S. bishops should not proceed with any vote, reminding DiNardo that while a bishops' conference "enjoys a rightful autonomy," its work "must always be integrated within the hierarchical structure and universal law of the Church." Ouellet also criticized the proposals as premature and said they should have been shared with the relevant Vatican departments. Furthermore, any future mechanisms "should incorporate the input and fruits of the college of bishops' work of common discernment" in the global meeting at the Vatican in February.[55]

DiNardo opened the assembly on November 12 by blaming the Vatican for the USCCB's being unable to proceed with the assembly's flagship proposals. He claimed that "at the insistence of the Holy See," communicated only the previous night, the bishops' vote on accountability measures would be delayed until after the summit of February 2019, adding that he was "disappointed." He did not say that the proposals were incompatible with canon law, nor that he had tried to keep them secret from Rome, nor that Ouellet had asked him a whole week earlier to postpone any vote. It was anyway doubtful that the bishops would have approved the proposals, which had plenty of other defects.

The Bronny-DiNardo attempt to deflect indignation onto Rome paid off handsomely. The *Washington Post* was typical in claiming that the Vatican had "blocked a plan by America's Catholic leaders to confront sexual abuse," and had "suggested that bishops should not be held accountable by laypeople in the church."[56]

Both claims were well wide of the mark. The Vatican had asked only that the bishops' accountability measures be universally agreed upon and in line with canon law. There was nothing wrong with laypeople serving on boards investigating bishops' misconduct, as long as their authority to do so had been delegated by Rome. "There may be a temptation on the part of some to relinquish responsibility for reform to others from ourselves, as if we were no longer capable of reforming or trusting ourselves," the nuncio, Archbishop Christophe Pierre, told the bishops, adding that while the assistance of laypeople was essential, "the responsibility as bishops of this Catholic Church is ours." As Francis expressed it on the flight back from Morocco on March 31, 2019, the laity and everyone else must be involved, but "the Church is not a congregationalist Church. It is the Catholic Church where the bishop must take control of this as the pastor."[57]

In a promising sign of future unity, almost all the heads of dioceses—with the exception of a handful of *viganista* bishops, who sent auxiliaries—turned out for the week's prayer and mediations by Father Cantalamessa at Mundelein Seminary near Chicago just after the New Year. Many of the bishops, unaccustomed to silent weeklong spiritual retreats, were bowled over by the experience.

As he had done with Chile's bishops, Francis offered spiritual guidance in a paternal eight-page "tribulation letter." He invited them to be aware of the time in which they were living and to seize the grace being offered them while being aware of the temptations that distracted them. "At times of great uncertainty and confusion," he wrote, "we need to be attentive and discerning, to free our hearts of compromises and false certainties, in order to hear what the Lord asks of us." He repeated the core principle: "ideas are for discussion, but vital situations have to be discerned."

He knew they had lost credibility, but he invited them to see that evangelical credibility—the kind that comes of being witnesses to the transforming power of God's mercy—could not be produced by means of "stern decrees or by simply creating new committees or improving flow charts, as if we were in charge of a department of human resources." It wasn't a shiny new, successful corporation that they were asked to create but a renewed apostolic body, one that could come about only through repentance and receptivity to the Holy Spirit. The sign and fruit of that renewal would be their unity.

Theirs was a time of trial, but also of grace; a time to be liberated of false certainties and "futile forms of triumphalism" and instead "to listen to the voice of the Lord." He warned them against playing the victim, recriminating and disparaging each other, and to quit "projecting onto others our own confusion and discontent," inviting them to instead "rid ourselves of all that stands in the way of a clear witness to the Gospel of Jesus Christ."[58]

The retreat didn't make the news. It produced nothing "concrete." But many of the bishops said afterward they had been struck by Father Cantalamessa's inviting them to imagine the barque of Saint Peter not as a rowboat driven by their efforts, but a sailboat carried along by the winds of the Holy Spirit. Their task was to set the sails, trust their wounded shepherd to captain them, and, when the time was right, listen for instructions being called out from the shore.

six

Close and Concrete

St. Joseph the Patriarch is a large parish of forty thousand people in seven barrios alongside the Jesuits' Colegio Máximo in San Miguel, a town an hour and a half outside the city of Buenos Aires. In the half century following the college's foundation in the 1930s, in what was then empty pampa, migrants arriving from the interior of the country and neighboring nations pitched their tarpaulins here, forming a classic Latin American periphery.

Over time it became what it is today, a working-class neighborhood of little brick houses with gardens. Although many of the streets are still unpaved—the dust turns to sticky mud in winter—there are streetlights and shops and football fields. Many people have jobs in the factories and warehouses, but most work in the informal sector, where income is uncertain, and people hover sometimes above but often below the poverty line.

When the parish was founded by Bergoglio in 1980, at the start of his tenure as the college's rector, the Colegio Máximo was bursting with dozens of young Jesuits in formation: what better way for them to learn to be missionaries and pastors? Each weekend he sent the students out to visit homes to pray, bless, and console; to untie knots that kept people from taking part in life and the Church; to invite children to catechesis; to uncover pockets of suffering and solitude; and to announce the closeness of

God. It was religious, not social, work, yet it led into community projects—communal cook-ins, job skills workshops, night classes—and regular neighborhood fiestas. The experience was decisive, both for the people of San Miguel and for the Jesuits who for the past thirty-eight years have served them, helping to form a people.[1]

Among the parishioners are a number who remember how Bergoglio used to say Mass for around three hundred of them that included cheerfully noisy back-and-forth "dialogue homilies." Some also remember the games on the grounds of the college, followed by a children's fiesta, and they recall what happened afterward, when they trooped back to the parish to make the devil explode and send an angel to heaven.

The Jesuits confected two life-size models, one of an angel and the other of the devil. The devil was made from rags and filled with firecrackers, while the angel was constructed of polythene with helium balloons tied to it along with a little sign with the address and telephone number of the parish. It was a way of teaching Saint Ignatius's famous "Two Standards" meditation from Week Two of the Spiritual Exercises, which contrasts Jesus's call and Satan's attempt to frustrate that call with temptations.

After catechesis and a tea-and-cake party, the children would process with the Jesuits from the college back to the parish church, the Jesuits trying to look solemn while the children excitedly shouted, "Let's burn the devil! Let's burn the devil!" Once they reached the parish they lit a fire under Satan, who exploded in a satisfyingly loud riot of firecrackers. Then each child wrote a prayer on a piece of paper. The prayers were put in a plastic bag that was attached to the angel, who was released and flew up into the air. (One time the Jesuits took a call from Uruguay, where the angel had landed.)[2]

Among the young Jesuits fanning out across the barrios at that time was the parish's pastor, Father Rafael Velasco, SJ. He oversees five churches with Sunday Mass and other liturgies, as well as social projects, schools, popular kitchens, and catechesis. The college is a spirituality center now, and the Jesuit students study in Córdoba, so when it comes to the "mission," Padre Rafa sends out dozens of young people in the parish. But the method and the experience are the same as when Padre Jorge sent him out. Under Rafa's guidance, and assisted by a young nun, Sister Gisela, the dozens of young missionaries form teams, and among them they cover the seven barrios in under a week. Just as the Jesuits did, they go from house to house, sitting and praying with people, learning about their lives.

Now, as I meet with them after Mass in July 2018 around a table with lit candles and listen to them reflect on the experience, it is obvious that their hearts are bursting with names and faces. Gisela and Rafa ask questions, but mostly they listen to the stories pouring forth. People who had stopped going to church years ago but who told of how God had been at work in their ups and downs. People with no jobs who lived alone. People in need. People who cried when they saw the missionaries, out of relief and joy. People who were inspired by them to visit others.

The young missionaries listened, prayed with them, read Scripture, and responded from their hearts, the best they could, depending on each situation. Sometimes they directed people to parish projects—like the couple who twice a week open up their house to cook for those in need, or the night school for people out of work—or they pointed to catechesis and programs that prepare people to receive sacraments. Sometimes they made a note for Rafa about a person's particular needs. "It's all mixed together," the Jesuit explains to me later. "The spiritual and the material, catechesis and life skills. The Kingdom of God is both. We announce Jesus *and* His kingdom. We share, and show the meaning of that sharing. And people's horizons change." When people experience God as close and concrete—that faith isn't an *idea*, but an *event*—they come to see that they belong. Their behavior toward themselves, and toward each other, changes.

These parish missions bear all kinds of fruit, but not always straight away. Some people might start coming again to Mass, to join baptism and marriage programs, to train as faith teachers. But this is the age of liquidity: believing and belonging often do not correlate. Yet Rafa and his young missionaries don't think of the church as only those who come through its doors on a Sunday. Nor do they confuse evangelization with proselytism.

The purpose of the mission is not to fill the pews but to make possible an encounter with the God of mercy. The locus of that encounter, for most people, is their own lives, especially in their needs and their anguish. Some are hungry, alone, in need of help of one sort or another—fear, addiction, a trauma they had thought was in the past—while others try to make sense of what is happening around them. Some are doing well but worry about others. Some are full of infectious joy.

Yet what seems most to matter about the mission isn't what the young went out to give but what they have brought back. It's a sense of belonging, of oneness. That the Kingdom of God is born in kinship and service. That

God is acting there. That Grace abounds. That, as Cardinal Bergoglio put it in 2011, "God is present in, encourages, and is an active protagonist in the life of His people."[3]

The missionaries themselves have had that encounter, and their joy is palpable.

"God is very happy and proud of us," beams Celeste.

"I feel really accompanied," says Agustín.

Lucas, who is good with words, quotes Argentina's new saint who gave his life among the rural folk of Córdoba. Faith is like fleas, as El Cura Brochero used to say, because you find more of both among the poor.

But then he hits on an idea of his own. "*Misionando, fuimos misionados*," he declares, and the others nod vigorously and clap, because he has nailed it. *In going out on mission, we were missioned to.*

The pressing question facing the Catholic Church in the early twenty-first century is how to preach the Gospel in a world in flux. In a mutable, technocratic, globalized world, one that is ever more pluralistic, fragmented, and secular, how do people pass on and catch faith? By what means do they wake up, as people have in every generation, to the news of God's coming among us, close and concrete?

The question is seldom posed that way. Usually people ask how the Church (as an institution) should respond to secularization, by which they mean the remorseless expulsion of Christianity from the law and culture of the West. It is a question underpinned by distress and a sense of loss. People pine for a time when church institutions were strong and prestigious, when faith was influential on culture. Now culture sees only a haughty, distant corporation—self-interested, clericalist, hypocritical, even abusive.

Catholics look around them and see the old ways of passing on the faith fraying and breaking as family, parish, charities, and schools fragment. "We are living and experiencing a true change of era," says Francis, "and the technological and cultural shifts that have marked this period of history have made the transmission of faith increasingly difficult."[4]

And every survey backs up the same story, that even in the culturally religious United States, the falloff has been dramatic: 6.5 former Catholics for every convert to the faith. In Europe, the world's least religious continent, Mass attendance averages less than 20 percent of the baptized, and most young people identify with no religion. In Latin America, Mass attendance remains on average comparatively high and Catholics are young and gently increasing in overall numbers. Yet there is great variation between, say, Peru and Paraguay, on the one hand, and Chile and Uruguay on the other, and overall the number of Catholics has been dropping as a proportion of the overall population.

Only in Latin America, however, has the Church asked, with a depth adequate to the challenge, how it must respond to this new era, and has put the answer in a document whose main author is now Pope Francis and which is named after the shrine in Brazil where a key meeting of Latin American church leaders took place in May 2007. Aparecida is essential to understand the evangelizing vision of the Francis pontificate. The Fifth General Conference of the Latin American Episcopal Council (CELAM) barely registered in the consciousness of the world's Catholics until the election of Francis. But people quickly saw the connection between Aparecida's diagnosis and discernment and Francis's first, programmatic document of November 2013.

Evangelii Gaudium (the Joy of the Gospel) was the pope's official response to the synod that had been convened a year earlier by Benedict XVI to discuss the "new evangelization." The question of that synod was the question that faces the Church: how to propose the Gospel in a secular, liquid world. Francis's answer, in his apostolic exhortation *Evangelii Gaudium*, was essentially Aparecida's.

That was why it startled many Catholics of the Northern Hemisphere. What the church leaders in Latin America grasped in May 2007 had not yet dawned on the Church in the north: namely, the definitive passing of that era in which Christianity was supported by law and culture, and the urgent need for a change in mind-set in order to evangelize in this new context. Aparecida called this a "pastoral and missionary conversion," and those who were there felt it as a Pentecostal wind, convinced it was the Holy Spirit's invitation not just to the Latin Americans but to the universal Church, which Francis's election subsequently appeared to confirm.

The shift represented by Aparecida has shocked the traditional Catholic heartlands of the wealthy to the north because their default setting has been a strategy of accommodation to the age. That accommodation takes many forms: a flaky, liberal Christianity of personal fulfillment and social justice that avoids the self-denying challenges of the Gospel; the idea that the Church needs to look more like the contemporary age, so that the age will accept it; or an angry rejection of the contemporary age, which justifies a timid, self-protective hunkering down. The focus has been, in each case, on the "values" the Church represents, ethical stances reduced to sexuality and bioethics on the right, or social justice issues on the left, as rivals to the reigning relativism. While it has not prevented the remorseless shrinking of Catholic ranks, the accommodationist approach offers some illusion of security, the protection of the "comfortable winter palaces" that Francis spoke of to Chile's bishops.

Impatient with this accommodation, younger, educated Catholics, many of them converts, want the Church to be more defiant, more radical in its opposition. Some opt for withdrawal into citadels of the pure; others dream of conquering the state to re-moralize society via some nationalist, authoritarian project in the name of "Western Christian heritage." Yet these stances are really another kind of accommodation. They are incapable of evangelization, strategies of resistance rather than renaissance. As the great Uruguayan thinker Alberto Methol Ferré put it: "The integralist does not question modernity, but sees it from the same perspective as the Enlightenment—just unfavorably."[5]

Rather than accommodating to modernity—whether through acquiescence or resistance—Aparecida called for an alternative modernity, built from the ground up, from the periphery, from those left behind. Rather than lamenting secularization, Aparecida saw Christianity's loss of cultural and political power as an opportunity to recover the gratuity of God's grace. Rather than defining itself as antiglobalization, it sought a globalization of solidarity. Rather than seeking to bolster the power and prestige of the Church's beleaguered institutions, it offered a paradox: that precisely those bodies of people that are weak in resources yet rich in mercy and witness are the most capable of evangelizing a liquid world, and can give God's Kingdom a new birth in our time.

I saw it, down in Argentina, that cold Sunday morning in July 2018 as I listened to eight young people in the parish founded by Father Jorge Mario Bergoglio, SJ, as they reflected on their four-day mission in the barrios of San Miguel. We were shivering a little because the heaters had died with a power cut just minutes into the meeting. But after a while we stopped noticing the cold.

For most of the 1990s Bergoglio was an auxiliary bishop in Buenos Aires, overseeing a lower-middle-class part of the city that included *villas miseria*, the shantytowns, as well as a number of sanctuaries and shrines that play such a significant role in the lives of ordinary Latin American people. After he became archbishop of the Argentine capital in 1998, his immediate flock was around three million—those who lived within the boundaries of the original city—but in reality it was far larger, for his was one of eleven dioceses in the so-called Buenos Aires Region, an ecclesiastical demarcation that includes the spread-out suburbs where thirteen million people, of whom perhaps 85 percent are Catholics, live their lives.

Aparecida called for dioceses within cities to work together to implement common urban pastoral plans. Around a thousand pastoral leaders and theologians from the eleven dioceses of Buenos Aires met each year between 2007 and 2013 to do just that. In the so-called PUBA (Buenos Aires Urban Pastoral) congresses, under Bergoglio's leadership, they would draw from their experiences of implementing Aparecida some key lessons for evangelizing a global world in flux. PUBA is so little known in the wider Church that few have spotted its significance as a laboratory of the pastoral and missionary conversion Aparecida called for, whose key lessons would find their way into *Evangelii Gaudium*.[6]

"After Aparecida, Bergoglio talked about how the transmission belts of faith were broken, and how we now have to go out," recalls Buenos Aires auxiliary bishop Juan Carlos Ares. Faith no longer reached people naturally through inheritance and culture, but had to now be the fruit of a personal experience ("encounter") with God's mercy in Jesus Christ. It followed that the Church's way of seeing and acting had to change. In *Evangelii Gaudium* Francis summed this up in terms of his dream of a "missionary option," such that the Church's structures and culture "can be suitably channeled for the evangelization of today's world rather than for her self-preservation." The purpose was to raise up authentic disciples. "Who is the chief beneficiary of the work of the Church: the Church as an organization or the People of God?" Francis challenged CELAM's coordinators in July 2013.[7]

At Aparecida the bishops had noted how the Christian Church came into existence two thousand years ago in a similar context of urban pluralism, which it made use of to grow. It wasn't, at that time, a powerful civic institution seeking influence in the circles of power; Christ's followers were often hounded and persecuted. Yet persecution and evangelization went hand in hand. Faith spread rapidly through chaotic cities because the Christians' "gaze of faith" allowed them to see God alive in His people, especially on the margins, and they went out to meet Him there. Now, too, evangelizing meant getting out from the parish, being on a permanent missionary footing, having a constant closeness to people. This implied a hermeneutic shift, a way of seeing. "We realized that we weren't taking God to the city, but that God lives in the city and we are going out to encounter Him," says Ares. "This was our pastoral conversion."[8]

Another bishop on the front lines of this transformation is Bishop Gustavo Carrara, who in Bergoglio's time headed his team of slum priests. Separately, Ares and Carrara warn against taking the city's Church as Aparecida's pinup; pastoral conversion, they stress, is *in via* in Buenos Aires as much as elsewhere. But when they explain the conversion involved and give examples of its practical implications, it is clear that Aparecida, via PUBA, runs in their veins.

One important idea is *santuarizar la parroquias*, as one of Bergoglio's sticky neologisms put it: to have parishes take lessons from the shrines. The city's sanctuaries are open all hours, take people as they come, and are down-to-earth. "For the people who come, God has to do with concrete needs, and concrete life is to do with God," Carrara explains. "Those who come are often outside church structures, they don't have their papers in order, and they come to express things about their lives they can't express elsewhere. In the sanctuary, they feel heard and loved." They are received by trained lay volunteers with a special gift for listening. The French theologian Christoph Theobald, SJ, calls such people "water-diviners" and says their listening charism is key to evangelizing in a context of non-belonging.[9]

At the PUBA congress of 2012 it dawned on Bishop Ares (who at the time ran the popular shrine of Saint Expeditus, a Roman soldier famous for "expediting" bureaucratic processes) that the shrine needed to be missionary, too. He began weekend missions outside the train station four blocks away, using prayer cards, tents, loudspeakers, and regular outdoor Masses to link the life of the shrine with the faith of commuters and street sellers. Prayers were gathered up and offered at Mass; people came to talk, confess, ask questions. Ares found a river of faith flowing outside church buildings, and the experience transformed him.

Now that he is in charge of forty-seven parishes, he asks them to do the same: to go out, to visit houses, to attend to needs and suffering where people are. It means carrying a table into the street to celebrate Mass; handing out news of special prayer services for the sick, the departed, young people, and the jobless; or teaming up with other parishes in reaching out at night to the homeless. Above all, he urges them to use the parish's patronal feast as an opportunity for prayers and fiesta out in the neighborhood, not just behind the churches' walls.

"The parish is the *barrio* and the *barrio* is the parish" is how Bishop Carrara puts it. The parish isn't just its buildings or the people at Mass on Sunday, but the ties among those who make up its community, only some of whom will be baptized Mass-goers. Key to forging those ties is to put the poor at their heart, as Aparecida urged, and to see them as subjects rather than just objects of evangelization. The peripheries will look different in the wealthy Barrio Norte from the *villas miseria*, Carrara says—in el Barrio Norte, the need that is seen is often the hunger of loneliness and anguish rather than material poverty—but there is need everywhere, and it is concealed, for suffering and need always hide out of shame.

Father Pepe Di Paola, Argentina's famous slum priest and a Bergoglio disciple, enunciates another important Aparecida principle. "No one stays outside," he tells me over a gourd of maté in his little office in Villa La Cárcova, a huge *villa miseria* next to San Isidro, one of Buenos Aires's richest boroughs. He likes Francis's famous image of the Church as a field hospital because it includes everyone in various states of disrepair. "Whether you've got flu or you've been shot or you're an addict, you're inside, you belong," he says, smiling.

Padre Pepe's crack addiction projects, born out of his former slum parish in Villa 21, have inspired dozens of similar ones across Argentina. The point is not just to realize that behind drug dependency are other factors— lack of work and schooling, legal problems, homelessness—but to see the addicted person as a belonging subject rather than a receiving object. "The response of a parish might normally be to send away the addict, but we say no, he stays within the community." You recognize the Kingdom of God, Francis likes to say, not only because the hungry are fed but also because they sit at the same table as everyone else.

When Carrara describes the missions of young people in the parishes of the *villas miseria*, they sound like what I heard in San Miguel, only here many of the missionaries are former addicts who with God's help have climbed their way back out of dependency and want others to know a different future is possible. "They come back saying, 'People told us: we thought our lives were going to end there, but then they met us.' They've met a person who has been through what they have been through and that gives them hope."

Carrara smiles as he says this. He's seen plenty of these resurrections: people left for dead at the side of the road who find they can be Good Samaritans, too. Too often the Church thinks of people who evangelize as professionals with certificates, and formation matters, of course. But the one really necessary qualification is the *encuentro*. To have had an encounter with mercy and to lead others there, says Carrara: that's what it means to be a missionary disciple.

Such conversions are the origin of faith. It's how the Church is born, and every day reborn, in the midst of secular, liquid modernity.

More than a document, it was a happening. Bergoglio saw it as a "grace event." To call it a Latin American Pentecost is not hyperbole. Just as in the Upper Room in Jerusalem, when the shattered and fearful disciples were visited by the Holy Spirit and emboldened for mission, Aparecida's effect was to unleash the missionary potential of the Church in Latin America, giving it new energy and direction at a time of fear and uncertainty.

It was in many ways a gift of Benedict XVI. Soon after becoming pope in 2005 he gave permission for the Church in Latin America to do what Saint John Paul II's men had opposed: assemble a new "general conference" organized by its continent-wide body, the Latin American Episcopal Council (CELAM). It was the fifth in CELAM's history, and the first in twenty-five years. To prepare, the Church across the continent swung into action, organizing consultations, reports, and surveys for the bishops to take into their discernment.

Aparecida took place over a fortnight in May 2007 at the vast shrine, against a backdrop of intense devotion by great crowds of poor people. It began not with a document but with open dialogue, collating the pastors' concerns about being faced with the change of era, and concluded in a remarkable consensus among the 130 bishop delegates for a new "continental mission" for the age. Aparecida represented, Francis said ten years later, "the effort to put Jesus's mission at the very heart of the Church, making it the yardstick for measuring the effectiveness of her structures, the results of her labors, the fruitfulness of her ministers and the joy they awaken—for without joy, we attract no one."[10]

The future pope's role was decisive. The archbishop of La Paz, Bolivia,

Edmundo Abastoflor, recalls how Bergoglio masterfully and patiently reconciled different groups, fashioning a final draft from thousands of amendments. The result was "the fruit of the synthesis and vision of Cardinal Bergoglio, who managed to carry everyone with him and produce that document which is crucial not just for Latin America, and which he took so personally."[11]

In Francis's first months, before the publication of *Evangelii Gaudium*, it was the Aparecida document that he handed to visiting heads of state so they could understand what he was up to. He told a delegation of Latin American bishops that as pope he would be "doing nothing else but apply Aparecida." It was his "manifesto," as Massimo Borghesi puts it, a great "baroque synthesis" of tradition and modernity of the sort that hadn't been seen since the great missionary era of the colonial period.[12]

At its heart was the insight that the greatest threat to the Church lay not outside but within, from the temptation of fearful self-enclosure when faced with the tribulation of change. The invitation was to follow the promptings of the Holy Spirit out to every human periphery. It was a journey of reorientation, "to free us from becoming a self-referential Church," as Bergoglio put it in a homily that he delivered at the shrine with his trademark slow-burn intensity. The image he used there of the crippled woman in the Gospel "who does no more than look at herself, with the people of God off somewhere else," was key to his thinking. It was not God who had abandoned his people. The Church, a self-referential, fearful, clericalist institution, had withdrawn from the people. An evangelizing Church was one that returned to the people, to encounter God in the lives of the people.

The homily captivated those present, convincing many that Bergoglio was anointed, that his vision was the one to guide the Church at this time. When Francis gave a précis of the same homily in his reflections at the preconclave gathering in Rome five years later, using exactly that diagnosis and even that image, many of the cardinals reached the same conclusion, and elected him pope days later.[13]

What made Aparecida—and Bergoglio, its great articulator—unique in the contemporary Church was this response to a world in flux. The bishops at the shrine considered the negative impacts of modernity, above all on the poor, including individualism, consumerism, the erosion of community and culture, the destruction of nature, the weakening of families and respect for life, as well as corruption and growing inequality, as the result of idolizing money. But rather than stop there, deploring the state of the world, they asked how the Church needed to change in order to save the world. Rather than *condemn* and *lament*, Aparecida sought to *discern* and *reform*. Faced with a world in flux, it invited the Church to rethink its mission.[14]

This attitude of humility was exceptional in the Church at a time when many church leaders in Europe and the United States, furious or anxious at losing ground, were focused on strategies for resistance and reconquest. At the 2012 synod called by Benedict to discuss the "new evangelization," the Latin Americans stood out from the gloom and victimhood of many Europeans and Americans. They quoted Aparecida and turned the conservative response on its head. "We do not speak of the new evangelization only because the others have changed," they said. "The moment has arrived in which to ask ourselves: What are the sins of the Church which have led us to a new evangelization?" For this self-interrogation, they added, "a *status quaestionis* of the Church in herself, and her place in the world, is inevitable." They called for a pastoral conversion, a term that had been common currency in Aparecida but was new to most at the synod.[15]

In order to change the world, the Church had to change. The problem wasn't just that the world was changing, for better or for worse, but that the Church had reacted to change by refusing to change, by putting up walls and turning in on itself. Rejecting attitudes that saw only "confusion, danger, and threats," or that sought to respond with "worn-out ideologies or irresponsible aggressions," Aparecida called for a shift in focus: to enable a "personal and community encounter" with the risen Lord, one that "raises up missionary disciples." It wasn't about big programs or new structures, but "new men and women": people transformed by the encounter with Christ.[16]

What emerged from Aparecida was this humble, discerning disposition, typified by Francis. What mattered in the change of era weren't the stormy seas but Christ's invitation to step out of the boat. For Bergoglio then and Francis now, the renewal of the Church was less a strategy and more a trustful waiting on God's directions, a missionary disposition, which involved humble listening and discernment. Put Christ and the poor at the center, and the rest would follow.

That meant being close and concrete. Aparecida called for a Church "visibly present as a mother who reaches out, a welcoming home, a constant school of missionary communion," as Bergoglio put it back in Buenos Aires. Evangelization was not a matter of plans and programs, of strategies, tactics, maneuvers, techniques, as if all depended on the power of the evangelizer. In the mind-set of the Gospel, Francis said in Asunción, Paraguay, in July 2015, "you do not convince people with arguments, strategies or tactics. You convince them by simply learning how to welcome them." As he had earlier put it: "Jesus didn't proselytize, he accompanied. . . . Closeness: that's the program."[17]

Bergoglio's speech at Aparecida named some of what kept the Church distant: laypeople barred from being missionary disciples by clericalism; people with complex personal lives kept from parishes by a black-and-white legalism; the marginalization of young people with a call to service and mission; as well as the isolation and distance of many priests and parishes where the administrative and juridical squeezed out the pastoral. If there is a scarlet thread running through Francis's pastoral reforms it can be found in this list. The task was to remove, one by one, all obstacles to the Church's proximity. Aparecida's concerns—for the Church to become missionary, to promote ecology, to bolster marriage and family and integrate the divorced and remarried, to help young people discover their vocations—have defined Francis's priorities as pope, a list he has steadily been working through since 2013.[18]

"A Catholic faith . . . that does not convert the life of the baptized would not withstand the trials of time," Aparecida warned. What were needed now were five clear directions. First, a discerning, humble response to the change of era that led inevitably to a program of reform. Second, a new kind of pastoral action that could offer the experience of God's mercy and an alternative modernity: the "Kingdom of God." Third, a resolutely missionary refocusing to enable an encounter with Christ, capable of raising up missionary disciples. Fourth, a Church that needed to become a welcoming, warm mother in response to the cold non-belonging of technocracy. And fifth, taking seriously the Church as the people of God, simultaneously evangelizing and evangelized.

It was as if everything in this era of change was geared, after all, not to the steady extinction of Christianity, but to its surprising rebirth.

Arriving at the shrine of Aparecida two years after the death of John Paul II, many church leaders in Latin America had watched with sadness how the

Church in Europe was nervously retreating from the fires it had lit at the Second Vatican Council. The United States offered another kind of desolation: bitter, argumentative, and divided, the Church there seemed to have been captured by a family-values moralism that was defined best by what it was against. But south of the Rio Grande, delegates at Aparecida had their own reasons for feeling discouraged: the sudden rise of Pentecostalism, the lack of formation of laypeople, as well as formidable social challenges.

Down in Buenos Aires, Bergoglio read the Church's difficulty in evangelizing in terms of a spiritual desolation that had led to the loss of what the great Swiss theologian Hans Urs von Balthasar called the "unity of the transcendentals."

The transcendentals in the Catholic tradition are truth, goodness, and beauty, the objects of the human seeking capacities of feeling, thinking, and desire, which are literally embodied in the incarnation of God. By beauty Bergoglio meant not just art and music, which are a vital part of the Christian offer, but the heart-captivating experience of an encounter with Jesus Christ. Beauty is the irruption of the divine in human history and in each human life; beauty is the resurrection; beauty is the unexpected mercy and gratuity of God, the discovery that God is close and concrete. Without beauty, truth and good fossilize, become dry and moralistic—truth without love. Yet without truth, beauty was a lie; without goodness, beauty and truth would be corrupted. The Church could only witness to the real Being of Christ, in short, by keeping together the transcendentals. As Bergoglio put it, "if one element is missing, Being breaks down, becomes idealized, becomes an idea: it is not real. They have to go together, not be split."[19]

Modernity had split them. But now, in postmodernity, with the collapse of the grand narratives of liberalism and Marxism with which Catholicism had entered into a great rivalry for most of the twentieth century, those competing narratives no longer held sway. People no longer wished to debate great abstract truths; they preferred to go shopping. The Uruguayan intellectual close to Bergoglio, Methol Ferré, had observed that the "atheist libertinism" of contemporary consumerism is a way of being that seeks beauty, yet in sundering the quest for beauty from truth and goodness, such culture ends in the shopping mall, in distraction, gratification, and self-indulgence.

Yet the quest for beauty is a sign that humanity is also seeking its source. Such a culture can only be evangelized by a Church that integrates true beauty: the mercy and gratuity of Saint Francis of Assisi or Saint Teresa of Kolkata. It was not by chance that Francis took the name of the first and canonized the second: Mother Teresa and *il poverello* were captivating not because they wrote wonderful books or because of the admirable institutions they founded. It was *who* they were; it was *how* they were. They had had an encounter that changed them. When they spoke of truth and did good, people paid attention; people were captivated. Such Christian witnesses showed what von Balthasar suggested, that precedence matters: the beauty of the encounter unlocks the heart so that truth and goodness can be grasped.

After he became archbishop of Buenos Aires in 1998, Bergoglio began to absorb the idea of the encounter with the beauty of God into his speeches and homilies. He often noted how people thirsted for encounter, how the true end of their beauty seeking was an encounter with Christ, which the Church was called to offer. To be credible in the contemporary world, Christianity had to reintegrate the beauty of mercy into its proclamation of the good and true. It had to become, therefore, a "culture of encounter."[20]

The main obstacle to this proclamation was what Borghesi calls "the moralistic drift that characterizes Catholicism in an era of globalization." It was the main reason that the Church was failing to evangelize, as Benedict XVI had seen, too. Determined to recapture Christianity from the iron cage of dogmatism and moralism, Benedict had written a famous line at the start of his first encyclical, *Deus Caritas Est* (God Is Love) in 2005, in which he declared that "being Christian is not the result of an ethical choice or a lofty idea, but the encounter with an event, a person, which gives life a new horizon and a decisive direction." The quote is repeated twice in the Aparecida document and again in *Evangelii Gaudium*, where Francis says he never tires of repeating the statement, which takes us to "the very heart of the Gospel."[21]

As pope, Francis has spoken of *el encuentro primario*, the "primary encounter." Aparecida called it *el encuentro fundante*, the "foundational encounter," and describes the amazement of the disciples at the "exceptional quality of the one speaking to them, especially how he treated them, satisfying the hunger and thirst for life that was in their hearts." Aparecida spelled out the different ways of having this meeting with Christ: in the sacraments, liturgies, prayer, and contemplation of Scripture. But the document also spoke of the encounter *outside*, in popular culture and among the poor. In *Evangelii Gaudium* Francis described popular religiosity as "a true expression of the spontaneous missionary activity of the people of God," and he gave the example of a mother of a sick child praying not in a church or even a sanctuary but in her humble house, gazing with love at a crucifix.

This focus on the "faith encounter with the person of Jesus" didn't just catalyze the bishops at Aparecida; it also united them, a sign of the action of the Holy Spirit. Professor Rodrigo Guerra López, who was at Aparecida as part of a CELAM think tank, witnessed how "the idea of going back to the roots, to the source, to a personal encounter with the concrete person of Jesus Christ . . . appealed to bishops from different parts of the Church: to the pastoralists as well as the more doctrinally focused, as well as to those close to the Charismatic Renewal and the other church movements."[22]

For Mexican cardinal Carlos Aguiar Retes, who was on Bergoglio's drafting team at Aparecida, this reorientation marked a clear shift. The call now was "to announce the Kingdom, not a morality. The morality is a consequence." Where for centuries the Church's pastoral action was geared to imparting the knowledge of doctrine and the fulfillment of commandments, now "we have to be worried first about discovering God, this God of mercy who opens His doors to you, and this God of mercy that you have to communicate." The Church needed "to offer an experience of life which is fulfilled in us; and we have to show that mercy." That way of mercy—the way of beauty, of encounter—was nothing less, Aguiar Retes told me, than "the evangelizing strategy of Jesus."[23]

In *Evangelii Gaudium*, Francis moved decisively to emancipate the Church from the ethicists, to make clear that Christianity was not "a titanic effort of the will, the effort of someone who decides to be consistent and succeeds," as he had put it in a 2001 speech. "No. Christian morality is simply a response. It is the heartfelt response to a surprising, unforeseeable, 'unjust' mercy. . . . This is why the Christian conception of morality is a revolution; it is not a never falling down but an always getting up again." A few months before his election, in November 2012, he gave an example: the adulterous woman saved from stoning by Jesus in chapter 8 of John's Gospel. The Gospel does not say whether she returned to her sinful, promiscuous life, said Bergoglio, but "you can be sure that she didn't, because whoever encounters such great mercy cannot deviate from the law. It's the consequence."[24]

Was it because Christian morality was so often reduced to an ethical idea and a lofty precept, Bergoglio wondered, that contemporary humanity had succumbed to relativism, in which man becomes the measure of what is good and bad? Instead of condemning relativism, the Church had to realize that "only the presence of a God who loves and saves us will catch people's attention." That was also what Benedict XVI saw, says Cardinal Donald Wuerl, former archbishop of Washington, D.C., who chaired the October 2012 synod on the new evangelization. Benedict called the synod because the Church had "overcomplicated" its message, taking refuge in the comfort zone of an ethical response precisely at the time when it most needed to witness to the transforming effect of the encounter with a loving and merciful God. "Benedict was saying to that synod: 'Pay attention!' You have to look and you have to speak differently," he recalls, adding that this was precisely what Francis has done.[25]

Benedict saw that the Church had to restore the primacy of the encounter, of grace and mercy, and that Latin America, after Aparecida, would be the source of that transformation. "Benedict believed it was still time to open up paths, it was the right moment for Latin America," recalls the Mexican cardinal, Carlos Aguiar Retes, who was with Benedict on his visit to León, Mexico, in March 2012, when the German pope made the decision to step down. Benedict had seen in Aparecida that the Church's future was in Latin America, and he expected his successor to come from there. He didn't know it would be Bergoglio, yet after he stepped down in 2013 to allow the transition to take place, he had a quick word with the archbishop of Buenos Aires as he arrived in Rome for the conclave, reminding him he was under obedience, and that if elected, he had to accept.[26]

In its sharp critiques and passionate, joyful prose, *Evangelii Gaudium* opened the doors of the universal Church to Aparecida's Pentecost wind, shattering its defensive winter palaces of ethicism and desolation. It was impossible to pick up Francis's November 2013 exhortation and fail to notice a new tone. Some called it *pastoralità* (pastorality); others said it breathed the Holy Spirit. It was close, concrete, and personal. It was human, joyful, and energetic. It wasn't about deploring or lamenting, but changing and acting.

Evangelii Gaudium barely mentioned the Second Vatican Council, yet virtually every page took it for granted. It skirted around the postconciliar debates by neither seeing the Church as an island of grace in a world of sin, nor expressing optimism about modernity, but going to the heart of Vatican II's vision of a Samaritan Church walking lovingly alongside humanity. But Francis was also unafraid to incorporate developments since the Council. One of these was the Catholic Charismatic Renewal, the Pentecostal-type movement that had exploded in the Church since the 1970s, emphasizing worship, spiritual gifts, and the expectation of surprises.

In the years running up to Aparecida in Buenos Aires, Bergoglio had grown close to the Renewal and used to pray often with evangelical pastors. Aparecida's concluding document spoke in classically charismatic terms of the need for a personal encounter with Christ and the role played by the Holy Spirit (mentioned forty-four times) in opening minds and hearts to God's law. Now, in *Evangelii Gaudium*, he sought to restore the place of the Holy Spirit that had been diminished over the centuries by a lopsided focus on freedom from sin rather than the new life in Christ that followed conversion. In close to fifty references to the Holy Spirit and its freedom, fearlessness, and newness, and using classically Pentecostal language such as "personal encounter with the saving love of Jesus," *Evangelii Gaudium* showed that the Renewal was now at the heart of the universal Church. At Pentecost 2019, Francis gave that idea concrete expression when he launched a Vatican-erected body under the Dicastery for Laity, Family and Life called CHARIS to promote and unify the international Charismatic Renewal. The new body signaled the desire of the Church's first charismatic pope that the Renewal be a "current of Grace" for the whole Church.[27]

There was also a core Ignatian understanding in *Evangelii Gaudium* that the joyless moralism of so much Christianity and its inability to evangelize were the result of a resistance to the promptings of the Spirit that came from turning away from Christ. The "sweet joy of evangelizing," said Francis in *Evangelii Gaudium*, followed an openness to the promptings of the Holy Spirit, "who frees us from self-centeredness cloaked in an outward religiosity bereft of God"—in Ignatian terms, from desolation into consolation. That self-centeredness, the result of fleeing from modernity into a refuge of ideology and identity, had led many to feel queasy at all this talk of trusting the Spirit. "It is like being plunged into the deep and not knowing what we will find. I myself have frequently experienced this," Francis sympathized. But faith called for trust. There was "no greater freedom than that of allowing oneself to be guided by the Holy Spirit . . . letting him enlighten, guide and direct us, leading us wherever he wills."[28]

Francis saw *Evangelii Gaudium* as "the evangelizing breath that the Church seeks to have today," an updating of Saint Paul VI's great 1975 exhortation, *Evangelii Nuntiandi*, in the light of the experience of Aparecida. It was a bold bid to restore the centrality of grace and encounter—words that each appear about thirty times in the document—to the Church's proclamation, while organizing a full-frontal assault on the obstacle to that goal, the moralistic deviation of "Christians who know doctrine but lack faith" and "who think of the faith as a system of ideas, as an ideology."[29]

Rather than simply tell Catholics where the Church had gone wrong, he invited them to see for themselves. If, as *Evangelii Gaudium* began, "the joy of the Gospel fills the hearts and lives of all who encounter Jesus," why did the Church so often appear grim-faced and detached? How had faith degenerated into ideology?

Ideology, in a famous definition by the theologian Karl Rahner, is "a fundamental closure in the face of the 'wholeness' of reality, one that turns a partial aspect into an absolute." In Christianity, it means more importance is placed on doctrines and laws than on Christ himself; a static view of the Church and its doctrine as unchangeable, outside history; institutional pride, including a reluctance to admit mistakes and weaknesses; and a tribal mentality that defines itself by who is outside and what it is against. In a 2008 address in Buenos Aires, Bergoglio had defined fundamentalism as a neurotic reaction to instability and uncertainty, an inability to trust reality. "Whoever takes refuge in fundamentalism is a person who is afraid to set out in search of the truth," he observed. "He already 'has' the truth; he has acquired it and now uses it for his defense, because he sees any questioning as a form of aggression against him."[30]

Now, in *Evangelii Gaudium*, Francis challenged "those who long for a monolithic body of doctrine guarded by all and leaving no room for nuance." He warned that where the God of love is obscured it is because "doctrinal or moral points based on specific ideological options" are being preached instead of the Gospel. And he pointed to those "who trust in their own powers and feel superior to others because they observe certain rules or remain intransigently faithful to a particular Catholic style of the past."

This stung in the Anglo-Saxon world above all. Just as many reactionaries of the nineteenth century had become Catholic more out of fear of revolutionary liberalism than a love for Christ, so a number of high-profile converts in the UK and the United States had openly argued that for conservatives in this age, the Catholic Church was a natural home for refugees from liberal Protestantism and secular relativism. But Francis wasn't Pius IX. He wasn't going to allow reactionary lobbies to turn the Church into a fortress. "In some people," Francis observed, "we see an ostentatious preoccupation for the liturgy, for doctrine and for the Church's prestige, but without any concern that the Gospel have a real impact on God's faithful people and the concrete needs of the present time." This, he wrote, is "a tremendous corruption disguised as a good." It may be dressed in Catholic clothes, and be punctilious about tradition and doctrine, but the rigidity, pride, and self-righteous moralism of "closed and elite groups" shows that their proclamation lacks the truth of Christ Himself, who may have withdrawn to draw strength from prayer, but who never turned His back on the world.[31]

Evangelii Gaudium also pulled the rug out from under the conservatives' diagnosis of the Church and modernity. Prominent commentators had long argued that the Church's post-1960s decline was a result of its excessive compromise with the contemporary age following the Second Vatican Council, to which the solution was to restore obedience, loyalty, and fidelity to tradition—in other words, a restoration. But Francis saw the cause of the Church's shrinking in its self-enclosure, its retreat from the world into a distant, moralistic, and self-serving institution. The need for the "primary encounter" with Christ demanded bringing to the forefront the Good News of a forgiving God whose healing love is not a reward for good behavior but "precedes any moral and religious obligation on our part." Evangelization "should not impose the truth but appeal to freedom" and "should be marked by joy, encouragement, liveliness" as well as attitudes on the part of the evangelizer such as "approachability, readiness for dialogue, patience, a warmth and welcome which is non-judgmental."

Francis also called for a "poor Church, for the poor," to go out as sheep among wolves. Converted by mercy, a poor Church would seek every chance to offer what it had freely received, mercy, by "touching the suffering flesh of Christ in others." For what best communicates "the heart of the Gospel," said Francis, are "works of love directed to one's neighbor." *Evangelii Gaudium* emphasized in particular two signs of the Kingdom of God in today's world: the inclusion of the poor and the need for dialogue in society, both themes stressed in Aparecida's discernment of the "change of era."[32]

What mattered was to go out. When he was with Italian church leaders in May 2016, Francis quoted a Brazilian bishop who in his era was the icon of an evangelizing, charismatic Church of the poor: "When your boat starts to put down roots in the calm of the pier, set out to sea." What Hélder Câmara meant, said Francis, was not that you have a mission to fulfill but that you are essentially a missionary, for "in the encounter with Jesus you have experienced the fullness of life, and therefore you desire with your whole being that others recognize themselves in Him."[33]

To consider how much Jorge Mario Bergoglio has changed over the years, ask Mario J. Paredes. The Chilean-born, New York–based Hispanic leader and entrepreneur was taught by Bergoglio back in the late 1960s, around the time of the Jesuit's ordination as priest, at the Universidad del Salvador in Buenos Aires. Paredes recalls Bergoglio as a standout figure, a formidable teacher, widely read and deeply knowledgeable about culture, a refined man (*un hombre exquisito*) in every sense. But warm and approachable he was not. Paredes recalls an unsmiling figure: ascetic, disciplined, courteous, taciturn, distant.

In 2010 he met Bergoglio, by this time a cardinal, in Buenos Aires, at the presentation of a new edition of the Bible, and met a very different man: compassionate and concerned for the poor, but still reserved and slightly glum. Then, three years later, he met Francis in Rome a week after his election, in the company of a delegation of the Catholic Association of Latino Leaders (the meeting had been in Benedict's diary; Francis kept it) and was bowled over by the further transformation. The warm, gracious, smiling, joyful, tactile person he encountered was almost another person altogether, between-the-eyes proof of the grace of the papal office.[34]

The story of Bergoglio's metamorphosis has been told often, in competing narratives that do not always agree on who he was before, nor how and what changed, or when. Too many stories rest on one-dimensional snapshots: as provincial and rector, he could be very serious, and a little dour, yet also (as the people of San Miguel remember) a lot of fun; authoritarian, yes, but compassionate and close to people. Argentines remember his scowl as archbishop of Buenos Aires—that was certainly his public image—yet in the shantytowns of Buenos Aires they say he was as he is now: warm, smiling, delighting in people.

But all can agree he has changed—often. The Córdoba "exile" in his fifties and his subsequent ministry as auxiliary bishop were years of suffering that softened him. Politically, the economic collapse of 2001–2002 led him to assume an outspoken, prophetic role on political and justice matters that contrasted with his time as Jesuit provincial, when he steered his order away from collaborating with organizations seeking social change. As a Jesuit, he had been hostile to the Charismatic Renewal, saying you couldn't replace liturgy with a "samba school." But as cardinal he embraced it, encouraging mass Catholic-evangelical meetings, praying in the charismatic style, and displaying a marked new boldness and reliance on the Holy Spirit. The Pentecost experience of Aparecida in 2007 produced in him a new stage: a conviction that Latin America now had a continental mission to the universal Church, and that he was the servant of that call. At the end of all these changes came the greatest of all: an experience of light and freedom on the night of his election in March 2013, which changed him in ways that amazed people like Paredes who had known him in Buenos Aires.

Cardinal John Henry Newman, canonized by Francis in October 2019, famously observed that "to live is to change" and that "to be perfect is to have changed often." What matters in the spiritual life is ultimately this openness to be changed, which requires trust—or as Christians say, "faith." What blocks it is the fleeing from this openness: trusting, rather, in ideology, structures, or an idealized sense of self. A saint is one who has moved out from those "false" selves to become what God calls her to be.

Because he was at one time prone to it, Francis is quick to spot this rigidity in the young, especially in those who never knew the liturgy prior to the Second Vatican Council yet idealize it. It was important not to reject restorationists but reach out to them, as Benedict XVI had, but there could be no going back on the inculturated liturgy of the Second Vatican Council. "To speak of the reform of the reform is an error," Francis told Father Spadaro. He added: "Sometimes I've met very rigid people . . . and I've wondered: why this rigidity? If you scratch a little, you find that the rigidity always conceals something: insecurity, but also other things."[35]

They should "pay attention when a seminarian takes refuge in rigidity: this always covers up something bad," he told the Italian bishops. The rigid are seeking out strong structures to compensate for their insecurity, and "when they feel confident the illness begins to emerge." Rigid, authoritarian types are to be avoided in selecting candidates to the priesthood; it was better to accept "a muddled young man with normal problems, who gets on people's nerves, for all his contradictions will help him to grow," he told Dominique Wolton.

Francis also warned bishops against accepting men into seminaries who could be unchaste or part of a gay subculture: "if you have the slightest doubt, it's better to refuse them," he said. In a book interview in 2018 he repeated the warning: "Homosexuality is a very serious issue that must be adequately discerned from the beginning with the candidates, if that is the case," he said, for priests and religious are called to "live in complete celibacy," and it is "better that they leave the ministry or their consecrated life than that they live a double life."[36]

The context of the remarks suggested that Francis was concerned above all with open displays of "gay behavior." He mentioned a bishop who in response to discovering a network of gay priests in his diocese had reformed the seminaries, as well as a religious superior concerned by gay men in his congregation expressing their affection with each other. Francis clearly approved of the first example, and in relation to the second had insisted that "this kind of affection has no place" in the priesthood and religious life. In each case, Francis saw not just sinful behavior but self-serving cliques, signs of clericalism. But critics pointed out that he didn't appear to acknowledge that as long as the Church made it impossible for clergy to admit they were gay, the "ecclesiastical closet"—a major component of that clericalism—would continue.[37]

To counter clericalism meant better discernment of vocations and formation. Badly formed priests whose hearts are not changed in seminary turn out to be "little monsters" who then "shape the people of God," Francis warned at a meeting of religious orders in 2014, adding, "this really gives me goose bumps." To the Jesuits in Myanmar, he said the principal criterion for assessing a vocation was "Can the candidate discern? Will he learn to discern? If he knows how to discern, he knows how to recognize what comes from God and what comes from the bad spirit, then this is enough for him to go on. Even if he does not understand much, even if they fail him at the exams . . . it is OK, as long as he knows spiritual discernment."[38]

"Discernment" appeared thirty-seven times in new guidelines for the training of priests published at the end of 2016 by the Vatican's Congregation for the Clergy. The first major makeover of priestly formation in more than three decades, at the heart of document, called "The Gift of the Priestly Vocation," was not some heroic, idealized notion of the priest as a spiritual executive or moral policeman but humility, docility to the Holy Spirit, and capacity for change. "The gradual inner growth along the journey of formation," the document boldly declared, "should principally be aimed at making the future priest a 'man of discernment,' able to read the reality of human life in the light of the Spirit. In this way he will be able to choose, decide and act according to the will of God." It wasn't enough to know the right things. Francis needed priests who knew God.

Discernment is likewise front and center of both the process of deciding to become a priest and the training that should be given by seminaries. That means one-on-one "personal accompaniment" in order "to carry out vocational discernment and to form the missionary disciple." The priest of the future "by listening and careful discernment of situations" learns to walk with people in their complex realities, "showing the beauty and demands of Gospel truth without falling into legalistic or rigorist obsessions."[39]

Wherever there is fervor and a desire to bring Christ to others, said Francis in *Evangelii Gaudium*, "genuine vocations will arise." But, he told the German weekly *Die Zeit*, lack of priestly vocations is "an enormous problem" in many parts of the world. "How many seminaries, churches and monasteries will be closed in the coming years due to a lack of vocations?" Francis rhetorically asked the Italian bishops, describing Europe as a land once "fertile and generous" in producing priests and nuns, that was now in a period of "vocation sterility."[40]

He was aware of pressures to introduce a married priesthood, which was a matter of discipline rather than doctrine; in the first three centuries of Christianity, there had been no norms in favor or against, and priests were married. In later centuries, many were married before committing to continence when they became priests. Today, too, there are formerly Anglican, married Catholic clergy, and marriage can be chosen by priests in the twenty-three Eastern Rite (formerly Orthodox) Churches in communion with Rome. But Francis shares the views of most bishops that celibacy should remain obligatory for those choosing priesthood in the Latin Church. Lived prayerfully, it is a gift and source of growth, the best vessel for a Christ-like availability for service and mission. "I won't do it," he told reporters on the plane from Panama who asked about the possibility in January 2019. "I don't want to appear before God with this decision."[41]

But where the pastoral need was overwhelming and the alternative was a lack of sacraments, he was open to it in remote mission areas such as Amazonia. Brazil's bishops at the synod on the Eucharist in 2005 had floated a proposal to ordain *viri probati*—that is, men of proven virtue, who would in most cases be older and married—in areas such as Pará, where the diocese of Xingu had just twenty-seven priests to cover eight hundred parishes in an area the size of Germany. After they petitioned Francis in 2014, he encouraged them to develop proposals that could then be considered at the synod of October 2019 on Amazonia. On the flight from Panama, Francis cited the "interesting" argument put forward by some theologians that ordinations of *viri probati* would confer the power to sanctify but not the other two powers (governing and teaching), saying it was something "to study, to think, and to pray about." He was always open if there was a precedent. "In the Church it is always important to recognize the right moment, to recognize when the Holy Spirit demands something," Francis told *Die Zeit*.[42]

Yet the Aparecida–*Evangelii Gaudium* vision of renewal didn't depend solely on more and better priests, but on raising up "missionary disciples" in general, some of whom would choose priesthood or religious orders. That meant creating a culture in the Church in which young people were helped to discern God's calling to them whatever their state of life. In choosing for the synod of October 2018 the theme of vocational discernment and young people, Francis wanted to make clear that all young people had "the right to be guided in life's journey," as the synod's preparatory document put it. In following God's will, wherever that might be, lay the source of happiness and fulfillment. But discernment was a skill that had to be practiced, and learned, with help from guides. Using the three verbs in *Evangelii Gaudium* "to recognize," "to interpret," and "to choose," the document made clear that discernment required "the hard, personal experience of interpreting the movements of the heart to recognize the action of the Spirit."[43]

"Discernment" appeared forty-eight times in the synod's concluding document, which had two whole chapters dedicated to the "mission to accompany" and the "art of discernment." Rejecting a crude notion of conscience that was common among the rigorists as merely the mechanism for applying rules and norms, the document portrayed conscience as the seat of human desire for truth, goodness, and beauty, which were discovered fully in the free encounter with Christ. Finding God's will was the way Jesus helped others; the Church's mission was to do the same. That could be almost anywhere: in prayer, retreats, pilgrimages, and Bible reading, but also in "the fraternal experience of life in common" as well as in "the encounter with the poor with whom the Lord Jesus identifies."[44]

It isn't good enough to divide people into worthy and unworthy; what is needed, Francis said in *Evangelii Gaudium*, is attentiveness to "God's saving love, which is mysteriously at work in each person, above and beyond their faults and failings." To show the face of Christ, the Church would need to walk with people as they progressed in the spiritual life by degrees, attentive to the conditions and limitations life imposes, recognizing that "a small step, in the midst of great human limitations, can be more pleasing to God than a life which appears outwardly in order but moves through the day without confronting great difficulties."[45]

Francis knew this would involve a rethinking of the black-and-white, one-size-fits-all approach that had come to characterize so much seminary formation. "The Church will have to initiate everyone—priests, religious, laity—into this 'art of accompaniment' which teaches us to remove our sandals before the sacred ground of the other," he said, before calling for compassionate listeners who could awaken "the desire to respond fully to God's love and to bring to fruition what he has sowed in our lives."[46]

A German missionary appointed to head a remote territory in southern Peru came to Rome in 2017 to attend a "baby bishops" course, where he met 114 other newly minted successors to the apostles. Bishop Reinhold Nann was struck by how few university theologians, canon lawyers, and "church managers" there were among them, and how most were, like him, practical pastors. It struck him that "Francis has triggered a sea change, a kind of return to the Gospel message. Suddenly, the poor and outsiders—but also the pastor of souls (*Seelsorger*) who goes out to the peripheries—find themselves center stage."[47]

Francis's *Seelsorger* bishops are often contrasted in news reports with the "culture-warrior" types favored by his two predecessors. It is a shift that some conservatives, fearful of accommodation or assimilation, misread as softening the Church's prophetic, countercultural witness. Yet for Francis the issue is the proclamation of the Gospel in its integrity, not carved up to suit ideology or traded in pursuit of political gains. He wants that proclamation to rely not on the power of words but on the power of its own attractiveness; the Gospel should be proposed and not imposed. The Church "does not need apologists for her causes nor crusaders for her battles but rather humble and confident sowers of the Truth," he told the Vatican's Congregation for Bishops. A bishop was, first, a "witness to the Risen One," who safeguards doctrine "not to measure how distant the world is from it, but to fascinate the world, to captivate it with the beauty of love, and seduce it with the freedom that the Gospel gives."[48]

When Saint John Paul II addressed the U.S. bishops in Chicago in October 1979, he stressed loyalty to papal authority and fearless orthodoxy in the public square. Thirty-five years later, in September 2015, Francis in Washington, D.C., warned bishops against "making . . . the Cross a banner of worldly struggles" and a temptation "to think back on bygone times and to devise harsh responses to fierce opposition." He was warning against temptations in desolation—to lament and condemn—as well as against putting their faith in the power of money, law, and the blandishments of politicians.

The Church grows, he told the bishops in Mexico City's cathedral in February 2016, by embodying mercy and through close contact with its faithful people, not by the "seductive illusion of underhand agreements." Unless they could speak to people of knowing Jesus, "then the words with which we recall Him will be rhetorical and empty figures of speech . . . mere babbling orphans behind a tomb." He told Colombia's bishops in Bogotá in September 2017 that they were neither technicians nor politicians but pastors. "I ask you to keep your gazes always fixed on concrete men and women," he told them. "Do not talk about 'man,' but about human persons, loved by God and composed of flesh and bones, history, faith, feelings, disappointments, frustrations, sorrows and hurts."[49]

For John Paul II, the nonnegotiable criteria were loyalty, courage, and obedience. He appointed many manager-type bishops, strong on discipline, and canon lawyers and ethicists who could fearlessly articulate clear arguments. Benedict XVI preferred to appoint good teachers, leading to a disproportionate number of theologians. But Francis took a different approach. A great theologian or intellectual or lawyer can always be sent to teach at a university or to staff a diocesan office, Francis made clear to the nuncios, but if he wasn't also a pastor, he shouldn't head a diocese. "It can't just be: Does this person have a doctorate or has this person had experience governing?" says Cardinal Wuerl, who since resigning as Archbishop of Washington, D.C., continues to sit on the Congregation for Bishops. "Francis is saying, add into that: Does this person have pastoral experience? Does he demonstrate pastoral skill?"[50]

Wuerl is one of an all-important body of between twenty and thirty cardinals from around the world who fly to Rome twice a month for the so-called Thursday Table at the Vatican's bishop-making department. Among other English-speaking members of the Congregation are Blase Cupich of Chicago and Vincent Nichols of Westminster; while Cardinals Rubén Salazar of Bogotá, Colombia; Francisco Robles Ortega of Guadalajara, Mexico; and Juan José Omella of Barcelona pick bishops for the Spanish-language world. The Table also includes key curial cardinals: Pietro Parolin, the secretary of state; Beniamino Stella from the Congregation for the Clergy; and Lorenzo Baldisseri, secretary general of the synod.

The pope cannot know more than a few of the hundred-some new bishops he appoints each year, and he relies therefore on the decisions of these cardinals, who sift reports and shortlists from papal nuncios who have taken soundings in the local Church, sizing up who among the up-and-coming clergy might one day be among the successors of the first apostles. There are more than five thousand bishops in the world, and every year many hundreds reach the age of seventy-five, when they must offer their resignations. Some are replaced immediately, others after more years of active service.

But the pope can be clear about the criteria they should use: that bishops be "shepherds close to their people," pastors who "smell of sheep," watchful men who can nurture their flocks. The nuncios and the Congregation of Bishops know the pope has a particular horror of ambitious, worldly bishops with a princely, clericalist mentality, and they are on the lookout for "gentle, patient and merciful" pastors who love poverty in both the interior sense of having the freedom to follow the Lord's will, as well as the external sense, of living lives of simplicity and austerity. In February 2014, Francis urged the Congregation to cast their nets wider, citing the prophet Samuel, who, in seeking Saul's successor as Israel's king, rejected the sons Jesse offered him and sent instead for the youngest, absent one. "Little Davids" had to be truffled out: "it's not enough to go fishing in the fish ponds, on the reserve, or in the nursery of 'friends of friends,'" Francis warned.[51]

In October 2016, the C9 made changes to the questionnaire used by nuncios to assess bishop candidates. Alongside the usual questions about loyalty to the magisterium, prayerfulness, and their ability to teach and govern, the new questionnaire asked: Do they embrace poverty and live simply? Are they content to stay in the chancery, or do they go out in search of people in need? Are they pastors, rather than managers? These changes, according to one briefing, were intended to make the process more "pastoral," "biblically inspired," and "spiritually based."

A corollary of closeness was stability. The Council of Trent's demand that bishops be resident in their dioceses is more relevant now than ever in an age of liquidity, Francis told the Congregation in 2014. He urged newly appointed heads of dioceses not to give "the scandal of 'airport bishops,'" dashing around the world. "The flock needs to find a place in their Pastor's heart," he told them; if not, the bishop will be constantly buffeted by the waves as he searches for an ephemeral compensation, and he will offer no shelter. As ever, Francis asked no one to do what he had not done. As archbishop, he had seldom left Buenos Aires, and when he did, he usually cut short his visits to get back to his "spouse." As pope, he has set an example by remaining in Rome during the summer heat, going neither to the papal summer palace of Castel Gandolfo nor to the mountains, as popes traditionally have done.[52]

But he didn't mean that bishops should stay behind a desk. Speaking to Latin American bishops in Bogotá, Colombia, in September 2017, Francis urged them to follow the example of the sixteenth-century Peruvian saint Toribio de Mogrovejo, who spent eighteen of his twenty-four years as archbishop of Lima touring his vast diocese, which at the time extended from Panama to Chile. Francis takes seriously his role as Bishop of Rome and makes frequent surprise visits to poor parishes or centers that care for the vulnerable, and there are usually parishioners from the city's parishes at his seven a.m. Mass in the Santa Marta. He greets them warmly afterward, standing at the door like a village parish priest. Their bishop may be the pope, but he can still carry the smell of his flock.[53]

Because of the intimate link between the Bishop of Rome and the Church in Italy, the pope traditionally appoints the president and the secretary general of Italy's powerful bishops' conference (CEI). Francis offered to renounce this right, but the Italian bishops, after discussing the matter, opted for the status quo. So he asked the CEI president, Cardinal Angelo Bagnasco of Genoa, to poll the bishops on their favorites for the secretary general role. Bagnasco came back with a list of front-runner consensus candidates, which Francis, taking his cue from the prophet Samuel, ignored, stunning the Church in Italy in December 2013 by naming a man who was reportedly last on the list.

Bishop Nunzio Galantino, until then shepherd of the obscure Calabrian diocese of Cassano all'Jonio, liked to be called "Don Nunzio" rather than "Your Grace." He lived in the seminary rather than in the bishop's palace, and he asked the people of his diocese before his installation to give money to the poor rather than gifts to him. In appointing Galantino for a full five-year term as secretary general (Francis has since put him in charge of APSA), the pope was making a dramatic statement, matched only by his May 2017 choice of Cardinal Gualtiero Bassetti of Perugia-Città della Pieve as CEI president to replace Bagnasco. Bassetti is clearly an *Evangelii Gaudium* kind of bishop, who gets out of the sacristy and into the street, not confining himself to the catechetical and sacramental but evangelizing. He also sits on the Congregation for Bishops, playing a key role in what has been the biggest shepherd makeover of any local Church: half of the bishops of Italy's excessive 226 dioceses have been appointed by Francis.

These appointments are key to Francis's attempts to wean the CEI—which manages vast sums of money and is a major player in Italian public life—off culture wars and power strategies. The result was that in 2016 the CEI barely mobilized against civil unions (including for gay couples) as it had in 2007, while maintaining its clear opposition to adoption by same-sex couples. The so-called Progetto Culturale, an attempt to win back political and social elites devised by Cardinal Camillo Ruini (an ally of Sodano), has been dropped.

In contrast with the heavyweight, fiery intellectual Cardinal Angelo Scola, Francis named Mario Delpini as archbishop of Milan in July 2017. A priest of the diocese, Delpini is a man of spartan habits who rides a bicycle and as vicar-general lived in a modest home for retired clergy. Known as a good preacher who has written a pastoral guide that warns priests against clericalism, Delpini was nonetheless Scola's right-hand man, illustrating the point that in establishing guidelines for choosing bishops Francis was not attempting to impose a theology as much as a way of being a shepherd.[54]

Another Church in Europe that has strongly felt the Francis makeover has been Spain, the country Benedict XVI most had in mind when he called the synod of 2012 to consider how to re-evangelize secular Western nations. Francis knew the mind-set of the Spanish episcopate from giving a retreat to the bishops in 2006, and he was horrified by the princely trappings of some of its leaders, not least Madrid's archbishop, Cardinal Antonio María Rouco Varela, an immensely powerful figure who was close to Sodano and who is reported after the 2013 election of Francis to have said: "The conclave escaped us." Rouco was an icon of the angry gloom school, claiming at the 2012 synod that the Church in Spain had become a victim of a 1930s-style persecution, when priests were killed in large numbers and churches burned. He epitomized the victimism and desolation of the Church in Europe, blaming the culture for the Church's failure to evangelize.[55]

Within months of Francis's election, the pope replaced Rouco with Cardinal Carlos Osoro. "The Church is not persecuted in Spain, nor is it boxed in, nor is it afraid to go out to meet people where they are," the new archbishop of Madrid told *El País*. Cardinal Osoro is a man of dialogue, close to his people, approachable and affable, who has made care and advocacy for migrants a priority. He describes mercy as the "main beam" upholding the Church, and he has struck a new public tone of service and humility. "As a bishop," he says, "I come to proclaim Christ to all, and no one is further away than anyone else."[56]

Francis's bishops are striking a whole new tone in public life: of welcome and dialogue, rather than imperious condemnation. That means continuing to speak out on beginning-and-end-of-life issues such as abortion and euthanasia but also raising their voice on "midlife" humanitarian challenges, above all unemployment and migration, as well as ecology. The Osoro-Omella approach reflects *Evangelii Gaudium*'s understanding that the Church credibly preaches the Gospel more in its concrete attention to the poor than in its focus on legislative or ethical issues. "If those on the margins—spiritually and socially—do not find in the Church concrete commitment to action to assist them," Omella warned in Rome in 2017, "our message of prayer and catechesis and preaching ends up hollow." As a member of the Congregation of Bishops, he will help appoint close to half of the heads of the country's 116 dioceses over the next decade as a generation of bishops come up for retirement.[57]

The press dubbed Francis's Spanish appointees *obispos todoterreno*, "four-wheel-drive bishops," because they were willing to be out in all terrains and in all weather. In March 2016 the magazine *Vida Nueva* quoted a bishop describing how the Church is becoming "closer to the people, more ordinary, more merciful, more willing to dialogue." In line with the Spanish bishops' conference's 2016–2020 *Evangelii Gaudium*–inspired pastoral plan for "spiritual renewal and pastoral conversion," Cardinal Ricardo Blázquez called for Catholics to go out onto the street, "because the Gospel shines brightly wherever the sick are healed, the poor are treated by attending their many kinds of poverty, when sinners are treated with compassion."[58]

Among the episcopal appointments that best signal this shift toward "pastorality," the one-two punch of December 2017 stands out, when Francis filled two of global Catholicism's foremost posts in one swoop. He named Aparecida prime mover Carlos Aguiar Retes to head the world's largest diocese, Mexico City (population 9 million), and tapped Michel Aupetit, a medical doctor and bioethicist by background, to head the archdiocese of Paris (population 1.3 million). Both have taken their flagship dioceses in a strongly missionary direction. In his first message, Cardinal Aguiar spoke of the change of era demanding a pastoral renewal to move from "a flock that seeks the services of its shepherds" to "a community of missionary disciples where we all seek, in communion, to proclaim and transmit the Good News of God's Kingdom." Aupetit told his priests that an increasingly liquid society called for "a permanent adaptability to citizens in their work and in their way of life," and he announced the creation of a center to coordinate and promote missions throughout the diocese.[59]

The changes in Mexico City are particularly worth observing as a sign of the future. As the former CELAM secretary general, Aguiar had worked closely with Bergoglio in the Aparecida drafting team, and nowhere outside Buenos Aires has Aparecida been applied as vigorously as it was in Aguiar's former diocese of Tlalnepantla, in the outskirts of Mexico City. Hundreds of missions led women, young people, and the poor to become active as missionary disciples, and vocations to the priesthood and religious life doubled. Aguiar was also key to developing the Mexican bishops' response to the papal visit in February 2016, which commits them to developing an *Iglesia pueblo* to overcome clericalism and timidity, attend to the "loss of roots" of Mexican society, and to become a welcoming Church close to its people. The bishops' document, "Towards an Encounter with

Christ Redeemer," also committed the bishops to a fearless defense of their people from drug cartels and to speak up on human rights, inequality, and corruption.[60]

It was, however, in Lima, Peru, that Francis made his most dramatic appointment, replacing the reactionary, aristocratic Opus Dei cardinal Juan Luis Cipriani with his mirror opposite: Father Carlos Castillo Mattasoglio, a theology professor and humble pastor from one of Lima's shantytowns. Cipriani, a longtime energetic opponent of the option for the poor, was one of only 2 out of 133 at Aparecida said to have voted against the concluding document, before leaving the general conference in high dudgeon. Francis's appointment of Father Castillo—a parish priest who was a disciple of liberation theology's founding father Gustavo Gutiérrez—was the ecclesiastical equivalent of a hand-brake turn, not least because it was announced within a record twenty-five days of Cipriani's turning seventy-five.[61]

Castillo arrived for his March 2019 installation in Lima's cathedral from across the Rimac River and the church of San Lázaro, once attached to a leper hospital, symbolically connecting the center to what he called "the other bank." He said he wanted to create a church that was close to the people struggling in the flimsy houses and sleeping on cardboard, "the suffering Christs" who were calling them to be what Francis called "a field-hospital Church." In his first homily he asked Catholics to answer three questions: What in their heart of hearts did they want the Church in Lima to improve on? What "main peripheries" were the clergy called to attend to? And what forms should Lima's missionary Church take on in order to be a sign of hope?

At an earlier press conference to introduce his successor, Cipriani insisted to journalists that Francis's appointment should not be read as support for "liberation theology" while kicking out "the Opus Dei reactionary"; that would be to reduce the Church to a "henhouse" rather than the "body of Christ," he said. It was a gracious attempt at smoothing over the differences, but failed to convince.[62]

When it comes to Francis's "Little David" policy of naming peripheral figures to high Church office in order to overturn clericalism and careerism, nothing has been so eye-catching as his choice of cardinals. Known as "red hats" after their scarlet birettas, cardinals are advisers to the pope who vow to support his mission. They also directly determine the future direction of the Church, when those who are under eighty years of age at the time of a pope's death or resignation, normally around 120 of them, gather in conclave to elect his successor. The task of picking new "electors" as old ones reach the voting age limit is therefore among a pope's most important and delicate tasks. By changing the criteria for their selection to incorporate men on the missionary margins, Francis has carried out what is arguably, along with synodality, his most far-reaching reform.

In yearly consistories—ceremonies that confer the scarlet hats and titular churches in Rome on those the pope has named as cardinals—Francis had by February 2019 named fifty-eight "electors," approximately half of the total of the College of Cardinals, with anywhere between six and ten new cardinals expected to be named in 2019. That left forty-seven electors who had been named by Benedict and eighteen by John Paul II.[63]

Although Francis's predecessors considerably internationalized the college, the 115 cardinals who voted in the March 2013 conclave were still disproportionately weighted in favor of the traditional European center. With its declining population of 250 million Catholics, Europe had more than half of the electors (and within that bloc, half were Italians) while Latin America, with a growing population of 420 million Catholics, had just nineteen, followed by North America (fourteen), Africa (eleven), Asia (ten), and Oceania (one). By his fifth consistory in June 2018, Francis had reduced the Europeans from sixty to fifty-five, and within that bloc the Italians from twenty-eight to eighteen, compared to five years earlier.

The College of Cardinals was also far more diverse: as of February 2019, sixty-five countries had a cardinal elector, compared with forty-eight in the 2013 conclave. While keeping the United States and Canada steady, he has increased the proportion of red hats in Africa, Asia, Latin America, and Oceania to the point where the European component of the College of Cardinals in the fall of 2018 was now considerably less than half (43.6 percent), and was expected to fall further with the announcement of new cardinals at the end of 2019. Under the first Latin American pope, Africa and Asia combined have more red hats than Italy, and in theory Francis's successor could be elected by the required two-thirds majority without a single European vote.

But the bigger change has been overthrowing the implicit criteria for selecting cardinals. Paul VI, John Paul II, and Benedict XVI all made the College of Cardinals more global, yet they stuck to the logic that cardinal electors would normally be heads of major metropolitan dioceses. There was an unwritten rule that archbishops of these so-called cardinatial sees would always receive a red hat, as would heads of major Vatican departments; and because the limit of 120 electors set by Paul VI prevented expanding the College, the effect was to bolster the center. It also encouraged careerism, dangling a red hat at the end of a lifetime of ecclesial upward mobility.

Francis has torn up all three unwritten rules, bypassing traditional sees in favor of lesser places in the Catholic heartlands and, most dramatically of all, choosing cardinals in remote, far-flung, missionary territories, many of which are poor or suffering in some way. Although heads of major Vatican congregations still get red hats, the heads of many smaller departments do not, and while the archbishops of capital cities continue to be made cardinals, outside these there is no such thing as a "cardinal see." In Italy, for example, Francis has overlooked Turin and Venice in favor of Perugia and Agrigento, while in the United States, Los Angeles and Philadelphia have been passed over for Indianapolis and Newark.

Francis has described his selections as making the College more representative of the global Church, while helping Catholic communities even in small or distant countries feel that their voices are heard in Rome, not just for their sake but for the Church's. "The small Churches that grow in the periphery and are without ancient Catholic traditions today must speak to the universal Church, to the whole Church," he told the Jesuits in Bangladesh. "I clearly feel that they have something to teach us." The idea that truth can be glimpsed more easily from the periphery than from the center is an insight that has been dear to him since the 1970s, when he was impressed by Argentine philosopher Amelia Podetti's work on the change of perspective that occurs by paying attention to the marginal. It is essentially a Gospel principle. The standpoint of the excluded, from places of fragility and poverty—Christ's viewpoint—allows for a broader and deeper view; those in the "center," conversely, fail to grasp the fault lines and therefore the impending earthquakes of history.[64]

To curb gossip and speculation, Francis keeps the names he has chosen a carefully guarded secret. Those he appoints find out when everyone else does: when the pope reads their names aloud in St. Peter's Square. The "periphery picks" trigger delightful stories, when a humble missionary bishop laboring in the fringe of some tiny island nation hears the news from his mother or cousin who has heard it on the radio. Cardinal Charles

Maung Bo of Myanmar, for example, found out from his niece in Australia, who had seen it on TV.

The first reaction is often disbelief. Haiti's first ever cardinal, the bishop of Les Cayes—not the main diocese of Port au Prince—picked up his phone to find it flooded with congratulatory messages from well-wishers in France, but Chibly Langlois assumed there was a mistake until he went onto the Vatican's website. "At that moment, I took a deep breath. I told myself, if it is the will of God, passing through the pope, that I am to be a cardinal, then God's will should be done." Bishop Francis Xavier Kriengsak Kovithavanij of Bangkok was also cautious. "We better find out if this is true," he told reporters who called.

Louis-Marie Ling Mangkhanekhoun, an ethnic Khmu who is apostolic vicar of Vientiane, Laos, gave a former student short shrift when he phoned with the news. "He said congratulations on your election to be a cardinal. I told him not to tease your elder. It is not right." Later a nun called with congratulations. "I said, 'Are you crazy?'" He went to check the internet, thinking they had probably got his name wrong, and only when the nuncio and the Vatican called did he start to "feel positive." Then he realized he needed a visa.

"How come you choose to name us publicly without telling us first?" Panamanian cardinal José Luis Lacunza Maestrojuán asked Francis during the consistory of February 2015. "If you consult, people start talking, and then the rivalries and envy take over. People say, 'Why him and not me?'" was the pope's answer, adding: "To avoid all that, I decided to announce them all in one go." "Holy Father, you'll only have yourself to blame if one day you give someone a heart attack," Lacunza joshed. Francis was delighted at the idea. "If they survive, it means they're in good health and can carry on working," he answered, laughing.

Cardinal Kovithavanij of Bangkok still didn't understand why he had been chosen until he went to Rome in January 2017 with other bishops from Southeast Asia. The pope told them that the strength of the Church was in the local people of God, "especially the Church that is small, the Church that is weak, and the Church that is persecuted. This is the backbone of the universal Church." Kovithavanij realized it was true, that the Church's real resource lay in patience and perseverance. "This made me think that our poverty, suffering and persecution are the three columns that strengthen the Church," he said.

Conferring the red hat was also as much about opening the College to the gifts of a people as it was a recognition of the bishop who would wear it. The reactions of shocked joy of local people have become under Francis part of the narrative of cardinal-making. The day that Dieudonné Nzapalainga of Bangui in the war-torn Central African Republic found out he was a cardinal, he was in the remote parish of Bossembélé across the savanna, where news spread so fast that it took him four and a half hours to travel just a few miles down the crowd-thronged road. "It was like Central Africa had won the World Cup," he told Fabio Marchese Ragona. "It's as if God was winking at us, giving hope to our people."[65]

Individuals also matter: Jorge Mario Bergoglio is famous for his ability to read hearts, and the cardinal choices are often the result of a personal encounter. But there are also strategic criteria involved. He wants the universal Church to hear from shepherds close to their people in places of war and pain, or places threatened by terrorism and climate change: hence his naming of Iraqi Patriarch Louis Raphaël I Sako of the Chaldean Catholic Church, who has led his flock through years of war and religious persecution, or Italian Giuseppe Petrocchi, archbishop of L'Aquila, whose diocese was shattered by one of the most destructive earthquakes in Italy's history. Some play key roles in peacemaking on the interreligious front line, such as Cardinal Bo of Myanmar, where the Buddhist majority has driven out the Muslim Rohingya minority. In other cases there are geopolitical imperatives. In moving the global Church spotlight to a pastor beleaguered by drug cartels (Alberto Suárez Inda of Morelia, Mexico) or dictators (Baltazar Enrique Porras Cardozo of Venezuela) or hostile Muslim populations (Joseph Coutts of Karachi, Pakistan), Francis can help insulate the Catholics there from persecution.

The choices are carefully discerned, the result of Francis's David-spotting and Jesse-quizzing during bishops' visits to Rome or at the synods. As Father Antonio Spadaro puts it: "In some cases they express particular stories or dynamisms he thinks should be shared, or maybe conflicts with open wounds that the pope wants to touch, or a particular tone that he thinks will be of use to the Church."[66]

A dramatic example of opening up an area to its own periphery is Oceania, which in Vatican mental maps has traditionally been coterminous with Australia and New Zealand, where there are substantial Catholic populations. But in naming cardinals from the Pacific archipelago—Tonga, with just 150,000 Catholics, and Papua New Guinea, with 2 million—Francis has given a voice to missionary churches in poor countries where rising sea levels from climate change are wreaking havoc on the local economies.

What doesn't count now is the strength or wealth of the Church in a given country or area. Bangladesh and Mauritius have a combined Catholic population similar to a midsize parish in the United States, while 2017 red hat Anders Arborelius is the first Swedish Catholic bishop since the Reformation, and his mostly immigrant church is a tiny component of the whole population. In the case of Gregorio Rosa Chávez, auxiliary bishop of San Salvador and disciple of the slain martyr Saint Óscar Romero, the red hat didn't go to the head of the diocese, but to an auxiliary bishop. In another, the nominee didn't even have a diocese: Mangkhanekhoun has a flock of 14,500, six priests, and a mission to mountain-dwelling animists led by married lay catechists who teach the seminarians.

What effect will the periphery picks have on the next conclave? One predictable consequence is that the outcome will be less predictable. The "little David" cardinals are outside the liberal-conservative battles that have characterized intra-Catholic disputes in the rich world, meaning that the next papal election will perforce be concerned less with preservation and more with mission, as *Evangelii Gaudium* intends. The conclave's preoccupations are likely, too, to be more human: the defense of human dignity in situations of extreme suffering, or basic freedoms in contexts of persecution. A more pastoral conclave is likely to elect a pastor as pope.

By selecting as cardinals bishops who look more like the first apostles than Renaissance nobles, Francis has also helped to bury the declaration by Pope Urban VIII in 1630 that cardinals were the equivalent of princes. "A cardinal enters the church of Rome, not a royal court," Francis told the new red hats during morning Mass in St. Peter's Basilica in February 2014, before urging the cardinals to reject "habits and ways of acting typical of a court: intrigue, gossip, cliques, favoritism and preferences." Jesus, he told them, "did not come to teach us good manners, how to behave well at the table. To do that, he would not have had to come down from heaven and die on the cross." In the consistory of 2017, he asked the five new cardinals to focus on "the innocent who suffer and die as victims of war and terrorism; the forms of enslavement that continue to violate human dignity even in the age of human rights; the refugee camps which at times seem more like a hell than a purgatory; [and] the systematic discarding of all that is no longer useful, people included."[67]

While expanding the periphery, Francis has also used his red hats to bolster the pastoral conversion of the Catholic heartlands of Europe and the Americas. Africa and Asia remain the continents of the future, and growing fast; yet the Church there is still too young and—with the exception of the Philippines, whose cardinal archbishop, Luis Antonio "Chito" Tagle, is a star—unlikely to produce the next pope. Latin America, on the other hand, is now the gravitational center of the universal Church, the nursery of the evangelizing energy in *Evangelii Gaudium,* and home to the world's largest Catholic population, which is both young and steadily growing. In awarding eleven red hats to Latin American electors in his five consistories, Francis has bolstered Aparecida by appointing men closely identified with its vision: Mexico's Carlos Aguiar Retes, Peru's Pedro Barreto, and Sérgio da Rocha, president of the Brazilian bishops' conference.[68]

In the United States, on the other hand, the pope has sought through his choices of cardinals to rebalance a deeply divided and heavily ideological, culture-warrior episcopate, distorted in part by former nuncio Archbishop Carlo Maria Viganò. Naming Blase Cupich of Chicago, Joseph Tobin of Indianapolis, and Kevin Farrell (formerly of Dallas, now head of the new Vatican Dicastery for the Laity, Family and Life) as cardinals signals Francis's support for a more credible, ethical witness—in which immigration, gun control, the death penalty, poverty, and the environment are also Gospel concerns. The sole focus could no longer be on abortion, euthanasia, and religious freedom. Tobin, Cupich, and Farrell are men of dialogue, who have created a new pastoral openness to LGBT people and the divorced and remarried. In this way, Francis has nudged the leadership of the Church in the United States toward the "seamless garment" ethic spurned by Catholic conservatives in their bid to lock the Church into Republican family-values ideology. Tobin used his first Mass in Newark to call for Catholics to dial down the rhetoric on "hot-button issues" and to better integrate their faith with their daily life. To believe in Jesus, he said, "is not acceptance of a doctrine or a moral code, but of a person who lives now and is the source of life—and not just on Sunday morning."[69]

Francis's bold bid to set the Catholic Church on an evangelizing path has called forth a remarkable opposition from rigorists and the traditionalists, which to a remarkable degree echoes Jesus's conflict with the Pharisees and other religious elites.

Although the Pharisees accused Jesus of failure to uphold the law, in many respects—famously over divorce—they were more lax than Jesus was. The underlying issue was not adherence to law and tradition but how these were deployed, for what end and for whose good. As the Gospels depict them, the Pharisees saw themselves as the gatekeepers, the guardians, who derived their sense of worth and social standing from their fidelity and observances. Their goodness, or righteousness, was their achievement, not God's. God's covenant was Israel's possession, a way of demarcating Jews from everyone else, not a channel for saving humanity. In Francis's distinction, bad Pharisees (there were, in the Gospels, many good ones) were intermediaries, not mediators.

In his Jesuit writings, Bergoglio showed how in Jesus the law and the tradition become dynamic instruments for salvation—integrating, forgiving, healing—offered to all people, especially those who are poor and on the edge, rather than a wall-building exercise in the service of an exclusive religious nationalism. In challenging the Pharisees to conversion, Jesus was not setting out to change or water down the doctrine and the law, but to change their hearts, their way of seeing, that they might cease to arrogate the divine power and instead become its facilitators. He wanted His disciples to replace the narrow, fuzzy, myopic spectacles of the doctors of the law with the wide-angled lens of the heart of the Good Shepherd, to apply the law as an instrument not of control but of God's healing and grace, via discernment (the way of Jesus) rather than legalism (the way of the bad Pharisees). In the contemporary Catholic rigorists' desire for a clearly demarcated boundary between those "inside" and those "outside" the Church's economy of salvation, Francis saw a clear parallel with the elite religious "parties" in Israel at the time of Jesus.[70]

The point appeared to be proved by the ferocity of the opposition to Francis, which has come mostly from the self-certified "faithful" or "orthodox" Catholics, who feel betrayed, abandoned, and slighted by him. Jesus's parables—the elder brother of the prodigal son, or the vineyard workers who are indignant at receiving the same wage as those who worked less—describe the type: loyal, faithful people who have come to believe in their merit and wish to be recognized, who want the Church to declare that they are innocent and others are guilty. They expect, at least, a pat on the head from the pope, yet they find that he criticizes them for their rigidity and judgmentalism while reaching out to embrace those whose records should disqualify them from even getting close to him.

Just as the heart of Jesus's dispute with the Pharisees was over the boundaries of God's grace, the locus of Francis's tension with the rigorists has been access to the sacraments. In declaring that the Eucharist was "not a prize for the perfect but a powerful medicine and nourishment for the weak," *Evangelii Gaudium* echoed Cardinal Carlo Maria Martini's famous final interview, posthumously published in September 2012, in which the Jesuit archbishop of Milan said the sacraments "are not a disciplinary instrument, but a help for people at times on their journey, in life's weaknesses."

The boldest of Francis's homilies confronting Catholic Pharisaism came in his second consistory, in February 2015, at the midpoint between the two synods on the family. The bishops were wrestling with the possibility of opening the sacraments to some divorced and remarried Catholics; although media reports had framed the debate as a doctrinal battle, the Church's teaching on marriage as faithful, indissoluble, and open to children had never been in question. At the heart of the matter was the issue of the use of God's law, and the perennial temptation of religious people to harness doctrine and law to bolster their own identity, to justify themselves by condemning others, and in this way to become an obstacle to God's desire to heal and save all.

Francis explained the contrast between the two approaches using Jesus's scandalous healing of the leper in the first chapter of Mark. In curing the outcast, he observed, Jesus was forced to stay out of the towns; in sharing the lepers' suffering and rejection, He entered their perspective. From the standpoint of the lepers it was clear how Jewish cleanliness laws, when used to protect and justify the healthy and the righteous, were underpinned by a logic of fear and exclusion. This was the logic that Jesus overturned. "For Jesus, what matters above all is reaching out to save those far off, healing the wounds of the sick, restoring everyone to God's family," Francis told the cardinals, adding pointedly: "And this is scandalous to some people!"

He then deftly polarized a hermeneutical choice, standing it like a waymark before the 280 cardinals. "There are two ways of thinking and of having faith," he told them. "We can fear to lose the saved or we can want to save the lost." He added, "Even today it can happen that we stand at the crossroads of these two ways of thinking: the thinking of the doctors of the law, which would remove the danger by casting out the diseased person, and the thinking of God, who in his mercy embraces and accepts by reinstating him and turning evil into good, condemnation into salvation and exclusion into proclamation."

Even today. In their few mentions of the Pharisees, Saint John Paul II and Benedict XVI focused on their lack of integrity—external obedience yet cold hearts—or their doctrinal laxity, say, over divorce. But Francis was highlighting here their unhealthy attachment to law and doctrine, and relating their rejection of Jesus to contemporary attitudes within the Church that were harming the Church's credibility and capacity to evangelize. This was daring, eggshell territory for a pope.

But he had to go there, because the rise of rigidity and legalism in seminaries posed a major obstacle to evangelization. In a 2016 meeting with Polish Jesuits in Kraków, Francis warned of priestly formation that taught priests "to act within limits and criteria that are rigidly defined *a priori*, ignoring concrete situations," and he urged them to teach the art and spirituality of discernment to help priests walk with people. A few months later with the Jesuits in Rome during their thirty-sixth General Congregation to elect a new superior general, he spoke of his concern that "rigidity that is far from a discernment of situations has been introduced" into priestly formation.[71]

By "discernment of situations" Francis meant the ancient Thomist art of *discretio*, prudence in applying the law, that used to form part of priests' training, and that was at the heart of the Church's great pastoral traditions. Discernment is the opposite of legalism, because it starts with the concrete person and her needs and applies the law in ways that can assist her, rather than starting with the law and using it to divide humanity between those inside and those outside it. To follow Jesus is to emulate his way of applying God's law, not the Pharisees'.

For Francis, the surge of rigorism and legalism signaled a turning away from Christ, a sign that religion had become a moral code, a dead letter, an ideology. "A priest who does not pray has closed the door, has closed the path of creativity," he told clergy on a visit to the Italian diocese of Caserta. "If you don't have Jesus at the center," he bluntly told seminarians in Naples, "postpone your ordination. If you're not sure if Jesus is at the center of your life, wait a while, in order to be sure." In a retreat for clergy organized by the Catholic Charismatic Renewal in June 2015, he compared a priest in love with Jesus to a man or woman who cannot stop speaking about his or her lover. The ones in love with Jesus were those who spent time with Him in the evening, praying before the tabernacle, rather than watching television. He told them not to worry if they fell asleep, because then God could gaze on them as a father looks at his sleeping son, but they mustn't miss out on that time.

If prayer and knowledge of Jesus was one antidote to Pharisaism, the other was proximity to real-life situations. Asked by a Latin American friar where pastors should position themselves in contexts of huge social division, Francis was clear: "with those who suffer most, but without having contempt [for the wealthy]." Point of view was all. But adopting the perspective of the poor—as Jesus did in staying with the lepers—didn't mean hating the rich. "If there is any 'class struggle' in the Gospel it's between the mercy preached by Jesus and the rigidity of the doctors of the law," he told the friar, urging him to steer clear of power, money, and the political-religious factions of the day, and do what Jesus did: serve the people.[72]

This was the pastoral conversion at the heart of the call of Aparecida, reformulated in *Evangelii Gaudium*. Where you chose to be to a large extent determined what you saw. Only through real-life contact with sin, poverty, and suffering could the Church be purged of its Pharisaism, as Francis made clear in a homily in Medellín, Colombia, that was a coda to his homily to the cardinals. Speaking to a million people packed into the fields around the city's airport on September 9, 2017, he said Jesus's first disciples needed to be "purified" of their attachment to precepts, prohibitions, and mandates, or the rigorous fulfilment of rituals and practices. Because these stopped them from asking the discernment question—What pleases God?—Jesus led them out to lepers, the paralytics, and the sinners, whose healing required much more than norms or recipes.

Francis then challenged the Church to do the same: to be close and concrete, not distant and legalistic. People were hungry for God, hungry for dignity, yet they stayed away from the Church because of the attitudes of so many Catholics. "We can't be Christians continually putting up a 'Do Not Enter' sign," he insisted. Speaking against a backdrop of mountains and skyscrapers, he recalled the historic meeting of CELAM in Medellín in 1968 when the Church in Latin America had received the Second Vatican

Council and had urged an option for the majority poor. Now that Church had produced a pope who was recalling the people of God worldwide to the mission defined at Aparecida: to go out to humanity as missionary disciples, not lamenting or condemning, but asking God what He wanted them to do to heal and save and love.

"The Church does not belong to us, but to God," Francis said in Medellín. "He is the owner of the temple and the field, and *everyone has a place*, everyone is invited to find here, and among us, his or her nourishment— *everyone*." Then he announced the program, which was the same one that Padre Rafa had given the young people in St. Joseph Patriarch parish in San Miguel. The Lord was calling forth from His Church "missionary disciples who know how to see without inherited myopias, who examine reality through the eyes and heart of Jesus, and from there judge. And who take risks, act, and commit."[73]

seven

Saving Our Common Home

In October 2017, Francis took the Gospel not just to the ends of the earth, but about 220 miles beyond it when via video linkup to the International Space Station he asked the astronauts onboard a series of questions. He wanted to know from the three Americans, two Russians, and an Italian what they had learned up there, and how they saw the earth.

Lack of gravity caused the astronauts to move on the screen in slow motion, and because of the time-space lag, there were long pauses between the pope's questions and their answers in English, all of which had to be translated by the Italian astronaut, Paolo Nespoli. The effect of these pauses was oddly contemplative, like faith sharing.

When Francis asked how they understood Dante's verse that love is the force that moves the universe, the Russian cosmonaut Alexander Misurkin told him he had been reading Antoine de Saint-Exupéry's *The Little Prince* and was taken by what he had read there. "Love is the force that gives you strength to give your life for someone else," he told the pope. "It's clear you have understood the message that Saint-Exupéry so poetically explained," Francis enthused.

When it was mission commander Randy Bresnik's turn, he told the pope that what he most enjoyed in space was being able to "see God's creation maybe a little bit from His perspective." The U.S. Marine who had flown combat missions in the Iraq War said you couldn't come up here and not be touched in your soul at the indescribable beauty of the earth, when you meet the planet turning peacefully on its axis, without borders or conflict, so awesomely beautiful and fragile. When you see the planet that way, he said, it makes you think about "how we should collaborate to improve the lives of all."

Yes, yes! Francis said, his face lighting up as he absorbed the answer. Being in space shows you that fragility, and the speed at which the earth turns makes you realize that it's just a passing moment—that it can be destroyed in an instant. *Grazie, grazie!* he thanked the astronaut.

The "overview effect" was a term coined by Frank White in the 1990s to describe the cognitive shift that astronauts report when they view the earth from orbit or from the moon's surface. This recognition of the fragility, one-ness, and interdependence of humanity and the earth has a parallel in what the Christian contemplative tradition describes as an ecstatic, grace-filled moment, "a peak experience" where for a moment you get a glimpse of the world the way God sees it—not just the *what*, but the *how*.[1]

In the sixteenth century, long before space travel, at a time when new worlds were being opened up to Europe across the Atlantic, Saint Ignatius deployed the overview effect in his retreat manual. In the Spiritual Exer-cises he saw the Holy Trinity gazing on the earth much as Bresnik later would, with tenderness and compassionate concern. But God doesn't just see; He *acts*. He sends His son. Saint Ignatius asks the person on a retreat to follow in their mind's eye what happens next: the peaceful, fragile birth of the child in Bethlehem, the life of hardships and forced migrations, and how the divine family "journeys and labors" in the world.

In the Exercises, the world is more than just a backdrop to salvation; it is the place of the redemption act. Creation is God's workshop. In *Laudato Si'*, his encyclical letter on creation and ecology that was signed on May 24, 2015, Francis put it this way: "The God who liberates and saves," he says, "is the same God who created the universe, and these two divine ways of acting are intimately and inseparably connected."

Once the planet is seen as infused with divine creativity, creation can no longer be treated as just a thing. In a 2002 foreword to the monk-writer Thomas Merton's writings on nature, the American eco-theologian Thomas Berry observed that "an absence of a sense of the sacred" was the basic flaw in ecological efforts. "It has been said 'we will not save what we do not love,'" he wrote. "It is also true that we will neither love nor save that which we do not experience as sacred." *Laudato Si'* was Francis's bold bid to help humanity to love the earth, to glimpse its sacredness and be moved by its plight.[2]

Just as God in the Exercises looks down "upon the face and circuit of the world and on all its people, living in blindness, going to their death, and descending into Hell," so *Laudato Si'* films, scene by scene, the contemporary version of that descent. A throwaway culture generates an "immense pile of filth." Tropical forests vanish and oceans turn acidic. Typhoons triggered by a warming earth throw villages into the sea. Toxic waste turns coral reefs a sepulchral white. Unique species die out, never to be seen again. The poor, displaced by rising oceans and diminishing natural resources, crowd into cities to battle social breakdown and disease, while the rich, bombarded with trivia, their eyes shut to the suffering at their gates, live hamster-wheel lives in a bubble of consumerism and ignorance. Law, politics, and culture are powerless against the global forces of profit and plunder. It is a world crying out for a savior.

The salvation starts with the story that should have been. In chapter two of *Laudato Si'*, human beings, God, and the created world live umbilically bound together. Nature's rhythms are respected; all collaborate in its fruits. Pregnant with divine grandeur, the earth abounds in beauty and possibility, showing forth God's affection for His creatures and His attention to their needs. Jesus, the embodiment of that compassion, is so attuned to nature that even the winds and waves obey Him.

Sin turns human beings against one another and against their fellow species. Creation and humanity, conceived as partners, born in fellowship, are now rivals; reciprocity has become cruelty. "We have only one heart," writes Francis, "and the same wretchedness that leads us to mistreat an animal will not be long in showing itself in our relationships with other people."

Naming that wretchedness—the mental shift that has corrupted our relationship to the living world—is the task of the encyclical's "judge" or discernment chapters, three and four. They nail both the false consciousness that follows the rupture of man and nature (the technocratic paradigm) and the new consciousness that will be needed to restore gift and reciprocity (integral ecology). These are the crucible of the encyclical's argument and conversion narrative. Accept Francis's account of the fallen and redeemed mind-sets, and the call to action in chapters five and six—which answer the "now what?" question—follows naturally.

Francis is explicit that technology per se is not the issue. Technology is a gift to improve the quality of human existence; it can even be a place of encounter. "Who can deny the beauty of an aircraft or a skyscraper?" he asks in *Laudato Si'*. The problem is not the technology but the way we turn *potentia* into *potestas*. Humankind has failed to develop a moral sensibility capable of managing the power that comes with the *techne*. Having lost our sense of the sacred in creation, we are enthralled *by* technology and in thrall *to* it. It has mastered us. We have developed a hardness and indifference, an impatience with nature that reflects a heart gone cold. The power that technology brings is satanic, as John Navone's *Triumph Through Failure* puts it, insofar as it "tempts man to refuse to acknowledge and to accept the truth of his own reality and of reality in general."

Embracing the limits of that reality instills virtue: patience, compassion, tolerance, humility, forgiveness, and understanding. But in the technocratic paradigm, the yardstick of good becomes strength and efficiency, and human limitations are seen as impediments that technology must overcome. Whereas in an earlier age people intervened in nature as a matter of cooperation, "of receiving what nature itself allowed, as if from its own hand," writes Francis, now "we are the ones to lay our hands on things, attempting to extract everything possible from them while frequently ignoring or forgetting the reality in front of us."

In what Romano Guardini calls the technocratic paradigm, Francis offers a unifying account of many kinds of insensibility: financiers ignoring the real human lives that lie at the bottom of complex mortgage refinancing schemes, corporate behemoths trashing forests in poor countries in the quest for profit, shareholders driving down wages to maximize returns.

But the paradigm also accounts for the tedious monotony of urban existence, the distance of the state and political elites, the depersonalization of social interaction, the leveling of cultures, the shrinking of community, the failure to recognize the humanity of migrants or the unborn or the disabled, as well as the misanthropic green thinking that wants to reduce the numbers of humans as predators or parasites on the natural world. It lurks behind the practical moral relativism that flows from what the encyclical calls a "misguided anthropocentrism" that "sees everything as irrelevant unless it serves one's own immediate interests": slavery; sexual abuse; trade in blood diamonds, drugs, and human organs; the mistreatment of the elderly; abortion; and so much else. Laws and regulations cannot alone stem these evils, the pope warns, because when culture is corrupted and universal principles no longer obtain, laws come to be seen as arbitrary impositions or obstacles to be evaded.[3]

Laudato Si' is apocalyptic both because it unmasks the truth about what we hold as sacred, and also because it exposes human helplessness to solve the crisis by our own means alone. In language that is direct, simple, and compelling, the encyclical demands that we choose a new way, one that depends on an "ecological conversion." Our crises—ecological and political, human and natural—are interconnected in a deep sickness that demands a new way of thinking and living. Competitive behaviors that have fueled human progress are no longer strategies that can help us. A solution to environmental destruction can no longer be conjured like a rabbit from the hat of technological mastery that provoked the crisis in the first place. Only *metanoia*, a new heart, leading to a new way of seeing—the overview effect—can now save us. As in Saint Ignatius's "Two Standards" meditation, we have to choose between two ways of being human. One demands continued sacrifice of the weak until there's no one left standing. The other is the way of *Laudato Si'*, the way of mercy.

In *Laudato Si'* the environmental crisis isn't just an ethical lapse or a failure of awareness but the symptom of something much deeper: the out-working of the Fall. Depicting a world of people seduced into a merry-go-round of endless production and consumption, deprived of the joy God intends for us, *Laudato Si'* shows us humanity miserable and alone in a frigid night of blinking machines. But it also calls forth a radical gesture of loving defiance: to gaze on God's creation with the eyes of loving contemplation, and allow ourselves to be converted.[4]

When the archbishop of Huancayo, Peru, Cardinal Pedro Barreto, warned that *Laudato Si'* would come under fire, "because they want to continue setting rules of the game in which money takes first place," he knew what he was talking about. His battle over a polluting smelter in the Peruvian highlands had shown him not just the interconnectedness of the suffering of the poor and the ruin of nature, but also what happens when you confront those who profit from irresponsible mining.[5]

Growing up in Lima, Peru's capital, Barreto had never forgotten the glass-clear water and virgin mountain air of his childhood visits to the center of his country. He joined the Jesuits in Peru in 1961, just after Bergoglio did the same in Argentina. But Barreto found his true calling when he was sent in 2002 to the northern Amazon region of Jaén as vicar, and later bishop, of the missionary territory there. He served the Wampi people and thought he would spend his life among them. But he had barely been there two years when John Paul II made him archbishop of the high-altitude city of Huancayo in the Mantaro valley of the central Andes, known as Peru's breadbasket.

On the morning I spent with him in April 2016, Barreto described for me his shock at the barren landscape of the Mantaro, and how the stench from the rotting river overpowered him when he arrived in his diocese in 2004. In his office is an old *Caretas* magazine from that time, with the archbishop on the cover. He is standing in a local field, holding up artichokes that had been banned from export because of their high lead content.

Only it wasn't the levels of lead in the vegetables that finally spurred him to act, but in the blood of children.

La Oroya, which sits at 13,000 feet, five hours' drive up into the mountains from Lima, in the region of Junín, is one of the planet's ten most polluted areas. For miles around the smelter, the hillsides are stripped of vegetation. The mountaintops stretching to the horizon are caked in a permanent covering of what looks like snow but turns out to be a 3.5-inch layer of tiny metallic particles left by noxious smoke belched night and day into the air since 1928.

Few in the area doubted that the smelter was the source of the havoc downstream in the Mantaro River valley. Nor that La Oroya—the name of the place, as well as the smelter—must be to blame for the high number of chronic illnesses and premature deaths among the five thousand people who worked and lived around it. Yet before Barreto got involved, nobody seemed able or willing to act.

Barreto schooled himself in the technical details and asked local universities to carry out scientific studies of air, water, and soil along the Mantaro. A survey of the area's six hundred children under the age of six showed all had shocking levels of lead in their blood, at least 40 milligrams per 100 milliliters. But the Lima government, anxious for foreign investment, appeared satisfied by the defense supplied by the Missouri-based Doe Run, which owned the smelter. The Americans did not deny the toxicity, but they used the old tobacco company defense that there was no scientifically demonstrable link between those lead levels and the lung diseases, persistent headaches, blood conditions, and premature deaths that plagued the workers and their families.

Barreto was a pastor, and his people were hurting. But when he formed a "dialogue table" commission to engage the smelter in talks about how to reduce toxic levels, he faced the hostility not just of its unions but even, at first, the local parish priests, whose people feared unemployment and the retaliation of their bosses more than what they called the "bad winds" from the smelter chimneys. Barreto thought often in those years of Easter, of Jesus's impotence: wanting to save people, yet being hated and rejected. "It's like when Jesus gazes on Jerusalem and cries, saying 'Jerusalem, Jerusalem, how I have wanted to gather you as a hen does her chicks, and you didn't want me to.' It's a loving reproach. I lived that in a little way."

As his environmental coalition pressed for change, Barreto found himself pilloried in posters and road signs on the main road between Huancayo and Lima, which passes by the smelter. There were protests in which demonstrators carried a coffin with Barreto's name on it. Sometimes it was more than just threats, but he doesn't like to speak about them. So the next day, when his driver, who doubles as the bishop's de facto bodyguard, takes me to Huancayo's tiny airport, I coax the stories from him. By the time I board my flight, I am amazed that the archbishop is still alive.

The year after John Paul II named him archbishop of Huancayo, the pope died, and Barreto found himself in Rome for the bishops' synod on the Eucharist called by Benedict XVI. In his speech, Barreto linked the sacrament of bread and wine with the words priests use to consecrate the Eucharist at Mass, when they offer up "fruit of the earth, work of human hands." What if the fruit were polluted, he asked, if it had lead in it? Some thought the link was strained, the kind of lefty thing you'd expect a Latin American Jesuit to come up with, and a year later, preparing for the great continent-wide "Fifth Conference" of CELAM in Aparecida, Brazil, in May 2007, Barreto faced similar pushback from some of his brother bishops, who said this was politics, not religion.

But once he got to Aparecida he was bowled over. From Mexico's low-wage factories, the maquiladoras, to the polluted aquifers of Patagonia, all the bishops, it seemed, had an environmental story or concern. Benedict XVI, in an address to Brazilian youth before opening the general conference, spoke of the devastation of Amazonia and its native peoples. Then, at the shrine, he gave a speech that was applauded close to twenty times in which he said the option for the poor was implicit in a faith in a God who became poor for us.

Although it appalled a small minority of bishops, the affirmation healed a long-standing wound left by the John Paul II years, when potentate cardinals in Rome had dismissed the option for the poor as warmed-over Marxism. Now, in the general conference, the two priorities—ecology and the poor—began to converge. The Amazonian bishops' searing testimonies dovetailed with the scientific data, and a clear picture began to take shape that the Church couldn't ignore: the planet's pain was borne by the land and the landless, while far-off foreigners reaped the rewards.

Among many who were converted to the ecological cause during the assembly was the archbishop of Buenos Aires, who for the first time used his famous metaphor of the *cultura del descarte*, the "throwaway culture." Until Aparecida, his grasp of the environment issue, in his own account, had been limited, but when he heard the Brazilian bishops speak of the deforestation of Amazonia, he quickly got it. The Argentine and the Peruvian Jesuits—Bergoglio had first met Barreto in the 1980s—worked together in Aparecida to draft the relevant paragraphs of the document, casting the natural world as a precious gift of God needing protection from "economic and technological powers." Unmasking the link between environment and culture, nature and justice, theology and ecology, they showed that there could be no lasting response to the crisis of the environment without restoring a sense of the sacred.

Noting how Latin America was affected by global warming "caused primarily by the unsustainable way of life of industrialized countries" and how the culprits were, in many cases, agribusiness and extractive industries that "fail to respect the economic, social, cultural, and environmental rights of local peoples," Aparecida called for a new, ecologically sustainable and socially just model of development to replace the casino capitalism that was ripping up the natural world.

You can easily see the straight line from Aparecida to *Laudato Si'*. There aren't two crises, one social and the other environmental, but two aspects of the same crisis. Call it the overview effect: to understand what was happening in the Mantaro River downstream of La Oroya, you had to grasp why parents of children dying of lead in their lungs didn't want to argue with the American corporation that paid their wages. How, then, can you proclaim God's Kingdom in such circumstances? How can you avoid proclaiming a new social order, one that rejects human sacrifice as intolerable? "The dynamic of the Fifth Conference was taking us to a pastoral, and implicitly ecological, conversion," Barreto recalled. "That's the conversion you're seeing now, under Francis, in the universal Church."

When Barreto met Bergoglio again three years later in Buenos Aires, for a CELAM conference on ecological spirituality, the conflict over La Oroya had reached an impasse. Under public pressure, the Peruvian government had refused the U.S. company's conditions for reinvesting, so the smelter declared bankruptcy, leaving 3,500 employees with pending claims. Many of the migrant workers had returned home, while those remaining at La Oroya were being assisted by church projects to retrain for scarce job opportunities in the Peruvian sierra.

Barreto saw three lessons.

First, if foreign investment doesn't come with a strong ecological commitment at the start, it will wreak havoc.

Second, the ecology issue couldn't be separated from the model of production and wealth creation; it had to be part of the wider Catholic commitment to development and justice.

Third, given that the restraints had to come from somewhere, common action was needed on all political levels—local, national, and international. On behalf of the poor, the state and international bodies had to stand up to businesses that thought only of their shareholders.

Barreto was struck at that 2010 meeting by how engaged the bishops of Argentina had become on the issue. A lay expert adviser, Dr. Pablo Canziani, a charismatic Catholic who was also an atmospheric physicist, had been invited by Bergoglio in 2003 to create an environment program at the Catholic University in Buenos Aires (UCA), of which the cardinal was chancellor. Canziani would be one of many whom Francis enlisted in the drafting of *Laudato Si'*.[6]

At around the time Barreto was beginning his battle over La Oroya, the bishops in Argentina asked Canziani to head a UCA-based team to investigate the environmental impact of the two giant foreign-owned pulp mills near the Uruguayan town of Fray Bentos. Because Fray Bentos is separated by just a few miles of river from an Argentine town with the sonorous Guaraní name of Gualeguaychú, the inhabitants of the town, which means "river of the big jaguar," were up in arms.

As at La Oroya, the case for the investment was compelling. Fray Bentos had been economically depressed since a British corned-beef plant had closed its doors in 1979, and the pulp mills, the largest-ever foreign private investment in Uruguay, would generate eight thousand jobs for the town. Yet the effects on fish stocks, water, tourism, and air quality of the Spanish- and Finnish-owned mills—one of which was already up and running— would be devastating for its neighbors across the river.

What came first, jobs or nature, Uruguyan livelihoods or the Argentine environment? The conflict pitted *gualeguaychuenses* against *fraybentinos* in years of protests, mobilizations, and counterdemonstrations, dragging in the governments not just of Argentina and Uruguay—who argued it out at the International Court of Justice at The Hague—but of Spain and Finland. The conflict didn't die down until 2010, following a series of agreements that led to joint environmental controls.[7]

With the support of Gualeguaychú's bishop, Jorge Lozano, Canziani organized a thorough study of the environmental impact of the Botnia and ENCE mills, interviewed the residents of the river town, and detailed the legal and practical options. He sent his substantial report to Cardinal Bergoglio, then president of the Argentine bishops' conference, who called Canziani at home on Good Friday, not long before the afternoon Veneration of the Cross, to ask him a series of technical and procedural questions about the report. Canziani could see that the cardinal, who as a young man had trained as a chemist, had an excellent grasp of the technical complexities and underlying issues.

Gualeguaychú, it turned out, was just one ecological drama among many in Argentina. Bishops from all over the country had begun to seek Canziani's counsel on issues affecting the people of their dioceses, including deforestation, water contamination, and the selling off of natural resources to multinationals. In response to the rising tide of interest, Canziani began hosting a regular program on a Catholic radio station interviewing priests, bishops, and scientists on environment issues affecting Argentina.

In 2009 the bishops of the vast southern Argentine region of Patagonia teamed up with their counterparts on the Chilean side of the Andes to make a joint UN submission calling for an end to the foreign commercial exploitation of its vast freshwater reserves. In a fierce Christmas message that would be quoted in *Laudato Si'*, the Patagonian bishops on the Argentine side blasted multinational companies who "after ceasing their activity and withdrawing, leave behind great human and environmental liabilities such as unemployment, abandoned towns, the depletion of natural reserves, deforestation, the impoverishment of agriculture and local stock breeding, open pits, riven hills, polluted rivers and a handful of social works which are no longer sustainable."[8]

Two years after the CELAM meeting in Buenos Aires, Gualeguaychú's Lozano convinced his brother bishops to dedicate a whole day of their plenary meeting to the issue. Canziani gave a presentation on the science of climate change with theological input from his UCA colleague Father Eduardo Agosta Scarel, a Carmelite friar who was also a meteorologist and climate change expert. The bishops peppered the experts with questions. Bergoglio listened carefully, took copious notes, and made astute queries. It was the last time Canziani saw his bishop before he emerged in white on the balcony of St. Peter's.

Shortly after that election in March 2013, Francis told the president of what was then still the Pontifical Council for Justice and Peace that he was contemplating a new social encyclical on ecology. Cardinal Peter Turkson was taken aback. A fortnight later, after Francis asked Turkson how the draft was going, he told the Ghanaian cardinal: *Scrive!*—"Get writing!"

Turkson handed the first draft to Francis eighteen months later, in August 2014. At that point the document was a third bigger than *Evangelii Gaudium*. Francis confided to journalists on the flight from Korea that month that he had to "build on solid data" because "if the pope says that the earth is the center of the universe, and not the sun, he errs, because he is affirming something that ought to be supported by science, and this will not do." Banishing Galileo's ghost, Francis was determined to listen respectfully to the evidence and base his climate change assertions on an overwhelming expert consensus.

But he also needed to rewrite it. The draft he had been given started with a long theological introduction, typical of papal documents aimed at church leaders. But Francis needed to trigger behavior change in humanity as a whole. In 2013, the Latin American Jesuits, who had made a commitment to ecology part of their mission, had analyzed the "interior resistances" that stopped people hearing and acting on the crisis. They found that many regarded global warming as a complex scientific question that didn't concern ordinary people. There was a widespread belief that technology would somehow solve it, and that the planet was an unlimited resource. The key challenge, the Jesuits concluded in "Healing a Wounded World," was blindness, a lack of seeing, because "those responsible for the problems and those affected by them tend to be different people and human groups."[9]

Put that Jesuit list of resistances alongside *Laudato Si'*, and then watch the encyclical take them down, one by one. The final obstacle—that those most affected by climate change were those who benefited least from the consumerism that led to it—was a constant theme in the encyclical, which sought to bring the two worlds together to hear and listen to each other. Francis deployed the classic "see-judge-act" structure beloved of Latin American documents, says Bishop Mario Toso, part of Turkson's team, because Francis "wanted to involve the largest possible number of readers, including nonbelievers, in a thought process that to a large extent can be shared in by all."[10]

The pope kept tight control of the drafting process, requesting the assistance of experts but allowing no one preeminence. He had learned from the experience of the previous papal social encyclical, Benedict XVI's 2009 *Caritas in Veritate* (Love in Truth). Because everyone knew it had been drafted by a group that included a brilliant economist, Professor Stefano Zamagni, that name gave an excuse for libertarian Catholics in the United States to declare that Catholics could simply ignore anything in *Caritas* that reflected Zamagni's thinking.[11]

Laudato Si', in contrast, avoided being identified with a single person or school of thought. Some names, naturally, leaked out, among them Professor Hans Joachim Schellnhuber of the Potsdam Institute for Climate Impact Research in Germany and Leonardo Boff, the Brazilian Franciscan theologian and ecologist. (Boff let slip that the pope had asked him to send documents to the Argentine ambassador in Rome, a former pupil of the pope's, rather than to the Secretariat of State, to prevent its subsecretaries intercepting and burying them.) But in the main, the names of those consulted, around two hundred people, were kept successfully under wraps.[12]

Between August 2014 and the encyclical's publication ten months later, it went through two further drafts, each worked on by Francis with help from a group of theologians that included his Aparecida and *Evangelii Gaudium* amanuensis, Archbishop Victor Fernández. It was then looked over by various Vatican congregations, and sent for translation in March 2015. After a final revision Francis signed the encyclical on the feast of Pentecost two months later, and released it in June, which would allow time for it to have maximum impact on the climate meeting of world leaders in December.

Its title, kept secret until days before its release, was not Latin, as many thought, but medieval Italian, the opening words of Saint Francis of Assisi's "Canticle of the Sun," his great hymn of thanks for creation, which began: "*Laudato si', mi' Signore*"—"Praised be you, my Lord." The encyclical's subtitle, "On Care for Our Common Home," captured the vast scope of its subject—as did (despite efforts to reduce it) the document's size. At 42,000 words on 180 pages, with 250 paragraphs compared to just 79 in Benedict's *Caritas in Veritate*, it was three times as long as the first social encyclical in 1891, Leo XIII's *Rerum Novarum*. In fact, *Laudato Si'* was by a long shot the fattest Catholic social encyclical ever, dubbed the *Summa Ecologica* in deference to Saint Thomas Aquinas's vast *Summa Theologica*.[13]

The fears it raised were just as big, especially in the Church of the world's chief polluter and global capital of climate denial. The institutes and business schools funded by wealthy American Catholics were already furious that the pope had seen fit in *Evangelii Gaudium* to criticize the notion that markets automatically generate wealth for all. Now they feared the pope would use his authority to attack U.S. capitalism and consumerism as ungodly because it hurt the planet. They weren't wrong.

They began to move the document into their line of fire at the end of 2014, following rumors it was shortly to be published. Visiting the United States just before the encyclical's release, the C9 president, Honduran cardinal Oscar Andrés Rodríguez de Maradiaga, was stunned by the viciousness of right-wing Catholic attacks, which he said reflected "a vision of capitalism that doesn't want to renounce damaging the environment for the sake of profits." *Our Sunday Visitor,* a right-of-center weekly sold in parishes nationwide, was moved to complain in an editorial of "venom-spewing, ideologically based commentary" from conservative Catholics that included mockery of the pope and calling into question his mental state.

Doubtless they were thinking of *First Things*, the highbrow journal that had under John Paul II been famous for berating Catholics for their lack of deference to the papacy, but which now sought to persuade them that ignoring the papacy was the right thing to do. Six months before the encyclical was even out, an article in the journal denounced Francis as "an ideologue and a meddlesome egoist" whose "megalomania sends him galloping into geopolitical—and now meteorological—thickets, sacralizing politics and bending theology to premature, intemperate policy endorsements." A more subtle—and ironic, given the efforts Francis had made to defer to scientific evidence—approach was to call up Galileo's ghost. Because the pope wasn't qualified to say if climate change was man-made, Professor Robert P. George of Princeton claimed, Catholics were "bound by the moral norms" in the encyclical but free in conscience to disagree with him on the empirical evidence he appealed to.[14]

Conservative politicians, trapped between Tea Party rejection of global warming and their self-image as faithful Catholics, also scrabbled around for moral reasons to ignore Francis. Rick Santorum, a 2012 presidential candidate who had described the idea of any human role in climate change as "patently absurd," said Francis would be "better off leaving science to the scientists and focusing on what we're really good at, which is theology and morality," while Republican front-runner Marco Rubio claimed to defer to the pope on "moral issues," but when the pope strayed into "political areas" such as the economy and climate change he was "just a person."[15]

None of this was new. During the previous high noon of globalization, Leo XIII in 1891 had faced similar pushback when he looked out on an impoverished mass of workers and a tiny number of stratospherically wealthy capitalists and said it was time for just wages and trade unions to right the balance. Businessmen scoffed: What did the pope know about the technical workings of the free market? But Leo in *Rerum Novarum* [On New Things] was no more claiming a specialist knowledge of economics than Francis, 124 years later, was pretending to be an authority in climate science. Yet both popes were adamant that because an issue had a technical or scientific dimension didn't make it a morality-free zone. The free market may set a worker's wages, but it could not determine if those wages were just; equally, Francis was not equipped to monitor the impact of fossil fuels on climate change, but he could say that global warming was a moral issue that demanded a conversion of minds and hearts.

But first, the Vatican had to decide whether man-made global warming was real. Ignoring intense lobbying by the fossil-fuel industry via the Chicago-based Heartland Institute that argued there was no proven link between emissions and global warming, the encyclical deferred to the stark November 2014 Synthesis Report of the Fifth Assessment Report of the UN Intergovernmental Panel on Climate Change (IPCC), which reflected a nearly 100 percent consensus among scientists that fossil-fueled growth had led to dangerous and unsustainable global warming with catastrophic effects on the natural world.

But just as Leo XIII didn't need experts to tell him that the urban poor were destitute, Francis didn't rely on scientists alone to tell him what was happening. More than 10 percent of the encyclical's footnotes—21 out of 172—carried moving quotes from developing-world bishops who had seen at first hand the effects on their communities of deforestation, toxic waste, rising seas, and typhoons.

Laudato Si', it turned out, was about far more than ecological destruction. It was about a whole new form of relativism thrown up by technocracy. Francis had trailed his thinking in a speech to the European Parliament at Strasbourg in November 2014, when he warned of what happens when technology takes over morality and consumerism is uncontrolled. *Laudato Si'* confronts, head-on, the atheism behind the "throwaway culture." No wonder some were nervous.[16]

For all that the captains of capitalism would claim he was a raving radical, Francis was in fact pushing out from a path firmly forged by his predecessors. Saint John Paul II had called for an "ecological conversion" of the Church through "concrete programs and initiatives," and Benedict XVI set an example by installing a thousand solar panels on the roof of the Vatican's audience hall and a hybrid engine in one of the popemobiles. But Benedict's greatest achievement was to engage theologically with the rising ecological awareness. Noting in *Caritas in Veritate* how nature expressed "a design of love and truth," a "grammar" that "sets forth ends and criteria for its wise use, not its reckless exploitation," he observed that the logic of gift underpinning the moral intuition behind ecology was incompatible with the ethic of sovereign autonomy.

In a series of addresses, Benedict observed how insisting on respect for the given order of the natural world ran counter to the contemporary attitude toward sexuality and human life. Permissive laws that upheld a woman's "choice" assumed that choice alone could specify what was good without reference to transcendent criteria, such as the sacred value of life. Yet when mining corporations pouring toxic waste into rivers claimed it was a necessary price to pay for jobs and consumer goods, progressives were appalled.

If creation were merely raw material without intrinsic value, subject only to cost/benefit analysis, then these choices were justified; but if humanity and creation were governed by a logic of gift, in which the right response to creation—whether human or natural—was respect, why did the same thinking not apply in both cases? Benedict called for the development of a "human" ecology to supplement a "natural" one, as a way of connecting with contemporary sensibilities.[17]

His arguments were compelling and clear, but they were aimed more at challenging ecologists than converting Catholics. In the hands of the culture warriors, "human ecology" became simply another stick to beat up liberals in rows over gay marriage or abortion laws. Yet the more pro-life, pro-family groups, especially in the United States, appealed to "human ecology," the more exposed was their own lack of commitment to natural ecology. Many saw no contradiction in arguing against abortion and gay marriage on the one hand while on the other defending a free-market model of unrestrained consumption, the right to carry guns, and the death penalty. By Benedict's own logic they could hardly argue against the killing of an unborn baby as the unacceptable price of a woman's autonomy if the plundering of the rain forest and the impoverishment of the landless were an acceptable price for unchecked consumption.

Francis gently challenged this schizophrenia at a Vatican conference on male-female complementarity in September 2014, organized by prominent American conservatives, among them Professor George. The conference was an astute bid to respond to the deconstruction of marriage and sexuality by showing that maleness and femaleness ran through all cultures and faiths, as well as the natural world. (Jonathan Lord Sacks, the former chief rabbi to the UK, told a riveting account of marriage that began with what he claimed was the first ever act of copulation—by prehistoric Scottish fish.) To loud applause, Francis described how the collapse of family and marriage under pressure from a "throwaway culture" advanced under "the flag of freedom" had caused "spiritual and material devastation to countless human beings, especially the poorest and most vulnerable." But he went on to point out that this was "an ecological crisis; for social environments, like natural environments, need protection." Equating the two environments was a subtle but clear shift, and the applause was more muted.[18]

But although Francis needed, for the sake of the Church's credibility, to challenge American conservative double standards, his main aim was to take ecology where science couldn't: into the realm of the sacred. Science could pinpoint the "is" but not the "ought"; it could inform, but not move to act. While compelling data could shout and sound the alarm, it could not ask people to care about what they did not love.

This was a point made by climate scientists themselves. One of the great oceanographers of modern times, Walter Munk, remarked in a Vatican conference in 2014 that global warming could only be overcome by "a miracle of love and unselfishness." Media stories of endangered minorities and species appealed to classically liberal moral concerns but often left religious people unmoved. A Stanford University study a few months before the encyclical came out showed that a message centered on purity and protecting God's creation from desecration would resonate deeply with religious sensibilities, moving people both to accept the evidence and to act on it.[19]

That meant providing a new narrative that transcended liberal ecology, one that could take the polarity of respect for nature on the one hand and respect for human uniqueness on the other, and create a new synthesis beyond the dialectically opposed ideologies of biocentrism and anthropocentrism. *Laudato Si'* called this new thinking "integral ecology" because it offered a unified moral narrative. Humankind was called to be a custodian of creation, rather than its arrogant overlord; human creatures were a fellow species, interconnected with and biologically dependent upon God's other creatures. From this converted viewpoint flowed an ethical conversion. Thus *Laudato Si'* would be the first authoritative Catholic document unequivocally and emphatically to teach the intrinsic goodness of nonhuman animals, in this way making animal welfare a pro-life issue.

Integral ecology also enabled Francis to position the global Church at the heart of a drive to respect the divinely gifted design of love and truth in every "environment." Whether in the natural world, the family, or urban spaces, integral ecology offered a lens with which to judge the misuse of human autonomy and the idolatry of power. It was a challenge both to pro-life, pro-family conservatives to respect the integrity of the natural world, and to environmental campaigners to safeguard the institutions and laws that protect human life and family. In this sense, *Laudato Si'* was key to Francis's evangelization call. The purpose of the Church in the contemporary world was not to dominate but to serve, to reveal a loving Creator whose son gave his life "so that the world might be fashioned anew according to God's design," as the Second Vatican Council put it.

"People are expecting a policy paper," Father Michael Czerny, SJ, then the number two in Turkson's team, told me shortly before the encyclical came out. "What they're going to get is the Gospel."[20]

Laudato Si' wasn't addressed to the bishops and faithful, or even—as some encyclicals had been—to all people of goodwill, but to all earthlings. The pope was inviting every human being to join in a new great task of collaboration with their Creator and with each other, one that was about "ecology" in the original Greek sense of *oikos*, meaning "home." In the church of San Damiano in Assisi, Jesus had appeared to Saint Francis to ask him to repair His Church. Now a pope named after Saint Francis was asking humanity to repair God's world.

Francis's genius, thinks Canziani, was to discern the moment when science and religion were reaching out to each other over climate change, ready for a partnership that could enable new ways of seeing among the mass of citizens of the world, and so halt the hurtling train of consumption and destruction. That new lens starts with a conscience-stricken, anguished realization that something vital has been lost, and triggers a determination that things have to be done differently to get it back. The old-fashioned word for this is "conversion."

Understanding what got lost and when is crucial to the encyclical's backstory. Nature was once upon a time something awesome and sacred, to be respected and cooperated with. But then came the triumph of science and industry on the backs of a population explosion and economic activity allied to the raw power of *techne*. "We went from one extreme to the other without finding the midpoint," Canziani explains in his office in Buenos Aires, "and now we're on a path of destruction." That loss is the theme of Romano Guardini's extraordinary 1950s texts, *The End of the Modern World* and its accompanying essay, *Power and Responsibility*, which took as their subject what the German theologian saw as the central question of the age: the mind-set of power shaped by technocracy.

In a 1989 lecture at the Colegio del Salvador in Buenos Aires on the need for a new political anthropology, Bergoglio quoted the books, describing Guardini as "the prophet of postmodernity" for identifying how the rapid development of technology over two hundred years, accelerated by globalization, had brought humanity to a fork in the road of history. Guardini's thesis was key not just to the narrative of *Laudato Si'*, which regularly quotes *The End of the Modern World*, but also to how Francis saw the encyclical's purpose: to help humanity grasp that the choice was annihilation or conversion.[21]

The German theologian's account centers on the radical sundering of Creator and created. Where pre-moderns saw nature as an expression of the divine, of which they, too, formed an organic part, now people asserted themselves *over* nature in search of their well-being. As the world ceased to be God's creation, it could be possessed and plundered with new know-how. Guardini saw a paradox in the autonomous rationality that underpinned this shift: that man's bid for power would render him ever more subject to a power not his own. Such a power would increasingly enslave humankind by tempting it with limitless possibility, like the forbidden fruit offered by the serpent in Eden.

Guardini foresaw that power itself would become increasingly depersonalized, emptying itself of moral sensibility, of empathy and compassion. Man had come to believe the lie that he, not God, was the author of his own creation, and over time his freedom would be undone, ironically, by his autonomy. Foreseeing that humanity "will be free to further his lordship of creation, carrying it even to its last consequences," Guardini observed that this mastery would be open to him because he "has permitted himself utter freedom: the freedom to determine his own goals, to dissolve the immediate reality of things, to employ its elements for the execution of his own ends." Increasingly he would do these things "without any consideration for what had been thought inviolate or untouchable in nature." The effect would be to sunder the very bonds that held people together.[22]

Rejecting the optimism of the postwar world, Guardini predicted with remarkable clarity that the forces that had led to Auschwitz and the gulag would accelerate as family, tribe, Church, and nation continued to fall apart. The era of the totalitarian state would give way to the totalitarianism of economic and corporate power: with the dissolution of the bonds holding people together in families, institutions, and nations, humanity would be increasingly destabilized and dominated by the forces of technology and rootless finance. Guardini saw at the end of the road what the sociologist Zygmunt Bauman would memorably call "the liquid society," and even named its symptoms: a time of mass migrations, social breakdown, and the collapse of grand narratives, in which fluidity takes over from stability as the new norm of human existence. It is to this world—ours now—that Francis in *Laudato Si'* has offered the Church's first comprehensive response.

Francis discerns with Guardini that the real drama of postmodernity turns not on technology per se but on the mind-set of power that flourishes in a technocratic age. In the incarnation, Guardini observed, God had revealed true power, which is the power of service, in which freedom is subject to and constrained by the essence of things and the limits of human nature. Jesus's unmasking of the false power of domination and violence was the triumph of the Cross, his kenosis, which Guardini calls "supreme power converted into humility."

Hence the hidden hope of *Laudato Si'* which reveals an alternative destination for modernity just at the moment when humanity awakens in ecological awareness to the false promises of technocracy and consumerism. Francis trusts that the very technocracy laying waste to the Christian legacy will also awaken the Church from its slumber. As love disappeared from the face of the public world, foresaw Guardini, it would throw into relief "the courage of the heart born from the immediacy of the love of God as it was made known in Christ."[23]

This revelation would be accelerated and assisted by secularization. As the unbeliever learned to live honestly without religion, the Church, unshackled from law and culture, would be better able to contradict the surrounding ethos. The authentic Christian witness—concrete and close, authentic and "organic"—would contrast ever more with the temptation "to erect a culture on rational and technical foundations alone." The drama of Western postmodernity would unfurl in the ever starker contrast between the technocratic paradigm on the one hand and a renewed Christianity on the other. Either humanity would be saved by integrating and subordinating the new power of the *techne*, or it would surrender to that power and perish.

Guardini closed with an intriguing intuition: that as people become ever more governed by forces they cannot control, they would turn to a "great man." His imagined leader—whether in the world of politics or religion, he does not say—understands "how to subordinate power to the true meaning of human life and works." Free from the modern dogma of progress, comfortable with technology but not in thrall to it, he would be capable of establishing an authority that respects human dignity and a social order in which "God is acknowledged as the living norm and point of reference for all existence." The great man (or woman) needed for our time, he concluded, would be able to grasp "Christianity's inmost secret: humility."

Is Francis that "great man"? In his Mass of inauguration on the Feast of Saint Joseph, March 19, 2013, the new pope's homily was precisely on this topic of authentic power as service, a power of nurture that can midwife a new social order.

It was a social order in which government had an important role, checking the forces of technocracy and protecting the various environments, human and biological, urban and rural, that are necessary for human flourishing. Just as Jacques Maritain's "integral humanism" in the 1940s offered a postwar Catholic vision of a liberal European democracy open to God, in contrast to the prevailing liberal individualism and socialist collectivism, Francis's "integral ecology" offers a vision of social and economic organization underpinned by the gift logic of the Christian tradition as an alternative to the dominant technocracy. It is integral because it respects the organic links of existence. In speaking of the "environment," writes Francis in *Laudato Si'*,

> What we really mean is a relationship existing between nature and the society which lives in it. Nature cannot be regarded as something separate from ourselves or as a mere setting in which we live. We are part of nature, included in it and thus in constant interaction with it. Recognizing the reasons why a given area is polluted requires a study of the workings of society, its economy, its behavior patterns, and the ways it grasps reality. Given the scale of change, it is no longer possible to find a specific, discrete answer for each part of the problem. It is essential to seek comprehensive solutions that consider the interactions within natural systems themselves and with social systems. We are faced not with two separate crises, one environmental and the other social, but rather with one complex crisis that is both social and environmental. Strategies for a solution demand an integrated approach to combating poverty, restoring dignity to the excluded, and at the same time protecting nature.[24]

A reinvigoration of the very purpose of statecraft, therefore, was called for. Government could no longer remain distant in a nominalist bubble or be reduced to an ineffectual referee overseeing a Darwinian struggle of rivals, but must act to foster many "ecologies" in the face of the techno-cratic tide. That meant, for example, protecting the value and vocation of work by containing the power of corporations and creating jobs through small-scale businesses and producers; fostering the values and identity of peoples and cultures and their ancestral lands; bolstering urban spaces where communities can flourish; as well as ensuring decent housing, good public transport, clean air, and the integration of run-down urban areas.

In chapter five of *Laudato Si'* Francis asked: If increased production and consumption led to a deterioration in the quality of life of the poor and the degradation of the environment, why call it progress? If a com-pany swells its profits at the expense of future resources or the health of the environment, should we consider this growth a success? Creativity was needed, along with an openness to new possibilities, to consider ways of investing that created jobs, made energy more efficient, and reduced con-sumption in the rich world to allow poorer places to develop. "We know how unsustainable is the behavior of those who constantly consume and destroy," he argued, "while others are not yet able to live in a way worthy of their human dignity."

The idea that decreased growth in rich parts of the world was nec-essary to allow poorer places to prosper went directly against the core dogma of trickle-down economics. Popes had long been skeptical of the idea that the rich becoming fabulously wealthy was—to use a different watery metaphor—a rising tide that lifted all boats. As Francis pointed out in *Evangelii Gaudium*, rather than the money trickling down, the glass of wealth just got bigger. *Laudato Si'* did not enter into the complex question of wealth cre-ation. Its role was to name the reality of the very poor staying poor while the rich got richer and to call for it to be addressed. But for many on the Catholic right in America, even that was intolerable.[25]

Yet the evidence was clear: the shift in wealth from labor to capital, along with the stagnation of wages and spiraling corporate profits, the increase in inequality and the growing exclusion of the poor, showed that globalization had gone wrong. Coordinated global policies were needed that started from the planet as a whole. Developing countries were owed a great debt, the pope said in *Laudato Si'*, because the countries where the most important reserves of the biosphere are found were fueling the devel-opment of richer countries at the cost of the former's present and future. Hence wealthy countries should pay their "ecological debt" to poor countries "by significantly limiting their consumption of non-renewable energy and by assisting poorer countries to support policies and programs of sustainable development."

Like the Trinity gazing down upon the earth, Francis affirmed the planet as a single "homeland" that called for "one world, with a common plan." For the economist and professor Jeffrey Sachs, this was the most important phrase in a document he praises as "magnificent" and "breathtaking." The year of the encyclical, 2015, two common plans would be agreed upon that Francis would continually refer to: the United Nations' Sustainable Development Goals and the Paris COP21 climate agreement. "We must achieve what we have agreed upon," he told finance ministers around the world in May 2019, "for our survival and well-being depend on it."[26]

After listing all the areas in which not just cooperation but "a global consensus" would be necessary, Francis called for a "true world political authority" capable of enforcing such international agreements. The idea— greeted with derision in some quarters—was based on a long-standing social Catholic principle mooted by John XXIII and endorsed by Benedict XVI in *Caritas in Veritate* in precisely the words Francis used. The principle here was "subsidiarity," namely, that governance should be at a level appropriate to the task. Usually this was a call for higher authorities to devolve down, but it could equally signal the need for new oversight bodies. It had long been axiomatic to the Vatican that only agreed global rules implemented by transnational authorities were capable of meeting border-blind challenges, not just to police drug trafficking, tax evasion, and terrorism, but to coordinate policies of common human concern such as migration and the environment.

"Politics must not be subject to the economy, nor should the economy be subject to the dictates of an efficiency-driven paradigm of technocracy," Francis declared as a general principle, adding that it was time to reject what he called "a magical conception of the market, which would suggest that problems can be solved simply by an increase in the profits of companies or individuals."

Francis in the final chapter of the encyclical urged humanity to accept "that we have a shared responsibility for others and the world, and that being good and decent are worth it." He went on to earn a standing ovation from religious and ethically committed people everywhere when he added: "We have had enough of immorality and the mockery of ethics, goodness, faith and honesty. It is time to acknowledge that lighthearted superficiality has done us no good."

Both the planet and the poor—the link made so strongly in Aparecida—had suffered from this egocentric culture of gratification. "The mindset that leaves no room for sincere concern for the environment is the same mindset that lacks concern for the inclusion of the most vulnerable members of society," Francis wrote. The lack of concern was creating a state of lawlessness. Where the state failed to take responsibility, business groups or organized crime syndicates stepped into the vacuum. Corporations concerned only with financial gain and a politics concerned merely with retaining or increasing power would fail to rescue humanity from the abyss it faced; yet the state often shirked its duty to rein in companies. Mindful, perhaps, of Gualeguaychú and La Oroya, Francis warned that "politics and the economy tend to blame each other when it comes to poverty and environmental degradation." That was no longer good enough.

Having argued in *Laudato Si'* that a lack of agreement on curbing global warming was a failure of technocratic politics, Francis invited the world's leaders to prove politics could raise its game. *Laudato Si'* was the first papal document ever to be released with a view to influencing a specific political event, the weeklong meeting in early December 2015 in Paris of 190 world leaders.

It was known as COP21 because it was the twenty-first yearly session of the "Conference of the Parties" to the 1992 United Nations Framework Convention on Climate Change. Efforts to meet that convention's goals through global agreements had thus far stumbled, and the opportunity for action was fading fast. *Laudato Si'* had put presidents and prime ministers on notice: humanity could not tolerate nations putting their own interests before the global common good. "Those who will have to suffer the consequences of what we are trying to hide," Francis warned, "will not forget this failure of conscience and responsibility."

He repeated this now-or-never, do-or-die message in one-on-one meetings with world leaders over the following months, as well as in a chain of high-profile interventions on his trips. In addresses in Latin America, before the U.S. Congress, at the world headquarters of the United Nations, and finally in a speech at the UN's African base in Nairobi, Kenya, days before the summit opened, he held political leaders' feet to the fire, urging them, in effect, to examine their consciences before the tribunal of history.

Failure to reach agreement would be "catastrophic," he said in Nairobi, where he called for a new global energy system that made "little or no" use of carbon. He asked the world's leaders to deliver a threefold agreement that would lessen the impact of global warming, fight poverty, and ensure respect for human dignity. The presidents of the world's five continental associations of Catholic bishops meanwhile backed his call for "an enforceable agreement that protects our common home and all its inhabitants." Ecclesiologically, this was an historic first, the first glimpse of a future of regional patriarchates.[27]

By then the Church's base was being mobilized by an unprecedented start-up network of hundreds of organizations in the Global Catholic Climate Movement (GCCM), formed at the end of 2014 by Tomás Insua, a young Argentine studying climate change policy at Harvard's Kennedy School. While working for Google Buenos Aires, Insua used to spend weekends in church projects among the poor. His ecological conversion came after the tech giant sent him to its office in Singapore, from where he traveled with his wife to the Philippines. There they saw the aftermath of history's most devastating typhoon, Haiyan, which had slammed into the islands in Tacloban in late 2013, killing more than 6,000 and displacing a staggering 4.1 million people. "It opened my eyes wide," he told me, "to see that climate change is about social justice."[28]

At Harvard the following year studying climate policy, Insua was thrilled at the news of the pope's forthcoming encyclical but dismayed to find that secular green groups and other faiths and denominations were far more excited about it than were the Catholics. Of the 1,500-odd organizations taking part in the global climate march in New York in September 2014, just two or three had anything to do with the Catholic Church, while on campus, he found the Protestants and Hindus far more engaged than his coreligionists. After meeting with Canziani in Buenos Aires that fall, Insua put together a network to leverage global parish-level pressure for a deal in Paris a year later.

The GCCM launched in January 2015 with the backing of the archbishop of Manila, Cardinal "Chito" Tagle, who presented Francis with the network's foundational statement as he arrived in the Philippine capital from Colombo, Sri Lanka. The cornerstone of the papal trip, which would set a new record for the largest-ever gathering of humanity—more than six million people at the closing Mass in Manila—was a visit to the typhoon-devastated area that had so moved Insua. Francis braved a tropical storm to reach Tacloban, cutting short his trip to avoid the worst of the weather from a new hurricane that tore down scaffolding at his Mass venue, killing a pilgrim. In the howling wind and rain he met the typhoon victims, whose pain, he said in a homily, had silenced his heart.

He made no mention of climate change, but he hardly needed to. The angry winds spoke for him. For a country averaging twenty-two typhoons a year, a future of more high-intensity storms from a warming planet was an appalling prospect. Ever since "What is happening to our beautiful land?," the Filipino bishops' 1988 cri de coeur quoted in both *Evangelii Gaudium* and *Laudato Si'*, the Church in the world's fourth-largest Catholic country had been at the forefront of the call to action on climate change. Now the Filipino bishops led the mobilization for the GCCM-organized global petition, which, by the time Insua presented it to President François Hollande in December, had gathered close to a million signatures.

A few weeks earlier, the global climate march had again taken place across the world. This time around 40,000 of the 800,000 taking part were Catholics mobilized by the Church. The GCCM petition, along with Francis's pressure on COP21, was key to producing the Paris Agreement—particularly the more ambitious target of limiting the increase in global temperature in this century to 1.5 degrees Celsius, to be achieved mainly by polluting nations pledging to pull away from fossil fuels.

On the night of December 8, 2015, as the world's leaders in Paris haggled, a three-hour slideshow of stunning photos of the natural world was projected onto St. Peter's Basilica in Rome. It was the Feast of the Immaculate Conception, marking the moment when Jesus's mother, Mary, was created, full of grace. It was also the opening of the Jubilee of Mercy, a year called by Francis to celebrate God's loving embrace of His creation. As yawning lions and electric-blue fish slid over the venerable façade, the square filled with the squawking and clatter of birds and insects. There could be no doubt, now, where the Catholic Church stood on the great issue of the age.

Like a windhover, *Laudato Si'* circled above the climate summit. Al Gore, the former vice president and Nobel Prize–winning activist, said later that the encyclical had been crucial in leading the world to commit to addressing the climate crisis ahead of the Paris Agreement. Lord Nicholas Stern, the World Bank economist, said it was "quite extraordinary in changing the weight of the argument." Stories circulated of Francis making urgent phone calls to break eleventh-hour deadlocks, urging whatever was needed—boldness, flexibility, or generosity—for the sake of the agreement. The pope had a "huge role to play" in the world coming together in Paris, says Professor Sachs, who was stunned by how many country delegations mentioned the encyclical in Paris. The Philippine delegation in particular used the GCCM petition to help raise the ambition in Paris, persuading Catholic-majority nations that what had been seen as an unfeasible target the year before, the Holy See–backed target of 1.5 degrees, was now the benchmark of global ambition. "The common wisdom is that without *Laudato Si'*," says Tony Annett, a climate change specialist at Columbia University's Earth Institute, "it is far from sure that the Paris Agreement would have been signed."[29]

It wasn't just the activists and the experts who were impressed. *Laudato Si'* was by a long shot the most widely read papal document in history. Even three years after its publication it was the most quoted encyclical in the Church's history. Far outside the Catholic fold, people were blown away by its tone, at once tender and caustic, apocalyptic yet hopeful, the way that it didn't just give a reading of the situation but spelled out concrete actions, something unprecedented in the history of papal social teaching. According to Professor Sachs, "it's a papal encyclical, but it's also a document you can teach in a sciences graduate course, in a public policy course, in a theology course, in a moral philosophy course, in a diplomacy course—and every one would meet the standards of rigor. It is a most remarkable document, and an essential document for our time."[30]

Its impact on the Church has been mixed so far—especially in the United States. A Yale University study a month before the Paris meeting showed a significant increase in the number of American Catholics who recognized global warming, and a Georgetown University poll revealed that Catholics were now more likely to be concerned about climate change than any other U.S. Christian group. There were new shoots of activity across the U.S. Church: talks in parishes and schools that led to "green teams," religious orders disinvesting in fossil fuels, and solar panels placed on the roofs of diocesan buildings. Four years after the encyclical, the Catholic bishops of California issued a major pastoral letter modeled after the encyclical that linked care for creation with a condemnation of abortion and euthanasia.

But while the organizers of the Yale study later said Francis had had a "significant impact on public opinion" on climate change during and after his September 2015 visit, six months afterward it was not clear how much more likely Catholics were than other Americans to buy fewer presents, let alone recycle, compost, carpool, switch off lights or the air-conditioning. Such acts, *Laudato Si'* had urged in its final chapter, were capable of changing the world, for "they call forth a goodness which, albeit unseen, inevitably tends to spread." It wasn't just the Americans who were slow to change their habits, even after Francis the following year declared the care and contemplation of Creation an eighth work of mercy, alongside feeding the hungry and comforting the afflicted. In February 2019, the pope told moral theologians that it was rare, in the sacrament of reconciliation, to hear someone confess to an act of violence against nature and creation. "We do not yet have awareness of this sin," he told them. "It is your task to do this."[31]

Yet it was clear, now, where the Church stood. The decision by U.S. president Donald Trump in June 2017 to withdraw from the Paris Agreement was described as "deeply troubling" by the U.S. bishops, whose call for the U.S. government to recommit to combat climate change quickly gained the support of close to eight hundred major Catholic institutions, including dozens of dioceses, hundreds of parishes and religious communities. Worldwide, more than fifty major Catholic organizations, including banks with more than $7.5 billion on their books, have stepped away from dirty energy. And the Church played a key role in the COP24 summit in Katowice in December 2018 in holding world leaders' feet to the fire.

Francis, too, has kept up the pressure, speaking out on the blight of plastics in the seas and convening meetings at the Vatican of oil company executives and investors, telling them that the world has to switch to clean energy if it is to avoid catastrophe. "Civilization requires energy," he warned them in 2018, "but energy use must not destroy civilization." At a second meeting a year later, he secured from Royal Dutch Shell, ExxonMobil, BP, Total, and Chevron, among others, pledges to support "economically meaningful" carbon pricing regimes.[32]

On April 16, 2019, Francis met a pigtailed Swedish teenager with Asperger syndrome in St. Peter's Square. Sixteen-year-old Greta Thunberg, inspiration of climate protest strikes across the world, had become the conscience of a new generation demanding from adults that they act. Decades separated them, but the old pope and the teenager were driven by the same passion. Beaming, Francis had just one message to her: "Go on, go on, continue," he told her. Thunberg was overjoyed. "Thank you for standing up for the climate, for speaking the truth," she told him. "It means a lot."

eight

La Patria Grande

July 8, 2015. Ashen-faced as he gripped the rolling staircase, Francis was braced for the worst as he came off his short flight from Quito at El Alto, the airport above Bolivia's capital, La Paz. Awaiting him at the bottom of the staircase with a *chulpa*, a traditional Aymara welcome gift of a handmade wool bag for coca leaves, was Evo Morales, a fiery former trade unionist and the country's first indigenous president.

Since taking office in 2006, Morales had relentlessly attacked the Church, painting it as a colonial import, and excluding it wherever possible from official acts, replacing Catholic rites with official venerations of the Inca fertility goddess Pachamama. Negotiations over Francis's visit, the second leg of his three-nation visit to South America in July 2015, had been stormy: the president was furious with the bishops' efforts to prevent his politicization of the visit, and no one quite knew what surprises he would spring when Francis arrived.

But the pope wasn't nervous about Morales.

Two years earlier, when La Paz's archbishop, Edmundo Abastoflor, had greeted Francis at the Vatican after his election, the two men had embraced warmly. They knew each other well from Aparecida. Like every other bishop of a Latin American capital, keen for Francis to visit, Abastoflor issued an invitation. The only problem, the pope told him, was that the last time he had traveled to Bolivia's capital he had nearly died.[1]

Back in La Paz, the Jesuits confirmed the story to Abastoflor. When he was twenty, Bergoglio had part of his lung removed following severe tuberculosis, and as a result he had reduced breathing capacity. In Buenos Aires, at sea level, his condition had not impeded him. Two decades on from that operation, however, the then Argentine Jesuit provincial had flown to La Paz for a meeting. As he stepped off the plane in 1979 at El Alto, at 13,600 feet the world's highest airport, he lost consciousness. Only a rapid application of an oxygen mask and transfer by plane to lowland Cochabamba had saved his life.

So when Francis's visit to Ecuador, Bolivia, and Paraguay was being put together by the Vatican, Abastoflor naturally made plans for the pope to fly from the Ecuadorian capital, Quito, directly to the lowland Bolivian city of Santa Cruz, where major events were planned. But to his amazement, the message came back that the pope would first fly to La Paz, even if only for a few hours, to visit Morales in the presidential palace and to speak in the cathedral.

Abastoflor was stunned. If Bergoglio had collapsed in his thirties, how much more likely was it that Francis, in his eighties, would do so again? The archbishop left nothing to chance. An air ambulance was on standby close by at El Alto, ready to whisk the pope to a hospital in Santa Cruz or to specialists in Brazil because no one—including, it turned out, Francis himself—had any idea what would happen when he disembarked. Assuming he made it to La Paz, the plan was for the pope to rest briefly in the archbishop's residence. Abastoflor made sure the room was well oxygenated. He also ordered air tanks to be discreetly hidden inside the flower arrangements at the cathedral.

"It's always surprising what the pope can do at his age," the Vatican spokesman, Father Federico Lombardi, told journalists in Quito the day before the trip, after noting that several people in the Vatican entourage had awoken with headaches due to altitude sickness but not, amazingly, Francis. Yet Quito, at 9,200 feet, was still a lot lower than El Alto at 13,600 feet.

There was visible relief on Francis's face as he reached the bottom of the stairway in the cold, thin air, and Morales placed the *chulpa* around his neck. The welcome ceremonies over, Francis climbed into the archbishop's car for the forty-minute journey to La Paz. On the way he asked for a bunch of flowers he could leave as an offering of thanks to the Virgin in the cathedral, because, he added, in a low voice, "I'm alive."

Why had he taken the risk? Abastoflor is in no doubt: it was important to Francis that he meet Morales and the bishops in their city, even if only briefly. "One only needs to come close, to be a neighbor," the pope had said in his pre-visit video message, in which he spoke of bringing the mercy and tenderness of God to all. That included, as it turned out, risking his life to accept an anticlerical president's invitation to his home.

The week Francis spent in the low-oxygen altitudes and steaming low-lands of three Andean nations would be the first of seven visits to the Americas over the following years that have constituted a master class in missionary evangelization. The trips had a single, overriding message: that only when the Church abandons its focus on institutions and pro-grams and learns to go out to encounter the Lord in His people, and above all the poor, can God's Kingdom come into being. From his home-land, the pope has shown the Church how to be close and concrete in a technocratic, liquid world.

Standing before a spectacular altar made of 32,000 corncobs, 1,000 squashes, and 200,000 coconuts, he told a crowd of a million people at Mass in the park of Ñu Guasú in Asunción, Paraguay, that evangelization was not about arguments, strategies, or tactics, but learning how to welcome people. It was like the seed that does not force its way into the soil and does not dominate it, but is received, and gradually grows. That is how the Christian communities needed to be, he said: "true centers of encounter between us and God, places of hospitality and welcome."

The "great challenge," he told the bishops in Bogotá, Colombia, two years later in September 2017, was how to speak to today's men and women about the closeness of God. The Church's task was to be what he called "the sacrament of this divine intimacy and the perennial place of this encoun-ter." Nobody listened to words anymore; to preach the love of God meant to perform it. Only in proximity does the follower of Christ "learn how to make tangible God's passion for his children."[2]

Coming close meant going out, taking risks, being vulnerable. Arriv-ing in Cartagena, Colombia, at the end of his four-day, ten-speech visit to the war-scarred nation, Francis was greeting crowds on his way to a shelter for the homeless when the popemobile stopped abruptly, causing him to hit his head against the metal bar that holds the glass roof of the vehicle. There was barely a front page in the world that the next day didn't carry the picture of the blood on his white cassock and the shiny bruise under his eye covered with a tiny Band-Aid, alongside the story of the matter-of-fact way he had got patched up and moved on. That shot said everything he had tried to convey in *Evangelii Gaudium* about preferring "a Church that is bruised, hurting, and dirty because it has been out on the streets" to "a Church that is sick from being confined and clinging to its own security."

Missionary evangelization meant going out to the edges, to places of pain and rejection, because Christ tended first to those who cried and dreamed. But Francis was also convinced that Latin America's unique synthesis of faith, politics, and culture needed to be of service to the world at this time, that the Lord had anointed the Church at Aparecida and was calling forth its gifts.

Hence he chose to start his 2015 American odyssey in three nations that were looked down upon by modern, cosmopolitan Latin America. Ecuador, Bolivia, and Paraguay had large numbers of poor, indigenous, and Catholics, and some of the highest Mass attendance rates in the world (in Paraguay's case, over 70 percent). In their popular devotions and strong social solidarity, they offered a reserve of religiosity that the universal Church badly needed, illustrating the circular paradox of *Evangelii Gaudium*: in taking the Gospel to the poor, who was evangelizing whom? In his pre-visit video, Francis asked Ecuador, Bolivia, and Paraguay to pray that the Gospel reach "the most distant peripheries." There was a pointed irony to his request.

The center–periphery dynamic also determined the itineraries, which saw Francis flip-flop between the capital and outlying areas (Quito/Guayaquil, La Paz/Santa Cruz, Asunción/Caacupé) while alternating presidents' palaces and cathedrals with slums and elderly homes, prisons and hospitals. It was the pattern that was etched into all the journeys that followed. Most dramatic of all was Mexico in February 2016, where he spent more time in the country's poverty-stricken bordertowns, in the company of Tzotzil Mayan Indians in the far south and the migrants and prisoners of Ciudad Juárez in the far north, than in the federal capital, in the company of bishops and politicians.

It was harder to do the same in the United States because the visits to Washington, D.C., New York, and Philadelphia in September 2015 were determined by specific invitations: from the U.S. Congress, the United Nations, and the World Meeting of Families. But he could at least ensure dramatic juxtapositions: lunching with the homeless right after speaking to America's political class, and meeting migrants on the afternoon of his address to the United Nations in New York.

Significantly, the U.S. visit came at the end of a ten-day marathon that had begun with three whole days in Cuba, so that even his arrival—by air to Washington, D.C., from Havana—broke through history-hardened borders of suspicion and mistrust. The original plan had been to land in the United States from Mexico, just as Donald Trump, in early campaigning for the presidency, was inflaming rallies with pledges to build a wall on the border, but logistically that wasn't possible. The next best thing was a huge transborder Mass at Ciudad Juárez the following February, which people could take part in via video link at the Sun Bowl over in El Paso, Texas. Before the Mass, Francis dramatically prayed by a tall cross at the top of a ramp on the banks of the river dividing the two nations.

On the plane back to Rome from Mexico, Francis was asked about Trump's plans to build a wall. The candidate should be given the benefit of the doubt, he said, but "building walls instead of bridges is not Christian; this is not in the Gospel." (Pro-Trump evangelical leader Jerry Falwell, who had spent his life telling political leaders how Jesus wanted them to run the country, snapped back that "Jesus never intended to give instructions to political leaders on how to run a country.")

The moving visit to Colombia in September 2017, to consolidate its historic peace process between the FARC (Revolutionary Armed Forces of Colombia) and the government, was followed with Chile and Peru in January 2018, and Panama in January 2019 for a World Youth Day that included the other Central American nations. Together with its tiny neighbor Uruguay, this left Argentina as the only Latin American country with no visit in the diary as the pontificate turned five. The pope's periphery-first policies began (to the chagrin of his countrymen) at home.

Being a missionary open to the Holy Spirit meant being ready to go off course, to respond to the moment, to improvise, to inhabit the ordinary spaces of the world, as when, in Santa Cruz, Bolivia, in 2015 he used a Burger King as an improvised sacristy to vest for a vast outdoor Mass, or when, on the flight from Iquique, Chile, to Lima, Peru, in 2018 he married the two LATAM airline staff. Just like Jesus hearing the cries of a blind man over the crowds, Francis later spotted an elderly lady holding a cardboard sign on a narrow street in the Peruvian city of Trujillo. The sign read: "My name is Trinidad. I am 99 years old. I cannot see. I want to touch your dear hand." Francis stopped the popemobile, went over to her, and told her: "Trinidad, I am Pope Francis." He tenderly caressed her face and drew the sign of the cross on her forehead. (In a video that went viral, she told reporters it was "a miracle of God.")

Days before arriving in the United States from Cuba, Francis singled out the island's missionary house churches, *las casitas misión*. Laboring under tight state restrictions, the Church had fewer than four hundred priests serving a population of eleven million, while Sunday Mass attendance, which still carried the whiff of political disobedience, was less than 5 percent. Speaking in Holguín—a poor city in the center of Cuba, close to where Christopher Columbus first landed in the New World in 1491—Francis praised the two-thousand-odd *casitas misión* in Cuba as "small signs of God's presence in our neighborhoods" that offered space for prayer, catechesis, and community. God "never wearies of visiting us in the marketplace, even at the eleventh hour, to propose his offer of love," Francis later told the U.S. bishops in Washington, D.C. In Philadelphia, he called for "creativity in adapting to changed situations" and being "open to the possibilities which the Spirit opens up to us." This was the message of Aparecida and *Evangelii Gaudium*: changing times called for a missionary flexibility, for finding God outside the sacristy.

Each American visit advanced key objectives of the pontificate: pastoral conversion, the culture of encounter, focus on the peripheries, missionary discipleship, bolstering the family, and building bonds of belonging across social divides. But the scarlet thread uniting them was the shift in focus of *Evangelii Gaudium* out to the poor, *los descartados*, the throwaway folk. In the context of liquidity, the task was not to cling to little islands of privilege and continuity but to launch life rafts to save the drowning. In the sweltering heat of Havana's cathedral, Francis told clergy and religious that when they served the least, the most abandoned, the sickest, "you are serving Jesus in the greatest way," because God's love was "like a disabled child who tries to kiss you and dribbles on your face," like the men and women who "burn away their lives" caring for "discarded material."

"The Lord wants an evangelizing Church, I see that clearly," Francis told the Jesuits in Lima in January 2018, recalling how he had spoken before the 2013 conclave of "a Church that goes out, a Church that goes out proclaiming Jesus Christ." He believed the Lord was now asking for "a poor Church for the poor" because "they are the center of the Gospel. We cannot preach the Gospel without the poor. So I say to you: it is along this line that I feel the Spirit is leading us."

There was strong opposition, he told the Jesuits, but nothing to worry about. It was a good sign; a confirmation, even. "This is the road. Otherwise the devil would not bother to resist."[3]

The dream of Latin American continental unity known as *la patria grande* had been on the pope's mind right from the start of his Andean journey in 2015. In the car on his way to the Ecuadorian capital's new "bicentennial park," named for the two-hundredth anniversary of Spanish-American emancipation, Francis peppered the archbishop of Quito, Fausto Trávez, with questions about moves to integrate the economies of Peru, Ecuador, and Bolivia. "We are so alike, so similar, that we should be a single nation," Trávez, a Franciscan, recalls telling Francis, "yet we have spent our time in wars and arguments." As he blessed the crowds through the wound-down window, Francis spoke to Trávez about what kept the nations apart. It was the theme of his homily at the bicentennial park: how Latin America's great future was held back by "a futile quest for power, prestige, pleasure or economic security."[4]

At the Mass celebrated for 800,000, there were readings and prayers in Quechua and music from the funeral of the last Inca emperor, Atahualpa. Francis linked the continent's yearning for unity with the Church's embrace of its mission to evangelize, showing the connection between pastoral conversion and political integration. True unity, he said, came neither from imposing ideologies nor from uniformity in thought and culture, but through a Gospel-revealed common recognition of the innate dignity of all people as children of God. Thus the continent's independence, an attempt to be free of subjugation to powers that did not respect that dignity, was at the same time an expression of a Gospel-implanted desire.

For Francis the pastoral and the geopolitical were inextricably bound, just as they had been for Saint John Paul II in his bid to liberate Eastern Europe from the Soviet yoke. What the Berlin Wall was to the Polish pope, the Mexican–American border and the Florida Strait were to the Argentine pope. But he was also concerned with the borders within Latin America, so often the focus of rival claims and territorial disputes that could escalate into war.

He was convinced that Latin America needed to come together, to fortify its Christian, humanist traditions in a strengthened alliance capable of withstanding the "ideological colonization" of globalized technocracy. In his hourlong speech to the popular movements in Santa Cruz, Bolivia—one of the most remarkable ever made by the pope—he spelled out what he called "the new colonialism" that appeared in both ideological and economic guises, among whose "different faces" was "the anonymous influence of mammon: corporations, loan agencies, certain free-trade treaties, and the imposition of 'austerity' measures which always tighten the belts of workers and the poor."

Before the crowd of union leaders, farmers, and social activists, he said Latin America could not allow "certain interests—interests that are global but not universal—to take over, to dominate states and international organizations, and to continue destroying creation." Francis was showing that the Church stood with the people against those dehumanizing forces, not as an outside agent but as "part of the identity of the peoples of Latin America," an identity that "some powers are committed to erasing at times, because our faith is revolutionary, because our faith challenges the tyranny of mammon."

There was an implicit critique of the ideology behind Morales's Movement for Socialism. "We do not love concepts or ideas; no one loves a concept or an idea. We love people," he told the popular movements. At a civil-society meeting in Asunción, Paraguay, he repeated the warning: "Ideologies end badly, and are useless. . . . They relate to people in ways that are either incomplete, unhealthy, or evil." Two months later, at a Mass in Revolution Square, Havana, he told a congregation that included Raúl Castro and leading communists that "service is never ideological, for we do not serve ideas; we serve people."

As rector of the Colegio Máximo in the 1980s, he had sought to isolate the Argentine Jesuit province from the marxisant ideologies that were prevalent at the time in most of Latin America. But he made an exception for the Jesuit-run Colegio Javier in Guayaquil, Ecuador's second city, where he lunched at the start of his July 2015 visit following a Mass celebrated for a million people in Samanes Park. The colegio, which had learned of his coming just a few months earlier, had spent the time energetically preparing with special songs, poems, and murals, so that the pope's arrival was greeted with an explosion of energy and creativity.

Colegio Javier's rector, Father Alfonso Villalba, had struck an isolationist path similar to Bergoglio's Colegio Máximo in the 1970s and 1980s, and their shared resistance to wider trends in the Society of Jesus was a bond between them. Over the years the Argentine rector had sent dozens of "scholastics," as Jesuits in formation are known, to Guayaquil to teach in the college and minister to the city's poor. The two rectors met more than once, but mostly they wrote each other long letters over the years, which Villalba—aware at the end of his life that Bergoglio was destined for greater things—burned before his death.

Francis came to Colegio Javier in July 2015 to greet the one remaining link with that past, a ninety-one-year-old Spanish Jesuit named Francisco Cortés, the college's former spiritual director, known as "Paquito," whom he hadn't seen since 1985. After an affectionate embrace, they spent some minutes alone.

In a hoarse voice in his simple room at the college, Paquito described for me a year later how grateful Francis had been for Javier at a time when the Jesuits, as well as Argentina, had been deeply divided. "We were neither ultraconservative nor of the left. It was very quiet here," Paquito told me.[5]

The old Spanish Jesuit, who had in his long life never met a pope until one came into his room, said he had only one question for Francis. "Why did you want to come and see *me*?" he had asked him, amazed. Clutching his arm, Francis said he had wanted to thank him for treating his Argentine students so well. Paquito took out a list he had prepared, with the names of dozens of scholastics Bergoglio had sent him over the years. Francis looked it over, nodding and smiling, while never releasing the old Spaniard's arm. "I give thanks to God," Francis told him. "They were difficult times."

The challenge for Bergoglio as provincial was that standing prophetically with the poor in the 1970s had become confused with Marxist sociologies of modernization and Cuba's model of socialism. He faced a similar challenge now, as a pope in Latin America: how to honor those who had died in defense of their people, without endorsing some of their political beliefs? A classic example was the Spanish Jesuit missionary and democracy activist Father Luís Espinal Camps, a poet and filmmaker who lived alongside striking miners in Bolivia and was at the front line of protests against the 1970s military dictatorship when he was brutally tortured and murdered by paramilitaries in March 1980. Worldwide, the news was eclipsed by the gunning down at the altar of the archbishop of San Salvador, Óscar

Romero, just days later, but Espinal's murder had deeply shocked the Jesuits in Argentina, where Bergoglio had just finished his term as provincial.

En route to La Paz from El Alto in July 2015, grateful to be alive, Francis had made a stop to pray at the spot where Espinal had been gunned down. In brief remarks to hundreds of people gathered at the site, Francis referred to him as "our brother" and focused on the reason he was killed. "Espinal preached the Gospel and that Gospel irritated. And so they eliminated him."

An hour later, after their long private meeting in the presidential palace in La Paz, Morales and Francis came out for the cameras. Morales's men had blocked the papal entourage and the Bolivian bishops from joining the pope for the meeting, possibly because of what was planned next. In front of the clicking cameras the president sprang a surprise, handing Francis a huge crucifix made out of a hammer and sickle, a replica, he told him, of one Espinal had made and kept by his bed. The pope was taken aback but not—he told journalists later, downplaying the incident—offended by it. Espinal, he explained, was an enthusiast of a Marxist version of liberation theology that the Jesuit superior general at the time, Father Pedro Arrupe, had opposed. "It was [Espinal's] life, his way of thinking," the pope said carefully.

In Chiapas, Mexico, in February 2016, Francis faced a similar challenge in acknowledging the legacy of Bishop Samuel Ruiz, known as "Tatic" (Father) to the Mayan Indians who made up 70 percent of his diocese of San Cristóbal de las Casas. A champion of the poor and ecology as well as a leading advocate of "inculturation," Ruiz had faced considerable hostility in Rome and from conservative bishops in Mexico. Francis chose to vindicate him in small but charged gestures: praying at his tomb and issuing a decree that allowed the three Mayan languages—Tzotzil, Tzeltal, and Cho'ol—to be used during the Mass. He did the same in Santiago de Chile in January 2018, when he constantly referred to Cardinal Raúl Silva Henríquez, who was an outspoken defender of human rights and social justice during the dictatorship of Augusto Pinochet and who was constantly blocked by John Paul II's nuncio and later secretary of state, Cardinal Angelo Sodano.

In vindicating these Latin American prophets, Francis was foregrounding a key tenet of Paul VI's 1975 apostolic exhortation *Evangelii Nuntiandi* that underpinned *Evangelii Gaudium*: namely, that there could be no evangelization without proclaiming justice, peace, and human liberation; there was no Jesus without the alternative social order He announced. If some liberation theologians in the 1960s and 1970s had confused the Kingdom of God with the political ideology of socialism, the problem over the last three decades had been the opposite: the defense of Christendom had become enmeshed with conservative ideologies, and the Church's prophetic social witness had been suffocated in the crackdown on liberation theology.

Nowhere was this truer than in the blocking of the sainthood cause of Salvadoran archbishop Óscar Romero, slain at the altar in March 1980 by paramilitaries acting on the orders of the government after he spoke out against its violent suppression of political protest. Romero was not only, obviously, a martyr in the classic sense of the term, but he was also a transparently holy man whose final years and death remarkably echoed Christ's. John Paul II's secretary of state, Cardinal Sodano, and his Latin American curial allies—especially the Colombian prefect of the Pontifical Council for the Family, Alfonso López Trujillo—had notoriously blocked the canonization on political grounds, under pressure from local bishops who were enmeshed with the regime and the nation's wealthy families. The delay had become a major scandal in Latin America that Bergoglio was determined to put right. He reportedly told a Salvadoran priest in 2007 that "to me [Romero] is a saint and a martyr. . . . If I were pope, I would have already canonized him."

John Paul II, who knew Romero was a saint, delayed the canonization under pressure from Sodano and López Trujillo, while Benedict opted to move slowly, holding inquiries and reviews to appease opponents until he finally approved the cause on the eve of his resignation. Three weeks after his election, Francis authorized the canonization. "[Romero] was defamed, slandered, soiled—that is, his martyrdom continued even by his brothers in the priesthood and in the episcopate," Francis told Salvadoran pilgrims in the fall of 2015.

At a huge Mass in St. Peter's Square in October 2018, Francis declared Romero a saint, together with Pope Paul VI and a handful of others. In his homily he contrasted a worldly religiosity based on the observance of commandments and clinging to security with the total, self-giving, sacrificial love that Jesus asks of His followers. In asking for the grace "to leave behind wealth, the yearning for status and power, structures that are no longer adequate for proclaiming the Gospel, those weights that slow down our mission, the strings that tie us to the world," Francis was holding up the example of Romero to all those churchmen who had preferred the maintenance of an unjust social order to the Kingdom of God. But he was also sending a clear message to the Vatican: that the Church's recognition of its saints and martyrs should never be subordinated to political concerns.

Speaking to the bishops of Central America in Panama in January 2019, Francis held up Romero as a model pastor, one who accepted being vilified by his peers as the price of being close to his people. "Romero was not an administrator of human resources, nor a manager of people or organizations," he told them. "Romero felt, he felt with the love of a father, friend and brother." Romero lived simply, in poverty, he said later, because he did not want the Church's strength to depend on alliances with the powerful and political influence, but "only on the true strength born of the embrace of the crucified Jesus."[6]

In addition to hallowing the Latin American Church's modern prophets, Francis held up missionary heroes from its colonial era, the roughly three centuries between the conquest and evangelization in the sixteenth century and independence in the nineteenth. Of these, none meant more to him personally than the Jesuits who had created the impressive network of missions known as "Reductions" in Paraguay, which then included what is today northern Argentina and western Brazil. The Reductions were home to hundreds of thousands of Guaraní until their late-eighteenth-century suppression on the orders of Charles III of Spain, who soon after expelled the Jesuits. The missions were "among the most significant experiences of evangelization and social organization in history," Francis told a meeting of civil-society leaders in Asunción, Paraguay, in July 2015. There "the Gospel was the soul and the life of communities which did not know hunger, unemployment, illiteracy or oppression." They showed, he said, that "today, too, a more human society is possible."[7]

Francis discussed the legacy of the Reductions enthusiastically with Asunción's archbishop, Edmundo Valenzuela, in the car on the way to the national shrine of Our Lady of Miracles, Caacupé. Once there, the combination of posters and music from the film *The Mission*, the unmistakable Paraguayan harps, and the cries in Guaraní from thousands of delighted descendants of the inhabitants of the Reductions, all proved emotionally overwhelming for Francis, who needed some time in the sacristy to compose himself. A doctor was sent for, but it was a different heart issue.[8]

Valenzuela was moved by how Francis used Paraguay's past to point to its future. "He understood that in our people the Spirit of God has sowed many seeds—of goodness, justice, love, solidarity—but they're still seeds, and he came to wake us to that," he told me. In Michoacán, Mexico, where Francis celebrated Mass with the pastoral staff and chalice used by the beloved sixteenth-century bishop "Tata" Vásquez, he urged the Church to follow the example of the pastor who spoke up for and organized the wretched Purhéchepas Indians. Today, he said, the Church was similarly called to free the people of Morelia from the bondage of modern-day drug lords.

In Washington, D.C., Francis canonized the California missionary Junípero Serra, who "learned how to bring to birth and nurture God's life in the faces of everyone he met." In Cartagena, Colombia, he held up the seventeenth-century Saint Peter Claver and his team of Jesuits who defended the dignity of black slaves. Claver "had the genius to live the Gospel to the full, to encounter those whom others considered only material to be discarded," Francis said, adding that in that encounter was born the modern campaign for human rights.

But his greatest colonial missionary hero was the sixteenth-century Peruvian pastor Saint Turibius of Mogrovejo, who spent most of his twenty-two years as archbishop of Lima crisscrossing his vast diocese, learning Quechua and Aymara, infuriating Spanish colonial officials with his denunciations of their injustices, and ending his life in a hut, surrounded by native people playing pipes to accompany his final journey. Turibius had presided at the third Lima council beginning in 1582 that organized the missionary evangelization of South America. One of its main tasks was drawing up a trilingual catechism in Spanish, Quechua, and Aymara that would later be translated into Guaraní and used by the Jesuits in the Paraguayan missions.

Turibius exemplified to the Church in the late sixteenth century what Romero did in the late twentieth: a bishop who held together the encounter with Christ and the proclamation of His Kingdom; one who stayed always close to his people, defending them from the wolves. Turibius showed "there could be no evangelization without charity," Francis told Peru's bishops, because for him "charity must always be accompanied by justice." Indeed, the pope added, "there can be no evangelization that does not point out and denounce every sin against the lives of our brothers and sisters, especially those who are most vulnerable." In Peru, Francis himself had done precisely that, denouncing human trafficking in Puerto Maldonado and femicide in Trujillo, modeling a Church that expressed its closeness to the people by naming and shaming the conditions and forces that held them down.

In a 2017 interview to mark the tenth anniversary of Aparecida, Francis said there had been great progress in the "people's awareness of belonging." The Church in Latin America was more able to judge the present using its own lenses, rather than ill-fitting foreign ones. But he lamented the waning of the *patria grande*, which he described as the "true project of Latin America." It was held back by corruption, drug trafficking, and the continent's subservience to the "international monetary system," he said. "We were looking for a path towards the *patria grande*," he told Peru's bishops, "when we came up against an inhuman liberal capitalism that harms the people."[9]

As for the Church, he observed in the same interview, Catholicism in Latin America was "still very much halfway there" in terms of pastoral conversion. It was often still too distant. Clericalism, the legacy of the national era, was still too common. The call to lay discipleship still "has to be discovered and developed and given its proper weight."

Francis saw these two incomplete Latin American journeys—the Church's pastoral conversion, mapped out at Aparecida, and the continent's historic journey to the *patria grande*—as intertwined. A static, bureaucratic, ritualistic, formalistic Catholicism was incapable of generating the bonds necessary to counteract the dissolving trends of globalization: hence the urgent call in Aparecida, and again in *Evangelii Gaudium*, to pastoral conversion, to being close and concrete.

To understand the link in Francis's mind between Latin America's pastoral conversion and its destiny in the *patria grande*, there is no greater source than a landmark 1981 essay by the Uruguayan intellectual and longstanding Bergoglio collaborator Alberto Methol Ferré.[10]

"El Resurgimiento Católico Latinoamericano" (The Latin-American Catholic Resurgence) argued that as a result of Vatican II the Church in Latin America could now *shape* modernity, as it had in the days of the Hapsburg colony, when the Gospel had been key to the formation of Latin

America's symbiotic civilization and created the foundations of the continent's underlying unity. The Church could be once again a *complexio oppositorum*, an agent of integration, a mechanism of synthesis, fashioning a new culture out of discrete elements just like the one that had flowered in the age of Turibius and the Jesuit missions.

The Church's cultural fertility—its *generativity*—came about, Methol argued, because it was neither assimilated to modernity nor rejecting of it. It could create an *alternative* modernity, capable of holding together Spanish and Creole, Creole and Indian, black and white, on the basis of a shared human dignity revealed by the Gospel. That colonial experience of the Church, faithful to tradition without being traditionalist, modern without being modernist, showed what an evangelized modernity could look like again today: a model of globalization that was distinct from and capable of containing the prevailing technocracy. This destiny had been identified back in the 1970s by Amelia Podetti, who was convinced that Latin America's role in the contemporary world was to create a globalization that was an alternative to that of the superpowers, "for its mission and its destiny are to think through and live out unity."[11]

In Methol's reading, Latin America's colonial journey toward this unity was interrupted, ironically, by emancipation from Spain, and what would be at least a century of fragmentation and subservience to foreign powers and cultures. The trauma of the independence period led to three ruptures. The first was between elite and *pueblo*, as the Creole leaders grabbed common and Church lands, leading to gross economic inequalities and the impoverishment of ordinary people, and a greater social and political distance between the cosmopolitan urban wealthy and the rural poor. With the loss of its lands and rural missions, the clergy became dependent on urban elites for their maintenance, while the bishops were appointed not by Rome but by the state. Hence the second rupture: the Church became increasingly clerical and distant from the ordinary religiosity of the people. The third was the weakening of the bonds of civil society and between nations, which led to the fragmentation of Latin America into isolated, often feuding, nation-states, which in the nineteenth and early twentieth centuries often went to war with each other with devastating consequences.

All three traumas reversed the openness to the Spirit that went hand in hand with the Church's pastoral and missionary option for the poor in the colonial era. As the Church was knocked back and turned in on itself from the late eighteenth through the twentieth centuries, it became a "depen-dent society," incapable of overcoming society's contradictions because it was polarized between factions favoring assimilation and those favoring resistance, much as in the contemporary Church in the rich world. "The Integrist is a Catholic defeated by the Enlightenment, who closes in on himself," wrote Methol. "The Modernist is the same, but who is open. One is frozen, the other dissolves."

Methol saw in the Second Vatican Council—which reconciled the Church with the contemporary age by sifting modernity, integrating what was of the Gospel—the chance for the Church to disentangle itself from the dead-end cycle of assimilation and rejection, and to resume its colonial-era role as agent of reconciliation. The Church's contemporary mission was now to heal the three ruptures of the national period. The first was its own task of reform: to abandon clericalism and commit itself once again in humble service to the *pueblo*, to open up to the voice of the poor and the traditions of popular religiosity that had developed outside clerical cul-ture. The second was to promote a new national-popular economics and politics, rooted in the values and interests of the *pueblo*, that sought to overcome gross economic inequalities and social exclusion, a true politics of the common good. Finally, and as a corollary of the first two, it meant resuming the frustrated journey to continental unity through dialogue and integration, which in turn implied a rejection of the "ideological coloniza-tion" of globalized technocracy.

All three aims were at the heart of the "continental mission" agreed upon in Aparecida, and central to Francis's messages on his American trips. Francis's notion of a "culture of encounter," which he promoted in meetings with politicians and civil society leaders, was his contemporary version of the colonial-era role Methol had seen the Church playing, as a "shaper of culture" by holding together the polar contrasts of the time. Aparecida had "perceived a divorce between the faith and concrete social practice of believers," Bergoglio noted in January 2008, adding that it would be pri-marily the task of laypeople to transform social structures, counteracting the narcissism of contemporary individualism, combating exclusion, vio-lence, and corruption. Hence the task of the formation of people, in prayer and discernment, the lack of which, Bergoglio warned, could lead all too easily to "a fundamentalist religious subjectivism or a syncretism of wishy-washy, superficial Christians."[12]

Francis's frequent references to colonial missionary activity were not nostalgia. He was convinced that the Church in Latin America was now called to play a similar role as in that era, in helping to forge a people. It could only do that by belonging to the people, by being *in* and *of* the people. That meant inculturation, which in turn implied a respect for popular devotions and religiosity. The greatness of the colonial missions led by Turibius and the Jesuits was that they sowed the seed of the Gospel within existing cultures. Restoring this capacity for inculturation had been the great achievement of the 1979 CELAM meeting at Puebla, Mexico, which, inspired by Paul VI's 1975 *Evangelii Nuntiandi*, treated with a new respect the faith-culture of ordinary people that had preserved the seeds of the Gospel sown by the colonial-era Church.

Bergoglio described this faith-culture as "the foundational cultural synthesis of Latin America, produced in the sixteenth and seventeenth centuries, which jealously safeguards the variety and interconnectedness of Indian, black and Europe substrates." In a famous homily he had given at Aparecida, Bergoglio had made a declaration of popular rather than papal infallibility when he spoke of "people and pastors making up this holy, faithful people of God which enjoys an *infalibilitas in credendo*." To CELAM officials in Bogotá, Colombia, Francis in September 2017 praised "the popular piety of our people, which is part of its anthropological uniqueness and a gift by which God wants our people to come to know him," adding that "the most luminous pages of our Church's history were written precisely when she knew how to be nourished by this richness and to speak to this hidden heart." A few months later, he gave thanks at the conclusion of his visit to Peru for "the faith of God's holy, faithful people, which does us so much good," telling the bishops: "If you do not touch the faith of the people, the faith of the people does not touch you."

This evangelized popular culture was central to how Francis saw the Church's pastoral role in building Latin America's future. He had long spoken of the continent's distinctive culture and mind-set in terms of a hermeneutic, referring in his writings to the way the people had "a soul, an awareness, a way of seeing." In the Basilica of Our Lady of the Assumption in Santiago de Cuba, Francis spoke of "the soul of the Cuban people . . . forged amid suffering and privation which could not suppress the faith." In Bogotá, he spoke to CELAM leaders of "our mestizo soul." Both neoliberalism—individualism, consumerism, globalized technocracy—and the sub-Marxist ideologies of what he called "adolescent progressivism" were alien to this "soul." Latin America, he told civic leaders from the continent in Rome in March 2018, "was born *mestizo*, will remain *mestizo*, will only grow as *mestizo*, and this will be its destiny." This was Latin America, he said, "a *Patria Grande* in the process of becoming."[13]

To many Americans and Europeans, of both the left and the right, this language sounded suspiciously populist, while to some Argentine liberal intellectuals it smacked of Peronism's Manichean division of society into *pueblo* and *anti-pueblo*. Noting that on Francis's trips in 2015 he had used the word "people" 356 times and "democracy" only 10, one liberal Italian historian claimed that Francis was a nationalist Catholic of the old school, holding Latin America back from the Enlightenment of liberal democracy. It was ironic that while politically Republican free-market conservatives in the United States criticized Francis as a socialist and populist nationalists such as Steve Bannon deplored him as a globalist, the European liberals excoriated him as a "populist" of a pseudofascist kind, "imbued with visceral anti-liberalism."[14]

Francis's use of the term *pueblo* was indeed illiberal: he conceived of the Latin American people not as an amalgamation of autonomous individuals, but as a community, a fraternity, and a culture. But while it had political implications, *el pueblo* for Francis was not a political category. It was not coterminous with a nation, class, or clan, nor with the messianic category used in demagogic political ideologies from the French Revolution's "general will" to the fascist *das Volk* and *il popolo* in Germany and Italy. Even less was it synonymous with the Marxist distinction between the proletariat (the people) and the oligarchy.

The Argentine theologian who most influenced Bergoglio, Father Lucio Gera, used the term *anti-pueblo* to describe "oligarchies" that pursued their own self-interest rather than serving the common good. But he didn't mean an economic class per se: you could be rich and still be part of *el pueblo* if you saw yourself as belonging. *Anti-pueblo* was, in essence, a mind-set: an attitude of scornful or distrustful self-witholding, what Bergoglio, as a Jesuit, referred to as an "isolated conscience."

In an address in at the Buenos Aires cathedral in 2002 before Argentina's political dignitaries, Cardinal Bergoglio had pondered the Gospel story of Zacchaeus, the short-of-stature tax collector of Jericho who after encountering Jesus promises to give back to the people much more than he has taken. Bergoglio saw that in calling Zacchaeus down from his syca-more tree, Jesus is inviting him to come down from his self-sufficiency, the false personality that he had constructed on the basis of his wealth and that kept him at odds with *el pueblo*. After meeting Jesus, Zacchaeus chooses to work patiently and in solidarity alongside the mass of ordinary people. He remains a tax collector, but one who serves, not exploits, no longer arro-gant and isolated, for his heart has turned—Francis told young people at the shrine of Maipú in Santiago de Chile—"from materialism to solidarity." He who was *anti-pueblo* is now *pueblo*.

El pueblo is a "mythical and historical" concept that cannot be explained in terms of logical categories, Bergoglio wrote in a 2010 essay on Argentina's destiny. A person lives in a society (or a city, or a village), and is the citi-zen of a country; but he or she *belongs to* a people. That people is not yet one; becoming a people is a journey—lengthy, arduous, and sometimes painful—toward a transcendent horizon, toward ever greater solidarity and fraternity, in an entity that transcends all differences while respecting diversity. This becoming-a-people is the patient process described in *Evan-gelii Gaudium* 220: one that happens by means of a "culture of encounter," integrating disparate elements in a kind of Baroque symphony like the art and architecture of Latin America's colonial period.[15]

Francis's energetic denunciation of clericalism and his horror of spiritual worldliness have to be understood against this backdrop. In calling his disciples to build a people, to work for the good of all, Jesus needs "men and women of the people," not "grandees who look down upon others," as Francis says in *Evangelii Gaudium*. Clericalism is a form of corruption, a priest's way of detaching and distancing himself from God's people, just as a politician becomes corrupt when he stops serving the people and seeks his own good. Clericalism, like corruption, is *anti-pueblo*.[16]

There is an insidious form of corruption in the Church that occurs when wealthy donors fund bishops' expensive projects and receive prefer-ential treatment in return. Even though, in such instances, bishops are not benefiting personally, Francis did not hide his pain about the times when the Church distanced itself from *el pueblo* in identifying with the well-off, allowing wealthy donors privileged access over others.

In Guayaquil, Ecuador, Francis was taken by the city's then bishop to a ten-foot-high modern Divine Mercy sanctuary that the bishop had opened in 2013 with donations from local businessmen, who had gathered there to receive the pope. This wasn't popular religiosity; the shrine was far away from where the poor lived. Greeting some disabled children, the pope stayed barely five minutes, joking acidly that he wouldn't charge for blessing them.

A meeting at the St. Francis church in Ecuador's capital, Quito, the next day, had been intended to bring together the "social pastoral" workers, people serving slum dwellers and the indigenous in the rain forest, together with representatives of those communities. Yet in the end only about fifty of the seven hundred who were present were people working with the marginalized, and the native peoples were merely a token presence. Most of the congregation was made up of businesspeople, politicians, members of church movements or think tanks financed by the wealthy who had muscled their way in through connections. "You could see he was frustrated," says one person who was present. "He had been led to expect a large number of indigenous people he could engage directly." Even though there were only a handful of them, Francis made sure in the speech to highlight their presence, while stressing in his speech the importance of including native peoples, Afro-Ecuadorians, women, and civic groups.

It was even worse at New York's St. Patrick's Cathedral.

Francis, who had amazed America by being driven around in a small black Fiat, arrived at New York's JFK Airport on the evening of September 24, 2015, and transferred (after a helicopter ride) from the Fiat to the popemobile. Riding up Fifth Avenue for evening prayer at St. Patrick's, he turned to Cardinal Timothy Dolan behind him at one point and asked: "How much did you have to pay for that seat?" to which Dolan laughingly answered: "Seven years of Peter's Pence!"

They were joshing, but the pope's joke had a bite. Although the Vespers was intended for the clergy and religious of the city, the front half of the cathedral was packed solid with wealthy donors and VIPs, with the front pews reserved for those who had contributed more than half a million dollars each to Cardinal Dolan's $177 million cathedral renovation fund, and who in return might get to shake the pope's hand. The biggest donors of all—the megarich—got to read the prayers of the faithful. Because the cathedral had given so many tickets to donors, religious and priests struggled to get a place. According to a member of the cathedral staff close to him, Francis was shocked to find himself facing row upon row of suits and diamonds. He asked the MC as he arrived: "But where are the priests and religious?"[17]

Speaking over the donors to the men and women in habits behind them, Francis in St. Patrick's warned clergy and religious not to seek respite in worldly comforts, for such behavior "alienates people who suffer material poverty and are forced to make greater sacrifices than ourselves, without being consecrated." As ever, the issue for Francis—who used to spend his downtime Saturdays in Buenos Aires among the poor of the shantytowns—was the temptation of distance. "Closeness to the poor, the refugee, the immigrant, the sick, the exploited, the elderly living alone, prisoners and all God's other poor, will teach us a different way of resting, one which is more Christian and generous," he told them.

Another way of the Church distancing itself from the people was by investing great efforts in legislative battles, aligning itself with Republican Party agendas. In Washington, D.C., Francis warned the bishops that the Church "falls into hopeless decline whenever we confuse the power of strength with the strength of that powerlessness with which God has redeemed us." This was not naïveté: there was a battle between light and darkness being fought in this world. "Woe to us, however, if we make of the cross a banner of worldly struggles and fail to realize that the price of lasting victory is allowing ourselves to be wounded and consumed."

The Church could only credibly evangelize from powerlessness, by going as sheep among wolves. Politically, the Church sought only the liberty to preach and act according to the Gospel. "She has no need for alliances with this or that party," Francis told the bishops in Bogotá, "but only the freedom to speak to the heart of every man and woman." To CELAM in Bogotá in 2017 he spoke of his conviction that solutions to the complex problems posed by "this difficult and confused, yet provisional moment that we are experiencing" would be found "in that Christian simplicity hidden to the powerful yet revealed to the lowly."

In the summer of 2017, Francis read books by Zygmunt Bauman, the Polish sociologist and thinker who had famously identified and analyzed the "liquid society." Bauman had died in January of that year, just four months after meeting Francis at the interreligious leaders' gathering he had hosted the previous September at Assisi. The ninety-one-year-old prophet and the eighty-year-old pope had had an intense discussion. Bauman told him he had worked all his life to make the world a more hospitable place, but he had seen so many false starts that he had become pessimistic about what he called the "negative globalization" of the early twenty-first century. But Francis had given him hope. "Thank you, because for me you are the light at the end of the tunnel," the Polish thinker told him. The pope laughed: "nobody has ever told me I was at the end of a tunnel!" But Bauman insisted: "yes, but as a light."[18]

Bauman's analyses heightened the pope's sense of urgency about the "change of era" that was making the transmission of faith so hard. "Experiences of family are disappearing, and everything is slowly breaking up, growing apart," he explained in Cuba's second city, Santiago. A few months later in Tuxtla Gutiérrez, Mexico, he warned of "destructive ideologies that destroy the nucleus of the family, which is the base of every healthy society."

After the pope read Bauman this language became more stark and apocalyptic. In a lecture in the Pontifical Catholic University of Chile in the capital, Santiago, he warned that "points of reference that people use to build themselves individually and socially are disappearing," making it hard to build a nation, or indeed any community. "Without the 'us' of a people, of a family and of a nation, but also the 'us' of the future, of our children and of tomorrow, without the 'us' of a city that transcends 'me' and is richer than individual interests," he warned grimly, "life will be not only increasingly fragmented, but also more conflictual and violent."

There was little in Francis's speeches that expressed confidence in the liquid economy and even less in the technocratic state to deal with its consequences. The Church, as the sex abuse crisis had shown, was also an institution in crisis. Yet Bauman had seen in Francis a counterforce to the wall-building tribalism and fear then sweeping the Western world. Where was the pope's hope?

The answer was the margins. Francis saw a new world being born from the edges, from places of poverty, pain, and exclusion, where God was making Himself felt in the tears and dreams of the poor—above all, in Latin America, among the indigenous peoples who were still close to nature, and in the continent's appalling prisons.

Against the devastation of cultural and human ecology, Francis counterposed "the profound wisdom" of Latin America's native peoples and their threatened lifestyles. In Chiapas, Mexico, the pope addressed the

Mayan people directly: "Today's world, ravaged as it is by a throwaway culture, needs you!" he told them. In Bogotá he urged people to learn from
the wisdom of their own native people: "the sacredness of life, respect for
nature, and the recognition that technology alone is insufficient to bring
fulfilment to our lives." In Santiago's La Moneda Palace he said that from
the Mapuche people of the south "we can learn that a people that turns its
back on the land, and everything and everyone on it, will never experience
real development." In Puerto Maldonado, Peru, surrounded by representatives of the different Amazonian peoples—he called out the names of
twenty-two peoples, as if to give them agency—he told them: "Those of us
who do not live in these lands need your wisdom and knowledge to enable
us to enter into, without destroying, the treasures that this region holds."

Amazonia was a reserve not just of biodiversity but of a culture "that
must be preserved in the face of the new forms of colonialism," he said in
Puerto Maldonado. Against the attempt to make of the Amazon "a name-
less land, without children, a barren land—a place easy to commercialize
and exploit," he affirmed that "this is not a land of orphans. It has a Mother.
This good news has been passed on from generation to generation thanks
to the efforts of so many who share this gift of knowing that we are God's
children."

Echoing much of what Bauman had documented over many years, he
went on:

> On a number of occasions, I have spoken of the throwaway culture. A
> culture that is not satisfied with exclusion, as we have grown accustomed
> to observe, but advances by silencing, ignoring and throwing out every-
> thing that does not serve its interests; as if the alienating consumerism of
> some is completely unaware of the desperate suffering of others. It is an
> anonymous culture, without bonds, without faces, a throwaway culture.
> It is a motherless culture that only wants to consume. The earth is treated
> in accordance with this logic. Forests, rivers and streams are exploited
> mercilessly, then left barren and unusable. Persons are also treated in the
> same way: they are used until someone gets tired of them, then aban-
> doned as "useless" . . . False gods, the idols of avarice, money and power,
> corrupt everything. They corrupt people and institutions, and they ruin
> the forest. Jesus said that there are demons that require much prayer to
> expel. This is one of them. I encourage you to continue organizing into

movements and communities of every kind in order to help overcome these situations. I likewise encourage you to gather, as people of faith and vibrant ecclesial communities, around the person of Jesus. Through heartfelt prayer and hope-filled encounter with Christ, we will be able to attain the conversion that leads us to true life.

You could see Francis's attempt to rebuild modernity from the margins in the visits to prisons he included in every Latin American trip. Prisons offered powerful moments for challenging the sacrificial dynamic of the throwaway culture with the Gospel logic of inclusion and rehabilitation, while modeling for the Church the kind of radical missionary activity Christ was calling it to.

Prisons contained those rejected by an increasingly punitive, unequal society based on exclusion. The extraordinary rise in the rates of incarceration in the West over the past decades, a rate out of all proportion to levels of criminality, showed that prisons were increasingly places of retribution rather than rehabilitation, the result of a "penal populism" aimed at appeasing fears that—as the clerical sex abuse crisis showed—were not alien to the Church itself.[19]

The prisons Francis went to showed different dimensions of the same social tragedy. At Palmasola in Santa Cruz, Bolivia, many of the four thousand inmates were detained indefinitely prior to trials that never came. In Philadelphia's Curran-Fromhold Correctional Facility, a windowless, concrete bunker of sliding metal doors, nearly half the inmates had mental problems. Not long before Francis visited Cereso No. 3 in Ciudad Juárez, Mexico, more than two hundred prisoners had died in just one year's riots involving rival gangs. In San Joaquín, a women's prison in Santiago de Chile where most were being held on drug-trafficking charges, those who entered when pregnant or with infants had to give up their children when they reached the age of two.

Francis always began by refuting the lie that those inside were bad and those outside good. "I always ask myself why them and not me," he told journalists on the flight back from Lima. It is painful, he told the prisoners in Philadelphia, "when we see people who think that only others need to be cleansed, purified, and do not recognize that their weariness, pain and wounds are also the weariness, pain and wounds of society." Critiquing the idea that "everything will be resolved by isolating, separating, incarcerating, and ridding ourselves of problems, believing that these policies really solve problems," he told the prisoners of Ciudad Juárez that prisons were "a sign of the silence and omissions which have led to a throwaway culture, a symptom of a culture that has stopped supporting life, of a society that has abandoned its children." In Panama, he spoke of how society puts labels on people that "freeze and stigmatize not just the past but also people's present and future."

But Jesus offered a different way of looking at people, a gaze that created new life and a new history. In Ciudad Juárez, Francis offered himself as one who had experienced that mercy. "The man standing before you is a man who has experienced forgiveness. A man who was, and is, saved from his many sins. That is who I am. I don't have much more to give you or to offer you, but I want to share with you what I do have and what I love. It is Jesus Christ, the mercy of the Father."

And because Jesus was there, among them, even being in prison meant they could never be deprived of new possibility. "Jesus is stubborn," he told them. "He gave his very life in order to restore the identity we had lost, to clothe us with the power of his dignity." He urged them to pray to see themselves in this new light, and so find the strength to make a new start. He told the women prisoners in Santiago that they could "reject all those petty clichés that tell us we can't change, that it's not worth trying, that nothing will make a difference." Jesus "comes to meet us, to restore our dignity as children of God," he said in Philadelphia. "He wants to help us to set out again, to resume our journey, to recover our hope, to restore our faith and trust."

In the youth detention center of Las Garzas in Panama, Luis Oscar Martínez, a twenty-one-year-old detainee, told the pope that he had always felt an emptiness inside, the lack of a father's tender gaze, until he found it in God. But then he fell away into crime, and now he was completing his sentence and dreaming of being an international chef and refrigeration expert. "That someone like you could take the time to listen to someone like me, a young person deprived of liberty," Luis said, breaking down. "There are no words to describe the freedom I feel at this moment!"

The pope's third message was even more radical: that the powerless prisoners, stigmatized and forgotten, could be the agents of that change to which Christ was calling society. In Ciudad Juárez, a grim Mexican border city scarred by easy money, exploitation, and violence, where brutal gangs called a truce for his visit in February 2018, the pope urged prisoners to "work so that this society which uses people and discards them will not go on claiming victims."

It had to do with a capacity to dream and to cry. "This is a place where we shed tears, we weep out of a sense of helplessness in the face of injustice, murder, and the failure to settle conflicts through dialogue," Francis said at the Ground Zero memorial in New York, pointing to the flowing water. "To weep over injustice, to cry over corruption, to cry over oppression: these are tears that lead to transformation, that soften the heart," he said at the Mexican border Mass. Standing before the mutilated Christ of Bojayá in Villavicencio, he told victims of Colombia's long civil war that he had asked for the grace of tears, so that "we can all look and walk ahead with faith and hope."

If crying named the pain of the injustice, dreaming created an alternative. "Don't bend or yield. . . . Open up and dream!" he told young Cubans in Havana. "Dream that with you the world can be different. Dream that if you give your best, you are going to help make this world a different place." In Ciudad Juárez he invited workers "to dream of a Mexico that your children deserve: a Mexico where no one is first, second, or fourth; a Mexico where each sees in the other the dignity of a child of God."

Dreams, like prayer and tears, opened up processes that let the Holy Spirit in. The pope came to Washington, D.C., to remind a nation of its dreams: Lincoln's dreams of liberty, Martin Luther King's dreams of full rights for all, the dreams of Dorothy Day and Thomas Merton for justice and reconciliation. These were all "dreams which lead to action, to participation, to commitment," Francis told the U.S. Congress, "dreams which awaken what is deepest and truest in the life of a people."

nine

This Turbulent Family

At the first synod called by Benedict XVI, in October 2005, the recently named archbishop of Wellington, New Zealand, stood up to prise open what the Vatican regarded as a nailed-down issue. The bishop delegates had to submit their speeches in advance, and John Atcherley Dew knew the synod's General Secretariat didn't like his. But conscience impelled him to raise the matter of those who, in his view, were being barred from sacraments unfairly.

Dew's concern was for divorced Catholics who had entered second (civil) marriages without an annulment, especially abandoned partners who had either never left the Church or who had returned to it after a long absence, who had been unable, for whatever reason, to obtain a declaration of nullity of their former marriage. Without that declaration, church law treated them, indiscriminately, as adulterers, and therefore excluded them from the two vital sacraments of confession and the Eucharist unless they either left their spouse, or refrained from having sex with them.

The archbishop of Wellington was not questioning the doctrine of marital indissolubility: Jesus had spoken firmly against divorce. Second marriages, unless the first had been declared null, were not recognized. Nor was he questioning the law regulating the sacraments: no one can receive Communion in a state of mortal sin. His concern was for the many divorced and remarried who were not in a state of mortal sin.

Their exclusion was painful not just for the couples involved but for their children, who failed to understand why the Church was punishing their parents when it seemed obvious that God was seeking to assist them, by means of His grace. There was also a credibility gap: how could the Church preach God's mercy yet treat His people harshly and indiscriminately? Dew's speech movingly described many couples' yearning for the Eucharist. It was like a physical hunger for food, he said; the Church could no longer ignore their suffering.

"This isn't able to be discussed because 'we believe in the indissolubility of marriage and there's nothing we can do about it' was the message I was given," Dew recalls as the reaction of the synod's General Secretariat. The bishop delegates, for their part, were divided: some were annoyed that he had raised the issue; others were appalled that he had had his knuckles rapped for saying what many believed. Copies of his actual speech, rather than the Secretariat's airbrushed version, soon reached the journalists covering the synod, who reported that a fifth of the 250 bishops failed to vote for the proposition affirming the existing practice. It was clear that many bishops believed that civil remarriage could not be so easily equated with adultery, and that they were calling for a different pastoral response.

Among them was a tall, soft-spoken Latin American cardinal with an Italian surname. "This topic can't be swept under the carpet anymore," he told Dew over coffee the day after his speech. The Kiwi was heartened, but he hadn't a clue who the man was and didn't see him again for the next eight years, until the early morning of March 14, 2013, when on his television screen in Wellington, he watched the same man on the balcony of St. Peter's bowing his head to ask for the crowd's blessing. "I thought, 'Oh my goodness, this is the cardinal who approached me!'"[1]

In Buenos Aires, Cardinal Jorge Mario Bergoglio had grown increasingly troubled by the way the Church failed to prepare people properly for lifelong marriage and then, when the marriage failed, forced the divorced into a laborious and expensive annulment process that could take years, and excluded them from the Eucharist if they remarried in the meantime. Believing that if the Church was going to ask people to make a lifelong commitment, it should equip them much better, Bergoglio sought to improve and extend marriage preparation and catechesis.

He was also concerned about those whose marriages had failed. He sought to speed up and simplify the Buenos Aires marriage annulment process, and he encouraged his priests to trust their judgment in the confessional and in distributing Communion. His views were captured in the Aparecida document's call for a special accompaniment of the separated and divorced, a study of the factors leading to marriage breakup, and nullity tribunals that were accessible to all and effective in processing cases.[2]

But like every other bishop, he was hamstrung by the universal norms. The last time the issue had been formally discussed by the universal Church was at the 1980 synod on the family, shortly after John Paul II's election. Divorce and cohabitation at the time were rising sharply, but the far-reaching collapse in Western marriages was yet to come. Bishops from a number of countries, including Germany and England, raised the plight of the remarried in their speeches, and the synod's relator, or chair, Cardinal Joseph Ratzinger, recognized their desire to take part in the life of the Church as a major pastoral challenge. But the Church in most Western countries still looked to law and culture to support the institution of lifelong, faithful marriage that was open to children, and the bishops were keen to give a clear message to the state that it should stay that way.[3]

Despite this desire to maintain the status quo, John Paul II's 1981 postsynodal apostolic exhortation *Familiaris Consortio* moved decisively in a new direction. The 1917 Code of Canon Law, then being revised in the light of the Second Vatican Council, had described remarriage after divorce as "bigamy," and threatened those who "persisted" in it with excommunication as notorious public sinners. But in *Familiaris*, John Paul II made clear that, to the contrary, the divorced and remarried could not be excommunicated: they remained part of the Church. He also urged a "careful discernment of situations," noting how there were cases, for example, of abandonment, or people needing to marry again for the sake of children.[4]

What did it mean, to distinguish between these cases? By encouraging such people to implore God's grace, the pope clearly believed not all of them could be considered mortal sinners. And if such cases involved what moral theologians called "diminished subjective culpability," it would follow they should not be excluded from confession and Communion. But having walked to that door and peered through it, John Paul II quickly slammed it shut. He insisted that to be absolved in confession (which, in the case of mortal sin, was needed before one could receive the Eucharist) a person must abjure their civil spouse. If that were impossible without creating further harm—say, to the children of the new union—they must cease to have conjugal relations. To admit the civilly remarried to the sacraments would lead the faithful into "error and confusion regarding the Church's teaching about the indissolubility of marriage," the Polish pope declared.

Some might not be in mortal sin, in other words, but the greater good demanded their exclusion. In support of this argument, John Paul II added a startling new doctrine. The divorced and remarried were outside the sacraments, he said, because "their state and condition of life objectively contradict that union of love between Christ and the Church which is signified and effected by the Eucharist." This became known, after its original Latin, as the *ipsi namque* clause, and it was troubling to theologians who were concerned for doctrinal continuity because it had appeared nowhere in the synod and had no provenance in the Church's teaching documents on marriage. The metaphorical description of the Church as the "bride of Christ" had never been wrapped into eucharistic theology, and certainly it had never been used to bar the remarried from receiving the sacraments.[5]

Thereafter, any attempt in synods to reopen the question was slapped down, for fear of undermining the defense of the Christian understanding of marriage in civil law. It was a telling example of what Aparecida would diagnose as the Church's drift toward legalism and moralism in response to secularization.

Meanwhile, divorce rates soared, especially in Catholic countries, as liberalization of laws made it easier to leave a marriage than a mortgage. In the United States, where a third of Catholics were divorced, sacramental marriages fell by 60 percent between the early 1970s and 2010. By the time bishops got around to introducing mandatory marriage preparation classes—usually a hopelessly inadequate half-day or a few hours here or there—the gap between the high ideals of lifelong marriage and the capacity for Catholics to meet them had grown alarmingly. Yet the annulment process continued to operate on the increasingly doubtful assumption that people understood what they were undertaking when they got married.

When three German bishops of the Upper Rhine issued a joint pastoral letter in 1993 that proposed a discernment process to look at complex cases, John Paul II's doctrinal prefect, Cardinal Ratzinger, ordered them to rescind it, and the following year, in a major instruction, reaffirmed *Familiaris*. But as a pastor, Ratzinger was more nuanced. As archbishop of Munich in the 1970s, he had allowed Communion for remarried who were convinced in conscience of the invalidity of their first marriages, and even in the 1990s, he had agreed that no general norm could cover all individual cases. As pope, Benedict XVI spoke often of how the issue pained him, telling a big family meeting in Milan that there were no "simple solutions," and calling for "further study and clarification."[6]

The issue bubbled off radar in the small-group sessions at the October 2012 synod. Some quoted the former archbishop of Milan, Cardinal Carlo Maria Martini, whose death and posthumous interview on the eve of the synod posed challenging questions about whether the Church was offering its sacraments where they were most needed. He singled out the divorced and remarried as a prime example. The sacraments, Martini pointed out, were channels of God's grace, not a reward for the righteous but medicine for the sick. He presented a picture of a shrinking flock failing to reach out to the lost sheep, and he warned that if the Church did not change its attitude toward so-called patchwork families, it risked losing the next generation. To deal with the "disciplinary and doctrinal knots" that obstructed evangelization, Martini had in 1999 called for "a more universal and authoritative instrument, where such knots could be "examined in freedom, in the full exercise of episcopal collegiality, in listening to the Spirit and looking to the common good of the Church and the whole of humanity."

The question of Communion for the remarried came up again at the General Congregations, the pre-conclave cardinals' discussions in early March 2013, along with the issue of the ordination of married men. How could the new pope enable the Church to discern these questions gently, in the face of resistance? What was the "universal and authoritative instrument" that would allow him to do so?[7]

On his flight back from Rio de Janeiro in July 2013, Francis announced out of the blue that the next synod would consider access to the sacraments by the remarried "within the larger context of the entire pastoral care of marriage," including annulment reform. Family breakdown was devastating society, he explained, and the Church "has to go out to heal those who are hurting, with mercy." Only by means of "deep reflection," he told *Corriere della Sera*, could the issue be tackled. That meant a discussion in freedom. "I was the rapporteur of the 2001 synod and there was a cardinal who told us what should be discussed and what should not," Francis told *La Nación*. "That will not happen now."[8]

In October 2013, the Vatican announced Francis's mechanism: a two-part synod on marriage and family in the modern world. An initial two-week "extraordinary general assembly" of around 190 senior church leaders, heads of bishops' conferences and the like, in October 2014 would be followed by an "ordinary general assembly" lasting the normal three weeks in October 2015, with about three hundred delegates sent by bishops' conferences. The first would set the parameters for the discussion; the second would decide on the ways forward. A post-synod exhortation would presumably follow in 2016.

A three-year synod process, with a total of five weeks of discussion and debate, and bishops voting twice on the same issue? This would be the longest and most wide-ranging process of church deliberation since the Second Vatican Council in the 1960s. And with Francis's reforms taking the synod out of the Curia's control, it would entail far more than a talking chamber. Bishops began to realize that this was Martini's "universal and authoritative instrument," a collegial mechanism of discernment that—unlike the synod since the 1970s—would have the authority to change pastoral policy.

Disagreement broke out at once among the Germans. When the archdiocese of Freiburg leaped ahead by announcing a general pathway for divorced and remarried Catholics to receive Communion, the prefect of the Congregation of the Doctrine of the Faith, Cardinal Gerhard Müller, sought to cut it off at the pass, explaining at length in *L'Osservatore Romano* why any such move was impossible either now or in the future. The C9 cardinal Reinhard Marx of Munich in turn pushed back, telling Müller he had no right to close off the discussion in advance. The Vatican's spokesman Father Federico Lombardi meanwhile reminded the Germans that this was an issue that the universal Church would deliberate on, and that they should all hold fire.

Francis asked another German, the octogenarian theologian and cardinal Walter Kasper, to address the entire College of Cardinals in February 2014 as a prelude to the synod in October. Cardinal Kasper was one of the three Upper Rhine bishops who had been slapped down by Cardinal Ratzinger in 1994, leading nervous conservatives to assume at once that Francis was siding with "the liberals." But that was to misread him. Francis's aim throughout, but especially at this pre-synod stage, was to create the conditions for an authentic discernment. Many cardinals were asking, why tamper with what is settled? Discernment meant asking: what is God's will here? By asking them to listen to Kasper for two hours, Francis hoped to prise open hearts and minds, that they might at least see that there was a problem to be faced.

Kasper scoured church history for precedents that could enable the synod to steer between the Charybdis of legalism and the Scylla of laxity. The example of the *lapsi*, Christians in the early Church who denied their baptism under persecution but later asked to be readmitted, offered one example of a "penitential path" back to Communion that could be a model for the divorced under specific conditions: "after the shipwreck of sin, not a second ship but a lifesaving plank," as Kasper put it.

A number of cardinals—many of them retired, eminent figures from the John Paul II era, but also men like George Pell and Raymond Burke—left the synod hall fuming. Rather than accept the need for discernment, they had set their faces against even a discussion. Like the minority at the Second Vatican Council, the rigorists took pride in resisting not just any opening on the issue, but the process itself, which they would cast from now on as a conspiracy to undermine church teaching. They penned essays for two books rushed out in advance of the October assemblies that dismissed any possibility of change and which tried to frame the issue as one of fidelity to Christ versus surrender to modernity. "Every opponent of Christianity wants the Church to capitulate on this issue," Pell wrote. This beleaguered frame justified not asking the question, "What does God want?" by claiming, "This is what our enemies want."[9]

Most of the cardinals were not in this rigorist camp and understood the challenge of reconciling God's mercy with a clear witness in favor of the indissolubility Jesus taught. Yet few were persuaded by Kasper's proposal of a penitential path on the Orthodox church model, which allowed for the blessing of a new union following a recognition of failure. Many were also uncomfortable with the idea that a marriage could die. Kasper himself seemed too anxious to win an old argument, and to assume Francis was on his side. A number of leading cardinals felt steamrollered.

Cardinals Timothy Dolan of New York and Vincent Nichols of Westminster, for example, said the question involved not just the doctrine on marriage but the meaning of the Eucharist. "I don't see for myself where the area of maneuver opens up without quite a radical rethink of one or the other," Nichols told journalists at an eve-of-synod press conference.

But unlike the rigorists, Nichols went to Rome "intent on listening to what people have to say."[10]

Francis now made a key strategic decision. Having suggested on the Rio flight that annulment reform was a matter for the synod, he changed his mind when he spotted a conservative strategy to take the synod down that road of nullity jurisprudence to steer it away from the issue of Communion. Cardinal Müller had seized on Francis's airborne observation that marriages were more likely nowadays to be invalid because of the loss of the Christian understanding of marriage in culture, and declared himself in favor of revising nullity law in the light of this shift. His flexibility on this point—at odds with Cardinal Burke, who had adamantly opposed any revision—gave away the plan: to obviate the need to discuss the Communion issue by making the question essentially about annulment. More declarations of nullity would bring back the remarried to the Communion rail and so avoid the discernment question altogether.

Francis was wary of loosening the legal grounds for nullity, which could weaken the witness to indissolubility and potentially introduce divorce by the backdoor. He also believed that the low take-up of annulments was a question not primarily of jurisprudence but of time, cost, and accessibility. (In his own family, his niece, María Inés Narvaja, had been unable to marry her future husband because the case was stuck in Rome. After four years of waiting, they had married in a civil ceremony. "That's the best news you could have given me," her uncle told her.) One statistic said it all: American tribunals granted around half the 60,000-odd annual declarations of nullity worldwide, despite having just 6 percent of the Catholic population. Applying for a declaration of nullity in much of the rest of the world was cumbersome, expensive, and arduous, especially for the poor, who seldom applied, or gave up along the way. It was the issue of access to tribunals and the process itself that needed reform, not the jurisprudential grounds for nullity.[11]

Because those were technical matters, and given the consensus among bishops that the process needed to be speeded up and made easier to navigate, Francis felt able to hand annulment reform over to an eleven-member expert commission with a technical brief to devise procedural changes that could be then fed into the second synod. Its secretary was Monsignor Alejandro Bunge, Francis's go-to canon lawyer, whom he had brought over from Buenos Aires to work in the Rota.

Closing off Müller's attempted sidetrack would now force the synod to discern. The issue was not legal but pastoral: how the Church treated the wounded while upholding Jesus's teaching on indissolubility. But it wasn't a matter of a compromise between two ideals. It was through holding together truth and mercy that the Church would rebuild marriage and the family.

In the run-up to the synod a story came out from Argentina that the pope had contacted a woman who had reached out to him. Jacqui Lisbona wasn't divorced, but for nineteen years she had been married to a man who was. A new priest had taken over her parish and told her she could not receive Communion, and further that when she went home to her husband and two daughters she was resuming an irregular situation. In Francis's call to her, she told a local radio station, he had lamented that there were priests out there "who are more papist than the pope" (which in this case was rather more than a catchphrase). He urged her to find a different parish to go to confession and receive the Eucharist, and he thanked her for helping him understand such cases better. The Vatican press office refused either to confirm or deny the woman's account.[12]

In September, he witnessed the marriage of twenty couples from his diocese of Rome. Among them in St. Peter's Square were some who had been cohabiting and one who had a child. Francis took them as they were. Marriage, he told them, was "real life, not some TV show." And he gently pointed out what made a Christian marriage. The love of Jesus, he said, would help them whenever their own love "becomes lost, wounded or worn out."

At the vigil the night before the synod's opening he made clear his reason for calling it: to restore and strengthen the family, which "continues to be a school unparalleled in humanity, an indispensable contribution to a just and supportive society." A fragmenting, liquid world cried out for strong families more than ever because humanity needed roots, he said, adding that the deeper those roots, "the more possible it is in life to go out and go far, without getting lost or feeling a stranger in a foreign land."[13]

Creating a mechanism of authentic discernment was not easy: bishops were accustomed to being told what to think, and many assumed that unity meant they couldn't disagree openly. But it was better to yell at each other in public, even to the point of throwing punches, as they did in the early church councils, than to plot in private, Francis had laughingly told priests in Caserta, Italy, in July 2014. He gave the same message to the 190-odd bishop delegates (known as "synod fathers") on their first morning, October 5. The "general condition," he said, was to "speak up." Content would no longer be policed: "Let no one say, 'This you cannot say.'" Then came two further stipulations: "You need to say all that you feel, with *parrhesia*"—freely and boldly, with apostolic courage—and "listen with humility and accept with an open heart what your brothers say."[14]

Speak up, speak out freely, listen humbly—any Jesuit would recognize this as "discernment in common," the method by which apostolic bodies discern the will of the Holy Spirit. Cardinals who had taken part in the conclaves would also have recognized it. Freedom, honesty, patience, and plenty of prayer time were necessary to create a serene space in which the spiritual movements could become palpable.

That space was not just the synod hall, but the presence of the pope himself. They could proceed "calmly, and in peace" because "the presence of the pope is a guarantee for all and a safeguard of the faith," Francis told them. This was ancient doctrine, the authentic meaning of papal infallibility. In the spiritual storms of the next two weeks, the truth of the faith would never be at risk, however turbulent it might at times feel, because Saint Peter was with his apostles. In fact, he was waiting to greet them as they arrived, mixing freely with them during breaks, and tapping them on the shoulder for chats over coffee. It was all very different from popes at previous synods, presiding like Supreme Court judges. Francis, recalls Cardinal Nichols, "created this sense of absolutely being together, and therefore of welcome and of openness."[15]

There were various format changes. An hour was scheduled at the end of each afternoon for free discussion, and the synod fathers were encouraged to use their four-minute slots to respond to others, or speak as the Spirit moved them. Their written speeches were distributed to each other beforehand, but not—as in previous synods, albeit in edited form—to journalists. "To know *what* people have said is fine, but not *who* said it," Francis later told Mexican TV, "so he can feel free to say what he likes." Access to the *what*—general summaries of points and themes that had arisen—was supplied at the daily media briefing by press-office collaborators who sat in on the synod each day, so reporters knew what was on the delegates' minds. But without the *who*, it was impossible for them to assess which

way, for example, the Communion debate was leaning. The synod's organizers saw this as a necessary restriction to preserve the synod as a mechanism of discernment. "We are not here to achieve majorities for particular
positions," the archbishop of Paris, André Vingt-Trois, chided reporters at
the first press conference, "but to work towards the objective of allowing a
volonté commune [a common will] to emerge in the Church."[16]

That was the Aparecida model, which was clearly guiding Francis's synod
reform, as two protagonists of that assembly close to Francis, Mexican archbishop Carlos Aguiar Retes and Argentine archbishop Victor Fernández,
confirmed. Feeling free to speak about what mattered to them, unafraid of
being in the next day's headlines or of being ticked off by the curial heavyweights, energized the synod fathers. "People are saying what they think,
and passionately," a delighted Cardinal Francesco Coccopalmerio, who
had once been Cardinal Martini's private secretary, told journalists after a
couple of days of speeches. Almost everyone said the same, whatever their
stance on the Communion issue. On the issue of freedom, at least, the synod
had come quickly to a *volonté commune.*[17]

Liberated from the straitjacket of having to rehearse familiar doctrinal
positions to demonstrate their orthodox bona fides, pastors could finally
be pastors and discuss the plight of their flocks. "We had been looking
at the juridical, wanting to defend it to the maximum," recalled the archbishop of Quito, Fausto Trávez, "but at the synod we said: let's look with the
eyes of mercy, with our feet on the ground."[18]

What that meant was an approach "that starts from the true situation
of people and trying to figure out what's going on here," as the archbishop
of Gatineau, Québec, Paul-André Durocher, put it. Inductive rather than
deductive reasoning enabled the members of the synod to be honest about
categories in Catholic teaching and law that did not respond to real life.
The cardinal archbishop of Vienna, Christoph Schönborn, a formidable
Dominican theologian and pastor who had edited the monumental *Catechism of the Catholic Church,* provided a striking example when he spoke
of glimpses of God's grace in second unions, which the adjectives "adulterous" or "irregular" failed to capture. He told of one such patchwork family in which parents provided lovingly for their children, taught them to
pray, and took them to church. In spite of the chaos, the family produced
a priestly vocation. Before sitting down, Schönborn revealed that he had
been that child.[19]

Among the other signs of pastoral conversion was the surprise return of two casualties of John Paul II's long war on relativism: the language of graduality, which recognized that God led people in sometimes small steps, over time; and the internal forum, which back in the 1970s and 1980s allowed for greater on-the-ground flexibility in attending to human needs and circumstances. Both had been increasingly squeezed out in the previous twenty years but were now making a comeback under Francis. As Durocher put it, Jesus dealt with "individual cases," and "we need to reflect on how to do this in the Church." God, he pointed out, "is perfectly merciful and perfectly just and we have to strive to do that." This was precisely Francis's objective: to bring truth and mercy, the universal and the particular, into a better tension.[20]

But at the end of the week, a crisis erupted that made this much harder, when two paragraphs of the fourteen-page summary of the synod discussion thus far found their way into the press. Reuters ran a story about a "dramatic shift in attitudes toward gays and same-sex couples," while veteran Vaticanist John Thavis described an "earthquake" in the Church's attitude toward gay unions. According to John Allen, it was the first time a summit of Catholic bishops had declared that "relationships that don't accord with Catholic teaching, including same-sex unions, can have positive moral value."[21]

But that wasn't what the synod had said. The *relatio* was supposed to capture the mind of the assembly as a whole, yet the topic had been barely touched upon inside the hall. An Australian couple invited to address the synod had praised friends who welcomed their gay son's partner to a Christmas celebration (which led Cardinal Burke to complain in the media that children should never be exposed to the "evil" of gay relationships), but in claiming that gay people "have gifts and qualities to offer to the Christian community," the post-discussion *relatio* implied that homosexuality itself (rather than gay people) was per se a gift. Even more controversially, it claimed of gay unions that "mutual aid to the point of sacrifice constitutes a precious support in the life of the partners," implying that gay and straight unions could in some way be compared. Both notions were well beyond the pale for most of the delegates, especially those from Africa, for whom the *relatio* was expressing views that directly contradicted their public positions back home.

The rigorists pounced: here, surely, was proof that the Communion issue was part of a broader bid to "open up Catholic teaching . . . in a radically liberalizing direction, whose fruits we see in other Christian traditions," warned Pell. Burke claimed, without providing evidence, that the synod's General Secretariat had manipulated the process, a claim that quickly became an article of faith among conservative commentators. The soft-spoken, ultra-dignified president of the Polish bishops' conference, Archbishop Stanisław Gadecki, regretted in pained tones that the report should have focused on what he called "good, normal, ordinary" families.[22]

What had happened? It was never going to be easy for the drafting committee to take 280 speeches from 114 bishops' conferences across the world and collate them, along with hours of free discussion, into a fourteen-page summary translated into five languages, and all in just forty-eight hours. Although it lacked sufficient references to Scripture and Church teaching, the document was mostly good, holding in admirable tension the differing views. On the topic of sacraments for the remarried, for example, it accurately echoed an emerging consensus that any opening "would not be a general possibility, but the fruit of a discernment applied on a case-by-case basis, according to a law of gradualness, that takes into consideration the distinction between state of sin, state of grace and the attenuating circumstances"—very close to a formula that, in the end, the second synod later endorsed.

But all agreed that the paragraphs on homosexuality did not reflect the mind of the synod. How did they get in there? The synod's Hungarian relator, Péter Erdő, who was opposed to any opening on Communion, publicly blamed his special secretary, Italian archbishop Bruno Forte, even pointing to him in a press conference: "He who wrote the section must know what it is talking about," he said testily.

Forte told journalists it was vital to recognize the dignity of every person, including gay people, but made no comment on what had gone wrong in the drafting. In fact, he had been as astonished as anyone else to see the paragraphs—they had been added after he had signed off on the document and handed it in. When he found out, according to a Forte collaborator, he alerted the pope, who told him not to worry, the document wasn't supposed to be published and could be altered before it was read out. But almost at once it appeared on the synod's website, with the *New York Times* reporting that the positive language on gay unions and cohabitation was "a striking departure from traditional Catholic preaching that such couples are 'living in sin.'"[23]

Francis's cherished discernment space had been attacked and undermined. But he took it in stride. When a synod staff member complained to the pope that Burke's well-oiled media operation was exploiting the outrage over those few lines to attack the synod, Francis just smiled and told him, "You need to pray more, no?"

The main result of the *relatio* fiasco was to feed conservative fears of a permissive agenda being secretly concocted by a devious pope's liberal allies. Archbishop Forte, fumed George Weigel in *First Things*, had crafted the midterm report as a sop to "an international media eagerly awaiting the Great Catholic Cave-In to the sexual revolution," the result of which had been to "put iron into the spines of many synod fathers." Jaundiced eyes began to see yellow everywhere: even the six extra people Francis named to the drafting committee to make it more representative of the global Church were seen as proving a conspiracy to "stack the synod" because they included noted papal allies such as Cardinal Donald Wuerl of Washington, D.C.; the Jesuit superior general Father Adolfo Nicolás; and Bergoglio's Aparecida collaborators, Archbishops Aguiar Retes and Fernández. The reason for adding them was more prosaic: after the midterm upset, Francis needed men he could trust to compose a final report that genuinely reflected the mind of the synod.[24]

On the Communion for the remarried question, that mind was still far from being made up. The issue surfaced about forty times in the 189 speeches, and there were sharp exchanges halfway through the first week, but mostly it was sidestepped. Of the ten small groups into which delegates divided in the second week, two were opposed to any opening, three were in favor with some reservations, while five didn't address the issue at all. Moderates such as Nichols had begun to see that the problem lay in the attempt to resolve the issue either way, "and in that sense, squeeze out the space for the constructive and purposeful intent of the synod."[25]

The midterm report was heavily revised in the light of the *modi*, or amendments, submitted by the small groups, which were made public at the insistence of synod fathers who were anxious to show the world they were correcting the midterm report. All talk of the gifts and qualities of gay people (now deemed to need "pastoral attention" rather than a full-on "welcome") was removed, as was any comparison of gay unions with marriage. On the Communion issue, meanwhile, the report kicked the can to the next synod, noting that both positions had passionate advocates and needed "further study." At the end of the fortnight, sixty-two paragraphs in the final document achieved more than 50 percent of the 181 votes, and of these, all but three paragraphs got more than two-thirds. The failing three referred to the gay issue and Communion for the remarried.

Did the three paragraphs fail to get a two-thirds majority because they still went too far—or because the revisions were too extreme? It was hard to know; probably both. But the lack of consensus unquestionably reflected the fears that had arisen in the meeting. Outside the synod, the very public retreat from the midterm *relatio* led to inevitable headlines that the synod had delivered a defeat for the pope's more "merciful" vision, a narrative respun by conservatives as a story of "orthodox" leaders foiling an underhanded attempt to liberalize doctrine. Yet both narratives missed how similar the final report was to the midterm one in its nuanced language of welcoming, dialogue, and discernment. "The openness remains," Cardinal Luis Antonio Tagle of Manila assured the news website *Crux*.[26]

For Francis, what mattered was the process: the movements of the spirits and the temptations. It was clear that the first synod had been rich in both. Rising at its conclusion to give one of his most remarkable addresses, Francis named moments of consolation ("listening to the testimony of true pastors, who wisely carry in their hearts the joys and the tears of their faithful people"), as well as the temptations in moments of desolation he had observed in the course of the assembly.

Referring to Satan's attempts in the Judean desert to lure Jesus away from His mission, he named two temptations in particular: "to transform stones into bread to break the long, heavy, and painful fast" and "to transform the bread into a stone and cast it against the sinners, the weak, and the sick." These were Jesus's charges against the Pharisees: on the one hand, they tolerated men casting off their wives; on the other, they laid legalistic burdens on people while doing nothing to lift them. Thus Francis critiqued both "hostile inflexibility"—to remain enclosed within the letter of the law, resistant to the "God of Surprises (the Spirit)"—as well as the progressive or liberal temptation of "destructive niceness" (*buonismo distruttivo*), which "in the name of a deceptive mercy binds the wounds without first curing them and treating them." For Francis it was clear that if the synod path ended up in either of those ditches, it would have failed to stick to the route the Spirit was inviting them to walk.

For the first time since his election Francis now solemnly spelled out the formidable authority of the pope. He did so, above all, to remind them of the charism of unity that Jesus had entrusted to Saint Peter. The pope, Francis reminded them, was "guarantor of the obedience and the conformity of the Church to the will of God, to the Gospel of Christ, and to the Tradition of the Church," and by the "will of Christ" the supreme pastor and teacher and lawgiver. Those who had set up a contradiction between defense of doctrine and the pope were rejecting God's gift of the papacy (Christ's appointment of Saint Peter to lead the apostles) as an agent of unity and reconciliation.

He then sketched a counter-vision of a pastorally converted Catholicism where truth and mercy, the universal and the particular, were held together in compelling combination in a Church that was close and concrete.

> This is the Church, the vineyard of the Lord, the fertile Mother and the caring Teacher, who is not afraid to roll up her sleeves to pour oil and wine on people's wounds; who doesn't look at humanity as if from a glasshouse, judging and categorizing people. This is the Church: One, Holy, Catholic, Apostolic and composed of sinners who need God's mercy. This is the Church, the true bride of Christ, who seeks to be faithful to her spouse and to her doctrine. It is the Church that is not afraid to eat and drink with prostitutes and publicans, the Church whose doors are wide open to receive the needy, the penitent, and not only the just or those who believe they are perfect! The Church that is not ashamed of the fallen brother and pretends not to see him, but on the contrary feels involved and almost obliged to lift him up, to encourage him to take up the journey again, and to walk with him toward a definitive encounter with her Spouse, in the heavenly Jerusalem.[27]

*　*　*

The language of the questionnaire was stodgy because, even in the era of Francis, the synod still spoke in impenetrable Vaticanese, and most local churches were frankly unaccustomed to asking people for their views. Nor was it clear if a summary of each country's answers could be published or not. But it was remarkable that the consultation of the people of God was happening at all. The questionnaire that followed the first synod had been sent to every bishops' conference by the synod's General Secretariat with a request that it be discussed widely. Suddenly, *experience mattered.*

Hundreds of thousands of Catholics' responses, collated by bishops' conferences and submitted to the synod's General Secretariat, eventually generated eighty-five paragraphs tacked onto the sixty-one of the 2014 synod's final *relatio*, adding challenges such as economic insecurity, aging, disability, and gender ideology to the working document of the 2015 synod. The resulting *instrumentum laboris*—dubbed, inevitably, the *instrumentum laborious*—waddled awkwardly across the synod fault lines. The divorced and civilly remarried Catholics should follow a path of pastoral counseling and penance under the guidance of a priest, but the question of access to the sacraments required further discussion. Gay people needed pastoral care, which could mean a warm hug or a stern lecture, depending on the pastor, but their unions were not to be spoken of.

"We are on high seas, so there is some turbulence," the synod's skipper, Cardinal Lorenzo Baldisseri, admitted with understatement. The Catholic Church, rebuilt in the nineteenth century to supply absolute certainties in an uncertain world, was not used to disagreements left hanging, and the tension was palpable. Books slid off printing presses, petitions sucked in signatures, and social media turned blue with accusation and countercharge. The debate had polarized, and each side saw the other as marshaling forces. What conservatives dubbed a "shadow synod" was organized in October by the German bishops, who invited sympathetic French and Swiss counterparts to a closed-door "study day on family issues" at the Gregorian University that was intended to help coordinate responses. But the Africans were active, too, holding pre-synod meetings in Rome in February and again in Accra, Ghana, in June, to marshal arguments against any opening on either gay unions or sacraments for the divorced.[28]

In many ways, Germany and Africa symbolized the polarization.

The Church in Germany, wealthy and organized, made clear where it stood in a report, saying that a "large majority" of the country's sixty-six bishops favored divorced Catholics in new unions receiving Communion in "particular justified instances." Cardinal Reinhard Marx of Munich, the bishops' conference president and C9 member, said the Church in Germany was "not a subsidiary of Rome" and had no need to wait for the rest of the Church before setting its own pastoral policy. The statements provoked grumbling that German Catholicism had become too worldly, too dependent on taxpayer subsidies (more than $6 billion in 2011) for its schools and hospitals, and too anxious to be credible in a culture where homosexuality and divorce were the norm.

Yet the same could be said, in reverse, of Africa, where both were culturally taboo. The Church in Africa was fast growing, poor, and young; in many ways it was the future. But it was also under pressure from Islamic fundamentalism, which equated Christianity with godless Western secularism. African bishops anxious to identify Catholicism with traditional tribal family culture accused German and Belgian bishops of promoting the kind of decadence that was being imposed by international agencies. In response, the Germans expressed frustration that cultural taboos in Africa were impeding a proper discussion of European pastoral challenges. African bishops "should not tell us too much what we have to do," Cardinal Kasper told a conservative reporter outside the synod hall, leading South Africa's Cardinal Wilfrid Napier to accuse him of a lack of respect toward African Catholicism.[29]

Was it even possible to have a universal response to these questions? How much latitude could or should each Church have? As Francis had made clear in *Evangelii Gaudium*, local bishops needed freedom to be able to respond to their own challenges without being straitjacketed by Roman centralism. But latitude in implementation wasn't the same as pluralism of interpretation: the Gospel needed to be inculturated, not cherry-picked. The Church was a "reconciled diversity," not a loose, Anglican-style federation of autonomous churches. Francis had called the synod precisely because of these polarizations, to create space for the Holy Spirit to forge a new, creative consensus that would allow the Gospel to shape culture, rather than being shaped by it.

The pope led the way in the synod interregnum by identifying both with the concerns over colonialism *and* the concern for the Church to be relevant to people's lives. In Manila in January 2015, he issued a ringing defense of the family from the "ideological colonization" of gender ideology, and on the flight home praised Paul VI's 1968 encyclical *Humanae Vitae*—which famously upheld the ban on artificial contraception in marriage—as a prophetic rejection of rich-world attempts to restrict the number of poor. In the same press conference, he refuted the idea that large families caused poverty and deplored the declining birthrate in Western countries, while adding—in an expression that some large

Catholic families claimed was offensive—that this didn't mean "breeding like rabbits."[30]

In February, Francis served up his stunning address on Jesus and the lepers to the new cardinals, contrasting a fear of losing the saved with a desire to save the lost. He urged them to reject the thinking of the doctors of the law ("which would remove the danger by casting out the diseased person") and adopt God's thinking ("who in his mercy embraces and accepts by reinstating him and turning evil into good, condemnation into salvation and exclusion into proclamation"). It was a sharp challenge. What did they care more about, policing their borders or saving people?

His messages in 2015 came back time and again to this hermeneutic of integration, stressing that people in a second union were not excommunicated and should be involved in parish life, in teaching the faith, serving the poor, listening to the Word of God, and working for justice and peace. In a long television interview in March 2015, he explained that a divorced and remarried person could be a great catechetic teacher or godparent to a baptized child; their bad example, paradoxically, made them a good example, because they both acknowledged their failures yet remained in the Church, confident of Christ's mercy. "When we speak of integration we mean all this," he told Valentina Alazraki, "and then we mean to accompany interior processes."

Yet he was adamant that integration wasn't the same as a willy-nilly opening up of the sacraments to the remarried. He told *La Nación* before Christmas 2014 that "Communion alone is not a solution; the solution is integration." Conversion could not be circumvented by simply opening the door to confession and the Eucharist, as he made clear on the flight from Mexico in February 2016, when he critiqued remarried couples who went to receive Communion as if it were their right. "All the doors are open, but you cannot say that these people can receive Communion," he said. "This would not allow them to proceed down the path of integration."[31]

Commentators claimed to be baffled at where the pope stood, but there was no contradiction. Francis was consistently in favor of whatever brought the Church alongside individual people in their concrete reality—which is what he meant by integration—and against anything that treated people as an undifferentiated category. Some of the Germans appeared to do the latter with their general opening to the Eucharist for the remarried, as much as some rigorists did in their blanket opposition to any opening. This was why Francis was resisting both an unqualified "no" and a "yes" on the Communion question: each shut out God's grace and the Holy Spirit's freedom of action, the first by keeping the doors closed, making change hard, the second by opening them so wide there was no need for change. Neither the lax nor the strict priest witnesses to Christ, he told clergy in March 2014, because "neither takes seriously the person in front of him." While the rigorist "nails the person to the law as understood in a cold and rigid way," the indulgent "only appears merciful, but does not take seriously the problems of that person's conscience, minimizing the sin."[32]

For Francis, the objective of the Church's outreach was to facilitate the encounter with Christ and conversion. The divorced and remarried needed to be invited on a journey that involved accepting *both* that they had failed *and* that they were unconditionally loved and forgiven. Because they were neither righteous victims who had done nothing wrong nor sinners forever severed from God's forgiveness, they could change and start again. The Church was a place of forgiven sinners. As Francis would put it at the vigil on the eve of the synod, the Church could walk at people's sides "because she herself has first experienced what it is to be reborn in the merciful heart of the Father."

The bigger picture here was Aparecida. The Holy Spirit was calling the Church to pastoral conversion in response to liquidity and secularization: not to relax her rules and her criteria, but to come close to people in their daily lives and to offer mercy. It was the same approach underlying his reforms to the Church's system for investigating the validity of marriages, the result of a yearlong study by his eleven-member handpicked commission of canonists and theologians.

He announced the reforms a few weeks before the opening of the 2015 synod. Judgments, known as "sentences," no longer needed rubber-stamping by a second tribunal, and in cases where the evidence was uncontested and the nullity clear, bishops could now act as judges. The changes meant that, rather than taking years, a decision by the Church could be available in slam-dunk cases in less than forty-five days. The process would also be easier and cheaper. By scrapping the jurisdiction requirements that made the process complicated for immigrants—who no longer had to return to the diocese where they had married to begin the process—and reducing fees to close to zero in many cases, annulments suddenly became feasible in a whole new way for the poor, for migrants, and in the developing world.

The reforms did not alter the jurisprudence: a declaration of nullity was still possible only if the necessary prerequisites for consent and validity were lacking, such as free will, maturity, full knowledge, and an openness to children. A judicial process, too, was still necessary "because marriage is indissoluble when it is a sacrament," Francis explained on the flight from Philadelphia, "and this the Church cannot change. . . . Either it wasn't a marriage, and this is nullity—it didn't exist. And if it did, it's indissoluble. This is clear."

But making the investigation easier and quicker meant, in practice, that many, many people would now be able to celebrate their second unions sacramentally and to find their way back to the Communion rail. After *Mitis Iudex Dominus Iesus* (Lord Jesus, Gentle Judge) went into effect in December 2015, it led to dramatic increases in nullity applications, with the Church in the UK and the United States a year later reporting increases in applications of 50 to 70 percent after decades of decline, not least because of the relaxation on jurisdiction requirements: immigrants could now apply from the countries they had made their home.[33]

In countries where tribunal coverage was patchy, the effect was especially marked. Argentina, where huge distances between inter-diocesan tribunals had long made the process impractical for poor working people, saw a tripling in the number of its tribunals in just nine months, while in Bolivia, where half of marriages ended in divorce, the "abbreviated process" effectively introduced the possibility, for the first time, of nationwide access to annulments. This was especially important, the president of the Bolivian bishops' conference, Ricardo Centellas, told me in Potosí in April 2016, because gunshot weddings were common among the Quechua and Aymara people following the birth of a child out of wedlock. Now, with the brief process, "what we're hoping is that people whose marriages have failed will be able to live in peace and remake their lives, because there are many cases where it's really clear that there was no marriage."[34]

In his homily on the Sunday morning before the opening of the second synod the next day, Francis went back to the reason he had called the gatherings in the first place: because he was convinced that God was calling forth a new commitment to marriage in our time.

Like Saint Ignatius imagining the Holy Trinity surveying the wreckage wrought by Satan, Francis painted a picture of technocracy's triumph in the solitude of countless men and women trapped in selfishness, sadness, and violence, enslaved by pleasure and money, "alone, misunderstood and mis-heard." He saw people trapped in diabolical paradoxes: a globalized world of luxurious mansions and skyscrapers, yet lacking the warmth of homes and families; of ambitious plans and projects, but little time to enjoy them; of sophisticated means of entertainment, but a growing interior emptiness; of "many pleasures, but few loves" and "many liberties, but little freedom."

But God had a plan, the old plan: "the loving union between a man and a woman, rejoicing in their shared journey, fruitful in their mutual gift of self." Jesus had restored that plan in recalling humanity to lifelong marriage. Indissolubility didn't mean handcuffs, but a fruitful pledge, "not simply to live together for life, but to love one another for life." In this way, said Francis, "Jesus re-establishes the order which was present from the beginning."[35]

This was the synod's task now: to revivify that truth and help people live it, to defend permanence, fidelity, and openness to life by taking seriously the heart's longing and the human capacity for committed love. But the Church didn't just point to the destination and watch with arms crossed as people struggled to get there, handing out membership cards when they arrived. The Church was called to be Christ's presence: to be with people when they fell and failed, because no one ever reaches anywhere important without at some point stumbling along the way, and when they looked up from the ground, they needed to see an outstretched hand and an encouraging smile.

As three-hundred-odd bishops trailed by the world's media arrived in Rome for the three-week synod on the family in October 2015, an unusually handsome forty-three-year-old monsignor in the Vatican's doctrine department held a news conference alongside a Catalan man in a checked beige blazer. Krzysztof Charamsa, a Polish curial official known until then only for his conservative, straitlaced theology, wanted the world to know that he was in love. Giggling shyly in his clerical collar as he rested his head on his boyfriend's shoulder, he delivered a carefully stage-managed message for the synod: that "offering gay believers total abstinence from a life of love is inhuman."

Il coming out di Charamsa, as the Italian media called it, ran for a day or two but quickly fizzled. It was hard to make the case for allowing priests to have sex in a celibate priesthood, and even harder to make the case for homosexual love in an all-male priesthood; and anyhow, the attempt to pile pressure on the synod by two well-educated, elegantly dressed European men made the Church look less like an oppressor than a victim.

Others arriving in Rome also had "messages" for the synod, the noisiest and most strident being the pop-up "rad-trad" lobbies bankrolled by family-values entrepreneurs. Church Militant, Lifesite News, and Voice of the Family were out in force to save the Church from "homosexualism," a flood barrier of rigor to keep out the incoming modernist tide. The liberals were out, too, among them the Global Network of Rainbow Catholics and Future Church, who wanted women priests, gay unions, and more democracy. Next to the family-values warriors, they seemed aged and polite, less angry than disappointed at the slow pace of change.

In the circus of competing press conferences and declarations, the synod fathers seemed doubly determined to carve out a serene space for discernment. C9 president Cardinal Óscar Rodríguez de Maradiaga said it was wrong to see the meeting in terms of "two opposing sides defending absolute positions" when in reality "we all seek the unanimity that comes from dialogue, not from ideas defended at all costs." For his part, Archbishop André Vingt-Trois of Paris pleaded with the 270 voting synod fathers to refrain from using the media to promote their points of view, for "we do not want to live this time as a test of strength in which the cameras and the microphones will be the arbiters."

In his opener, Francis stressed that what mattered was not negotiating an agreement like a parliament but walking together "to read reality with the eyes of faith and with the heart of God." The synod, he reminded them, was "a protected space in which the Church experiences the action of the Holy Spirit," one that called for "apostolic courage, gospel humility and trusting prayer."

But barely had he finished the speech when the turbulence began again—this time from the conservative wing. The opening address by the chair, or relator, Hungarian cardinal Péter Erdő, caused outrage by claiming the Communion issue had been settled by the previous synod. Pell then stood up to lambast changes to the synod's format that he alleged had been engineered to secure a liberalizing outcome. It later emerged that he had, that morning, handed the pope a private letter signed by thirteen cardinals who were hostile to any opening on Communion. Echoing Pell's claim that the synod had been manipulated, the signatories repeated the familiar warning that liberal Protestant churches had paid for surrendering to modernity in their empty pews. It was a curiously wordly argument, as if the purpose of the synod was to swell congregations.

The pushback was swift. The synod secretary general, Cardinal Lorenzo Baldisseri, rose to rebut Pell's claims one by one, showing there had been no conspiracy or stacking. Francis then, unusually, took the floor to make a series of forceful remarks that were loudly applauded. "Basically, he said, 'I'm the pope, I've made the rules for the synod, and you were notified about this, so this is the way it's going to be,'" recalls Cardinal Dew. "That sent a very powerful message to people that he meant that this is about synodality, it is about listening to one another, and again, trusting in the power of the Holy Spirit at work among those gathered there."

When the "Letter of the 13" later leaked, it triggered a new wave of indignation at attempts to "rig" the synod, but this time the wrath was directed against the conservatives. "The general opinion I detected among the bishops was a sense of disgust," Bishop Marcello Semeraro, the C9's secretary, told reporters. Many of the signatories quickly backtracked, claiming they hadn't signed it or had signed a different version, and the letter's prime movers, Pell and Napier, claimed to be satisfied with Baldisseri's explanations. But the damage had been done. To add to the list of conservatives behaving badly, the Polish bishops—who wore their intransigence on the Communion issue as a badge of loyalty to Saint John Paul II—were reprimanded for breaking the explicit rules against publishing reports of the speeches with names attached.[36]

It emerged that Francis had stood up to accuse Pell's rebels of a "hermeneutic of conspiracy" that was "sociologically weak and spiritually unhelpful." The words exactly echoed his 1984 writing, "On Self-Accusation," in which, using the Spiritual Exercises, he described how the devil sowed suspicion and suppositions in some people's hearts in order to divide them from the community. Over time, they developed an attitude of suspicion, so that everything came to be interpreted according to a "crooked measure" that sees reality through the lens of victimhood. Religious who are tempted in this way become "collectors of injustices," and ultimately fall into a "conspiracy theory," victim mentality.

In sociology, the conspiracy theory, from the hermeneutical point of view, is the weakest type of hermeneutic there is. It cannot stand up to serious reasoning. It is an elementary cause of someone being led astray, occurring in the type of person who basically longs for a simplistic goodies-versus-baddies set-up (with themselves as the goodies). Becoming disconnected from objective reality, they wall themselves up in a kind of defensive ideology. They swap doctrine for ideology, and exchange the patient pilgrimage of God's children for a victim complex of a conspiracy against them by "others"—the baddies, their superiors, the other members of the community. They end up trapped in a web of words.[37]

Others, too, had spotted the serpent's tail in the rigorists' attitudes. The archbishop of Brisbane, Australia, wrote of the "fear, even the panic this Synod seems to have provoked in some," which "doesn't look like the Holy Spirit to me: red-eyed joylessness cannot be of God." Mark Coleridge, whose synod blog became a must-read for journalists, went on to describe what he called "a whiff of fear, even a kind of paranoia, with some determined to ride into battle to 'save the Church,'" adding, "That kind of partisan spirit can turn brothers into enemies. The Spirit of God does the opposite."[38]

If the effect of the midterm report debacle in the first synod had been to put bishops on the defensive, pausing pastoral conversion as delegates retreated into hardened positions, the failed conservative coup had the opposite effect. The rigorists having been exposed as fear driven, the atmosphere now became more creative and merciful. Pastoral responses both to the divorced and to gay people began to emerge.

This was assisted by Baldisseri's process changes: delegates had more time each week in the thirteen language-based small groups, reducing inputs in the synod hall to just three minutes, and encouraging delegates to speak from pastoral experience rather than on abstract principles. When Cardinal Nichols asked the English-language group he chaired to speak about their own families, it "totally transformed" the discussion. "Suddenly we realized that every bit of the saga of family living was in the room," he recalls.[39]

Dew, too, saw a "real conversion" happening in the small groups. "People were listening to one another and the message was starting to come through that this is about being a merciful Church . . . really helping and walking with people." The archbishop of Chicago, Cardinal Blase Cupich, noted a growing awareness that "conscience was not just about identifying objective right or wrong," but "was a subjective action, by which a person comes to understand where God is calling them to." The discussion was moving away from seeing the issue as simply one of obedience to and application of church teaching, toward how the Church could better help people live that teaching by becoming aware of God's grace in their lives. That meant speaking less in the arcane language of moral and ethical categories. "The greatest contribution that the bishops can make to families is to act and speak like families act and speak," Cupich said. "That is a very key thing and I find that happening."[40]

The Communion issue landed mainly in the third week, when the synod came to discussing the final part of the *instrumentum laboris*, on "wounded families." Again, lived experience proved crucial. Among the stories that most affected the synod was a Mexican bishop's account of a child making his first Communion who took the host and broke it into three, taking two pieces back to his parents who, because they had remarried, could not receive it. The archbishop of San Juan, Puerto Rico, also made an impression with his poignant description of the divorced and remarried standing week after week in the Communion line with their arms crossed, publicly humbling themselves.[41]

A middle way was beginning to emerge. Only a few now continued to advocate Kasper's Orthodox-style penitential route back to the sacraments, while on the other extreme were a handful of East Europeans who opposed flexibility under any circumstances. The Polish conference president, Archbishop Stanisław Gadecki, warned on his website that "many supporters of this modernity"—the choice of words spoke volumes—"are in fact thinking about changing doctrine, yet are calling it a change in church discipline." Archbishop Tomasz Peta of Astana, Kazakhstan, was blunter: the very idea of relaxing eucharistic discipline, he said, showed the "smoke of Satan" had entered the synod.

Between these positions, most delegates were looking for a solution that would retain the general norm but allow greater pastoral flexibility in its application. But the reports from the thirteen small groups showed little consensus on what that might look like. The Spanish-speaking group led by Cardinal Rodríguez de Maradiaga urged a pathway of reintegration that didn't exclude the Eucharist, and a similar position was taken by the

English-language group moderated by Nichols, which called for a pathway of "reverential listening." Two groups moderated by conservative curial cardinals George Pell and Robert Sarah rejected any change to existing discipline, while the others were paralyzed and polarized. In the archbishop of Montevideo's Italian-speaking group there were "two completely opposed positions," Cardinal Daniel Sturla told me.[42]

The eleventh-hour breakthrough came from a most unlikely place: the single German-language group, Germanicus, moderated by Cardinal Christoph Schönborn and packed with heavyweights on both sides of the argument, including Kasper, Marx, and Müller. Despite their historic disagreements, they united in irritation at Pell's remarks to *Le Figaro* that the synod's battle over Communion came down to a duel between Ratzingerians and Kasperites. To show that theological consensus was possible, the Germans invited a learned eight-hundred-year-old to join the discussion. "When Cardinal Kasper and Cardinal Müller and Cardinal Schönborn are all talking about Saint Thomas [Aquinas], that is very interesting!" Marx later told journalists.

Müller, who the year before had vigorously opposed any opening, now conceded in a magazine interview that Communion could not be completely ruled out, "at least not in extreme individual cases" and that "in certain cases in the conscience area it is possible to give it." This turnaround from his intransigence the year before gave many a chance to jump off the fence. "'If the head of CDF says it is OK, it must be OK,' was the thinking," wrote the Jesuit commentator Father Thomas Reese.[43]

Having established the principle, they hashed out mechanisms that would allow for *discretio* (discernment) in the application of the law, eventually settling on an agreement that the internal forum could be used to admit some people to Communion on a case-by-case basis following a lengthy process of examination of conscience. This wasn't just a theory: Schönborn had long operated such a scheme in Vienna in line with Cardinal Ratzinger's admission that the general norm couldn't apply in every case. Essentially, his fellow Germans agreed that this was the way forward.

News spread quickly around the synod hall that, in Nichols's words, "the Germans had found a way forward that respected both the need for doctrinal integrity and pastoral sensitivity." The idea of a case-by-case discernment "has been gaining ground among synod fathers," reported the veteran Spanish Vaticanist Juan Vicente Boo.[44]

The synod sausage machine now got to work processing over a thousand *modi*, or amendments, to the *instrumentum laborious*. It was intense work by the pope's handpicked ten-man drafting team, headed by Erdő and Forte but including representatives from each continent whom he trusted, among them Dew, Wuerl, and Fernández. Francis dropped in at one point to encourage them. He told them he was deeply worried about the family. "Give me something that I can really work with, something that's for people," he asked. Collated, sifted, and folded into a final document, the *relatio finalis* was again reviewed and further amended before it went to the vote.

Some 263 synod fathers gathered on October 24 to vote on the final document: a two-thirds majority (177 votes) was needed to pass each of the ninety-four paragraphs. As they were read out, the synod fathers pressed buttons marked either *placet* or *non placet* and another, *confirmo*, to register their choice. An hour and a half later, the result was clear: the contentious three paragraphs had thin majorities, but all ninety-four paragraphs had passed. "If I believed in miracles before," said Father Tom Rosica, the English-language assistant who had been summarizing the synod each day for the press, "I saw it happen today."[45]

The applause, recalled Coleridge, was "prolonged and spontaneous" and "signaled many things: wonderment, gratitude, appreciation, relief, weariness. I found it strangely moving." Others reported a sense of peace in the hall, a sign, in Ignatian discernment, of a body being in tune with God's desires. After a round of wrap-up speeches of thanks from synod officials, Francis "rose to speak in that disarmingly ordinary way of his," Coleridge wrote, "and made another cracker of a speech."[46]

He did not hold back about what the synod had laid bare: "the closed hearts that frequently hide even behind the Church's teachings or good intentions, in order to sit on the chair of Moses and judge, sometimes with superiority and superficiality, difficult cases and wounded families." The allusion to the guardians of the law in Matthew 23:2 could not have been clearer, nor his following remark, that the synod had sought to "rise above conspiracy theories and blinkered viewpoints." It had shown, he said, that "the true defenders of doctrine are not those who uphold its letter, but its spirit; not ideas but people; not formulae but the gratuitousness of God's love and forgiveness," a gratuitousness that was in contrast with "the recurring temptations of the elder brother (cf. Lk 15:25–32) and the jealous laborers (cf. Mt 20:1–16)."[47]

The speech was spun on traditionalist websites as a bitter screed taking vengeance on conservatives, but it was nothing of the sort. Francis was celebrating a spiritual triumph; the bad spirit had been driven out by the good. The synod was not a political contest between two parties in favor of or against Communion for the remarried, but a spiritual battle between fear and trust, legalism and mercy, Pharisaism and Christianity. The latter had, finally, won through, and Francis was clear who should get the credit. "Many of us have felt the working of the Holy Spirit who is the real protagonist and guide of the Synod," he said.

The language of pastoral conversion was on almost every page of the final report. "The Church starts from the concrete realities of today's families, all in need of mercy, starting with those who suffer most," the report said, likening the Church to "a lighthouse or a torch carried in the midst of the crowd to bring light to all those who have lost their way or who find themselves in the midst of a storm." It called for "vocational discernment" programs to prepare couples for marriage and a host of practical suggestions for supporting marriages and families through testing times. Here, finally, was a Church of pastors rather than policemen. A Mexican synod father who had worked in pastoral care of the divorced and remarried was delighted to see a change of attitude and a change of language breaking out in the Church. "I believe that's what we got, and that's why I'm leaving completely satisfied and totally happy."[48]

The gay issue had been too hot to go anywhere near. Belgian bishop Johan Bonny said he had tried raising it but "there was no way of discussing it peacefully" in his group chaired by the stiffly traditionalist Guinean curial cardinal, Robert Sarah, who had famously likened homosexuality to Islamic terrorism. How the Church might better walk with and integrate gay people was left for another day, just as once the issue of the remarried had been.

Paragraph 85 on the divorced and remarried was a clear advance from 2014. It offered the German-Austrian formula of an internal-forum discussion with a priest leading to "the formation of a concrete decision on what is blocking the possibility of a more full participation in the life of the church and on steps that might foster it and make it grow." There was no mention of Communion at the end of the road, to avoid conditioning the discernment or implying that this was the objective. But nor was it excluded, as it had been in *Familiaris* and as conservatives had wanted.

The shift in the main body of the synod was visible in those who, like Cardinal Nichols of Westminster, had started out in October 2014 unable to reconcile the integration of the remarried with the defense of indissolubility and the Eucharist. But they had come to see the whole question in a new way: by putting the person before, not outside, the law. At the British seminary in Rome, the Venerable English College, Nichols expressed his frustration with those at the synod who "were trying to make everything into a doctrinal issue," adding, "Not everything is a matter of doctrine; not everything is decided by doctrinal dispute." Asked if the synod now meant that remarried divorcés could receive Communion, he said, "The very nature of this is that it's not as simple as yes-no." It had to be a journey open to God's grace, "and it's not for me or for the priest who is doing the accompaniment to preempt or foreclose that pathway."[49]

The recovery of this pastoral attentiveness to the concrete situation was the synod's signal achievement. An attempt by Cardinal Pell and the Polish bishops to claim that the *Familiaris* settlement was unchanged because there was no specific reference to Communion was pure legalism: the synod had rejected by a clear majority the conservative attempt to reiterate the *Familiaris* ban in the final *relatio*. It had also endorsed a case-by-case discernment that left open the possibility of readmission to the sacraments. Far from being new, this was the Church's very own pastoral tradition, yet it felt new because that tradition had been sidelined by the Church's slide into moralism.

Cardinal Schönborn said, "There is no black or white, no simple yes or no," on the Communion question. The situation of each couple "must be discerned" as Saint John Paul II had called for in *Familiaris Consortio*. As Antonio Spadaro, SJ, tweeted, the synod had moved from the binary logic of the door (open versus shut) to that of the face: each case was a real-life person, a soul before God on a journey, for whom general norms were a guide but could only take you so far. That was the meaning of mercy.[50]

ten

Mercy and Its Discontents

It is a striking feature of the Gospels that although the common people accepted Jesus enthusiastically, he raised alarm among those who saw themselves as guardians of the tradition and truth. The hostility to Francis from traditionalist and conservative groups in the Church that erupted during the Jubilee of Mercy of 2016 offered some striking parallels. It wasn't just that at the moment that ordinary people, inside and outside, were captivated by Francis's extraordinary ability to communicate the mercy of God, various kinds of influential Catholics—scribes (writers, journalists, professors) and doctors of the law (including cardinals)—became bilious, at times vicious, in their opposition to him. It was the fact that mercy was the reason for that opposition.

All post–Vatican II popes have faced fierce criticism from traditionalists and rigorists. Saint John Paul II, a hero to Catholic conservatives, was considered a heretic for praying with people of different religions at Assisi and for stepping inside a mosque. Benedict XVI, who was scorned by rigorist ethicists for daring to suggest that the use of a condom in the context of AIDS prevention could be the beginning of a moral awakening, received so much hostility from the right that a book (*Attacco a Ratzinger*) was written about it by leading Vaticanists. Yet the sheer ferocity of the mobilization against Francis was without precedent in recent times. He is rebuked for his "doctrinal ambiguities," dismissed as a socialist or a liberal, denounced as a dictator or a "danger" to the Church, and is regularly the target of charges of heresy by provincial academics issuing lofty denunciations in Latin to lend them a veneer of authority.

The reason is mercy. Francis called 2016 the special year of favor at the end of 2015, and halfway through it he released his post-synodal apostolic exhortation on the family, *Amoris Laetitia*, an inspired holding-together of truth and compassion that reflected the consensus of the synod and communicated the heart of the Gospel. It was *Amoris* that called forth from the Catholic Church an outpouring of Pharisaism, triggering letters, declarations, denunciations and petitions, charges of heresy, of causing confusion, of undermining teaching and causing chaos. In a long survey of what it called "the war against Pope Francis," the *Guardian* in October 2017 saw in the *Amoris* battle the most serious crisis since Vatican II triggered the breakaway of Archbishop Marcel Lefebvre.[1]

Yet it was easy to confuse the stridency of the critics with their number. "I don't think people are scandalized by the pope," observed Cardinal Blase Cupich of Chicago. "I think they're being *told* to be scandalized." The vast gulf between the hysteria of the pope's small circle of critics, with their fevered talk of schism, confusion, and crisis, and the quiet affection and admiration for Francis from the overwhelming majority of clergy and faithful, remains one of the most remarkable features of this pontificate. Yet while they may be few in number, the critics' fury cries out for an explanation.[2]

One conservative commentator highly critical of Francis had such a strong reaction to a daily homily the pope gave at the Santa Marta in February 2017 that he wrote a book claiming that the pope was "misleading his flock." Reading the summary of that homily caused something to "snap" in Philip Lawler, he recalled at the start of *Lost Shepherd*. Although Francis had frequently "forced" interpretations of Scripture and was "insulting" toward "tradition-minded Catholics," this was different: here the pope had turned the reading "completely upside-down" and was clearly engaged in "a deliberate effort to change what the Church teaches."

What was it that so upset him? The homily was on the passage in chapter 10 of Mark's Gospel in which the Pharisees challenge Jesus over divorce, asking if it is lawful for a husband to put away his wife. In the homily Francis explains why Jesus did not answer the question directly, refusing to enter into their "casuistic logic" ("because they thought of the faith only in terms of 'Yes, you can,' or 'No, you can't'"), and instead focused on the

Pharisees' hardness of heart that led them to advocate divorce. Jesus, said Francis, avoids all casuistry; he "speaks the truth, without casuistry, without permissions: the truth: 'From the beginning of Creation, God made them male and female.'" For this reason "they are no longer two, but one flesh." And this, the Pope affirmed, "is neither casuistry nor permission: it is the truth. Jesus always speaks the truth." Francis went on to explain that Jesus was "even clearer" later with his disciples, to whom he spelled out that "whoever divorces his wife and marries another, commits adultery."

The rest of the homily developed the idea that Christians were called to move, like Jesus, "from casuistry to the truth and to mercy." Casuistry, a form of legalist reasoning that was concerned with prohibitions and exceptions, was seen by Jesus as hypocritical, because it replaced obedience to the fullness of God's truth with a human set of laws that were used to justify human desires. The way of the Christian was instead to ask for the grace of God to respond to the truth, which is always accompanied, in Jesus, by mercy, "because He is the Incarnation of the Mercy of the Father, and He cannot deny Himself." Finally, the pope imagined "someone with a casuistic mentality" asking which was more important in God: justice or mercy? But this is "a sick thought" because "they are not two things but a single one, only one thing. In God, justice is mercy and mercy is justice."[3]

This was, admittedly, complex stuff for a 7 a.m. homily, but it was astonishing that anyone could believe his exegesis in some way changed church teaching or subverted the Gospel. The theology on the relationship between justice and mercy was precisely Saint John Paul II's in his 1982 encyclical *Dives in Misericordia* (Rich in Mercy), who wrote of how in Jesus "true mercy is the most profound source of justice." Yet Lawler could see the homily only in terms of the pope wanting "to promote his own view of divorce and remarriage," as if Francis repeating Jesus's teaching against adultery was somehow negated by what came afterward. Lawler's resentment appeared to rest on his sense of grievance that when Francis critiqued "tradition-minded Catholics" he was critiquing those who believed in law and doctrine, and that he did so because in some way he wished to subvert them.

When otherwise intelligent religious people so badly misread the pope it suggests a "hermeneutic of suspicion," or what the ancients called *invidia*, the word from which comes "envy" but which means "not-seeing," or "looking in a hostile manner." It is what accounts for the Pharisees' fear and suspicion of Jesus, a hostility that led them consistently to judge him as a threat rather than a source of salvation.

Although they were impressed by His teaching and powers, the Pharisees' response to Jesus was governed by emotions, above all fear. What they most feared was the topic of Francis's homily: the way Jesus treated law and tradition, which He never separated from God's truth or His mercy. But they also feared his open and unconditional embrace of sinners, whom He treated as friends without first demanding repentance, showing God's concern to heal and relieve all forms of human suffering, including sin, not by condemning or excluding, but by loving them. For the Pharisees, to love the sinner appeared to relativize the sin: Jesus was therefore a *skandalon*, an obstacle, one who "confused" the people and disregarded holy tradition, and who, by appearing to disdain boundaries, left them exposed. So great was their fear that eventually the Son of God was crucified by the Roman occupying power at the instigation of Jewish religious elites, as the ordinary people looked on in horror.

The *invidia* of Francis's critics, their incandescent rage at him, their bizarre misreadings of him, are as much a story of this pontificate as of the extraordinary boldness of his proclamation of God's mercy. The ferocity of the criticism against Francis within his own Church proves, if nothing else, the power of that proclamation today; and is a reminder that when a pope—or any disciple—truly imitates Christ, they can expect to share something of His fate.[4]

In September 2014, Francis removed a hotheaded traditionalist South American bishop in a feud with the local Church hierarchy. The story was widely covered, yet few knew how it ended, and how the pope's mercy triggered in Rogelio Livieres Plano a remarkable turnaround.

Since being named bishop of Paraguay's second-largest city by Benedict XVI, Livieres had been a high-handed conservative reformer who wanted Ciudad del Este, on Paraguay's eastern border with Brazil, to be a beacon in a local Church he regarded as compromised by dubious left-wing theologies. He even created his own seminary to train the kind of zealous clergy Paraguay needed. But his recruitment of an ultratraditionalist priest with a shocking record of sexual abuse to run the seminary appalled his fellow bishops and put him at odds with his own faithful. Father Carlos Urrutigoity had collected a string of sexual misconduct allegations from his native Argentina to Pennsylvania during a three-decade career in the outer fringes of Catholic traditionalism, a movement that plays down the significance of the Second Vatican Council and seeks a return to Renaissance-era ritual. Livieres ignored the criticisms, and put Urrutigoity in charge of his seminary to promote the pre–Vatican II form of the Mass.

The more local Catholics learned about Urrutigoity's past—his expulsion from a schismatic group in Argentina, a sex abuse lawsuit, and the scandal-ridden history of a traditionalist order he had set up in the Scranton, Pennsylvania, diocese, which was eventually suppressed by the local bishop—the more alarmed they became. But Livieres dug in, and continued to claim that Paraguay's bishops were corrupted by liberation theology. When bishops and local lay Catholics complained to Benedict XVI, Livieres, a member of Opus Dei, defended himself in a letter portraying the Church in Paraguay as left-wing and loose on doctrine, and insisting that Urrutigoity was innocent. When the letter leaked to the national media, relations with the bishops hit a new low.

Livieres made Urrutigoity his vicar-general in early 2014, triggering a fresh wave of outrage. There was a new pope now, and Francis acted, not least because by then the intra-episcopal feud had broken out in spectacularly public fashion. After a radio interview in which the archbishop of Asunción, Pastor Cuquejo, had called on the Vatican to investigate Urrutigoity, Livieres hit back on national TV accusing Cuquejo of being homosexual and telling him to "shut up and go away."

In July of that year, the pope dispatched a Spanish cardinal and an Uruguayan bishop to Ciudad del Este. Alarmed at the deficiencies they found in the formation the seminarians were receiving and the stories about Urrutigoity, Cardinal Santos Abril y Castelló and Bishop Milton Tróccoli shut the seminary and banned further ordinations. Livieres responded with a ten-page self-defense. When the pope asked him to resign, he refused. Francis suspended him in September. The Vatican was circumspect in its statement, citing "serious pastoral reasons" and "the greater good of preserving the unity of the local Church."

Livieres did not go quietly. He ranted at "earthly devils" for his ouster and claimed to be a victim of "ideological persecution." On his website, he joined the traditionalist campaign against the first family synod then getting under way in Rome, lambasting "the Jesuits" and "Cardinal Kasper" for seeking to justify in the name of mercy what was none other than "grave disobedience against the law of God." Opus Dei's office in Rome vigorously distanced itself from opinions it said were "entirely and exclusively his own."

In April of the following year, Livieres was taken gravely ill and hospitalized in Buenos Aires, where he was visited by the local Opus Dei head, Monsignor Víctor Urrestarazu, who carried a message from the Casa Santa Marta. Francis had sent Livieres a warm blessing and wanted him to know that if the bishop had offended him in any way, he forgave him with all his heart.

The effect on Livieres, say those close to him, was akin to a lightning bolt. Struck to the core, he begged to have his confession heard. Then he wrote Francis a long, humble letter, enclosing a gift, which he asked Monsignor Urrestarazu to give to the pope in person on his visit to Asunción in July 2015. Following the huge outdoor papal Mass at Ñu Guazú, Francis met with Paraguay's bishops and other senior church people in the nunciature. There the pope was given the letter. Deeply moved, he shared its contents with the other bishops.

It was a letter of abject contrition. Livieres had come, painfully, to see his pride and errors, his arrogance and his self-isolation. He now professed his fidelity to Pope Francis and begged his fellow bishops to forgive him. Long the target of his contempt and insults, the bishops were bowled over. Moved to tears, Francis said this was the highlight of his visit, and he promised to carry Livieres's gift with him always.

Shortly afterward the new bishop of Ciudad del Este, Guillermo Steckling, along with the new archbishop of Asunción, Edmundo Valenzuela, visited Livieres in the hospital in Buenos Aires. Livieres had been operated on and was dying, but the meeting was joyful. Valenzuela, thrilled Livieres had returned to the communion of the Church, made sure that when he died shortly afterward, in August, he was buried in his cathedral in Ciudad del Este with all the bishops in attendance. Francis told people in Rome he was sure Livieres was in heaven.

A few months later, at the end of November 2015, shortly before opening the Jubilee of Mercy, the pope was in Nairobi, Kenya. In an event with young people, he pulled out of his pocket two things he said he always carried with him. One was a rosary. The other, he confessed, "may seem a little odd."

The Vatican correspondents sighed. They expected him to produce the little crucifix he kept in a specially made cloth pouch in his cassock and to repeat the amusing, macabre story he had shared the previous year: how he had stolen the cross from a dead priest's coffin back in Buenos Aires in 1996 during his wake. (The priest had been a very popular confessor, and Bergoglio, then vicar-general, had brought flowers to put in the coffin next to the body. When no one had been looking, he had yanked the crucifix from the rosary in the dead priest's hands, whispering to him, "Give me half of your mercy!")

But to the journalists' surprise it wasn't the crucifix the pope brought out but a miniature *Via Crucis*, a pocket-size leather case that contained little silver badges depicting Jesus's passion and death. What no one knew was that this was the gift the dying Livieres had sent the pope with his letter.

"It's the story of God's failure," Francis explained to the Kenyan young people. "A little Way of the Cross. The story of how Jesus suffered from the time he was condemned to death until his burial. With these two things, I try to do my best, and thanks to these two things, I don't lose hope."[5]

"The Holy Spirit wills something," Francis told the magazine *Credere*, explaining where the idea of a holy year dedicated to the theme of mercy came from, and it had long been a plant uncurling in the warm soil of his discernment, whose seed had been planted by Aparecida.

A few months after that 2007 gathering, a fired-up Bergoglio had given an interview in Rome to the magazine *30Giorni* in which he said the Church should not be afraid "to depend solely on the tenderness of God." In a world largely deaf to the Church's words, "only the presence of a God who loves and saves us will catch people's attention," he told Stefania Felasca, adding that the Church's evangelizing fervor would return insofar as it witnessed to "the One who loved us first." But this wasn't easy, he said, because God's mercy didn't fit human plans and schemes.

He made the point with the Old Testament story of Jonah, the reluctant prophet who was swallowed and later regurgitated by a whale. Jonah had at the time been on a ship bound for Tarsis, fleeing God's instruction to evangelize the wicked city of Nineveh. What Jonah was really fleeing, said Bergoglio, was God's mercy, which was unacceptable to him. For Jonah, the archetypal religious fellow, the world was neatly divided into the righteous and the unrighteous, the saved and the wretched. In the same way, said Bergoglio, there were nowadays "those who, from the closed world of their Tarsis, complain about everything or, feeling their identity threatened, launch themselves into battles only in the end to be still more self-focused and self-referential." As a description of the defensive, moralistic Catholicism that had arisen in response to secularization as opposed to the outward-looking, evangelizing Church of Aparecida, the Book of Jonah could hardly be improved on.[6]

To underscore the link between mercy and evangelization, Francis asked the Vatican body in charge of the "new evangelization" to organize the Jubilee. Benedict XVI had created the pontifical council to take forward the conclusions of his 2012 synod, but it had largely drifted since then. Now Francis gave it a mandate. "In the present day, as the Church is tasked with the new evangelization, the theme of mercy needs to be proposed again and again," Francis wrote in his ten-thousand-word bull establishing the Jubilee, *Misericordiae Vultus* (The Face of Mercy). Its motto was Jesus's words: "Be merciful, just as your father is merciful."[7]

Francis spelled out the challenge in the strongest possible terms. "Perhaps we have long since forgotten how to show and live the way of mercy," he wrote. The Church's very credibility was at stake in its acceptance or resistance of the need for this conversion; it had fallen into the mind-set of Jonah.

In *Misericordiae Vultus* Francis quoted Saint John Paul II: contemporary technocracy had no room for mercy. But this begged the question: if Western culture was now becoming detached from its Christian roots and reverting to paganism—as the widespread practice of abortion and divorce and a sink-or-swim mentality that trusted only in human and material power suggested—why was the Church not exploding with converts and vocations? Why was it not notorious for its mercy, infamous for its compassion, scandalous in its standing with the outcast?

There was no shortage of such witness. Yet this was not the face of the Church the world saw, which was a far cry from the early Jesus movement, "an island of mercy," as the historian Rodney Stark describes it, in the midst of the squalor, misery, illness, and anonymity of ancient cities. The mercy of Christians scandalized and captivated the society of the time. Mercy was the single most important factor in Christianity's sudden expansion in its early centuries, before it became, in many respects, a law-and-order religion of precepts and power.[8]

The problem now was that, in recoiling from the modern world, many Catholics—among them, in particular, those taking refuge from relativism—looked to the Church to offer precisely those legalistic encrustations in which the Gospel of mercy had been buried from the time of Constantine onward and which the Second Vatican Council had sought to discard. As long as it offered moralism instead of mercy, the Church would be incapable of evangelizing the contemporary world. Hence *Misericordiae Vultus* made the embrace of mercy a life-or-death matter, declaring that wherever there are Christians, "everyone should find an oasis of mercy."[9]

Even the way he announced the Jubilee, during a penitential service at St. Peter's in March 2015 exactly two years after his election, showed that Francis saw its objective as purging the Pharisaism that had crippled the Church's capacity to convert. By responding to Jesus's merciful love, the sinful woman who washes his feet with her tears is born to new life, he explained in a homily on the episode in chapter seven of Luke. Simon the Pharisee, scandalized by Jesus's acceptance of her, "cannot find the path of love" because "in his thoughts he invokes only justice." Being a witness to mercy, Francis said, was "a journey that begins with a spiritual conversion. For this reason, I have decided to call an extraordinary Jubilee that is to have the mercy of God at its center. It shall be a Holy Year of Mercy."

Some liberal Catholics disliked the idea of mercy because of its connotation of judgment; why not "compassion"? But Francis was adamant: "Mercy is divine and has to do with the judgment of sin," he said firmly. God's mercy was His response to sin in the same way that compassion was His response to suffering. What made the world merciless was that it had forgotten sin and so did not offer "a hand to raise you up, an embrace to save you, forgive you, pick you up, flood you with patient, indulgent love; to put you back on your feet," he said in a book-long interview with Andrea Tornielli.[10]

Both conservative and liberal nervousness about the Jubilee reflected the contemporary view that truth and mercy were in contradiction, as if too much truth or justice reduced mercy, or too much mercy undermined the law. Yet Francis saw them as a polarity, a tension of poles pulling apart yet reconciled in God in a creative synthesis that amplified both. Mercy was not the downgrading of doctrine; it *was* doctrine, the truth of who God is. In Francis's traditionally Augustinian expression of it, mercy took for granted not just sin but the essential wretchedness of humanity.

There was nothing egalitarian about mercy. God's *misericordia* could be received only in humility, by those who acknowledged their *miseria*, their wretchedness, before their Creator, and their dependence on Him. Thus whatever humbled the Church, like the humiliation of the sex abuse failures, would make it more merciful, liberating it from the iron cage of self-reliance and casting it on the true power, the mercy of God. "The real poor," Francis said in his Lent 2016 message, "are revealed as those who refuse to see themselves as such," for they "use wealth and power not for the service of God and others, but to stifle within their hearts the profound sense that they too are only poor beggars."[11]

The loss of a sense of sin was narcissism. So while, on the one hand, the Church "condemns sin because it has to relay the truth," at the same time "it embraces the sinner who recognizes himself as such." The pope wanted the Jubilee to reveal that God's response to human suffering and sin was not condemnation but salvation in Jesus: mercy made flesh, the face of God's mercy. And he would spend a year showing it.

The Italian comic actor Roberto Benigni put it best at the launch of the Tornielli book, titled *The Name of God Is Mercy*: "The pope walks, walks, and never stops, he seems to toil and toil, he's pulling the whole Church towards Christianity, towards the Gospel, towards Jesus. If you think about the work he's doing, it's incredible."[12]

The Jubilee of Mercy wasn't about teaching an idea so much as a way to act. It was about emulating the way God interacts with and saves humanity. That action, as Francis expressed it continually throughout the Jubilee, is a four-stage dynamic: coming close ("welcoming"); sensing need ("discerning"); responding concretely and individually ("accompanying"); and a final stage that involves change, conversion, and belonging ("integrating"). The fourfold move is at the heart of *Amoris Laetitia*, and underpins, for example, the Vatican's advocacy for migrants.[13]

This fourfold dynamic is the way of the Good Samaritan, Jesus's parable about a kindhearted foreigner who goes to the aid of the victim of a roadside mugging, while the distracted, law-bound religious people pass him by. In the Christian tradition, the Samaritan is Jesus himself, the inn to whose care he entrusts the victim stands for the Church, and the coins that the Samaritan leaves the innkeeper to care for him symbolize the grace that God channels through the Church. That grace heals all kinds of suffering, whether by sin or by circumstance. Aparecida had spoken of the "Samaritan Church," and this was for Francis the model for the Jubilee. As he put it in *Misericordiae Vultus*, the Year of Mercy was to help the Church rediscover "the spirit of the Samaritan" that underlies the evangelizing, missionary thrust of the Second Vatican Council.

Back in the 1980s, when Jesuits were arguing about faith versus social justice, Bergoglio had contended that Jesus's parable of the Good Samaritan showed how poverty and wretchedness sought to conceal themselves, and how only personal contact could uncover them. Only by coming close to "the living wounds of Christ" could there be "awareness, apostolic action, and, finally, structural change." At the heart of the Samaritan-Church vision was the idea that there could ultimately be no justice without proximity. As he put it in *Misericordiae Vultus*:

> As we can see in Sacred Scripture, mercy is a key word that indicates God's action towards us. He does not limit himself merely to affirming his love, but makes it visible and tangible. Love, after all, can never be just an abstraction. By its very nature, it indicates something concrete: intentions, attitudes, and behaviors that are shown in daily living. The mercy of God is his loving concern for each one of us. He feels responsible; that is, he desires our wellbeing and he wants to see us happy, full of joy, and peaceful. This is the path which the merciful love of Christians must also travel. As the Father loves, so do his children. Just as he is merciful, so we are called to be merciful to each other.[14]

Nobody in the world showed better than Francis how to come close. Ever since his first General Audience in St. Peter's Square, when somehow in the chaos of thousands of jostling, cheering people he spotted a sick man and—to the alarm of his security detail—stopped the popemobile to go over to caress his face, Francis has shown an attentiveness and a responsiveness to suffering that has captivated the world. In St. Peter's Square, his tender embrace of Vinicio Riva, a neurofibromatosis sufferer with terrible boils on his face, remained the iconic moment, yet few could forget his response to Glyzelle Palomar, a twelve-year-old street girl in Manila, who after describing some of the horrors she had endured, asked him why God allowed children to suffer. The only answer we can give to that question, Francis told her, was silence or sobbing. "Certain realities in life," he told a stadium of thirty thousand, "can only be seen with eyes cleaned by tears."[15]

Another moment came at the end of his U.S. visit in September 2015, at Philadelphia's airport, when Francis spotted Michael Keating, who has cerebral palsy and uses a wheelchair. The ninety-second viral video of that encounter—the pope stopped the car, leaned over a guardrail, and tenderly kissed Michael's head—triggered not just donations to help the family cope, but media stories about their dedication to Michael, which in turn inspired and comforted others. It was just one touching gesture, yet it literally spread goodness and hope across the globe.

One day in St. Peter's Square, CNN's religion editor, Daniel Burke, found himself wondering how this happened. Tearing up from watching the pope embrace the elderly and the sick, he found himself full of the urge to do the same. Why? He found that scientists spoke of "elevation," the mimetic effect of gestures of tenderness that provoke the desire in us to be better people. "Edicts and rules may keep us from behaving like devils," Burke concluded, "but if you want us to be saints, it helps to show us how." It was a pithy explanation of why Francis has taught so much through an "encyclical of gestures."[16]

At their greatest, such gestures become teaching moments that unveil an unseen reality, one that can only be grasped in the gaze of mercy: that all belong, to God and to each other, and that division and separation constitute a great lie. It is the unveiling Jesus refers to in Matthew chapter 25 with his story of the shock of religious people on discovering that the God they worshipped was not a distant star in the galaxy but alive in the suffering poor they had either assisted or ignored.

"It is Christ's own flesh which suffers in his dearest sons and daughters," Francis told evangelical leaders in Bangui, Central African Republic, the forgotten war zone from where he pre-launched the Jubilee. That meant not being ashamed of the bodies of needy people. "When I give alms, do I drop the money without touching the person's hand?" he asked in a March 2014 homily. "Do I look my brother or sister in the eye?" Closeness, he told El País, "is to touch, to touch in our neighbor the flesh of Christ."[17]

A National Geographic photographer who spent six months documenting the pope and the Vatican discovered how attentive the pope was one day in St. Peter's. Dave Yoder was strategically placed close to a circle of bishops greeting the pope next to Michelangelo's *Pietà* when Francis traversed the arc toward him, shaking hands. An embarrassed Yoder pretended to examine his camera's settings, but "when I looked up, he was standing before me, hand extended, eyebrows raised, waiting for me to notice him. Status or occupation never seemed to concern him."[18]

Journalists experience the same attentive presence on the papal plane, as I saw when I joined the *vaticanisti* on the pope's overnight trip to Sweden at the end of October 2016. On the outward journey to commemorate the anniversary of the Reformation, he came among us as a pastor, greeting the seventy-odd reporters and cameramen one by one, moving slowly down the aisle, taking a letter here, a prayer request there, blessing a picture, recording a video message or inclining his head to receive a confidence, or laughing over a shared joke. When he reached me, we spoke about a young friend we had in common. "He has a good mind and a good heart," Francis told me. "Although it might be just for a few minutes, the pope is all yours," says Eva Fernández, Vatican reporter for the Spanish radio COPE, who has written a whole book on the pope's tenderness. "Whatever other concerns he has that day, at that moment what matters to him is what you want to tell him."[19]

He doesn't need to be physically present to be close. As cardinal, Bergoglio was famous for his "telephone ministry," and to this day he carries an address book stuffed with names and numbers. When he dials someone out of the blue—he punches in the numbers himself—in response to letters he has received, they are pastor's calls, consoling or encouraging, to people who are sick, in prison, or in refugee camps. The calls usually begin with disarming ordinariness: *Pronto, ciao, sono Papa Francesco. Come stai?* But thereafter, no call is ever the same.[20]

No issue has summoned from Francis God's gaze of mercy more than migration, arguably the most important and divisive phenomenon of the age. As with the question of Eucharist for the divorced and remarried, he advocates not a particular policy but a Samaritan proximity to the individual case, followed by discernment. He wants society to put on different lenses. "This crisis which can be measured in numbers and statistics, we want instead to measure with names, stories, families," as Francis put it in his February 2016 U.S.–Mexico border homily. Without closeness and mercy, "the other remains a stranger, even an enemy, and can't become my neighbor," he told migrants in Bologna.[21]

The pope is critical of politics that scapegoat migrants or try to shore up support by portraying foreigners as rivals, yet his response is not to call for the borders to be opened indiscriminately. He wants to change the focus away from the abstract question of open or closed borders, onto others: What are the needs of those arriving on our shores? How can countries best respond to those needs? Answering those questions demands, as at the synod, moving away from the door (open or closed border?) to the face: to the individuals. That could mean, for example, tempering an open-door policy by prudential restrictions to ensure proper integration.[22]

He has applied the lens of mercy to one group of migrants in particular: the persecuted and mistreated Rohingya of Myanmar. A Muslim minority in a Buddhist military state that has taken away their nationality, destroyed their communities, and massacred thousands of them, the Rohingya are among the most wretched people on earth. In speeches and homilies, Francis had long signaled that they had a protector in the Vatican, always using their name. But during an eggshell-delicate trip to Myanmar in November 2017, he carefully avoided using the term publicly while in the country meeting its president, as well as its foreign minister, Aung San Suu Kyi. Human rights groups were withering in their criticism. "The Rohingya have been stripped of so many things but their name should never be one of them," Human Rights Watch's Asia division reprimanded the pope.[23]

From Myanmar, he went to Dhaka in neighboring Bangladesh, where he met a small group representing 600,000 Rohingya refugees. They told him, through interpreters, their shocking stories, and when the organizers tried to silence them, the pope insisted they be allowed to speak. Then the leader of the world's Catholics asked the Muslim refugees to forgive him on behalf of their Buddhist persecutors, before adding through tears: "Let us not close our heart. Let's not look away. The presence of God today is called Rohingya." The sentence made headlines across the world.

He had not planned his words, he told reporters later. "I began to feel something. I cried. I tried not to show it. They cried too." He had not used their name while in Myanmar, he explained, because he did not want to close doors; he needed those meetings to address those with the power to affect the Rohingya's fate. Francis's relentless focus throughout the trip was on the Rohingya themselves. For their sake, he avoided using their name in Myanmar; for their sake in Bangladesh he publicly dignified their name in the strongest way a pope could. What appears inconsistent is consistent: for Francis the Rohingya weren't an issue, an abstract moral question, a political football, or an opportunity for virtue signaling; they were the wounds of Christ.[24]

His April 2016 visit to the Greek island of Lesbos, to stand with refugees from Syria's civil war, was one of the landmarks of the Jubilee. Tens of thousands were trapped in what was little more than a holding pen after a number of European countries closed their borders. "I want to tell you that you are not alone," he told the Syrian and Iraqi people at Moria refugee camp, urging them to not lose hope. In the company of the Orthodox ecumenical patriarch, Bartholomew I, and the archbishop of Athens, Ieronymos II, Francis issued a powerful joint declaration urging the world's nations to provide them safe harbor.

He had in mind the scheme developed by the Rome-based Catholic community of Sant'Egidio, the sponsor of the so-called humanitarian corridors that had facilitated more than two thousand vulnerable refugees to settle in Italy without making a treacherous sea-crossing. The previous month, Francis had praised the corridors in St. Peter's Square as a creative answer that combined solidarity with security.[25]

Barely a week before the Lesbos trip, he asked Sant'Egidio to ready a dozen refugees at the Moria camp to return with him to Rome on the papal plane. It wasn't easy to find people with their papers in order. In the end, the pope brought back three Muslim families, including six children, who had lost their homes in the Syrian war. The Economist described it as "one of the most eye-catching and arresting" gestures of his papacy.

It infuriated his right-wing critics, the ones who had resented that Francis washed the foot of a Muslim prisoner in Rome at the start of his pontificate. Although the reason the papal flight passengers were all Muslims was circumstantial—none of the Christian families could get their papers in order in time—there was an implicit rebuke to countries that had closed their borders to Muslim refugees in order (they claimed) to protect their Christian identity and culture. Asked on the plane why the families had all been Muslim, Francis said the only criterion was that they had their papers in order, but he added, pointedly, that all were children of God.

(A few weeks later, fifteen Christians who had been initially assigned to the papal plane came from Lesbos to Rome via Sant'Egidio's corridor. But they barely made the news.)[26]

Francis set aside a Friday each month during the Jubilee to visit "places of pain," among them a retirement home, a care facility for people in a vegetative state, a center for drug addicts, a safe house for trafficked former prostitutes, a neonatal unit, and a hospice for the terminally ill. What these places had in common, aside from being in Rome, was that they welcomed, accompanied, assisted, and integrated. The "mercy Fridays" visits were off the media's radar, but photos and anecdotes leaked out, supplying a year-long backstory of tenderness.[27]

Francis later recalled two stories that stayed with him, both about children who had died. One was the baby of an African prostitute who had been forced to give birth in the street in winter, another a woman in a hospital for the terminally ill who had cried incessantly over her child's passing. They had reminded him, he said, of the horror of abortion, "the habit of sending away children before they were born, that horrendous crime."[28]

It seemed odd, and to some, offensive, to link the two: surely one was a tragedy over which they had no control, while the other was a deliberate choice? But that was to think as the world did, to judge guilt and to divide people into sheep and goats. At the U.S. Congress in September 2015, Francis had warned against "the simplistic reductionism which sees only good or evil, or, if you will, the righteous and sinners," and had called on America to resist "every form of polarization that would divide it into these two camps." In his communications day message for 2016, Francis similarly called for the Church "to overcome the mindset that neatly separates sinners from the righteous," for while "we can and we must judge situations of sin . . . we may not judge individuals, since only God can see into the depths of their hearts." To judge was human; to save was divine.

On the eve of the Jubilee, Francis announced that all priests would now be able to absolve the sin of abortion, rather than seeking special permission to do so from their bishops, as some dioceses demanded. His letter of September 1, 2015, made no attempt to soft-pedal the gravity of abortion, which he made clear was the murder of an innocent. But because Western society had ceased to see it as such, leading to what he called "the loss of the proper personal and social sensitivity to welcome new life," there were now victims who needed attending to: not just the innocent lives extinguished, but grieving women racked by remorse and men with blood on their hands. Some had been persuaded of the lie that abortion was simply a medical procedure, while others knew what it involved but believed they had no choice. "I have met so many women who bear in their heart the scar of this agonizing and painful decision," Francis wrote. "What has happened is profoundly *unjust*; yet only *understanding the truth of it* can enable one not to lose hope."[29]

In framing the issue as one of injustice to which the response was to face the truth and hope for mercy, Francis was moving away from the futile ethical contest of rival abstract rights (pro-life versus pro-choice) to a battlefield-hospital logic, which focused on the wounds. "Understanding the truth of it" was not just that abortion was wrong, but that a corrupted culture did not see it as such; to concentrate on culpability and sinfulness was therefore at best pointless. What mattered, in this circumstance, was to offer a way out to people who had awoken to the truth and were crushed by guilt and grief. When Francis spoke about this to Dominique Wolton, he asked him to picture a woman who carried the physical memory of an aborted child, "and who weeps, who has wept for years without having the courage to go and see the priest . . . Can you imagine the number of people who are breathing at last? . . . At least let them find the Lord's forgiveness and not sin again."[30]

The indult produced unease among Catholic anti-abortion campaigners who worried that he was weakening the pro-life message. But mostly the fury came from pro-choice activists: how dare the pope imply that a woman who had had an abortion might need *forgiveness*? To move away from the ethics of abortion and onto the needs and wounds of those directly involved produced discomfort on both sides.

This pastoral shift, the focus on the concrete person rather than the abstract issue, was what lay behind the intense criticism from some Catholic conservatives of what they called the "confusion," "ambiguity," or "mixed messages" of the Francis papacy. To those whose religion was essentially a matter of law and identity, to move from the door to the face looked like relativism.

The arrows were especially sharp when Francis warmly received in the Vatican a Spanish transgender man who had reached out to him.

As cardinal, Bergoglio was familiar with the plight of gender dysphoria and trans people from a Discalced Carmelite sister in Argentina whom he had known since 1985. He regularly called and visited Sister Monica Astorga to give his support for her groundbreaking ministry to trans women, many of whom, shunned by society, turned to prostitution. When he visited her in Neuquén in 2009, he told her, "Don't leave them alone. This is the frontier work that the Lord has given you." From Rome, Francis has continued to encourage Sister Monica, likening trans people in letters to her to the lepers of Jesus's time.[31]

So when Diego Neria Lejárraga wrote to Francis at the end of 2014, Francis had a good sense of the pain the Spaniard wanted to share. Neria had grown up a girl in the Spanish city of Plasencia but waited until his mother died before having reassignment surgery at the age of forty. Eight years later, he was a practicing Catholic who had been insulted and spurned by a tiny yet angry minority in his parish who found his presence intolerable. When he received Neria's letter, Francis invited him to the Vatican in January 2015, together with his fiancée, the first time—at least on public record—that a pope had received a trans person. Francis hugged him and told him he was "a son of the Church." If someone in the parish tried to shun him, he told him, the problem was theirs, not his.

Later Neria said the meeting had made him feel clean and at peace, convincing him finally that God loved him as he was. He went on to write a book about his story and faith journey, *El despiste de Dios* (God's Slipup), and with the pope's support, to encourage other gender dysphoric Catholics not to give up on the Church but to feel at home there.[32]

Yet what Francis said to Neria wasn't all he had to say on the subject. In Manila the previous month, he deplored the "ideological colonization" of gender theory, which in a book interview he criticized as failing to recognize the order of creation. Elsewhere, he has often rejected the idea that gender could be different from the sex assigned at birth, and has made clear that gender is part of the created order deserving of respect: "Children are learning that they can choose their own sex. Why is sex, being a woman or a man, a choice and not a fact of nature?" he asked Dominique Wolton. Equally, he has deplored "the biological and psychological manipulation of sexual difference" that presents gender as a "simple matter of personal choice." At the end of the Year of Mercy, on a visit to Tbilisi, Georgia, he said the imposition of gender ideology via international agencies was part of a "global war against marriage." In October 2017, he critiqued advances in biotechnology that made it easier to change gender, and what he called the "utopia of the neutral" that sought to erase sexual difference. His comments earned rebukes from LGBTQ Catholic groups as ignorant and increasing the vulnerability of trans people to discrimination. They criticized him again when the Vatican's Congregation for Education reaffirmed Christian anthropology in a 2019 document called "Male and Female He Created Them."

Asked on the flight from Azerbaijan in October 2016 how he reconciled his rejection of gender ideology with pastoring a person struggling with their sexuality, the pope didn't blink. There was no contradiction, he said. "One thing is for a person to have this tendency, and even for that person to change sex, another thing is to teach in school in this way in order to change people's way of thinking," Francis told Joshua McElwee of the *National Catholic Reporter*. He then recounted some of Neria's story without naming him, referring to "he who was a she, but is a he," and praised a local retired bishop who had taken Neria under his wing and invited him to confession. Truth was truth and sin was sin, he said, but "we have to take each case, and welcome him, walk with him, study him, discern and integrate him. This is what Jesus would do today." Pastoral challenges such as these, he said, had to be solved, "always with the mercy of God—with truth, but always with an open heart."[33]

Because he had appeared to endorse gender reassignment by referring to "her" as a "he," while at the same time deploring gender ideology, Francis was again criticized from both sides—trans activists and family values conservatives—for creating "confusion." Yet this holding truth and mercy together in tension was at the heart of the Gospel: to be nonjudgmental wasn't to reject truth. As Sister Monica put it: "Jesus is at the center of the Gospel. And he discriminated against no one."

Just as in Francis's homily that so upset Lawler, Francis's right-wing, family values critics were revealing themselves as the relativists. In a classically Pharisaical move they casuistically treated the Church's embryonic thinking on gender dysphoria and gender reassignment therapies (which have received very little attention so far from Catholic theologians) as immovable teaching, while ignoring or downplaying the eternal teaching of Jesus about God, that no one was excluded from God's loving embrace.[34]

Francis told Father Spadaro in 2013 that everyone's life was full of weeds and thorns, yet "there is always a space in which the good seed can grow." Hence the ancient maxim that *de internis non iudicat praetor*: what was between a believer and God was no one else's business. It was why Francis had asked, back in 2013, "Who am I to judge?" And why he told Andrea Tornielli in *The Name of God Is Mercy*, "Before all else comes the individual person, in his wholeness and dignity. And people should not be defined only by their sexual tendencies: let us not forget that God loves all his creatures and we are destined to receive his infinite love."

This was the truth that the pope refused to water down for the sake of appeasing today's Jonahs in their fear-filled battles with the modern world. The Church's task was to open up its hospital to all, not turn sick people away to avoid scandalizing the healthy. As the pope had put it in a general audience at the start of the jubilee, "God's mercy always operates to save."[35]

Nothing in his pontificate better held in fruitful tension truth and mercy than *Amoris Laetitia*, his apostolic exhortation released in April 2016, midway through the Jubilee. It sought to make indissoluble marriage more accessible and attainable, while opening up the divorced and remarried to follow a path of growth and conversion. It also called forth from the Church a wave of Pharisaical fury that has persisted to this day.

Penned in ordinary language for men and women facing the concrete realities and challenges of modern family life, *Amoris Laetitia* grasped that marriage was no longer an economic institution anchored in law and the expectations of traditional culture, but had to be rooted in relationship, open to God's grace. The big shift in teaching in *Amoris* is the discernment of Aparecida: the transmission belts are frayed and broken; matrimony as an institution, at least as Christians understand it, will no longer be upheld by culture and law; ergo, lifelong marriage can only now be embraced as Gospel. The Church's task, in short, was not only to teach that exclusive, lifelong, man-woman love was what human beings were made for and longed for, but to show that it was possible, with spiritual growth and the cultivation of virtue in response to God's grace.

But to offer this shift of focus from law to Gospel the Church had to change. Rather than simply insisting on obedience to a precept, it had to become a channel of mercy that made possible the ideal to which it was calling humanity. *Amoris Laetitia*'s concerns were precisely those of Jesus: human relationships, with their suffering and setbacks, their dysfunctions and failures. Like *Evangelii Gaudium*, the exhortation was a polemic against the black-and-white, stone-throwing moralism that recoiled from such chaos. Such thinking, Francis wrote, closed off "the way of grace and of growth." Categorizing people's situations as regular or irregular was a way of avoiding the wounds: it ignored the power of grace, entrusted to the Church, which meant that all could have hope in lifelong love, however wounded or distant from the law. As he expressed the same idea in Bulgaria in May 2019: "Seeing with the eyes of faith is a summons not to spend your life pinning labels, classifying those who are worthy of love and those who are not, but trying to create conditions in which every person can feel loved, especially those who feel forgotten by God because they are forgotten by their brothers and sisters."[36]

Amoris also critiqued a church tendency to talk of marriage in an abstract fashion, divorced from the concrete struggles of human life. In proposing "a far too abstract and almost artificial theological ideal of marriage," the Church had failed to respond well to the current age in which "the fear of loneliness and the desire for stability and fidelity exist side by side in a growing fear of entrapment in a relationship that could hamper the achievement of one's personal goals." It wasn't enough to have a "correct" view; you had to have skin in the game. Marriage was a struggle, "a long and demanding apprenticeship" that required learning fidelity, patience, forgiveness, respect, and kindness through different phases; it was a "challenge to be taken up and fought for, reborn, renewed and reinvented until death."

That was why Jesus had insisted that marriage was for life. Learning to love needed stability, time, patience. Unless entered into and embraced as a lifelong project, marriage would succumb to "the culture of the ephemeral" that prevents growth. Rather than simply asserting indissolubility, Francis explained the reasons for it in light of marriage's role as a means of growth and redemption. The third chapter of *Amoris* summarized key church teachings on marriage and family since the Second Vatican Council, including the openness to life in marriage in Saint Paul VI's 1968 *Humanae Vitae*, but in such a way that rooted those teachings in the very purpose of marriage itself.

Chapter four, on conjugal love, was the jewel of the document, the basis for the Church's future catechesis on marriage. In the pope's own exegesis of Saint Paul's famous letter to the Corinthians on love, he offered dozens of insights into the emotional and erotic world of the marital partnership.

Only a pastor who had spent decades immersed in the lives of families could write about the intense negotiations that went on within them, how, for example, "love makes each wait for the other, with the patience of a craftsman, a patience that comes from God."

He didn't waste time lamenting horses that had long since bolted. Defensive indignation at the legal deconstruction of the family had frittered pastoral energy better spent helping people marry and stay married. The Church's task now was to rebuild marriage from below. From pastoral programs, to parenting, adoption, education of children, the challenges of aging and mixed marriages, to the formation of priests, *Amoris* was the most comprehensive attempt yet made by the Catholic Church to do for the family what *Laudato Si'* did for the environment: to plot a path back to ecological recovery. For this, the Church needed a new close and concrete pastoral approach, one that moved away from an abstract, lofty, spiritualized idealism and went in search of God's grace operating in the nitty-gritty of people's lives.

Saint John Paul II's 1981 exhortation had claimed that, because the union of Christ and His Church was signified by the Eucharist, those who had remarried were automatically barred from it. Without actually mentioning the *ipse namque* clause or its far-fetched extrapolation, Francis in *Amoris* noted instead that there was "no need to lay upon two limited persons the tremendous burden of having to reproduce perfectly the union existing between Christ and His Church." An idyllic or perfect marriage and family was a myth of advertising campaigns; it was far healthier "to be realistic about our limits, defects and imperfections, and to respond to the call to grow together." Everyone was wounded and faced failure; everyone was in need of mercy; everyone was offered God's grace. He quoted Saint John Paul II's *Familiaris Consortio* with approval: marriage was a "dynamic process . . . [that] advances gradually with the progressive integration of the gifts of God." It was time to take that seriously. "Many people feel that the Church's message on marriage and the family does not clearly reflect the preaching and message of Jesus," Francis said pointedly, adding that Jesus "set forth a demanding ideal yet never failed to show compassion and closeness to the frailty of individuals like the Samaritan woman or the woman caught in adultery."

The shift Francis was seeking was captured in the Second Vatican Council's final document, *Gaudium et Spes* (Joy and Hope), quoted almost twenty times in *Amoris*. That document had opened with a heart-lifting mercy overture, identifying the followers of Christ with the "joy and the hope, the grief and anguish of the men and women of our times, especially those who are poor and afflicted in any way." In *Amoris*, Francis saw families everywhere under pressure from poverty, migration, and unemployment; yet the Church had too often responded with rules and dogmatic declarations that "lead people to feel judged and abandoned by the very Mother called to show them God's mercy."

A better synthesis of truth and mercy was needed if Catholic teaching on marriage were to be faithful to Christ because mercy was "the fullness of justice and the most radiant manifestation of God's truth." While the Church had been good at teaching the ideal, it had not been so good at helping couples receive the graces needed to live it in practice. As Francis put it in what is arguably the document's key passage:

> We have long thought that simply by stressing doctrinal, bioethical and moral issues, *without encouraging openness to grace*, we were providing sufficient support to families, strengthening the marriage bond and giving meaning to marital life. We find it difficult to present marriage more as a dynamic path to personal development and fulfilment than as a life-long burden. We also find it hard to make room for the consciences of the faithful, who very often respond as best they can to the Gospel amid their limitations, and are capable of carrying out their own discernment in complex situations. We have been called to form consciences, not replace them.[37]

This was the *Amoris* project in summary: to urge the Church to facilitate openness to grace (mentioned more than fifty times in the document) through the fourfold mercy dynamic of welcome, accompaniment, discernment, and integration. Like Saint Augustine rebutting the Pelagians, Francis stressed both human frailty and limitless divine assistance. Married love "is not defended primarily by presenting indissolubility as a duty, or by repeating doctrine," Francis noted sharply, "but by helping it to grow ever stronger under the impulse of grace."

The Church needed to present the reasons and motivations for choosing marriage and the family, offer proper training and formation and support, and stay close and concrete. The second half of the document covered particular challenges or questions, such as parenting, relationships with siblings and grandparents, the education of children, and spirituality. Two of the chapters were about pastoral challenges: how parishes can prepare and accompany married couples, help them grow through crises, cope with challenges, and face tragedies such as death and divorce.

But it was chapter eight, titled "Accompanying, Discerning and Integrating Weakness," that would attract the most attention because it dealt with the celebrity issue that had so divided the synod. It was also the chapter that reflected most closely the pedagogy that Francis had been teaching throughout the Jubilee, and which contained the truth-plus-mercy gelignite that triggered an explosion.

"Something has changed in the Church's discourse," a delighted Cardinal Christoph Schönborn told journalists at the release of *Amoris Laetitia*, pointing out that nowhere in the document did the pope divide marriages into simple juridical categories of "regular" and "irregular." Francis, he said, "has looked on every situation with the heart of God and the gaze of Jesus." No one was outside the Father's love; no one was condemned forever. This was the new thing—yet a very old thing—the Holy Spirit had called forth in *Amoris*, one that was wholly in tune with the Church's tradition and Francis's predecessors.[38]

As editor of John Paul II's *Catechism of the Catholic Church* who had formed part of Benedict XVI's trusted inner circle of thinkers, Schönborn was not just a renowned Dominican theologian but one who was in tune with the thinking of the two previous popes. So when he declared *Amoris* to be an "organic development" of existing teaching based on a "profoundly Thomistic" theology of grace, Catholics listened. Saint John Paul II wasn't around to comment, but from his retirement, Benedict XVI did. The pope emeritus told Schönborn that John Paul II's *Familiaris Consortio* and Francis's *Amoris Laetitia* formed a "diptych." Benedict meant, presumably, that where *Familiaris* firmly defended indissolubility in law and culture, *Amoris* built it from below; where *Familiaris* called for those with broken marriages to be brought back into the Church, *Amoris* showed how it could happen: not by means of new law but by allowing the ancient pastoral practice of discernment to have effects in the external forum.[39]

It also recognized the principle of graduality that at the synod had come in from the cold. There was no doubt about God's purpose for marriage, but people got there at different speeds. Francis recognized that while "some forms of union radically contradict this ideal . . . others realize it in at least a partial and analogous way." Further, the Church "does not disregard the constructive elements in those situations which do not yet or no longer correspond to her teaching on marriage." Reprising his famous homily to the cardinals in February 2015, he said the logic of the Gospel was not to cast off but to reinstate, and so "the Church has the responsibility of helping [everyone] understand the divine pedagogy of grace in their lives and offering them assistance so they can reach the fullness of God's plan for them."

Hence, in the case of the divorced and remarried, "a responsible personal and pastoral discernment of particular cases" was called for, one that involved a lengthy examination of conscience under the guidance of a priest. As moral theologian Monsignor Philippe Bordeyne, rector of the Institut Catholique in Paris, pointed out, *Amoris* sought to form "a right judgment in the reality of what is . . . rather than what we would wish it to be." This was the proper role of conscience, whose task was not simply to work out where a person had departed from the Church's teaching, but to hear God's invitation in the here-and-now circumstances of life as it is.[40]

This required no new law. Certain bishops and theologians had lobbied for amendments to the rules on reception of the sacraments, but Francis had rejected them. Canon law made clear what was a valid marriage, and that to deliberately break a valid marriage was adultery. But while the law affirmed what was true, it was insufficient; the variety of situations and the complexity of lives called for far greater nuance and pastoral attentiveness. The Pharisees' answer when faced with this challenge, Francis said in December 2014, was simply to create ever more laws until they ended up with close to four hundred commandments, and so "made of God's gratuity a way of holiness that made everyone slaves." Jesus's answer, on the other hand, was more like the lullaby a mother sang to her child.[41]

Rather than more law, what was needed was more loving attention to reality, more Good Samaritan accompaniment, in order to open up the truth: to help a person or couple honestly to face their situation, and the options open to them; and from there to hear what God was asking of them. Francis warned against pigeonholing or rigidly classifying the divorced and remarried in ways that left no room for this "personal and pastoral discernment." Because of the "immense variety of concrete situations," he wrote in *Amoris*, what was needed was to look at the truth of a situation in the round, with the help of a wise priest. He then suggested five questions priests should ask to get at the truth about the breakdown of the marriage and the new situation. They were almost precisely those that Schönborn's clergy had used in Vienna over many years in their outreach to the divorced and remarried.[42]

In order to walk alongside people in such cases, *Amoris* made explicit what Saint John Paul II had called in *Veritatis Splendor* the "important pastoral consideration" that people could be morally good and persevere in grace even when certain aspects of their behavior were contrary to God's commandments. For this technical part, Francis relied above all on two moral theologians: Archbishop Víctor Fernández of Argentina's Catholic University, whose 2011 paper on the topic of ethical norms and human fragility clearly shaped *Amoris*; and Father Wojciech Giertych, OP, since 2005 the papal theologian, whose task was to ensure that the pope's output was theologically rigorous. Francis's reported dependence on the British-Polish Dominican for chapter eight in particular was significant: Giertych was a Benedict XVI appointee who appeared regularly on conservative Catholic media.[43]

"Because of forms of conditioning and mitigating factors," Francis wrote in *Amoris*, "it is possible that in an objective situation of sin—which may not be subjectively culpable, or fully such—a person can be living in God's grace, can love and can also grow in the life of grace and charity, while receiving the Church's help to this end." Such help could, in certain cases, Francis added in a footnote, "include the help of the sacraments," which, he reminded people in a line from *Evangelii Gaudium*, are "not a prize for the perfect, but a powerful medicine and nourishment for the weak."

He put this in a footnote precisely to show that receiving Communion or not—the issue over which the synod had split before finally coming together—was not the main point. What mattered was the journey away from casuistry, into truth via mercy. "*Amoris Laetitia* goes in a completely different direction," Francis told the Jesuits. "It does not enter into those distinctions. It raises the issue of discernment, which was at the heart of truly great classical Thomism." He confirmed this to the British theologian Stephen Walford: *Amoris*, he told him in a letter, "follows the classical doctrine of St. Thomas Aquinas."[44]

In other words, *Amoris* was responding to the need to distinguish between different pastoral situations highlighted by John Paul II in *Famil-*

iaris Consortio, and it did so using the traditional Thomist moral theology to which the Polish pope also appealed in *Veritatis Splendor.* Yet that wouldn't stop the critics from claiming *Amoris* was a "rupture," that Schönborn's Thomism wasn't true Thomism, and that, because of this alleged "discontinuity," the authority of the exhortation was in question. Yet not only was it excellent Thomism but, as the fruit of the biggest and most synodal church discernment process since the Second Vatican Council, *Amoris Laetitia* was arguably the most authoritative Church teaching in decades.

Francis never said this explicitly, and as an "apostolic exhortation," *Amoris* technically had a lower authority than an encyclical like *Laudato Si'.* But while Francis understood that there were "those who prefer a more rigorous pastoral care which leaves no room for confusion," he was convinced of God's will for the Church: the Good Spirit had finally prevailed in the synod. "I sincerely believe," Francis wrote, "Jesus wants a Church attentive to the goodness which the Holy Spirit sows in the midst of human weakness."[45]

Popes seldom ever speak that categorically, and usually only when the heart of the Gospel is at stake.

Sticking firmly to the legalistic lens, most journalists headlined, not inaccurately, that Francis was offering a "cautious opening" of the Communion door to remarried divorcées. They also reported that both sides were disappointed that the door was neither fully open nor fully shut. Liberals were unhappy not to have "a clear process that would permit Catholics who divorced and remarried outside the Church to receive Communion," as the *New York Times* put it, while conservatives claimed that if *Amoris* were read in the light of the Church's "constant teaching" set out in John Paul II's 1981 *Familiaris Consortio* there couldn't be a process at all.[46]

As a strategy—"Confused about *Amoris*? Stick to *Familiaris*!"—the conservative critique supplied an off-the-shelf justification for dissent in the name of orthodoxy. But it was naked legalism of the sort the Pharisees used against Jesus. The only thing that mattered was the law; the purpose of the law was clarity; any attempt to go beyond the law undermined or muddied the law; in which case, the duty was to clarify the law. "Does the Pope say the divorced and civilly remarried may be readmitted to Holy Communion?" rhetorically asked the conservative Bishop of Portsmouth, England, before answering in the negative. The chair of the U.S. bishops' working group for implementing *Amoris*, Archbishop Charles Chaput of Philadelphia, used the same tunnel logic: canon law hadn't changed, ergo nothing had changed. So, too, did Dutch cardinal Willem Eijk, who in claiming that the "traditional praxis" of 1981 "remains current" ignored both that John Paul II's praxis was far from traditional, and that Francis had indeed changed it.

But what was that change? The critics read the appeal to "discernment" and "conscience" as an excuse to opt out from the law, rather than apply it in ways that took into account particular circumstances not covered by the law. Chaput, for example, dusted off *Veritatis Splendor* to argue that "the subjective conscience of the individual can never be set against objective moral truth". Not only had *Amoris* nowhere implied otherwise, it had taken seriously what John Paul II had said in *Veritatis* about diminished moral culpability and the role of grace in moral development.[47]

Lincoln and Portland took their cue from Philadelphia, as did Alberta and the northwest territories in Canada. The bishops of each of these dioceses declared the impossibility of the divorced and civilly remarried under any circumstances to be readmitted to the sacraments unless they gave up sex. Such brazen episcopal rejection of papal teaching hadn't been seen in the Catholic Church since the heady days of *Humanae Vitae* in the late 1960s. The dissenters on that occasion could at least argue that Paul VI's decision to uphold the ban on contraception was an arbitrary act of papal authoritarianism, but in this case it was the College of Bishops themselves, authoritatively expressed by the pope, that had moved the ball.

In an interview with *La Civiltà Cattolica*, Cardinal Schönborn reminded Chaput that *Amoris* was an act of the magisterium, not mere opinion, and that all previous teachings needed to be read in the light of its contribution, not the other way around. Describing it as "the great document of moral theology that we have been waiting for since the time of Vatican II," the Viennese cardinal said it "develops the choices already made by the *Catechism of the Catholic Church* and *Veritatis Splendor*."[48]

Distinguished scholars associated with John Paul II agreed: *Amoris* involved no new law or doctrine on marriage, but an acknowledgment of what Saint Thomas Aquinas maintained, namely that no general rule could apply in every case. In *L'Osservatore Romano*, Rocco Buttiglione applauded *Amoris* as a development of *Familiaris*, and expressed frustration that while the body of the Christian people embraced Francis, "some of the learned class seem to have trouble understanding him." Moral theologians were also delighted. One of the Church's most distinguished, Professor Richard R. Gaillardetz of Boston College, said "Chapter Eight of *Amoris Laetitia* is the most well-developed reflection on the character of moral discernment and conscience formation to ever appear in an ecclesiastical document," adding: "This is not a repudiation of church doctrine. It is what doctrine looks like when it is actually put to the service of the life of ordinary believers."[49]

The dissenting dioceses could never be counted on the fingers of more than two hands, and outside the United States they were very rare. The heads of major archdioceses and presidents of bishops' conferences who reacted swiftly to the publication—Washington, Westminster, and Madrid, among others—were all enthusiastic, promising future guidelines for implementing it. The Germans showed unusual restraint in waiting some months before issuing theirs, which said that after a decision-making process carried out with the accompaniment of one's pastor, "in which the consciences of all parties must be highly engaged," a divorced and remarried Catholic can receive the sacraments of reconciliation and the Eucharist. The individual decision not to receive the sacraments in a given set of circumstances must be respected, according to the German bishops, "but so must the decision to receive."[50]

As the debates broke out, Francis let Schönborn speak for him. He trusted the Viennese cardinal almost as much as he distrusted the CDF prefect, Cardinal Gerhard Müller, who had spent his time since the release of *Amoris* backtracking from the position he had expressed at the synod, promoting himself as the document's authoritative interpreter, criticizing Schönborn, and claiming in a lengthy speech at a Spanish seminary that if the pope had envisaged allowing the remarried to take Communion, he would have explicitly said so. To no one's surprise, the pope had asked Schönborn, not Müller, to assure him of the document's orthodoxy.[51]

Help also came from home. In September 2016, the twenty bishops of the pastoral region of Buenos Aires, who oversee a Church of thirteen million faithful, sent Francis their draft guidelines for implementing chapter eight, asking him if they had understood *Amoris* correctly. Francis replied at once to thank them for a document that "clearly explains" its meaning, before adding, "There are no other interpretations." The letter was made public with the pope's permission, sending a clear message to bishops that Schönborn's was the correct—indeed the only possible—reading.

Cautious, nuanced, and deeply pastoral, the Buenos Aires guidelines beautifully captured the exhortation's thinking. For bishops like Oscar Ojea of San Isidro, the president of the Argentine bishops' conference, Francis had written *Amoris* thinking of pastors dealing with complex marital situations of the sort they had often discussed when Bergoglio was in Buenos Aires. When I asked Ojea in November 2016 to account for the attacks and misunderstandings, he was charitable. "You have to be a pastor to understand *Amoris Laetitia*, one who has spent a long time hearing confessions. If you've spent a long time behind a desk, you'll find it much harder."[52]

The fury of the deskbound had grown over the summer: accusations that the pope was allowing "adulterers to receive Communion" were served up by scholars and commentators who slammed what they called the pope's "false and heretical propositions." Father Thomas G. Weinandy, who for over a decade had disciplined dissenting theologians on behalf of the U.S. bishops, now became a dissident himself, resigning as a theological consultant to them after writing a public letter charging the pope with the crime of "confusing the faithful."[53]

Like the "ultramontanists" of the late nineteenth century demanding a declaration of papal infallibility, convert laymen led the charge—but this time to declare the pope fallible. The nephew of the atheist polemicist Christopher Hitchens, who had recently been received into the Church while working on a PhD on Samuel Johnson at Oxford, used the seventeenth-century Council of Trent to declare that the Church's teaching had been "consistent" over the centuries and could not now be changed. Like other critics, he betrayed Pelagian assumptions about grace, implying it was something external and one-off, rather than internal and constant, and spoke of faith as a kind of moral code that it was sufficient to assent to in order to comply with.[54]

The wider world only began to pay attention to the dissenters after four cardinals joined them in November 2016, in the so-called *dubia* letter. Three were long retired and very elderly; only the fourth, Raymond Burke, as *patronus* of the Order of Malta, at least in name, had any current church position. Nor were their views a surprise; they had opposed the synod from the start, and no one expected them to endorse its fruits. In Burke's case, there was also a large ego involved: he saw his repudiation of *Amoris Laetitia* in historic terms, as if he were a contemporary Saint John Fisher, the bishop martyred for resisting Henry VIII's divorce from Anne Boleyn.[55]

But if their views were predictable, their action was not. These were *cardinals*, who had pledged their obedience and service to the successor of Saint Peter, and who were using the media to excite public opinion against magisterial teaching, contrary both to tradition and Benedict's clear instructions. Their brazen repudiation of tradition and papal authority in the name of tradition and papal authority provoked astonishment and disgust across the Catholic world.[56]

In saccharine prose of courtly obsequiousness—"we permit ourselves to ask you, Holy Father, as supreme teacher of the Faith, called by the Risen One to confirm his brothers in the faith, to resolve the uncertainties and bring clarity, benevolently giving a response to the *dubia . . .*"—they challenged Francis to give a yes-or-no answer to the question of whether the divorced and remarried living *more uxorio* (that is, having sex) could now be admitted to Communion. The remaining challenges were attempts to drive a wedge between Saint John Paul II and Francis. Could it still be claimed that people whose living contradicted Jesus's teaching on adultery were in an "objective situation of habitual grave sin"? Were there "absolute moral norms"? Was an evil act still evil even if undertaken with good intentions? And could he agree with the sainted Polish pope that "conscience can never be authorized to legitimate exceptions to absolute moral norms"?

The cardinals knew the answers ("it depends" to the first; and "yes, obviously" to the rest) and Francis knew they knew. He liked criticism, which spurred reflection and change, but he made an exception, he told the Jesuits in Chile, for "resistance that comes from people who believe they possess the true doctrine and accuse you of being a heretic." In such cases, he said, "when I cannot see spiritual goodness in what these people say or write, I simply pray for them. I find it sad, but I won't dwell on this feeling for the sake of my own mental well-being."[57]

South African cardinal Wilfrid Napier, one of "Pell's rebels" at the 2015 synod, made the obvious point that it was "impossible" for Francis to respond because "discernment involves conscience more than law." It was the same reason Jesus did not respond directly to the Pharisees in the homily that so shocked Lawler: because to do so would be to accept the casuistic premise he was rejecting. Other cardinals lined up to critique the Gang of Four for sowing scandal and division and even urged them to give up their red hats. The C9 cardinals took the unusual step in February 2017 of pledging their full support for Francis and his teaching authority.[58]

Yet the traditionalist insurgency was sputtering to a halt. No one took Burke's threats in 2017 to issue a "formal correction of a pope's serious error" seriously; they knew he would never give up the princely privileges of being a cardinal for the sake of his conscience. The other signatories also made clear they were not keen on it. Then two of them died. Stripped de facto of his role as chaplain to the Order of Malta, Burke in 2018 continued to huff and puff that church authority "exists only in service of the tradition," while implying, of course, that he was the only valid interpreter of that tradition.

By then the train had left the station. More and more dioceses were producing guidelines and pastoral documents implementing chapter eight. Malta and Rome were followed by Belgium, India, and Brazil, all of which closely followed *Amoris* in not allowing any general relaxation of rules but calling for a discernment process that avoided both rigidity and laxism, and that did not exclude the sacraments at its conclusion. Even in Poland, where resistance in the synod had been strong, bishops were considering "allowing confessors to determine on a case-by-case basis whether remarried divorcees living in a state of objective adultery can receive Holy Communion," as the *National Catholic Register* curiously put it ("objective adultery" seemed to prejudge the case-by-case inquiry). In the United States, meanwhile, dozens of bishops began attending seminars organized by Boston College on how to implement the document using discernment criteria.[59]

In some cases, local Churches have produced sophisticated guidelines and processes to accompany the divorced and remarried into the life of parishes. As Cardinal Schönborn told *Crux*, where this much more "attentive" process exists, both for those getting married as well as the remarried being integrated into parish life, the Church was not loosening its discipline but being more demanding.[60]

In the ancient city of Braga, known as the "Rome of Portugal" for its strong Catholic presence, the archdiocese in 2017 published a sixty-page chapter eight process modeled on an Ignatian retreat as part of a bold new pastoral effort to bolster marriage preparation and accompaniment inspired by *Amoris*. The archdiocese has entrusted the task of accompanying remarried couples to an ad hoc group of Jesuits. When I spoke to two of them in March 2019, they were enthusiastic about the results, saying the process has galvanized their pastoral work. In many cases, the couples reached the conclusion that it would not yet be right for them to receive the Eucharist, that first their faith needs to be stronger and they need more involvement in parish life. The crucial change is that they now feel like active participants in the process, that their situation before God is their responsibility, and that whatever happens "they are part of the family," says Father Miguel Almeida, SJ, who adds that as a result "many people who were on the margins of the Church feel they belong again. All because of the pope."[61]

One of *Amoris*'s key interpreters, Monsignor Philippe Bordeyne, has given trainings on chapter eight for priests and laypeople in more than half of France's ninety-three dioceses. He reports a gap among both laypeople and priests between those who approved of the pope's pastoral understanding of fragile situations and those who feared he was fueling relativism by recognizing that grace operated in these complex situations. Observing that the resistance was greatest among young people, both lay and clergy, who had been raised in divorced or "patchwork" families, he notes that they "expect from the pope a rhetoric of the ideal, rather than a realistic view on the real situation of families." Conversely, those most pleased with *Amoris* are experienced pastors with a "realistic approach towards human fragility."

What matters, adds Bordeyne, is to begin where *Amoris* asks the Church to: by actively paying attention to the action of grace in people's lives, to understand how people grow under the effect of that grace—how they are included in God's plan of salvation. This idea provokes astonishment, he says, just as it did in the Gospels, when Jesus let sinners be part of the renewal of the Kingdom of God.[62]

The most high-profile casualty of the post-*Amoris* fallout was Cardinal Müller, prefect of the CDF, whose position became impossible after he went on a notoriously anti-Francis TV show on the U.S. Catholic network EWTN to criticize the Buenos Aires and Malta bishops' orthodox reading of *Amoris*. Francis accepted his resignation as soon as the German turned seventy-five a month later, moving up into his place the CDF official who had in practice long been his main collaborator there: Archbishop (now Cardinal) Luis Ladaria, a limelight-shy Spanish Jesuit scholar who had worked closely with Benedict XVI on some of his key texts.

Ladaria soon produced what would have been unthinkable under

Müller: a theological instruction on "certain aspects of salvation" in the light both of "the greater tradition of the Faith and with particular reference to the teachings of Pope Francis." The main concern of *Placuit Deo* ("It so pleased God . . .") was to rebut the contemporary versions of the ancient heresies of Gnosticism and Pelagianism that lay behind much of the rejection of *Amoris*.[63]

There were clues hiding in the document in plain sight. One was the presence of the landmark quote from Benedict XVI that being a Christian was not the result of an idea or ethical choice but the encounter with Christ. The other was the fact that Francis's teaching documents and speeches took up more than half of the footnotes, alongside early church Fathers such as Saints Augustine, Aquinas, and Irenaeus. *Placuit Deo* was marshaling the theological forces against mercy's two main discontents.

As heresies, Gnosticism and Pelagianism—which had dogged the Church in its early centuries and had never gone away—were not formal rejections of Christianity but distortions of it in ways that eliminated God's grace. They made holiness a matter not of relationship with Christ through prayer and sacraments, but of human effort or brilliance, reducing God to a distant lawgiver or ethical idea. *Placuit Deo* identified "neo-Pelagian individualism and the neo-Gnostic disregard of the body" as practical denials of the incarnate Christ as Savior, elitist distortions of Christianity that sought salvation in laws, rituals, and ideas.

A few weeks later, it became clear that *Placuit Deo*'s role had been to do the theological heavy lifting in advance of the pope addressing the people of God directly on the subject. *Gaudete et Exsultate* (Rejoice and Be Glad), released on Francis's fifth anniversary, was short and strikingly personal, using the intimate singular vocative *tú* in close to half of its paragraphs in the Latin-language versions in order "to re-propose the call to holiness in a practical way for our own time." In many ways *Gaudete* was the arrival point of five years of teaching and reform: the Gospel of Jesus Christ according to Francis.

The pope wanted to salute the holiness of the ordinary folk, "the souls whom no history book ever mentions" but on whom world history in reality turned, and to warn them against the seductive faux holiness of the Pelagian and Gnostic elites. Drawing on his second book of essays as a Jesuit, published in 1987, where he had used the French writer Joseph Malègue's description of a "middle class of holiness," Francis showed the

Christian spiritual life to be not a race of celebrity athletes, but the patient plodding of unknown people living lives in love, quietly bearing witness, and above all hoping in God's help. Holiness, as Francis powerfully put it, was "an encounter between your weakness and the power of God's grace."[64]

Previous popes had made clear that holiness was for all, not just for clergy and religious, but no pope had ever issued such a concrete, practical invitation to follow Christ in humility and mercy, to make ordinary sacrifices and gestures that showed God's power at work. And no pope had ever been in a position to salute his predecessor's decision to renounce the pontificate as "an act of holiness, of greatness, of humility."

Nor had a pope ever put women so firmly in the foreground of a teaching document. Francis saluted the "unknown and forgotten" mothers and grandmothers who daily transformed their communities, as well as the "genius" of great women saints such as Hildegard of Bingen, Bridget of Sweden, Catherine of Siena, and the "three Teresas" of Avila, Lisieux, and Kolkata. The example Francis held up in *Gaudete* of holiness in everyday life was a woman who faced different moments of decision in her day, choosing each time to make acts of charity, justice, compassion, and faithfulness. He also praised the holiness of men and women who "bring home the bread" for their families, acknowledging women as economic actors.[65]

If *Amoris Laetitia* was about making the Church a more effective channel of that grace, *Gaudete* was about opening up lives to welcome it. What mattered was not our strength, but God's mercy; the people's part was to open themselves, in humility, to His grace. That meant signaling the trapdoors, the two "subtle enemies of holiness." Francis suggested user-friendly ways of spotting neo-Gnostics: how they loved complex doctrines, had an answer to every question, reduced Jesus's teaching to a "cold and harsh logic that seeks to dominate everything," and were in love with abstraction. They were "incapable of touching Christ's suffering flesh in others."

Too much intellectual certainty about faith was often a sign that it was not Christ being proclaimed, but an ideology, he warned. In reality, "it is not easy to grasp the truth that we have received from the Lord," and it was "even more difficult to express it." Doubt and uncertainty were part of faith: people's questions, dreams, struggles, and worries "all possess an interpretational value that we cannot ignore if we want to take the principle of the incarnation seriously."

The same power Gnostics attributed to the intellect, Francis explained, the Pelagians placed in will, effort, and duty. Hence their obsession with the law, their punctilious concern for the Church's liturgy, doctrine, and prestige, and their obsession with right thinking. Yet "underneath our orthodoxy," Francis wrote with devastating directness, "our attitudes might not correspond to our talk about the need for grace, and in specific situations we can end up putting little trust in it."

Thus did Francis indict the critics of *Amoris* and account for their mercilessness. Today's neo-Pelagians paid lip service to grace, but by implying that people had all the grace they needed to obey all God's commands, they emptied the doctrine of its meaning. (Judging by the indignant reactions of *Amoris's* critics to *Gaudete*, the pope was on the money: rather than accept the invitation to rejoice and be glad, they snorted derisively or claimed to be victims of papal snark.)[66]

Coincidentally, anti-*Amoris* protesters, including Cardinal Burke, had assembled in Rome over the weekend before *Gaudete's* publication, insisting in a declaration that "forgiveness is based on an intention to abandon a way of life that is contrary to divine commandments." The implication was that the first was always conditional on the second, and the second was the result of human will or a one-time offering of grace. Francis wrote in *Gaudete et Exsultate* of the neo-Pelagians that they "tend to give the idea that all things are possible by the human will, as if it were something pure, perfect, all-powerful, to which grace is then added"; whereas, he said, quoting Saint Augustine, "in this life human weaknesses are not healed completely and once and for all by grace."

Grace was not a gas station where the tank was filled once for the journey, but more like a permanently attached fuel pipe, in which God's mercy is constantly available, not as a reward for changing but to enable and support that change. This was pure Saint Augustine. It was not knowledge or effort that could obtain God's love and mercy. Our relationship with God was not a transaction, but a grateful response to grace. Holiness was an encounter between human weakness and the power of God's grace; what blocked grace working more effectively was "the lack of a heartfelt and prayerful acknowledgement of our limitations." Where the heart was humble and open, accepting of weakness—which was much easier for those who were poor and had suffered—holiness grew through a humble reception of grace over time, step by step, within the constraints of circumstances and vulnerability.

Gaudete was about what it meant to live in holiness. It was also, necessarily, about Francis's own holiness. Mercy was the golden thread running through God's history with humanity. It was also his story. When he said that receiving mercy made people more merciful, that their merciful actions made them more receptive to grace, and that grace made them more sensitive to need and merciful in response, he was talking as much about himself as the holy heroes he named.

Holiness is a life lived growing in and for mercy. The authenticity of prayer—whether it is really of the heart, or simply going through the motions—can be gauged, he said, by how it changes how a person acts toward the poor, and how they see the poor. It was what Jesus named in the Beatitudes: a mind-set, a way of being, one that was patient, persevering, humble, hungering for a new way of being, identifying with the pain and sorrow of others—these were the fruit of the Holy Spirit, or grace, acting within a heart open to God.

"Our Lord made it very clear that holiness cannot be understood or lived apart from these demands," Francis wrote of the Beatitudes, "for mercy is the beating heart of the Gospel." The "great criterion" was "seeing and acting with mercy," a Beatitude upon which Jesus expanded in the twenty-fifth chapter of Matthew, meaning not just close-and-concrete actions that recognized the dignity of each human being—feeding the hungry, visiting those sick and in prison, and so on—but implicitly what Samaritan actions must spill into: the struggle for social change that promoted that dignity.

Francis then called out those who scorned such struggles as left-wing or political, as if they had nothing to do with the Gospel. He challenged pro-life activists who opposed abortion but regarded other life-ending or life-degrading injustices—human trafficking, the death penalty, and so on—as of lesser importance, as if life in those cases was less sacred. The specific example he gave stung right-wing American Catholics who had long argued that the plight of migrants was secondary to bioethical questions. For a Christian, said Francis, "the only proper attitude is to stand in the shoes of those brothers and sisters of ours who risk their lives to offer a future to their children." God was mercy, and therefore He responded with closeness and tenderness to all violations of human dignity and instances of misery; for anyone in the Church to give the opposite impression—or worse, to commodify that mercy—was to create a major obstacle to evangelization.

Gaudete was inspiring and uplifting, and often captivating: a defense of the humble holiness of God's poor against the hectoring religious elites, the neo-Pelagians and neo-Gnostics who had sought refuge in contemporary Catholicism as a fortress from which to combat modernity. The struggle Francis was asking Catholics to attempt was different. It was to embrace the call to mercy, but ever ready to ask for God's help in attending to the human weaknesses the devil was ready to exploit. Holiness demanded discernment, a constant seeking of God's will in the real, in the flesh, in the now. To discern was not to settle for a religiosity of rules or take refuge in concepts, but courageously to follow Christ, to be a channel of His mercy in a bruised and bruising world.

Only the following of Christ in freedom was capable of changing horizons. Discernment, the pope wrote, had to do with "the meaning of my life before the Father who knows and loves me, with the real purpose of my life, that nobody knows better than he." It required no special abilities or knowledge or virtue, but a willingness to grow in trust and be aware of the promptings of the Spirit and an ability to spot the bad spirit behind its angel wings.

All you needed to begin was your faith, as fresh as a green leaf, and God's mercy would come out to meet you—*primereando*, Francis liked to say, getting in there ahead of you, waiting for you with open arms, close and concrete.

Epilogue

As a new aggressive nationalist politics swept across the world, in early 2019 Francis concentrated on preparing the Church for the "change of era" he had spoken of after Aparecida, in which Catholics would need to evangelize while resisting the temptation to retreat behind tribal walls.

His New Year's messages warned of movements that scapegoated migrants and threatened the stability of international organizations, as well as "attitudes of rejection or forms of nationalism that call into question the fraternity of which our globalized world has such great need." To diplomats a week later, he somberly noted "the resurgence of nationalistic tendencies at odds with the vocation of the international Organizations to be a setting for dialogue and encounter for all countries."

Recalling how the League of Nations between the two world wars had been unable to withstand "populist and nationalist demands," he warned that states were now arming themselves and erecting new borders. He was particularly concerned about what he called "attempts to foment hostility between Muslims and Christians," and issued—yet again—an appeal to governments to assist those forced to migrate.

This was not just an outside threat but a problem within: more and more neotraditionalist and conservative Catholics—among them senior church leaders—were being seduced by a politics of identity that justified xenophobia and intolerance in the name of "Judeo-Christian civilization."

Francis saw obvious parallels with the 1930s. It was in his power, at least, to avoid repeating the Church's mistakes of that time, when fear of social disorder pushed bishops into the arms of nationalist, authoritarian regimes.[1]

In producing their usual scorecard of his achievements and failures at his sixth election anniversary, commentators missed an important landmark: by March 2019 Francis had steadily reached the end of the list of priorities he had outlined in his speech at Aparecida more than a decade earlier. The list was his response to the crisis in faith transmission triggered by the change of era, to which the Latin American bishops had responded with a pastoral and missionary conversion. His list included equipping the Church to become close and concrete in order to build up families and becoming synodal to hear God's voice and counter clericalism; it was also to become missionary in response to the disintegration of the bonds of belonging, and more pastoral and merciful in response to the anguish that resulted. Bergoglio had been particularly concerned with opening the doors for laypeople—especially women and the young—to take their place as missionary disciples.

He spent his sixth anniversary on his Lenten retreat with curial leaders. Then he went to Loreto on the Feast of the Annunciation and put out his third "apostolic exhortation," *Christus Vivit* (Christ Is Alive) following the previous year's synod on vocations and young people. He was troubled by young people's lack of roots; *Christus Vivit* sought to close the gap between the institution and the young people, to help the Church better accompany them as he had once been accompanied by Father Duarte as a teenager.

The pope saw young people less as objects of evangelization as its subjects: the young were not the Church's future, he wanted Catholics to understand, but its present, yet too often alienated from it, and needing—like the divorced and others outside the parish mainstream—to be listened to and given space. The Church needed to recognize the gifts the Holy Spirit was pouring out on the next generation. There were "young believers who are natural leaders in their neighborhoods and in other settings," he wrote, who may not come out of church environments or accept all Catholic teachings but who "have the desire and willingness to be encountered by God's revealed truth." They were often to be found on pilgrimages, and in shrines. Rather than overwhelm them with rules and moral strictures, the Church should learn to be open to the gifts of the Holy Spirit acting in them.[2]

Buried in the footnotes to this section was a reference to Father Rafael Tello (*Tayzho* in Buenos Aires pronunciation), a pioneering Argentine pastoral theologian and youth minister whom Bergoglio had first met as a teenager in the 1950s on a retreat for young people. Tello was one of the key post–Vatican II generation of "pueblo" theologians in Argentina who saw in the religiosity of the great mass of believers a reserve of evangelizing power tragically overlooked by a clericalist Church. Only when the Church learned to turn to the people, Tello believed, would this power be released.

Despite his influence and pastoral achievements—he founded the mass annual youth pilgrimage to the national shrine of Luján that today involves over a million people—Tello was an outlier, suspected, like so many other diocesan pastors working in the shantytowns in the 1970s, of being too close to the guerrillas. After losing his teaching posts and priestly faculties, he spent the rest of his life off the radar, pastoring to the poor in Luján and writing pastoral theology that shaped a generation of priests.

Not long after being named to Buenos Aires in 1998, Bergoglio publicly rehabilitated Tello, restoring his faculties as a priest. He was old by then, but had time at the end of his life to see Bergoglio in action. "For me the Church's biggest challenge is how to reach the immense majority of Christians whom the institutional Church doesn't reach," Tello wrote the archbishop of Buenos Aires just a few months before his death in 2002. "I believe you have the providential mission of beginning a reform in the Church. I ask God that you can carry it out."

A decade later, Bergoglio paid his own tribute, describing Tello at a book launch as "an admirable person, a man of God, who was sent to open up paths," adding that "no one who opens up paths is left without scars on his back." Alluding to the suspicion and calumny he had suffered, the cardinal gently observed that Tello "did not escape the fate of the Cross with which God marks the great men and women of the Church."[3]

Elected pope the year after that speech, Francis set about the reform Tello had hoped for, opening up new paths and turning the Church to the people it had failed to reach. Six years on, he had the scars to show. Although still wildly popular among ordinary Catholics, with approval ratings politicians can only dream of, in the media that had been so fascinated by him Francis no longer walked on water. On the left he was graded poorly for failing to change the Church's teachings, while traditionalists accused him of doing just that. The forces on the ecclesial and the political right inside and outside the Church were meanwhile joining hands under the banner of nationalist populism, and, having spotted Francis's weak flank, were hammering him over sex abuse.

As he entered his eighty-third year, the pope was magnificently indifferent to the fire and fury even as he carefully monitored the signs of opposition and resistance. But his Palm Sunday homily, which reprised his insights from his 1990 essay "Silencio y Palabra" ("Silence and Word"), showed he saw the spirits on the move, and how he needed to respond to the attacks. He spoke of the impressive silence of Jesus throughout his Passion, the way he "overcomes the temptation to answer back, to act like a 'superstar.'" In finding the courage not to speak, said Francis, "as long as our silence is meek and not full of anger," it will tempt the devil—who mistakes silence for weakness—out into the open. The real battle was the spiritual combat "between God and the prince of this world," he said, in which "what matters is not putting our hand to the sword but remaining firm in faith."[4]

The seeds he had planted in 2013–2014 were trees now, firmly rooted, budding and flowering if not yet fruiting. The lurid scandals of Benedict's years were a thing of the past. The "lobbies" growled but were impotent, the money launderers gone or in jail. Maybe next year the Vatican accounts would not just be audited but published. Meanwhile, the finances had settled enough for him to donate a huge $500,000 from Peter's Pence to help thousands of Central American migrants in Mexico struggling to reach the United States. (In the time of Trump, who said they were criminals, the gesture was as prophetically evangelical as it was charitable.) The new curial constitution, too, was complete, and it was now official: the Vatican existed not to police the Church but to evangelize humanity. Synodality and collegiality, too, were bedding down: the youth gathering of October 2018 had been the best yet. The October 2019 synod on the Amazon, meanwhile, involved a significant pastoral discernment with far-reaching implications: the recognition of an inculturated Church, including the ordination of married "elders," in order to ensure a Church that was present 24/7.[5]

But two areas above all demanded discernment and action. One was the 2018 wave of clerical sex abuse scandals, which challenged Francis to help the Church root out not only abuse and its cover-up but the clericalist corruption that produced them. The second was the trap set by Islamic extremists and Western nationalist wall-builders who fed off each other's hate to drive a wedge between the Muslim and Christian worlds. This year, 2019, was the eight hundredth anniversary of the historic meeting between Saint Francis of Assisi and Sultan al-Malik al-Kāmil during the Crusades, and something just as bold was called for now. But first came the abuse summit.

Popes are asked to be *alter Christus*, to model Christ to the world. As the first pope to take the name of the medieval saint who was thought to be most like Jesus, Francis was pledging to repair and reform the Church, to refocus it on Christ and outward to mission, and to combat spiritual worldliness, so that the Church be more like the poor: dependent not on its own resources but on Christ's. The friar of Assisi was also asked to help repair the world: to resist the violence of crusades, to build trust through dialogue and encounter, and to honor creation and all creatures as God's gifts. This was the "Francis Option" then, and now.

The modern-day Francis's "repair" task in the Church, it had become clear, was the reckoning with abuse: the desolation, the discouragement, and the lack of credibility that followed from the revelations of clerical deafness to victims in previous decades. The February 2019 summit of the world's leading bishops was intended to open the local Churches to the grace of conversion that Francis saw God offering at this time of tribulation. Policies and actions would flow from the gathering, of course; but what mattered to Francis was to respond to the Spirit acting in history, unveiling corruption and its causes. What the Spirit was unmasking now was the nature of abuse. As he would point out in his end-of-summit speech, abuse "is always the result of an abuse of power, an exploitation of the inferiority and vulnerability of the abused, which makes possible the manipulation of their conscience and of their psychological and physical weakness."

In the case of clerical abuse, priesthood was crucial to this manipulation. A means to serve had been corrupted to exploit and destroy; what led a young person to trust a priest—the goodness and mercy they represented—was the very thing that allowed them to be abused. So while conservatives blamed a failure of discipline and orthodoxy, and progressives pointed to an authoritarian ecclesiastical culture, Francis wanted to keep the focus on this diabolic corruption. To fail to grasp this was to fail to heal the roots of abuse. What the Spirit was unveiling, he told the bishops, was "the spirit of evil, which in its pride and in its arrogance considers itself the 'Lord of the World' and thinks that it has triumphed."

The text carried a footnote reference to Hugh Benson's dystopian 1907 novel of that name, *Lord of the World*. Francis appeared to be inviting comparisons between the bad spirit that drove priests to abuse and the novel's diabolic world leader, Julian Felsenburgh, "a strange, quiet figure of indomitable power and unruffled tenderness," as Benson painted him. The point, presumably, was plausibility. Evil was always parasitic on good; abusive priests wore the mask of the authority Christ had given them and used the trust it came with for their own gratification. Other categories of abusers—teachers or rock stars—had other kinds of power that enabled, concealed, and justified sexual abuse. But in the Church it was priesthood, reduced to an empty, formalistic parody of the real thing: as mere function or status that endowed a sense of superiority and entitlement. This corruption of the priesthood had a name: clericalism.

In insisting on a spiritual lens to account for the eroticization of power involved in sex abuse, Francis was following Jesus, who had little to say about sexual sin but much about the use and abuse of power by authorities, including religious ones. But just as important, Francis was making clear that he saw a battle under way; God was at war. The Spirit had been acting—as he had already said in his letter to the people of God in August 2018—in the victims' courageous testimonies, the tenacity of journalists, and the work of the Church's reformers like Father Hans Zollner and Archbishop Charles Scicluna. The pope's task now was to root out the defensiveness and evasiveness that still existed in clericalism's dark pockets, and to facilitate the transformation that was already under way. "The Lord is purifying his spouse and is converting us all to Him," Francis told the clergy of Rome in his annual Lenten talk. "He is blowing His spirit to make his spouse beautiful again after she was caught in flagrant adultery."

His allusion to chapter 16 of Ezekiel—the story in which he had long read his own conversion—showed how he saw the purification taking place. In shame and humiliation, old certainties and myths were crumbling; the machinery of arrogance and denial was breaking down. The old, clericalist dispensation no longer worked. The Church had been exposed, an adulterer in flagrante. Now, in the encounter of its *miseria* with God's *misericordia*, the Church was being redeemed. In the exposure of the Church's sins and its humble repentance—"struck dumb among the tears flowing at the monstrosity of sin and the limitless greatness of God's forgiveness"—Francis saw signs of nascent holiness.[6]

None of this, however, impressed the victims' groups. They saw talk of mercy and redemption as evasion; abuse was a crime to be eradicated by punishment, expulsion, and deterrence. For the pope and his advisers, ironically, it was the other way around: a purely juridical, corporate approach evaded the deeper reckoning. For "the Church, by her very nature, does not redeem herself from evils on her own, with human means and human strategies," wrote Gianni Valente in an article on the eve of the summit. Francis quoted the article approvingly in early April 2019, telling journalists on the flight from Morocco of the dangers of "becoming Donatist, making human regulations that are necessary, but limiting ourselves to these and forgetting the other spiritual dimensions, prayer, penitence, and self-accusation."[7]

Donatist? The schism in the ancient Church of Roman Africa was a warning from history. The anger and shame many contemporary Christians felt at the abuse revelations and their mishandling by bishops could be compared, *mutis mutandis*, with the disgust their forebears felt in the fifth and sixth centuries at leaders who had buckled under persecution. The Donatist heresy was that only the righteous—those tested and proved worthy—were fit to be priests, and even the validity of their sacraments hinged on this worthiness. But the Church fathers, led by Saint Augustine, argued that holiness resides in the faith of the Church, in God's grace rather than human goodness. Francis's point now was Saint Augustine's then: the power of change and conversion in the Church lay not solely or primarily in the externals of law and regulation, but on the grace offered to the Church itself.

The victims' groups calling for "zero tolerance"—by which they meant the blanket application of the penalty of laicization for all abuse or its cover-up—was one neo-Donatist alternative to conversion. Another was the rigorist stance of Archbishop Carlo Maria Viganò and his media and business allies in the United States, who were urging crusades of personal purification, purges of liberals and gays, and robust disciplinary measures.[8]

Both neo-Donatist strategies put their faith in the power of law and deterrence, or in moral discipline and intellectual assent. Yet Chile had shown that regulations and protocols without a changed consciousness were either a dead letter or offered cover to abusers. Equally, no history of the clerical sex abuse crisis could ignore that many of the most notorious abusers were also orthodox moralists and homophobic disciplinarians. As Francis wrote to the American bishops prior to their retreat, "many actions can be helpful, good, and necessary, and may even seem correct, but not all of them have the 'flavor' of the Gospel." It wasn't just the outside of the cup that needed to be washed. As Jesus had hinted, great effort to make the outside clean and gleaming was often an attempt to deflect attention from the dirt within.

The point was graphically made on the eve of the summit by a book called *Sodoma*. The agnostic gay activist Frédéric Martel's thoroughly researched exposé of the homosexual subculture of the Curia appeared, prima facie, to support Viganò's claim of homosexual networks at the highest levels of the Vatican. Yet the heroes of the *viganista* narrative—the homophobic bishops and cardinals—were in Martel's account the ones most likely to treat their vows of chastity with contempt, while the man Viganò tried to blame for the rot, Pope Francis, inconveniently emerged as the vigorous reformer determined to root out the hypocrisy.

Martel insisted he was not outing particular individuals but a culture, in which there was not a single gay lobby—the one Benedict XVI claimed in 2016 to have gotten rid of—but an elaborate honeycomb of interlocking networks that added up to one large closet. The closet had a number of implicit "rules," most obviously that "the more pro-gay a cleric is, the less likely he is to be gay; the more homophobic a cleric is, the more likely he is to be homosexual." Another was that gay double lives were a key to much of the Curia's internal politics, in which "lobbies" used gossip, blackmail, and score-settling to buy silence and secure complicity and promotions to curry favor.

As *Sodoma* related, the election of Francis—an obviously heterosexual yet gay-friendly pastor at ease with women, who abhorred this kind of clericalist corruption—represented a major disruption. After demoting and reassigning the worst offenders, it was little surprise he had enemies. As Andrew Sullivan put it in his review of the book, Francis's most determined opponents were often "far-right closet cases, living in palaces, leading completely double lives, backed by the most vicious of reactionaries and bigots on the European and American far right, and often smarting at their demotions."[9]

In the Closet of the Vatican, as it was called in English, was gossipy, rambling, cavalier with sources, and because of Martel's off-the-scale "gaydar" and his scorn for celibacy, easy for Vatican officials to dismiss. Yet many of his eye-popping stories could not be disputed: Vatican clergy making regular use of migrant prostitutes, the widespread use of the gay hookup app Grindr by traditionalist seminarians, or the higher than average HIV infections of priests and seminarians seen by the Gemelli Polyclinic all showed what many knew, that "lace by day, leather by night" was part of clerical culture within the Leonine walls. The hypocrisy had mushroomed above all under John Paul II, whom conservative Catholics lionized for his moral clarity.

One story told many others: the Polish pope's right-wing, homophobic family czar, Colombian cardinal Alfonso López Trujillo, was a predatory homosexual with a voracious appetite for violent sex with rent boys. After receiving complaints about him in the late 1980s, the Polish pope removed him as archbishop of Medellín and brought him to the Vatican, where he put him in charge of . . . the Pontifical Council for the Family. For years, until his death in 2008, López Trujillo waged rhetorical war on condoms and homosexuality on the conservative Catholic lecture circuit, while carrying on his dissolute existence and opposing the canonization of Oscar Romero.[10]

These weren't liberals questioning church teaching but conservatives defending it. Corruption and immorality, in other words, weren't primarily about lack of obedience to church teaching, as conservatives had long claimed. Lopez Trujillo, among many others—from Maciel to McCarrick—illustrated Jesus's use of the Greek word *hypokrytês* of the scribes and Pharisees of his day, for whom the authority of the priesthood and doctrinal rigor were masks that could be put on during the day and taken off when it suited their interests. Suddenly it was easier to understand Francis's Christmas speeches to the Curia, his tongue-lashing of "the hypocrites" who "hide the truth from God, from others, and from themselves," and his warnings against "the rigid" who "present themselves to you as perfect" but who "lack the spirit of God."[11]

So when, on the eve of the summit, the two remaining lace-and-homophobia *dubia* cardinals released a public letter to the bishops and religious-order heads arriving in Rome, it was hard to take seriously the claim by Raymond Burke and Walter Brandmüller that sex abuse was the result of a "homosexual agenda" rooted in relativism and hedonism "in which the existence of an absolute moral law . . . is openly called into question." You didn't have to read Martel to know that the celebrity abusers of the John Paul II era were appalled by the "homosexual agenda" and never questioned "an absolute moral law." Whether they knew Jesus Christ, on the other hand, was another matter.

In a Spanish TV interview shortly after the summit, Francis wryly joked that had he executed a hundred priest abusers in St. Peter's Square he would have been praised for doing "something concrete." But that was to "occupy spaces," he told Jordi Evole, whereas he wanted to "initiate healing processes that get to the root of the problem."

He wasn't afraid to use the law: a week before the summit he had laicized Theodore McCarrick, the first cardinal ever to be stripped of the priesthood for sexual abuse, and banished the eighty-eight-year-old to a friary in Kansas. But such exemplary punishments, while necessary to satisfy justice, did not get at the root of the problem. In order "to shed full light on the facts and to alleviate the wounds caused by such crimes," as he had put the summit's objective to the diplomats in his New Year's speech, the Church's leaders needed to become anti-abuse crusaders, with minds and hearts dedicated to the cause.[12]

Hence the format of a mini-synod, in which "we might listen to the Holy Spirit and, in docility to his guidance, hear the cry of the little ones who plead for justice," as Francis put it in his opening remarks. The church leaders from across the globe would sit through survivor testimonies, be guided through their obligations under the headings of responsibility, accountability, and transparency, and then silence, prayer, and liturgies of repentance would do the rest.[13]

Outside, the survivors' groups scoffed. What was there to discuss? Surely the pope can solve this "with the stroke of a pen"? But anyone who thought that abuse could be eradicated by giving orders risked being "very much disappointed," Father Hans Zollner warned. The moderator of the French-speaking group, the Jesuit archbishop Jean-Claude Hollerich of Luxembourg, agreed that Francis was wise to use a "synodal" approach, for "you can't change the Church by just giving orders from above. You have to change people's hearts." Hollerich, who said this toward the end of the summit, added that he had seen that change in his group, "a development in their consciences, in the bishops' thinking, in the course of these few days."[14]

Sotto voce, the organizers conceded beforehand that the gathering was aimed above all at the developing world. Many bishops in cultures with traditional sexual mores had bought into the Viganò narrative that abuse was a first-world phenomenon resulting from liberal attitudes to homosexuality. Some African bishops claimed at the start of the summit that clerical sex abuse wasn't "their problem," only to be rebuked by a formidable Nigerian nun, Sister Veronica Openido, who patiently listed her direct knowledge of sex abuse of minors by clergy in Africa since the 1990s, many of them women. Then came the harrowing testimony of an African woman victim. She was so young and trusting when the priest began raping her at age fifteen that at first she didn't know she was being abused. He beat her when she refused him, showered her with gifts when she gave in, and forced her to have three abortions rather than use condoms himself.

In all, there were eight speakers (three women, five men) with unsparing tales of childhoods of terror and shame and adult lives spent navigating dark craters left by the past. As the 190 bishops and religious leaders listened, horrified, their denial and resistance began to melt. An Italian woman who was abused for five years from the age of eleven by a priest had come to believe she was worthless, deserving of punishment. Only after forty years—after a shattered life and marriage—did she report it. It was an especially powerful account that left the pope in tears. Archbishop Scicluna, who set out a step-by-step lesson in how to report an abuse allegation, said it was "a narrative that transformed our hearts." The summit ended, appropriately, in a collective act of penance led by a Chilean survivor. Being overpowered physically, psychologically, and sexually by a man he considered close to a God of love and mercy had left him with the urge to destroy the person the abuse convinced him he was. "There are no dreams without the memory of what happened," he told stricken-faced bishops. Then he picked up a violin to play a Bach sonata that flooded the Sala Regia with pain and sadness.

In the final press conference, Zollner told journalists that a "quantitative and qualitative leap" had taken place, as a result of which Africans and Asians were "speaking now, in the same language, with the same determination" on the issue as Europeans and Americans. He said it had reached the heart level, "and if it reaches that level you can't be as you were before." The summit's organizers had shown how the procedures and guidelines already existed to ensure there was no place in ministry for anyone who had abused; the conversion of hearts and minds supplied the determination to make use of them.[15]

But outside, the neo-Donatists remained unimpressed. The *viganisti* accused the summit of "sidestepping" the issue of homosexuality and liberal moral theology and criticized its focus on abuse of power in clericalism as "Marxist" and "atheistic." The liberal media and victims' advocacy groups meanwhile lamented the lack of a new range of punitive measures. Changes in mind-set were all very well, scoffed Anne Barrett Doyle, but "conversion is unmeasurable, conversion is unenforceable." The victims' groups also reacted angrily to the pope's speech, accusing Francis of minimizing the Church's responsibility for abuse by referring to global child exploitation. They said he was deflecting blame by bringing the devil into it.[16]

In his speech to the summit, the pope had warned of a need to avoid "a juridicism provoked by guilt for past errors and media pressure" as well as of "a defensiveness that fails to confront the causes and effects of these grave crimes." But his preface to a collection of his "tribulation letters" on abuse that came out at the end of 2018 was more explicit. There Francis had warned of the temptation of "victimism," which "hides the appeal to vengeance, which only feeds the wrong it claims to eliminate."[17]

The irony was that, while the victims who had told their stories saw the real difference their presence had made, the groups that claimed to represent them were incapable of recognizing it. Yet it was because of that shift inside the synod hall that Francis felt able to ramp up the Church's commitment to combating the scourge of abuse outside as well as within its ranks. And far from evading the issue, it was because he was willing to boldly face the fact that diabolic dynamics of abuse had penetrated Catholicism that he could demand of the Church "an all-out battle" against "these abominable crimes that must be erased from the face of the earth." This was a mission that went to the heart of the Church's very purpose as Christ's body on earth.

If church leaders were still in denial, they weren't reading the news. Days after the summit ended, the lifting of reporting restrictions in the trial of Cardinal Pell meant the world now knew what Francis had been told in December: that the former finance czar had been found guilty by a second jury of raping two thirteen-year-old choirboys in the early 1990s. Two weeks later, as Francis was on his weeklong Lent retreat, the judge handed down his sentence: the seventy-seven-year-old Pell would be jailed for six years, and would serve at least half of that time. The verdict was shaky—the first jury had been mostly in favor of Pell—and the claims so lurid that many believed he had been framed or scapegoated, yet those who saw him as an autocratic bully were delighted that he had been finally brought down. His appeal in June 2019 was unlikely to settle the disagreements, not least because he faced charges over other alleged acts of sexual abuse.[18]

Francis had promised concrete outcomes from the summit and in the following months issued a barrage of new regulations. In March, Vatican state law and procedures were updated: diplomatic staff abroad would face severe punishments if found guilty of viewing child pornography (there had been cases), while a more victim-friendly, transparent process for dealing with claims was introduced. The new regulations, which borrowed from the best existing practice in the Catholic Anglosphere, were intended principally as an off-the-shelf model for local Churches to emulate.

Then, in May, Francis issued a sweeping new edict that required all Catholic priests and religious across the world to report clergy sex abuse and cover-up by their superiors to church authorities (usually the bishop, or, if the allegation concerned the bishop, directly to the Vatican) while providing whistle-blower protections for anyone who did. *Vos Estis Lux Mundi* (You Are the Light of the World) made clear that no one was above the law, redefined abuse in such a way as to include adults, and asked every diocese in the world to have in place a clear system for reporting abuse by June 2020.

Although the obligation to report and act on abuse allegations already existed, the genius of the edict lay in the way it prevented the often subtle pressures that inhibited disclosure in the Church. It was illegal now for a bishop to sit on an allegation, or for a Vatican department not to respond. The edict even specified timelines: the investigator must file a report every thirty days and complete his investigation within ninety days. But what mattered now was that everyone in the Church was a mandated reporter. It was against church law to ask a person with an abuse claim to stay quiet out of obedience or out of a misplaced concern for the community's reputation.

This was concrete action in good law: clear, universal, and radical, and with the express aim of eradicating sexual abuse. Yet Francis continued to insist, even in the edict itself, that law was not a substitute for what he called a "continuous and profound conversion of hearts... attested by concrete and effective actions that involve everyone in the Church" to confront abuse, a conversion that "becomes possible only with the grace of the Holy Spirit poured into our hearts."[19]

Benedict XVI had intended his six-thousand-word essay on abuse as a helpful contribution to the summit, but the manner of its release the week before Easter, and the way it was seized on by the *viganisti* as favoring their position, enraged pro-Francis theologians and commentators. The essay had originally been given to Francis and his secretary of state, Cardinal Parolin, who had raised no objection to it, but did nothing with it. A month after the summit, it was secretly released under embargo by the emeritus pope's entourage to anti-Francis conservative sites in the United States, circumventing the Vatican press office and the pope's staff.

In a coordinated spin operation, various high-profile *viganisti* rushed into print to praise the essay, which highlighted the impact of the sexual revolution of the late 1960s and homosexuality in seminaries, as well as weaknesses in post–Vatican II moral theology. Cardinal Müller, who had taken over from Burke as the unofficial leader of the opposition to Francis, declared the essay far superior to anything said at the summit; Benedict, he claimed, had nailed the true cause of the crisis in the wreckage of theological liberalism. On the other side, theologians and commentators lined up to blast the essay as "untimely," "regrettable," and hopelessly simplistic in its analysis, undermining the summit, Francis, and even Vatican II.[20]

This was not the ninety-two-year-old Benedict at his prime; anyone who cared about the emeritus pope and his reputation would have counseled leaving the essay in a drawer, which is probably why Francis and Parolin had done nothing with it. But it was hardly the critique of Francis and the summit's approach that both sides claimed. The reductive obsession with 1968 was hardly new, and offered an accurate account of the breakdown of morality and discipline in the 1970s that all the studies showed went along with the sudden spike in clerical abuse. In the final part, furthermore, Benedict offered strong support for Francis's critique of the neo-Donatists when he warned that some saw "the Church as something almost unacceptable, which we must now take into our own hands and redesign," insisting that "the field is still God's and the net is God's fishing net." This was precisely Francis's critique of the corporate-purgative remedies advocated by Archbishop Viganò.[21]

Why, then, the campaign behind its release orchestrated by Benedict's courtiers? They included Müller, who was a close friend of Benedict's long-time secretary and day-to-day live-in caretaker, Archbishop Georg Gänswein, as well as the dissenting *dubia* cardinal, Walter Brandmüller, among others. All three formed part of what is sometimes called the "Regensburg network" patronized by the royalist right-wing billionaire "Princess TNT," Gloria von Thurn und Taxis. The network has busily promoted the emeritus pope as a pastoral and theological alternative to the Francis papacy.

In 2016, Gänswein advanced his "two-popes" theory that the papacy now consisted of "an expanded ministry, with an active member and a contemplative member." This was why, he said, Benedict had the title of pope emeritus, wore a white cassock, and was called "His Holiness." This canonical oddity was, in fact, Gänswein's design: Benedict had told a German journalist in 2014 that before resigning he had wanted to be "Father Benedict," not "pope emeritus," but had been "too weak at that point to enforce it."[22]

Francis gently repudiated Gänswein's "two-popes" theory, joking on the flight back from Armenia that if in the time of the Avignon crisis there had been three popes, now there was only one. Benedict, he said, had pledged unconditional obedience to whomever the conclave elected and loyally supported the serving pope with his prayer and counsel. He was like a wise grandfather, "the man who protects my back with his prayer." Although Benedict had initially promised to remain "hidden to the world," Francis had urged him to see people, get out, and take part in the life of the Church.[23]

Notwithstanding the scheming of Benedict's courtiers, the 266th successor of Saint Peter enjoys a close relationship with the 265th, one that long predates Francis's election. This is the first time in history that a pope has had an ex-pope with whom to unburden. In a preface to a 2016 book on Benedict by Elio Guerriero, Francis described how with Benedict he enjoyed "friendly spiritual closeness, the joy of praying together, sincere brotherhood, understanding and friendship, and also his availability for advice." Francis visits far more often than people know—only a few times have they been made public—to bounce ideas off him, or to ask for his comments on drafts of papal documents. "You can't imagine the humility and wisdom of the man," Francis told a friend, Jorge Milia, early on in his papacy.

Benedict has spoken often of his affection and admiration for the pope, his "extraordinary human availability," and how touched he is by Francis's visits, gifts, and personal letters. "The human kindness with which he treats me is a particular grace of this last phase of my life for which I can only be grateful," he told Guerriero, adding: "What he says about being open toward other men and women is not just words. He puts it into practice with me." At the end of his sex abuse essay, he typically thanked Francis "for everything he does to show us, again and again, the light of God."

Benedict does not interfere; that is not his style. There's a joke making the rounds in Rome that says he didn't interfere even when he was pope. His weakness in governing—a defect he humbly admitted in his 2016 book interview with Peter Seewald—includes a reluctance to tell others what to do and a vulnerability to being manipulated. Yet he dislikes criticism of Francis and sends away those who complain to him with a flea in their ear, publicly reprimanding those who, like Brandmüller, criticize his decision to resign. But because traditionalist opponents look to him, his words can be inflammatory. When Gänswein read a letter from Benedict at the funeral of one of the *dubia* cardinals, Joachim Meisner, the retired archbishop of Cologne, the emeritus pope's talk of the Lord "never abandoning his Church, even if the boat has taken on so much water as to be on the verge of capsizing" was taken to be a critique of Francis, even though it almost certainly wasn't.[24]

Benedict does his best to insist on the continuity of teaching between the two pontificates, stressing that mercy was also at the heart of his and John Paul II's papacies. From the theological point of view, Benedict told the German newspaper *Bild*, "We are perfectly in agreement." In May 2018, Benedict also rejected what he called the "foolish prejudice" that Francis was a practical pastor with little philosophical and theological formation, while he was "the theoretician of theology, who little understood the concrete life of a Christian today." In fact, "Pope Francis is a man of profound philosophical and theological formation" whose writings show "the internal continuity between the two pontificates, even with all the differences of style and temperament," he said in a letter in response to a new collection of Francis's teachings.[25]

As a theologian in the late 1960s, Benedict had predicted a time when the Church "will no longer be able to inhabit many of the edifices she built in prosperity" and would become "the Church of the meek," "the Church of faith," transformed by the encounter with Christ. In this, both Benedict and Francis coincide with the forecast of Romano Guardini's *The End of the Modern World.* This was the shift seen and encouraged by Aparecida: a humbler and weaker Church, expelled from law and culture, could not rely on the traditional mechanisms of faith transmission but must facilitate the "primary encounter." As Francis put it in Rabat, Morocco, in April 2019, reformulating the famous dictum of Benedict's he so often quoted: "Being a Christian is not about adhering to a doctrine, or a temple, or an ethnic group, but an encounter with Jesus Christ."[26]

On the other hand, the German pope's prediction in a 1997 interview of a Church that would shrink to a mustard-seed body of "small, seemingly insignificant groups," as he put it, was poorly received in Latin America. Whatever Benedict meant by it—and this is debated—the notion of a smaller, purer Church was intolerable to Bergoglio and the leaders at Aparecida, for whom a poorer, humbler Church meant the opposite: one closer to the faith of ordinary people, and better able to connect with His presence among the poor. For the Latin Americans, the faith of ordinary people is the source of renewal, "the Church's immune system," as Francis put it to the Chilean bishops. A shrinking, middle-class Church of nostalgic cliques could only mean one that was rejecting its own immune system.

When I asked Francis about where he saw "popular religiosity" reinvigorating the Church in Europe he pointed to the crowds going on pilgrimages and visiting shrines, as well as the outpouring of faith at moments of tragedy. Here was the Holy Spirit moving among the people, outside the Church, yet which the Church was called to connect with and create space for.

I was recalling his words when a fire ripped through Paris's Notre Dame Cathedral just days before Easter. When vast numbers of praying, chanting crowds—many of whom had traveled long distances—appeared out of nowhere to keep vigil on the banks of the Seine, I saw what he meant. The expulsion of Christianity from law and culture does not mean a lack of religiosity, as France, deeply Catholic in spite of its laïcité, time and again proves. Some gloomy commentators in the United States saw the Notre Dame fire as an ominous symbol of Europe's lack of religiosity. Yet, if anything, the event vindicated its continued vigor. The praying multitudes moved the world, and, against all expectations, the *pompiers* miraculously saved all but Notre Dame's roof and spire.

Whatever their commonalities and contrasts, historians will draw a straight line from Benedict to Francis. So many of the Argentine pope's reforms built on the German pope's, just as Francis's great documents on evangelization, ecology, the family, youth, and holiness stood on his predecessor's shoulders. Indeed, the strange anomaly of the "two popes in the Vatican"—when they are photographed together, there is a visual shock involved, as if seeing double—underscores the interpenetration of the two pontificates. It was Bergoglio who in the 2005 conclave had asked the cardinals voting for him to switch their votes to Benedict. It was Benedict who allowed and opened Aparecida two years later, which produced the vision that answered the challenge of the Church in the contemporary world. And it was Benedict who, in resigning, paved the way for what he assumed would be a Latin American pope to implement Aparecida's Pentecost vision. The last pope of the Western European millennium opened the door of history to the southern wind now filling the Church's sails.

Francis has often spoken of that resignation as a prophetic act that has changed the papacy, and he will make sure—unless God wills otherwise—it is not a one-off. "I will do the same as he did," he told *La Vanguardia* in 2014, "and ask the Lord to enlighten me when the time has come, and what I have to do, and He'll surely tell me." He cannot contemplate doing so, however, while Benedict lives. When Benedict dies, Francis will be the first pope ever to bury his predecessor, a corporal work of mercy that will seal the bond between the two men that no amount of power plays by the "Ratzinger court" can undermine.

How will Francis know the right time? What will his discernment criteria be? He tells some that he will stand down once his reforms are irreversible; to others he says the sign will be when he no longer feels the gift of peace that came on him the night of his election. If and when that time comes, he will not wear white or be called an emeritus pope, but more likely the emeritus bishop of Rome. He may not even stay in the Vatican: he has renewed his Argentine passport in case he is able to pastor back in his beloved Buenos Aires. When speaking of future diary dates, he is careful now to say that either he or "the next Peter" will be there. But for now, he remains anointed. "It's a gift of the Lord," he told reporters on the way back from North Macedonia in May 2019 to explain why on trips he doesn't get tired: "It's all thanks to Him."

Back in the Santa Marta, he sleeps deeply, sometimes dozing off in front of the Blessed Sacrament at night. Barring his agonizing sciatica (which he treats with massages and injections), he is in good health. His face caves in from tiredness at times, especially when he fails to take his forty-minute naps in the afternoon; but he soon bounces back, full of laughter, when he has contact with people. Those around him are in awe at his energy and remorseless work ethic. But he is not frenetic, and gives off a deep peace. He likes to quote the old gaucho Don Segundo Sombra in the famous Argentine novel of that name: how in old age you're no longer a rushing stream carrying rocks, but move ahead steadily like a pool, calmly and kindly, making space and time for others.

There has been much talk of the Francis Effect, but it is as impossible to measure empirically as it is real. What so many cardinals, bishops, priests, and religious and missionary disciples have told me in the course of researching this book is usually some variation of what Cardinal Timothy Dolan of New York said on Francis's fifth anniversary. "People will approach me to say, 'I've been away from the Church for years, but Pope Francis is drawing me back,' or 'I'm not a Catholic, but I sure love this pope,'" he told *Crux*, adding: "He is helping people take a fresh look at the Catholic Church, and thereby come to know Jesus, and experience His love and mercy." To Dolan, the greatness of that achievement—to succeed, as it were, in the only thing that really matters in the Catholic Church: to evangelize—made evaluating the progress of this or that reform a secondary matter.[27]

In communicating so powerfully the "primary encounter," Francis has made it easy for people to return by going out to meet them first. "The pope seems to value the person as much as the institution," is how Chimamanda Ngozi Adichie put it in *The Atlantic*. A Nigerian who was alienated from her childhood faith by "a Church afraid of itself, of looking inward," Francis's humility and compassion have captivated her. Here is a pope who "seems able to say that most un-Catholic of things: 'I don't know.'"[28]

Humility is a constant of the Francis Effect. He has shown that the Church succeeds best when it faces its limits and failures, admitting its dependence on grace, and fails most when it holds itself arrogantly and distrustfully apart from the world. Haughty defensiveness is now more typical of the pope's critics than the Curia that serves him. In Rome, they speak of a new freedom, an openness, a more charismatic Church of joy and hospitality rather than one that is fearful and beleaguered. There is a new liberty to discuss and to criticize, to listen and to discern. The pope won't tell you what to think so much as help you encounter Christ and listen to the Spirit.

The Francis Effect offers a new way of being Catholic in our time, one that would quickly be recognized by the early Church. Christianity is not an idea, but an encounter. Holiness is not what you believe or know but who and how you are; faith isn't merely a set of beliefs but that primary encounter—in prayer, in life—with Jesus Christ. The visible sign of that encounter is a way of living marked by the mind-set and works of mercy.

The Francis Effect is to liberate Catholicism from its attachment to power and self-sufficiency, from its tribal superiority, and turn it outward, *ad gentes*, so that the Church lives no longer for itself but to serve humanity. The iconic image remains the foot-washing of the incarcerated, the act that so offended the traditionalists and the nativists. Honoring all as God's children—making Christ more visible, more accessible, more concrete—means a Samaritan Church, one that makes mercy a verb, known not for its angry lectures but for its bedside whispers, a Church that senses need and courageously responds, opening up channels of God's grace.

Nothing better summed up this "mercying" Church than the pope's almoner, Cardinal Konrad Krajewski, shinnying down a manhole in mid-May 2019 to restore the electricity supply of 450 migrant squatters in a disused government office in Rome. Risking arrest and electrocution, "Don Corrado" descended nine feet to the fuse box in order to get the power back to the families, who had been living without lights or hot water after being cut off over a large unpaid bill. Krajewski said it was an emergency, and a desperate situation; people were unable to run vital medical equipment, and children were falling over in the dark. He assumed all responsibility and said he would pay a fine if he had to. *La Repubblica* called him "the pope's Robin Hood." The Sheriff of Nottingham in the story was Matteo Salvini, the hard-line anti-migrant interior minister, who accused Don Corrado of "supporting illegal behavior" and reminded him that hardworking Italians struggled to pay their bills.[29]

The Francis Effect has been to re-equip the Church to evangelize like this, and the reform in Rome has made it easier. The name of the constitution mapping the Curia's reforms that finally appeared in 2019 was Jesus's commission to his disciples: *Praedicate Evangelium*, "Preach the Gospel." Thus a new dicastery for evangelization is now first among the Vatican departments, with all other dicasteries flowing out from it, including the once mighty Congregation for the Doctrine of the Faith. The primary task of the Church is to make known, in word and deed and witness, the merciful love of Jesus Christ. All else—clarification of doctrine, the priesthood, the sacraments, the Church's law, its ethical teaching, its charitable enterprise, its diplomacy—is the river that gushes from this source. *Praedicate Evangelium* makes clear not that the Church has a mission to evangelize, but that the mission to evangelize has a Church, and that its central body exists to make that easier.[30]

"Seeing with the eyes of faith is a summons not to spend your life pinning labels, classifying those who are worthy of love and those who are not, but trying to create conditions in which every person can feel loved," Francis said in Bulgaria in May 2019. He had shown the evangelizing power of this gaze just weeks earlier, when he appeared in the final episode of a BBC three-part series shown on Good Friday. *Pilgrimage* followed minor British celebrities as they walked together on the ancient Via Francigena pilgrim route from Canterbury to Rome. Among the eight pilgrims—who included a Muslim, a non-practicing Jew, a practicing Catholic, a lapsed Jehovah's Witness, and an atheist—was Stephen K. Amos, a gay comedian angry at what he saw as religion's rejection of him.

Arriving in the Eternal City, gawping at its treasures, the pilgrims learned that Francis would receive them in a private audience that would be filmed. Amos insisted on being allowed to challenge the pope and the Church's doctrines. The producers feared a diplomatic incident, but this was the era of Francis: the Vatican said fine, he could tell the pope whatever he wanted. As the pilgrims one by one introduced themselves, Amos spoke to Francis of his recent bereavements. "So me coming on this pilgrimage, being nonreligious, I was looking for answers and faith. But as a gay man, I don't feel accepted."[31]

The pope looked at him lovingly, with a furrowed brow. "Giving more importance to the adjective rather than the noun—this is not good," he told him. "We are all human beings and have dignity. It does not matter who you are, or how you live your life, or have this or that tendency—you do not lose your dignity. There are people that prefer to select or discard people because of an adjective; these people do not have a human heart."

As Francis spoke, Amos was in tears—as was everyone else. Later the two men hugged, and Amos breathlessly thanked him. Interviewed afterward he said the pope's answer had "blown his mind," that this was "what I've been searching for for a long time." In follow-up interviews, he said he had left Francis with joy in his heart, that his eyes had been opened to not judging religious people based on his negative experiences. He told how a door had opened, and the weight of his grief had lifted.

Amos's moving response to Francis stands, in some way, for the world's to this pope. It is not Francis per se who elicits the reaction, but the Gospel glimpsed in him: at such moments people see what it means to be humans created by a loving God. Hence—as Francis said in his Chrism Mass 2018 homily—it was not just untruthful, but inhuman, to confuse the adjective with the noun. "There is a distasteful habit, is there not, of following a 'culture of the adjective': this is so, this is such and such, this is like . . . No! This is a child of God. Then come the virtues or defects, but first is the faithful truth of the person and not the adjective instead of the noun."

Jesus, he said on that occasion, could have chosen to be a scribe or a doctor of the law, "but he wanted to be an evangelizer, a bearer of joyful news for His people." Closeness is crucial, he added, because it is the key to mercy, but also to truth, for truth is much more than "the definition of situations and things from a certain distance, by abstract and logical reasoning." Truth "makes you name people with their real name, as the Lord names them, before categorizing them or defining 'their situation.'"

This is why his famous question on the plane from Rio de Janeiro in July 2013, "If someone is gay and seeks the Lord and has good will, who am I to judge?" has been the iconic phrase of his pontificate as much as the foot-washing has been its iconic image. Recalling his comments in 2016, Francis said he was emphasizing the primary truth that "God loves all his creatures and we are destined to receive his infinite love." It is because of that "primary truth" that humanity is able to be in relationship with God.[32]

Because history is an arena of spiritual combat, it is no surprise that just at the moment the Church under Francis shows forth the universality of God's love, a wave of intolerance and populism is sweeping across the Western world, leaving the pope exposed as the master bridgemaker in an era of angry wall builders.

Yet he is no "globalist." Having spent two decades opposed to a disorderly globalization that rendered the world flat and unequal, warning of the bitter harvest of what technocracy was sowing, he is not surprised that in a world rendered rootless by consumerism and individualism, shorn of a deeper identity by loss of links with God and nature, beset by anguish, fear, and powerlessness, so many are turning to strongmen and ideologies that offer security and identity. But that doesn't stop him from warning where it will end and reminding the world what Christians really believe.

From the integuments of secularized Christianity the high priests of nationalist populism are constructing a pseudo-religion, one that dances around a golden calf of tribal egotism, setting "Judeo-Christian values" against the threat of "Islamization." While the nationalist-populists such as Vladimir Putin in Russia, Viktor Orban in Hungary, and Matteo Salvini in Italy insist that "Christian civilization" must build walls, the pope in Rome inconveniently insists that such a civilization cannot be Christian unless it keeps bridges and doors open.[33]

His clear stance has posed a major challenge for former Trump strategist Steve Bannon in his bid to construct a global far-right populist alliance. The thrice-divorced, non-practicing Catholic Bannon paints Francis, the world's most trenchant critic of globalization, as a globalist, while cultivating the Regensburg network around Benedict and urging Salvini to attack the pope. Through Cardinal Burke's Dignitatis Humanae Institute (motto: "defending the roots of Judaeo-Christian civilization"), of which he is a patron, Bannon has leased a monastery outside Rome, a "gladiator school" to train dozens of future populist nationalists. The plan has run into strong opposition from the local villagers of Trisulti, who object to the use of their local abbey for what reminds them of fascism.[34]

Francis never confronts the populists directly, yet counters them at every turn. It is not pro-life, he tells the media but not Trump, to separate and imprison migrant children, nor is it Christian to build walls to keep out the needy. Where Trump paints Mexican migrants as drug dealers or rapists, Francis describes them as fleeing war and misery. The attitude that sees migrants as the source of a society's ills "is an alarm bell warning of moral decline," he said after the European Parliament elections of June 2019.

In his holiness exhortation, *Gaudete et Exsultate* (Rejoice and Be Glad), he notes that "welcoming the stranger" is core Christian doctrine, not "a momentary fad . . . invented by some pope." A politician looking for votes might claim otherwise, he said, "but not a Christian." Against the claim to make their nations great again by keeping out foreigners, Francis offers a reminder that the progress of a people "depends above all on our openness to being touched and moved by those who knock at our door." The challenge of migration cannot be resolved by building walls and closing borders, he warned on the return flight from Rabat, Morocco, for you soon become a prisoner of the barriers you build. Quoting a novelist, he said bridges were God's invention, fashioned from the wings of angels to allow people to be in relationship.

In February 2019, he built one such bridge—immense in scope, bold in execution—across the divide with the Arab Muslim world. It was the eight hundredth anniversary of Saint Francis of Assisi's visit to Sultan al-Malik al-Kāmil. The first pope to take the saint's name went to the United Arab Emirates to lead the largest ever Christian act of public worship on the Arabian peninsula, and also to offer a way out of the polarization trap gripping the West, in which murderous acts of terror by Islamic extremists trigger populist jeremiads against Muslims and migrants.

The meeting came about because of Francis's closeness to the "pope of the Sunni world," the Grand Imam of al-Azhar in Cairo, Dr. Ahmed el-Tayeb. After talks with Muslim scholars and an address to six hundred religious leaders, Francis co-signed with el-Tayeb a groundbreaking declaration he had worked on with the Muslim leader for over a year. Francis later described it to young people as a big dream he had had with a friend.[35]

The Abu Dhabi "Document on Human Fraternity for World Peace" was a milestone in interreligious dialogue, but was much bigger than that. It was a bid by the primary leaders of the world's two biggest religions to harness the forces of faith to rescue humanity from fatal conflict. "There is no alternative," Francis told the religious leaders on February 4. "Either we build the future together or there will not be a future." He was urgent, apocalyptic: at this delicate historical juncture, religions were being called on to "contribute actively to demilitarize the human heart" by deepening "the capacity for reconciliation, the vision of hope and the concrete paths of peace."[36]

The el-Tayeb–Francis declaration took as its starting point humanity's fraternity as children of God, warning that everywhere truth was under assault. Materialistic individualism had desensitized the human conscience, weakening spiritual values and responsibility, leading to angst and the stockpiling of weapons. But the pope and the grand imam also saw an "awakening religious awareness" that had to be freed from the grip of those who would exploit it. "God, the Almighty, has no need to be defended by anyone," they said, "and does not want His name to be used to terrorize people."

The declaration boldly made clear that pluralism of religion was the will of God, along with diversity of color, sex, race, and language. Faiths were called, in other words, to cohabitation and cooperation, and thence to create tolerance, justice, and peace. Freedom of belief and worship and the protection of places of worship were vital, as were the rights and freedoms of all, including women, to education, work, and equal political and civic participation. "The first and most important aim of religions is to believe in God, to honor Him, and to invite all men and women to believe that this universe depends on a God who governs it," the pope and the Grand Imam declared. They commended their declaration for study across the globe, and to future generations, as "a witness to the greatness of faith in God that unites divided hearts and elevates the human soul."

The declaration was strong stuff in Wahhabi cultures in the Arabian peninsula, where Christians and women were second-class citizens and fundamentalism laid claim to Islam. But it also sent a clear shot across the bows of the Western populists who blasphemed by turning Christians into a hating tribe. As Francis said in his speech, "The enemy of fraternity is an individualism which translates into the desire to affirm oneself and one's own group above others." True faith, on the other hand, "consists in loving God with all one's heart and one's neighbor as oneself."

Then, before Easter, he went to Morocco, where Catholics comprise less than one percent of the population. His eighth visit to a Muslim-majority country came in the wake of Donald Trump's decision—pandering to U.S. evangelicals and pro-Israel donors—to reverse decades of U.S. foreign policy by moving the American embassy to Jerusalem. Now, with King Mohammed VI, Francis made a public appeal for Jerusalem to remain a place of encounter for Jews, Christians, and Muslims.

Meeting with migrants in Rabat, he reiterated his four-step strategy to create "spaces for conferring dignity"—welcoming, protecting, promoting, and integrating—and reminded them that "it is Christ himself who knocks on our doors." The next day, in Rabat's cathedral, he mapped out a future for Christian minorities. What mattered was not how many they were, but their capacity to "awaken wonder and compassion." Evangelization was not proselytism but witness. "We are Christians," Francis told the priests and religious, "because we have been loved and encountered." He pointed to the Abu Dhabi declaration on fraternity and said God's kingdom was born not in violence or power, but in "the power of the compassion poured out on the Cross for all mankind."[37]

Back in Rome, a week before he washed the feet of young prisoners at the start of the three-day Easter liturgies, he kissed the feet of politicians.

It was at the end of a two-day ecumenical retreat for the warring leaders of South Sudan at the suggestion of the Archbishop of Canterbury, Justin Welby, who is often in Rome these days, and hosted by Francis at the Casa Santa Marta. The retreat had come at a crucial juncture: the country was emerging shakily from a six-year civil war that had killed close to half a million people; a peace transition deal still held, but it was coming to an end.

Addressing South Sudan's president Salva Kiir Mayardit, his three vice presidents, and opposition leader vice president Riek Machar along with their officials, Francis spoke to them "as a brother," urging them to "stay in peace," and had some advice: they should always present a united front to the people, so that divisions were contained behind closed doors. Then he looked sorrowful, as if imagining the resumption of war: the horror, the hunger, the women raped, the children traumatized, the death and destruction. "I ask you from my heart, let's go forward," he said. "There will be many problems, but do not be afraid."

Then he told his interpreter to come with him and walked over to the president and, bowing before him, fell heavily on his knees, and kissed Mayardit's shoes. One by one, for what seemed an eternity, the eighty-two-year-old pope did the same with the others. The effort—he is a large man, and the pain from his sciatica can be intense—made his breathing heavy and labored. Machar, overwhelmed, made to stop him but Francis told him: "let me." Vice President Rebecca Nyandeng Garang could not contain her tears. Choking with emotion, Welby told them they had heard the prophetic call of Christ.

Francis later told a collaborator that he had felt, in that moment, the need to make a gesture. What came to him was God's chosen means of saving the world from destruction: the *synktákabasis*, God's coming down to come close. "By His self-abasement," Francis said a few days later, on Palm Sunday, "Jesus wanted to open up to us the path of faith and to precede us on that path."

On Holy Thursday, Francis went, as he had done each year, to a prison, this time to one an hour south of Rome. Hundreds of prisoners and officers cheered and clapped as he entered the Velletri detention center. In a brief homily, Francis explained that in Jesus's time this was a task for slaves, that Jesus "who had all the power, who was the Lord, makes the gesture of a slave" to show that all must be at the service of others. Then he washed the feet of inmates, including a Brazilian and two Africans.

Three days later in Sri Lanka, hundreds of Catholics would be massacred by Islamist suicide bombers as they celebrated the Resurrection, a reminder that Christians were by far the most persecuted group in the world, daily dying for their faith. It was also a reminder of how vulnerable the pope was to such an attack. But he wasn't going back to the armor-plated, bulletproofed Mercedes with tinted windows they still kept in the Vatican garage; as long as he is pope he will use the Ford Focus and the open-topped popemobile that swings him around the square, stopping to let children climb aboard or to get down to come close to someone who needs a token of God's passionate love for His creatures.

And that's his secret. He doesn't live for himself.

At the heart of the Spiritual Exercises that have shaped his life, Saint Ignatius observes that "the person will make progress in the spiritual life to the degree that they go out of self-love, self-will and self-interest." For twenty years, the Basque saint was a wounded walker ever more open to God's grace, who learned more and more how to "go out." He didn't reach Rome until late in his life, from where he sent out his spiritual sons, the first Jesuits, to the ends of the earth.

Now, half a millennium later, one of his sons had come back from one of those far corners to be pope, a wounded shepherd who has asked the Church to do what he has spent his life doing: to go out, to leave behind self-love, self-will, and self-interest, to have the freedom to respond to the Spirit that is transforming the world even in the midst of violence and confusion and destruction. It is now and always the only really free choice: whether to allow yourself to be looked upon, to accept God's love, in order thereafter to see beyond adjectives and to live for others.

Maybe that's why now, looking back on my meeting with Francis, I think of the freedom I found in that modest waiting room in the Santa Marta. "He is totally free!" Cardinal Marc Ouellet told me in Sydney back in 2013, shortly after Francis's election, in a tone of delighted astonishment. I didn't know what he meant then. But I do now. It is the inner freedom and fearlessness that Mark and Matthew meant when they said that unlike the doctors of the law, Jesus spoke with "authority."

Was it this that so endeared him to people, yet produced fear in some? It is the freedom that Gaston Fessard spoke of in his study of the Spiritual

Exercises that so influenced the young Bergoglio, in which the life of faith is a life of our freedom and God's freedom, united. It was this that had captivated me in Francis: a life spent freely choosing God's freedom over his own, which showed forth the awesome possibility of being loved and loving. And what would the Church look like, that looked like that? And we, how would we be?

Notes

one

1. "Quando il cardenale Jorge Mario Bergoglio visitò Tigliole," *Gazzetta d'Asti*, April 6, 2013.
2. Francis, *Gaudete et Exsultate*, 8, 12, and 16. See Lucia Capuzzi's biography, *Rosa dei due mondi* (Milan: Ed. San Paolo, 2014); and Orsola Appendino and Giancarlo Libert, *Nonna Rosa. La roccia delle Langhe da Cortemilia all'Argentina*, 2d ed. (privately published, 2016).
3. "El 'apostolado de la oreja' de los taxistas," *Zenit*, May 7, 2002.
4. Francis, "Address for the Meeting with the World of Labour," Piazzetta Reale, Turin, June 21, 2015.
5. Francis, "Homily, Mass and Canonization of the Blesseds, Homily of His Holiness Pope Francis," St. Peter's Square, October 14, 2018.
6. Lucia Capuzzi, interview with the author, Milan, May 17, 2016.
7. Vittorio Rapetti, interview with the author, Acqui Terme, May 16, 2016. See Vittorio Rapetti, *Laici nella Chiesa, cristiani nel mondo: Per una storia dell'Azione Cattolica nelle Chiese locali del Piemonte e Valle d'Aosta* (Rome: Isacem, 2010).
8. On Rosa and Mario's appearances in the *Gazzetta d'Asti*, see Vittorio Croce and Stefano Masino, *Una famiglia di nome Bergoglio: Le origini astigiane di Papa Francesco* (Asti: Ed. Gazzetta d'Asti, 2014). On Mario's (the pope's father) Salesian links, see Alejandro León, SDB, *Francisco y Don Bosco* (Madrid: Ed. CCS, 2014), 20.
9. Bergoglio, Letter to Father Cayetano Bruno, SDB, October 20, 1990. See also Francis, *La fuerza de la vocación. La vida consagrada hoy. Una entrevista con Fernando Prado*, CMF (Madrid: Ed. Claretianas, 2018), 58.
10. Bergoglio, "Homenaje con motivo del centenario de la llegada de los Salesianos a la Argentina," in León, *Francisco y Don Bosco*, 50–57.
11. Bergoglio recalled the accusation to Don Bruno in his letter of 1990. He defended himself in 2011 from the criticism by citing the example of Don Bosco. See Jorge Bergoglio and Abraham Skorka, *Sobre el cielo y la tierra* (Buenos Aires: Sudamericana, 2011), 165.
12. Francis, "Address for the Meeting with the Salesians and the Daughters of Mary Help of Christians," and "Address for the Meeting with Children and Young People," Turin, June 21, 2015.
13. On Shroud Man versus Vitruvian Man, see Nunzio Galantino, *Il rinnovamento missionario della Chiesa italiana* (Milan: Sao Paolo, 2018), 43.
14. The 2013 letter to Father Alexandre Awi is reproduced at www.portaluz.org: "Una traumática

experiencia padecida por Papa Francisco en su infancia, lo mueve a la 'Cultura del Encuentro'" (June 5, 2015). Bergoglio also described the disputes in his 1990 letter to Cayetano Bruno, SDB, in León, *Francisco y Don Bosco*, 37–45.

15. Francis, letter to Awi. See also Massimo Borghesi, *The Mind of Pope Francis: Jorge Mario Bergoglio's Intellectual Journey* (Collegeville, Minn.: Liturgical Press, 2018). Francis, *Evangelii Gaudium*, 217–37.

16. Quoted in Mark Shriver, *Pilgrimage: My Search for the Real Pope Francis* (New York: Random House, 2016), 37. See also Austen Ivereigh, *The Great Reformer: Francis and the Making of a Radical Pope* (New York: Henry Holt, 2014; Picador, 2015), ch. 1.

17. On Francis's "big politics," see his comments in the prologue to Antonio Spadaro, SJ, ed., *En tus ojos está mi palabra. Homilías y discursos de Buenos Aires, 1999–2013. Con una conversación con Antonio Spadaro* (Madrid: Ed. Claretianas, 2018), 27. Francis recalls his adolescent fascination with politics to Javier Cámara and Sebastián Pfaffen, *Aquel Francisco* (Córdoba, Argentina: Ed. Raíz de Dos, 2014), 36–38.

18. Ezekiel 16:62–63. All biblical quotations henceforth from *CTS New Catholic Bible*, London: Catholic Truth Society, 2007. Francis, *The Name of God Is Mercy: A Conversation with Andrea Tornielli*, trans. Oonagh Stransky (New York: Random House, 2016), 8. In relation to Ezekiel and sex abuse, see epilogue.

19. The pope used that phrase to the author when asked about Merton's influence on him. See Austen Ivereigh, "Pope Francis 'Meets' Thomas Merton," *The Tablet*, December 12, 2018.

20. Francis, "Carta . . . al periodista italiano Eugenio Scalfari del periódico 'La Repubblica,'" September 4, 2013.

21. Francis, "Encounter with the world of work," Ilva factory, Genoa, May 27, 2017.

22. Francis, "Encounter with the bishops of Liguria, clergy seminarians and religious of the region," San Lorenzo cathedral, Genoa, May 27, 2017; "Encounter with the young people of the diocesan mission," Shrine of Our Lady of the Guard, Genoa, May 27, 2017.

two

1. Jason Horowitz, "Ten Centuries Later, a Pope and Knights Do Battle," *New York Times*, January 28, 2017.

2. Frédéric Martel, *In the Closet of the Vatican: Power, Homosexuality, Hypocrisy*, trans. Shaun Whiteside (London: Bloomsbury, 2019), 26–30.

3. The description of Burke and his apartment come from *The Tablet*'s Rome correspondent, Christopher Lamb, who visited him there. "Who Is Trolling the Pope?," BBC Radio Four, February 18, 2017.

4. Darío Menor, interview with Burke ("A muchos les parece que la nave de la Iglesia ha perdido la brújula"), *Vida Nueva*, October 30, 2014; David Gibson, "Cardinal Burke Insists He's Not an 'Enemy' of Pope Francis," Religion News Service, August 22, 2016. See Burke's account to Josef Freiherr von Beverforde, KM, in early March 2017: "Internal Report of the Order of Malta: The view of Cardinal Burke," http://gloria.tv, April 27, 2017. Michael O'Loughlin, "Pope Francis: Demotion of Burke Not 'Punishment,'" *Crux*, December 7, 2014.

5. Burke's account in von Beverforde, KM, "Internal Report of the Order of Malta."

6. From the 1990s until, in effect, Francis's election in 2013, "Cacho" Caselli (nicknamed *el obispo*, "the bishop") was the intermediary between the Church and state in Argentina and the Vatican, first as Argentina's ambassador to the Holy See under the two presidencies of Carlos Menem in the 1990s, then as President Eduardo Duhalde's secretary of state for religion, and, finally, as an Italian senator with Silvio Berlusconi's Forza Italia. By placing himself as an intermediary at the center of a triangle between the Vatican, the government in Buenos Aires, and the Argentine Church, Caselli became not just personally wealthy but more importantly a powerful broker who was able to influence even bishops' nominations. See Marcelo Larraquy, "Una trama de poder, política y negociados," *Clarín*, June 26, 2016.

7. Improbable as it sounds, the plot was widely spoken of at the time, and has since been confirmed by a number of those who were involved, including Sarlinga, who was stood down by Francis in 2017 following a rash of accusations of money laundering and fraud. See Austen Ivereigh, "How the Pope's History with the Knights of Malta Could Be Linked to the Current Row," *Crux*, January 13, 2017. Also: Marcelo Larraquy, "La lenta agonía de los obispos conservadores," *Clarín*, February 2, 2014; Carlos Pagni, "De pronto, todo ha cambiado," *La Nación*, March 18, 2013; Mariano de Vedia, "La trama

política oculta de los años en que Bergoglio aún no era Francisco," *La Nación*, March 29, 2015; and Sergio Rubín, "Envuelto en un escándalo, renuncia el obispo de Zárate-Campana," *Clarín*, November 2, 2015.

8. Christopher Lamb, "Restless Knights," *The Tablet*, April 21, 2018. The details of Burke's ambitions come from a senior source in the order, who noted to me that "even Festing balked at Burke's bid to incorporate his institute into the Order." On the ICKSP, see the account by a former member, Eric Brende, "No One Expects the Inquisition," *Commonweal*, May 17, 2017. Brende notes that "outwardly, ICKSP (unlike the Society of Pius X) maintains unity with the larger, postconciliar Church," but "privately and unofficially" it denies that Vatican II carries doctrinal authority and seeks to create "a sort of parallel or shadow church within the church."

9. The press statement was shared with me by the order's communications director, Eugenio Ajroldi di Robbiate.

10. The mishandling by three knights (who later apologized) of complaints of abuse against the order's sacristan in the U.K. led to a church inquiry that was critical of the order. See Christopher Lamb, "Grand Master of Knight of Malta Caves in to Vatican Pressure," *The Tablet*, January 25, 2017.

11. Neil Weir, Luke Gormally, and John Haas, "Commission of Inquiry: First Report. Prepared for HMEH the Prince and Grand Master Frà Andrew Festing," January 2016, at http://wikileaks.org /popeorders/releases. Professors Gormally and Haas were publicly critical of Benedict XVI's comments in the pope's book-length interview with Peter Seewald, *Light of the World* (San Francisco: Ignatius Press, 2010). The Congregation for the Doctrine of the Faith at the time came down against Gormally on the AIDS-condoms question (see Sandro Magister, "Professor Rhonheimer Writes. And the Holy Office Agrees," *Chiesa*, December 22, 2010). The absence in their report of the views of ethicists more aligned with the magisterium, above all the CDF consultor Professor Martin Rhonheimer, is what makes it "one-sided." After looking at the report, Professor James F. Keenan, SJ, editor of *Catholic Ethicists on HIV/AIDS Prevention* (New York: Continuum, 2000), told me in an email of February 10, 2019, that Gormally and Haas "go beyond magisterial teaching in making obligations that the magisterium didn't make," especially the claim that the Church banned "the type of sexual act which is intrinsically incapable of being procreative," which postmenopausal women and their husbands would be surprised by. "There is no magisterial document that validates their claim," Keenan said.

12. See chapter 10. In his 2017 account to Beverfoerde, "Internal Report of the Order of Malta," Burke claims that he had not shared the pope's Freemasons mandate with the order because he thought it was covered by the "pontifical secret."

13. Letters of Francis to Burke (December 1, 2016) and Burke to Festing (December 6, 2016) at http://wikileaks.org/popeorders/releases/.

14. There are varying accounts of this meeting, which this summary merges. For Rummerstein's and Boeselager's, see Austen Ivereigh, "Knights of Malta Chief Says It Was Burke Who Asked Official to Resign," *Crux*, February 15, 2017; for Burke's, see Edward Pentin, "Cardinal Burke Firmly Rejects Account by Order of Malta's Acting Head," *National Catholic Register*, February 18, 2017; for Festing's, see his "Alternate Version of Events Leading to the Resignation of Fra' Matthew Festing," at http:// wikileaks.org/popeorders/releases.

15. As recalled by Festing in his "Alternate Version of Events."

16. Humberto Podetti, interview with the author, Buenos Aires, November 8, 2016.

17. Philip Pullella, "A popular pope, but how powerful? Francis still fights internal battles," Reuters, June 27, 2018. Juan Domingo Perón, *Conducción Política* (Buenos Aires: Punto de Encuentro, 2015).

18. Carlos E. Cué, "El Papa peronista, pero no kirchnerista," *El País*, February 29, 2016. An Irish Jesuit who taught at the Colegio Máximo at the time was surprised by how pro-Peronist were Bergoglio and his followers in the 1983 election. "Someone said to me that these Jesuits are from Radical families, but Bergoglio has turned them into Peronists." James Kelly, SJ, interview with the author, March 3, 2015.

19. Cámara and Pfaffen, *Aquel Francisco*, 38. I am grateful to a number of veteran *guardianes* in Buenos Aires, above all Norberto Monestes, who took the trouble to explain how they see Francis.

20. Francis, "'I Believe the Lord Wants a Change in the Church': A Private Dialogue with the Jesuits in the Baltics," *La Civiltà Cattolica*, October 17, 2018. For a crude attempt to portray Francis as "dictator," see Marcantonio Colonna, *The Dictator Pope: The Inside Story of the Francis Papacy* (Washington, D.C.: Regnery, 2017). The author was revealed to be a traditionalist English Knight of Malta and a Festing ally, Henry Sire. The order suspended him in March 2018, describing his account of the Order of

Malta conflict as "biased and one-sided" and the book as a "vile attack" on the pope. Christopher Lamb, "'Dictator Pope' Author Suspended by Order of Malta," *The Tablet*, March 22, 2018.

21. Statement by Fra' John Critien, January 3, 2017; Ed Condon, "The Vatican Has Destroyed the Order of Malta's Sovereignty," *Catholic Herald*, January 25, 2017. It was true that in 1953 the Holy See had recognized the order as a sovereign political entity, and that, as a religious order, the knights were subject to the jurisdiction of the Congregation of the Religious. But the corollary of that recognition was that political sovereignty could be invoked only in relation to political matters, such as its relations with states. In claiming that he wasn't accountable to the Holy See on an internal personnel issue, Festing was going well beyond those terms. The discussion was anyway academic: if the Vatican withdrew its recognition, the order would fast lose its raison d'être.

22. Festing, letter of January 14, 2017; Holy See Press Office communiqué, January 17, 2017; Keith Dovkants, "The Toffs Who Took on the Pope (and Lost)," *Tatler*, July 13, 2017.

23. Spadaro, ed., *En tus ojos está mi palabra*, 28.

24. Philip Pullella, "The Knights of Malta–Vatican feud: A tale of chivalry and sovereignty," Reuters, January 28, 2017.

25. Pope Francis, letter to Becciu, February 2, 2017.

26. Christopher Lamb, "Knights of Malta Called to Contribute to Order's Reform Ahead of Crucial Election of New Leader, Reveals Letter," *The Tablet*, March 28, 2017; Boeselager quoted in Lamb, "Restless Knights."

27. This quote is as one of the participants in the meeting recalls it.

28. Eugenio Ajroldi di Robbiate, Order of Malta's director of communications, email to the author, February 6, 2019. On the reform within the order, see Christopher Lamb's articles in *The Tablet*: "Pope Blocks Recruitment as Knights of Malta Tussle for Control of Order," February 1, 2018; and "Knights of Malta to Reform Governance Structure," February 12, 2018.

29. Interview with Antonio Caño and Pablo Ordaz, *El País*, January 22, 2017.

30. Pullella, "The Knights of Malta–Vatican feud"; *Die Zeit* interview quoted in Inés San Martín, "Pope Francis: I Do Not See Cardinal Burke as an Enemy," *Crux*, March 8, 2017. The pre-conclave lunch with the cardinals (the others were Santos Abril y Castelló, Antonio Cañizares, and Carlos Amigo Vallejo) is recorded by Gerard O'Connell, *The Election of Pope Francis* (New York: Orbis Books, 2019), 177–78. On Thomas More prayer: Francis, "'It Is Not Enough to Turn the Page. Life Must Be Given Anew': The Private Meeting of Pope Francis and the Jesuits in Ireland," *La Civiltà Cattolica*, September 13, 2018.

three

1. Francesca Immacolata Chaouqui, *Nel nome di Pietro: Ricchezze, affari, intrighi e scandali delle carte segrete della commissione del Papa* (Milan: Sperling & Kupfer, 2017), epilogue.

2. Antonio Spadaro, SJ, "A Big Heart Open to God: An Interview with Pope Francis," *America*, September 30, 2013; Francis, "Meeting with young people," Santo Tomás University, Manila, January 18, 2015. When Francis discussed the painting with Eva Fernández, he speculated that Matthew in the painting is the young man with his head down counting coins, rather than the bearded man who appears to be pointing at himself, as many believe. See Eva Fernández, *El Papa de la Ternura* (Madrid: Planeta, 2019), 19–31.

3. Bergoglio, "El sentido teológico de la elección," *Boletín de la Espiritualidad*, no. 4 (October–November 1968), 7–8. On Fessard, see Edouard Pousset, SJ, *Life in Faith and Freedom: An Essay Presenting Gaston Fessard's Analysis of the Dialectic of the Spiritual Exercises of St. Ignatius*, trans. E. Donahue (St. Louis: Institute of Jesuit Sources, 1980), 22–23. On Fessard and Bergoglio, see Borghesi, *The Mind of Pope Francis*, ch. 2.

4. Francis, "Homily, Holy Mass," Plaza de la Revolución, Holguín, September 21, 2015. On Bergoglio's personal credo, see Ivereigh, *The Great Reformer*, 92–93, 100–101.

5. Francis, "Press Conference During the Return Flight" from Rio de Janeiro, July 28, 2013.

6. Philip Pullella, "Vatican Prelate Admits Leaks; Says Woman 'Spy' Intimidated Him," Reuters, March 14, 2016; "El secretario de Balda admite que Chaouqui tenía 'cierta influencia' sobre el sacerdote y que 'les aconsejé cautela,'" *Religión Digital*, April 11, 2016.

7. Francis, "Interview of Pope Francis with Journalists During the Return Flight from the Holy Land," May 26, 2014.

8. O'Connell, *The Election of Pope Francis*, 174.

9. Francis, "Meeting with the young people," Kasarani Stadium, Nairobi, Kenya, November 27, 2015; Francis, *Misericordiae Vultus*, no. 9.

10. Austen Ivereigh, "What the Jesuit Pope Told the Jesuit General," *Crux*, May 13, 2017; Antonio Spadaro, "Pope Francis: 'There Is Corruption in the Vatican. But I'm at Peace,'" *Corriere della Sera*, February 9, 2017.

11. Alex Roe, "Why Nothing's Changed Since the Huge Corruption Scandal That Hit Italy 20 Years Ago," *Business Insider*, February 21, 2012; Philip Pullella, "Vatican Inspectors Suspect Key Office Was Used for Money Laundering," Reuters, November 3, 2015.

12. For many years the official figure was $250 million, but Cardinal Pell has confirmed it was $406 million. See Francesco Pelosi, "IOR: Ecco i veri risarcimenti per il crac del Banco Ambrosiano," *Lettera 43*, June 4, 2017. On the embezzlement case: Philip Pullella, "Prosecutor Freezes Accounts of ex-Vatican Bank Heads," Reuters, December 6, 2014. For an account of the Calvi era, see the terrifically detailed research of Gerald Posner, *God's Bankers: A History of Money and Power at the Vatican* (New York: Simon and Schuster, 2015).

13. Christopher Lamb, "Benedict Opens Up About Falling in Love and Reforming the Vatican," *The Tablet*, September 9, 2016. On the large amount of fake news on the Francis papacy, see Nello Scavo's meticulously documented *Fake Pope: Le false notizie su papa Francesco* (Milan: Ed. San Paolo, 2018). The damaging news stories and leaks come mostly from within the Vatican, usually from traditionalist lobbies.

14. The letter is described in Gianluigi Nuzzi, *Merchants in the Temple* (New York: Henry Holt, 2015) and has been separately confirmed.

15. Chaouqui, *Nel nome di Pietro*, 254.

16. See account in Shawn Tully, "This Pope Means Business," *Fortune*, August 14, 2014; plus COSEA papers in Nuzzi, *Merchants in the Temple*, ch. 1. I am grateful to Joseph Zahra, president of the Council of the Economy, for guidance.

17. Cardinal George Pell, interview with the author, April 1, 2017.

18. Cardinal Abril y Castelló told this story to Francesca Chaouqui, *Nel nome di Pietro*, ch. 3.

19. AIF reported in April 2016 that 4,800 IOR accounts had been closed since 2013. Joshua McElwee, "Vatican Financial Watchdog Registers Three-fold Increase in Suspicious Activity in 2015," *National Catholic Reporter*, April 28, 2016.

20. "Elena Guarino, the Salerno magistrate who led the investigation, told reporters the Vatican was fully cooperative," Philip Pullella, "Arrested Vatican Prelate in New Money Laundering Charge," Reuters, January 21, 2014; John Allen, "Vatican Court Condemns ex–Vatican Bank Officials for 'Mismanagement,'" *Crux*, February 6, 2018.

21. Detailed information about Ricca's past was published by Sandro Magister, "The Prelate of the Gay Lobby," *L'Espresso*, July 18, 2013. The pope's answer to the question about Ricca noted that people's past sins should not be held against them, and that "if someone is gay and is searching for the Lord and has good will, then who am I to judge him?" He went on to quote the Catechism of the Catholic Church that gay people must be integrated, not marginalized. Francis, "Press Conference During the Return Flight" from Rio de Janeiro, July 28, 2013. The lobbies' carping about the cost of the COSEA probe and recruitment of "expensive international stars" such as Brülhart can be found in Sandro Magister, "The Curia of Francis, Paradise of the Multinationals," *Chiesa*, January 17, 2014.

22. Christopher Lamb, "Vatican Challenges Met Police over Claim It Did not Assist on Soper," *The Tablet*, April 17, 2019.

23. Quoted in Alexander Stille, "Holy Orders," *New Yorker*, September 7, 2015; David Gibson, "Pope Francis Overhauls Vatican Financial Watchdog, Names Australian Cardinal as Comptroller," Religion News Service, February 24, 2014. On Brülhart, see Austen Ivereigh, "The Vatican's Quiet Reformer," *Crux*, April 29, 2017.

24. Jorge Mario Bergoglio, "Fervor apostólico," *Cuadernos de Pastores*, Año 5, no. 15 (September 1999), 28–31. He made the same distinction in a talk on politics in 2004 and in discussing Vatican diplomacy to the Spanish newspaper *El País* in his interview of January 22, 2017. Francis discusses the term and its origin in Francis, *La fuerza de la vocación*, 86–87.

25. Morning homilies: June 3, 2013; September 20, 2013; November 8 and 11, 2013; January 11, 2014.

26. Jorge Mario Bergoglio, *Corrupción y pecado: Algunas reflexiones en torno al tema de la corrupción* (Buenos Aires: Ed. Claretianas, 2005, 2013).

27. Claire Giangravé, "Vatican Tailors Try to Adapt to Francis's 'Papal Athleisure,'" *Crux*, June 13, 2017.

28. Pope to seminarians and novices: "there is no holiness in sadness," Vatican Radio, July 6, 2013. The Argentine bishop Juan José Iriarte is quoted in Yves Congar, *Power and Poverty in the Church: The Renewal and Understanding of Service* (New York: Paulist Press, 2016), 93. Originally published as *Pour une Église servante et pauvre* (Paris: Ed. du Cerf, 1963), Congar's little book is the best guide to Francis's curial reform.

29. "Address of Pope Francis to the Students of The Jesuit Schools of Italy and Albania," Vatican Information Service (VIS), June 7, 2013.

30. This is a common complaint. A senior American archbishop expressed to me in 2014 his frustration at no longer being able to secure Mass with the pope to reward donors.

31. Jeremy Kahn, "Pope Revamps the Scandal-Wracked Vatican Bank," *Bloomberg Markets Magazine*, May 5, 2015; Cardinal George Pell, "The Days of Ripping Off the Vatican Are Over," *Catholic Herald*, December 4, 2014; Michael Mullins, "Vatican Finance Czar Uncovers $1.5 Billion in Hidden Assets," *La Croix International*, February 17, 2015. Some perspective: Pell's figure of $3.2 billion means the Vatican is less wealthy than some of the Church's dioceses, such as Cologne in Germany, which at the end of 2013 reported €3.35 billion in stocks, funds, and property. "German Archdiocese of Cologne Reveals $3.8 Billion Fortune," Associated Press, February 18, 2015.

32. Philip Pullella, "Vatican Condemns Leaking of Documents Showing Power Struggle," Reuters, February 27, 2015.

33. Becciu, interview with Christopher Lamb, "Power Behind the Throne: New Cardinal Angelo Becciu," *The Tablet*, June 28, 2018.

34. Gianni Cardinale, "Mistò: 'La riforma voluta dal Papa dà risultati,'" *Avvenire*, July 26, 2017; and Domenico Agasso, "Vaticano, Mistò: 'La riforma dell'economia va avanti,'" *Vatican Insider*, May 5, 2018. Briefing del Direttore della Sala Stampa, Greg Burke, sulla XXV riunione dei Cardinali Consiglieri con il Santo Padre Francesco, June 13, 2018.

35. Galantino, *Il rinnovamento missionario della Chiesa italiana*, 72–73; Gian Guido Vecchi, "Galantino, nuovo presidente Apsa: 'Gestirò i beni della Chiesa per gli ultimi,'" *Corriere della Sera*, June 27, 2018.

four

1. Francis, interview with *Tertio*, December 7, 2016; Francis, *Evangelii Gaudium*, no. 32.

2. Adolfo Nicolás, interview with *Mensajero* reported in *Religión Digital*: "Francisco: "Le pido al Buen Dios que me lleve cuando los cambios sean irreversibles," April 4, 2017.

3. Cardinal Rodríguez de Maradiaga, interview with the author, Villanova University, April 13, 2018; Yves Congar, OP, *True and False Reform in the Church* (Collegeville, Minn.: Liturgical Press, 2011), 108); and Congar, *Power and Poverty in the Church*, 23. John W. O'Malley, *What Happened at Vatican II?* (Cambridge, Mass.: Belknap Press, 2008), 73–74, 186; Second Vatican Council: *Lumen Gentium*, nos. 9, 12; Robert Mickens, "The Calm Before the Storm," *La Croix International*, November 9, 2018; Massimo Faggioli, "From Collegiality to Synodality: Pope Francis's Post-Vatican II Reform," *La Croix International*, December 24, 2018.

4. Francis, "Homily, Mass for the Beginning of the Petrine Ministry of the Bishop of Rome," March 19, 2013.

5. Gerard O'Connell, "Pope Francis Washes the Feet of 8 Men and 4 Women of Different Religions and Countries," *America*, March 24, 2016; Congregation for Divine Worship, "Decree *In Missa in Cena Domini*," January 6, 2016, with accompanying commentary by CDW secretary Archbishop Arthur Roche, "I Give You An Example." See Edward Pentin interview with Archbishop Arthur Roche, "Archbishop Roche: Pope's Foot-washing Change Is a Return to Tradition," *National Catholic Register*, January 29, 2016.

6. Pope Francis and Father Fernando Prado, *La fuerza de la vocación*, 77.

7. Francis, letter to Cardinal Marc Ouellet, president of the Pontifical Commission for Latin America, March 19, 2016; Francis, "A Private Dialogue with the Jesuits in the Baltics," *La Civiltà Cattolica*, October 17, 2018.

8. Sergio Rubin and Francesca Ambrogetti, *Pope Francis: Conversations with Jorge Bergoglio*, trans. Laura Dail Literary Agency (London: Hodder & Stoughton, 2013), ch. 6.

9. Antonio Spadaro, SJ, *Il nuovo mondo di Francesco. Come il Vaticano sta cambiando il mondo* (Venice: Ed. Marsilio, 2018), 12. A "crucial meeting" of fifteen to twenty cardinals hosted by Cardinal Attilio Nicora on March 11, 2013, revealed that Bergoglio could probably count on twenty-five votes on the conclave's first ballot. Francis only knew of this gathering "much later," after his election, according to O'Connell, *The Election of Pope Francis*, 181–83.

10. Antonio Spadaro, SJ, interview with the author in Bogotá, Colombia, September 17, 2016; David Gibson, "Pope Francis Wants 'Absolute Transparency' as He Pushes Vatican Reform," Religion News Service, February 12, 2015.

11. Ermis Sagatta, "Maradiaga spiega la marcia dei disperati verso gli Usa," *La Voce e il Tempo*, November 22, 2018; Joshua McElwee, "Vatican Reorganization Would Be 'Decisive Shift,' Says Cardinal Gracias," *National Catholic Reporter*, October 30, 2018.

12. Francis, "Press Conference During the Return Flight" from Rio de Janeiro, July 23, 2013; Eugenio Scalfari, interview with Pope Francis, "The Pope: How the Church Will Change," *La Repubblica*, October 1, 2013; Cardinal Oscar Rodríguez de Maradiaga, "I Presagi del conclave," in Francesco Antonioli, *Francesco e noi* (Milan: Ed. Piemme, 2017). Francis refers to the C9 as "an advisory group of *outsiders*," using the same language as Cardinal Martini in his 2012 spiritual testament when he called for "twelve people outside the lines" to collaborate with the pope's governance. See Ivereigh, *The Great Reformer*, epilogue.

13. Inés San Martín, "Going Behind the Scenes with the Pope's Sounding Board," *Crux*, September 12, 2016; Alessandro Gisotti, "Mons. Semeraro: Francesco sta riformando la Curia con lo stile dell'ascolto," *Vatican News*, June 23, 2018.

14. Sarah's shenanigans are described by Rita Ferrone, "Cardinal Sarah Does It Again," *Commonweal*, February 27, 2018.

15. Francis, *Imparare a Congedarsi* (Learning to Say Farewell), *Motu Propio*, February 12, 2018; Andrea Tornielli, "'Vatican's Administrative Bodies Need a Change in Mentality,' Says Francis," *Vatican Insider*, May 2, 2014; Congar, *True and False Reform*, 268–69; Carol Glatz, "Pope to Seminarians: Using Church for Personal Ambition Is a 'Plague,'" Catholic News Service, April 3, 2017.

16. Cardinal Gerald C. Lacroix, interview with Gerard O'Connell, "Canadian Cardinal Spent 9 Years in a Colombian War Zone. Now He Serves a New Periphery," *America*, June 21, 2017; Christopher Lamb, "Archbishop of Melbourne on Healing the 'Hurting' Church," *The Tablet*, June 29, 2019.

17. This is a succint version of the breakdown between Bergoglio and the leadership of the Society of Jesus, which is detailed in Ivereigh, *The Great Reformer*, ch. 5. The best source on Bergoglio's Córdoba exile, including Francis's own reflections on that period, is Cámara and Pfaffen, *Aquel Francisco*.

18. John J. Navone, *Triumph Through Failure: A Theology of the Cross* (1984; repr., Eugene, Ore.: Wipf & Stock, 2014), originally published as *La Teologia del Fallimento* (Rome: Paoline, 1978), the version Francis read. He mentions the influence of the book in conversation with Ambrogetti and Rubín, *Pope Francis: Conversations with Jorge Bergoglio*, ch. 6. Navone's comment was made to Daniel Burke, "The Pope's Dark Night of the Soul," CNN.com, September 21, 2015.

19. "Formación permanente y reconciliación," in Bergoglio, *Meditaciones para religiosos*, 82–92. At the end of the 1980 essay he lists the four principles later enumerated in *Evangelii Gaudium*, ch. 4, as Christian principles for reconciling or uniting a body, that is, which avoid the elitist temptations he names here. They are: the whole is greater than the parts, unity is above conflict, reality comes before ideas, and time before space.

20. Pope Francis, "Address for the Presentation of the Christmas Greetings to the Roman Curia," December 21, 2013, and December 22, 2014; *The Spiritual Exercises of Saint Ignatius of Loyola*, trans. Michael Ivens, SJ (Leominster, UK: Gracewing, 2004), nos. 45–61.

21. Martel, *In the Closet of the Vatican*, 388.

22. Ivereigh, "What the Jesuit Pope Told the Jesuit General"; Francis, "Address for the Presentation of the Christmas Greetings to the Roman Curia," December 22, 2014.

23. Spiritual Exercises, nos. 136–148, 315; Francis, "Address for the Presentation of the Christmas Greetings to the Roman Curia," December 21, 2015.

24. Francis, "Address for the Presentation of the Christmas Greetings to the Roman Curia," December 21, 2017.

25. Austen Ivereigh, "Pope Francis Puts His Finger on the Post-Brexit Challenge," *Crux*, June 27, 2016; Francis interview: "El peligro en tiempos de crisis es buscar un salvador que nos devuelva la identidad y nos defienda con muros," *El País*, January 21, 2017.

26. Spadaro, "A Big Heart Open to God"; Massimo Faggioli, "From Collegiality to Synodality"; and "Synodality and Its Perils: Baby Steps Towards a More Representative Church," *La Croix International*, April 3, 2018; International Theological Commission, "Synodality in the Life and Mission of the Church," March 2, 2018, no. 4.

27. On the unique experience of synodality in the Latin American Church, see Silvia Scatena, "Da Medellín ad Aparecida: La lezione di un'esperienza regionale per una ricerca di forme e stili di collegialità effettiva," in Antonio Spadaro and Carlos Galli, eds., *La riforma e le riforme nella Chiesa* (Brescia: Ed. Queriniana, 2016), 248–67. The impact of Bergoglio on Aparecida and vice versa is discussed at length in chapter 6.

28. Francis, "Address for the Ceremony Commemorating the 50th Anniversary of the Institution of the Synod of Bishops," October 17, 2015.

29. The synods on the family are discussed in detail in chapter 9.

30. International Theological Commision, "Synodality in the Life and Mission of the Church," March 2, 2018; Francis, apostolic constitution, *Episcopalis Communio*, September 15, 2018.

31. Pope Francis with Dominique Wolton, *The Path to Change: Thoughts on Politics and Society*, trans. Shaun Whiteside (London: Bluebird, 2018), 22. *Evangelii Gaudium*, nos. 16, 26, 32; *Amoris Laetitia*, no. 3.

32. Gerald O'Collins with John Wilkins, *Lost in Translation: The English Language and the Catholic Mass* (Collegeville, Minn.: Liturgical Press, 2017), vii. O'Collins offers a devastating critique of the 2010 translation, and a compelling case for the rejected 1998 one.

33. Francis, apostolic letter in the form of *motu propio*, *Magnum Principium*, September 9, 2017; Francis, "La lettera del Papa al cardinale Sarah," October 15, 2017; Marx quoted by Christa Pongratz-Lippitt, "German-speaking Bishops Move to Take Full Control over Liturgical Translations," *La Croix International*, October 9, 2017.

34. Austen Ivereigh, "New Paths: What to Expect From October's Amazon Synod," *Commonweal*, June 18, 2019.

35. See Nicolas Senèze, interview with Father Hervé Legrand, "Pope's Decision on German Bishops Document Is in Line with Vatican II," *La Croix International*, June 6, 2018.

36. Francis spelled out this ambition in his "Address for the Presentation of the Christmas Greetings to the Roman Curia," December 22, 2016. It is not true that the Vatican workforce is principally clergy: some three-quarters of the 4,100 staff are laypeople, of whom 700 are women, both lay and religious. But only a tiny number of these have ever occupied senior, executive roles.

37. Elise Harris, "Women Inside and Outside the Vatican Sing the Praises of Pope Francis," *Crux*, March 10, 2019; Francis, letter to Maria Teresa Compte Grau, *Diez cosas que el Papa Francisco propone a las mujeres* (Madrid: Claretianas, 2018), 9; Francis with Wolton, *The Path to Change*, 278–81. Myriam Wijlens, "Women in the Church: A Canonical Perspective," *Osservatore Romano*, January 2, 2017; Pope Francis and Father Fernando Prado, *La fuerza de la vocación*, 77–78.

38. "Pope Francis: Woman Is the Image of the Church That Is Mother," *Vatican News*, February 22, 2019; Gabriella Gambino, interview by Alessandro Gisotti, "Gambino: Alliances Need to Be Created to Face the Abuse Scandal," *Vatican News*, November 30, 2018.

39. Rita Ferrone, "Francis's Words About Women," *Commonweal*, April 5, 2017; and "Better Together: Women, Men and the Diaconate," *Commonweal*, February 20, 2019.

40. "Pope Francis: The Church, like Mary, is woman and mother," homily, *Vatican News*, May 21, 2018; Congregation for Divine Worship, "Decree on the Celebration of the Blessed Virgin Mary, Mother of the Church in the General Roman Calendar," February 11, 2018.

41. Francis, letter to Compte Grau, *Diez cosas*, 9; Francis with Wolton, *The Path to Change*, 278–81. Wijlens, "Women in the Church: A Canonical Perspective"; Francis and Prado, *La fuerza de la vocación*, 77–78. The working document of the Amazon synod of October 2019 seeks to identify "official ministries" that can be done by women while calling for the Church to "recover the space that Jesus gave women." On the women deacons' report: Paul Moses, "Blessed, But Also Ordained," *Commonweal*, January 18, 2019. The historical evidence is solid that women were ordained, alongside men, by bishops, in order to carry out certain functions such as preaching and burying the dead, and that the diaconate

disappeared over time as the Church became clericalized, to the point where, by the twelfth century, a deacon was purely a stage toward priesthood. The Second Vatican Council restored the so-called permanent diaconate but only for men. Nowadays there are 43,000 permanent deacons in the Church, all men and mostly married, whose functions involve marrying and baptizing, preaching, and managing parishes. See "Witness" interview with Phyllis Zagano by Father Thomas Rosica, Salt & Light Media, June 18, 2017; Cindy Wooden, "Pope Says Study on Women Deacons Was Inconclusive," Catholic News Service, May 7, 2019.

42. Francis, letter to Cardinal Marc Ouellet, president of the Pontifical Commission for Latin America, March 19, 2016; Statutes of the Dicastery for Laity, Family and Life at www.laityfamilylife.va; Cardinal Farrell, interview with the author, December 13, 2017. On lack of lay participation, see Chris Lowney, "Fix a Disconnect That Hobbles the Church," *Crux*, April 5, 2017.

43. Junno Arocho Esteves, "Pope Names Members for Renewed Pontifical Academy for Life," Catholic News Service, June 13, 2017. Background: John Allen, "On Condoms, Has the Vatican Rejected the Pharisees?," *National Catholic Reporter*, December 23, 2010; Sandro Magister, "Pontifical Academy of Nonstop Fighting," *Chiesa*, February 20, 2010.

44. Ferruccio de Bortoli, interview with Pope Francis, *Corriere della Sera*, March 5, 2014; Austen Ivereigh, "Academy for Life No Longer an 'Enclave of the Ideologically Pure,'" *Crux*, June 10, 2017; and Francis, letter to the president of the Pontifical Academy for Life, "The Human Community," January 6, 2019.

45. John Gehring, interview with Sister Helen Prejean, "What Francis Did Is Just Huge," *Commonweal*, August 7, 2018; Junno Arocho Esteves, "Death Penalty Is Fruit of Laws Lacking Humanity, Mercy, Pope Says," Catholic News Service, December 17, 2018.

46. Francis, "Statutes of the Dicastery for Promoting Integral Human Development," August 17, 2016.

47. Carol Glatz, "Curia Reforms Put Priority on Evangelization, Synodality, Cardinals Say," Catholic News Service, April 23, 2019.

five

1. Andrew Sullivan, "Cleansing the Catholic Church of Its Sins," *The Intelligencer*, August 17, 2018.

2. For a superbly detailed critical analysis of Pennsylvania's findings, see Peter Steinfels, "The PA Grand-Jury Report: Not What It Seems," *Commonweal*, March 21, 2019.

3. The role of the arbitration and mediation program set up by Kenneth Feinberg at Dolan's request in 2016 in the McCarrick case was revealed by Paul Elie, "What Do the Church's Victims Deserve?," *New Yorker*, April 8, 2019.

4. See, especially, Laurie Goodstein, "He Preyed on Men Who Wanted to Be Priests. Then He Became a Cardinal," *New York Times*, July 16, 2018; and Boniface Ramsey, "The Case of Theodore McCarrick: A Failure of Fraternal Correction," *Commonweal*, February 16, 2019.

5. Jason Horowitz, Elizabeth Dias, and Laurie Goodstein, "Pope Accepts Wuerl's Resignation as Washington Archbishop, but Calls Him a Model Bishop," *New York Times*, October 12, 2018.

6. Juan Paulo Iglesias, "El papa en Chile: Una visita que dejó gusto amargo," *Infobae*, January 20, 2018.

7. He revealed his regular meetings with abuse victims in conversation with the Jesuits in Lima, Peru, on January 16, 2018, published as "'Where Have Our People Been Creative?' Conversations with Jesuits in Chile and Peru," *La Civiltà Cattolica*, February 15, 2018. "On Fridays—sometimes this is known and sometimes it is not known—I usually meet with some of them," he said. Greg Burke, the director of the Holy See Press Office, later confirmed that Francis meets with survivors "several times a month," either with individuals or in groups, always in the "strictest confidence."

8. Francis, "Discours du Pape François aux prêtres du diocèse de Créteil (France)," October 1, 2018.

9. Raphael Minder, "In Spanish Abuse Scandal, a More Open Vatican," *New York Times*, February 14, 2015.

10. "El exmonaguillo español que denunció abusos al Papa: 'Sufrí temblores y ataques de ansiedad,'" *El País*, September 13, 2018; Francis, "Press conference on the return flight from Dublin to Rome," August 26, 2018.

11. See my interview with Barros: Austen Ivereigh, "Controversial Bishops in Chile Deny Abuse Cover-up," *Crux*, January 17, 2018; Juan Carlos Cruz Chellew, James Hamilton Sánchez, and José

Andrés Murillo Urrutia, "Our Statement Regarding the Appointment of Bishop Barros and the Responsibility of Pope Francis," *Crux*, March 19, 2015; Philip Pullella, Interview with Pope Francis for Reuters, June 20, 2018, the full version of which was shared with the author. The Santiago archdiocese was ordered to pay "moral damages" to the three victims in early 2019 to the tune of $150,000 each, after the court found that "negligence by the Catholic Church had a great impact on the victims when institutional authorities dismissed the allegations instead of considering the possibility of investigating if there was an element of truth." Inés San Martín, "Chile Court Orders Church to Compensate Clerical Abuse Victims," *Crux*, March 27, 2019.

12. The others were Fathers Ariel Busso and Daniel Medina. See Juan Carlos Claret, "La crisis de la Iglesia chilena (I)," *Religión Digital*, December 4, 2017. The closeness of Busso to Francis has been separately confirmed to me.

13. Ivereigh, "Controversial Bishops in Chile."

14. After Collins resigned in March 2017 in frustration at what she called the "shameful lack of cooperation" from the Congregation for the Doctrine of the Faith in particular, she cited in various interviews its refusal of a commission request that all dicasteries respond directly to correspondence from abuse victims and its failure to distribute the commission's template for safeguarding guidelines to national bishops' conferences. In the first case, the CDF had objected that abuse victims should have primary contact with the dioceses. In the second, according to a senior Vatican official, the commission's guidelines were intended as a resource and were advisory, and the Pontifical Commission for the Protection of Minors never asked for the template to be sent.

15. Although the CDF takes responsibility for deciding how each case is handled, the process of investigation and trial is usually handled in a local tribunal. There are many reasons for the different sentences (laicization versus prayer and penance), not just the gravity of the offense.

16. Andrea Gagliarducci, "Pope Francis Completes New Vatican Office to Tackle Clergy Abuse," Catholic News Agency, January 23, 2015. The pope's remarks on clemency appeals were made during the "Press Conference on the Return Flight from Lima to Rome," January 21, 2018.

17. Cardinal O'Malley interview with the author, Casa Santa Marta, Rome, June 27, 2017; "Abuse-Enabling Bishops Who Resigned or Were Removed," at www.bishop-accountability.org, which notes that "in all cases, the disgraced prelate retained the title of bishop and remained active in the church." See also John Allen, "Catholic Bishop of Kansas City Convicted of Failure to Report Child Abuse Resigns," *Crux*, April 21, 2015; Mitch Smith and Laurie Goodstein, "2 Bishops Resign in Minnesota over Sexual Abuse Scandal," *New York Times*, June 15, 2015.

18. No one in the Vatican knows who was responsible for it going out. "It would have come from the Secretariat of State but they wouldn't have put it out unless the pope had asked for it," one official told me.

19. Archbishop Charles Scicluna, interview with the author, Oxford, November 16, 2018; Francis, apostolic letter issued *motu proprio*, "Come una madre amorevole" (Like a Loving Mother), June 4, 2016. A bishop was negligent if he had "objectively failed in a very serious manner to the diligence that is required by his pastoral office, even if not by a serious moral fault of his own." Robert W. Oliver, "Commento alla Letter Apostolica in forma di motu proprio *Come una madre amorevole*," *Monitor Ecclesiasticus* 131 (2016): 175–83.

20. O'Malley, interview with the author, Rome, June 27, 2017. For different accounts of what happened between the tribunal announcement and "Like a Loving Mother," see Nicole Winfield, "Pope's Abuse Accountability Tribunal Going Nowhere Fast," Associated Press, March 9, 2016; and "Pope Scraps Abuse Tribunal for Negligent Bishops," Associated Press, June 4, 2016; Carol Glatz, "Vatican Maze: Retracing the Path of Abuse Accountability Proposals," Catholic News Service, March 16, 2017; and Austen Ivereigh, "The Mysterious Case of the Missing Vatican Tribunal," *Crux*, March 8, 2017.

21. Saunders often shared with others (including me) his feeling of that pressure.

22. Austen Ivereigh, "Saunders Accusation Highlights Need to Tighten Abuse Commission Brief," CV Comment, *Catholic Voices*, June 1, 2015; "Saunders-Pell: Vatican Statements and CV Comment," *Catholic Voices*, June 3, 2015.

23. John Allen, "Marie Collins, Member of Pope's Sexual Abuse Panel, Criticizes His Response to Chile Scandal," *Crux*, October 5, 2015; Nicole Winfield, "Pope's Sex Abuse Commission Alarmed by Bishop Appointment," Associated Press, March 26, 2015; Austen Ivereigh, "Controversial Chilean Bishop's Appointment Continues to Divide Diocese," *National Catholic Reporter*, July 7, 2015; Joshua

McElwee, "Members of Vatican Abuse Commission Question Francis' Inaction in Chile," *National Catholic Reporter*, March 26, 2015; Philip Pullella, "Papal Sex Abuse Commission Members Meet over Chilean Bishop," Reuters, April 13, 2015.

24. John Allen, "Jesuit 'Man on a Mission' Sees Change Happening on Sexual Abuse," *Crux*, March 29, 2018; and "Quiet Progress of Pope's Anti-Abuse Commission a Hard Sell," *Crux*, February 18, 2018. PCM figures supplied by Monsignor Robert Oliver to *Catholic Voices*, Rome, April 23, 2018.

25. Juan Carlos Claret, "La crisis de la Iglesia chilena (y III)," *Religión Digital*, December 11, 2017. Author's translation.

26. The letter, dated February 22, 2018, was sent to various presidents of Latin American bishops' conferences. Joshua McElwee, "Cardinal Blames Barros Interviews for Bad Press During Pope's Chile Visit," *National Catholic Reporter*, March 9, 2018.

27. Francis, "'Where Have Our People Been Creative?'" The prologue was to *Las cartas de la tribulación* (Buenos Aires: Diego de Torres, 1987), a collection of letters written to the Jesuits by two of their superiors general, Lorenzo Ricci and Jan Roothaan, during the forty-one-year suppression of the order, 1773–1814. They are republished with extra material as Jorge Mario Bergoglio/Francisco, *Las cartas de la tribulación*, ed. Antonio Spadaro and Diego Fares (Barcelona: Herder, 2019).

28. Nicole Winfield, "Pope Shocks Chile by Accusing Sex Abuse Victims of Slander," Associated Press, January 19, 2018; Philip Pullella and Caroline Stauffer, "Key Cardinal Rebukes Pope over Abuse Comment in Rare Move," Reuters, January 20, 2018.

29. Francis spoke of his feelings after Chile to Philip Pullella (interview, Reuters, June 18, 2018) and to Andrés Murillo, as reported by Luis Badilla and Francesco Gagliano, "A sei mesi dal viaggio di Francesco in Cile. Come il Papa ha scoperto di essere stato usato da chi invece doveva aiutarlo nella preparazione della Visita," *Il Sismografo*, July 6, 2018.

30. Bergoglio, "Sobre la acusación de sí mismo," in *Reflexiones espirituales sobre la vida apostólica* (Buenos Aires: Diego de Torres, 1987; Bilbao: Mensajero, 2013), 118–26.

31. Philip Pullella, "Sexual Abuse Silence Deadly for Church: Vatican Official," Reuters, February 8, 2012.

32. Archbishop Scicluna, interview with the author, Oxford, November 16, 2018.

33. The summary of the Scicluna report is contained in the long footnote 24 of Francis, "Carta a los obispos de Chile," May 15, 2018, leaked at the time to a Chilean TV station and published in Bergoglio/Francisco, *Las cartas de la tribulación*. Almost eighty clergy in Chile had been publicly accused of sexually abusing minors since 2000; the Scicluna report suggested that number could be just the tip of the iceberg.

34. Francis, "Carta a los obispos de Chile," April 8, 2018, in Bergoglio/Francis, *Las cartas de la tribulación*.

35. See report on the three victims' press conference in *El Mercurio*, May 3, 2018; Cruz interview with Carlos Cué, "El Papa me pidió perdón, está espantado con los abusos, esto es un tsunami," *El País*, May 19, 2018; and Rosa de Alcolea, "Interview: Juan Carlos Cruz, Key Figure to Undertake the Path of Renewal in the Church in Chile," *Zenit*, March 7, 2019.

36. Francis, "Carta a los obispos de Chile," May 15, 2018, in Bergoglio/Francisco, *Las cartas de la tribulación*.

37. Jorge M. Bergoglio, prologue, *Las cartas de la tribulación*, 4; and Austen Ivereigh, "Discernment in a Time of Tribulation: Pope Francis and the Church in Chile," *Thinking Faith*, May 8, 2018.

38. John Allen, "Ex-Chancellor's Arrest Spotlights Big Picture in Chile Abuse Crisis," *Crux*, July 15, 2018. See also Inés San Martín, "On Chile, Pope Francis Is Way Past the Tip of the Iceberg Now," *Crux*, June 4, 2018; "Chilean Catholic Church Suspends 14 Priests over 'Improper Conduct,'" Reuters, May 23, 2018; and statement at the end of bishops' meeting with Francis by Mons Santiago Silva, president of the Chilean bishops' conference: "Editorial: Tiempo de diálogo y renovación," www.iglesia.cl, May 21, 2018.

39. Francis, "Carta al pueblo de Dios que peregrina en Chile," May 31, 2018, in Bergoglio/Francisco, *Las cartas de la tribulación*.

40. Juan Carlos Claret Pool, "Ante la remoción del obispo Barros," statement to media, June 11, 2018.

41. Royal Commission into Institutional Responses to Child Sexual Abuse, *Preface & Executive Summary*, 2017, 5, 67; Hans Zollner, "The Spiritual Wounds of Sexual Abuse," *La Civiltà Cattolica*, January 18, 2018.

42. Andrea Tornielli, "Abusi, Zollner: 'Le leggi non bastano se non cambia la mentalità,'" *Vatican Insider*, August 17, 2018.

43. "Bishop Robert C. Morlino's letter to the faithful regarding the ongoing sexual abuse crisis in the Church," August 18, 2018, published on the diocese of Madison website.

44. Francis, "Letter of His Holiness Pope Francis to the People of God," August 20, 2018. A superb reading of this is by James Hanvey, SJ, "The Spirit and the Letter," *Thinking Faith*, August 24, 2018.

45. "Bishop Barron Q&A About the Sexual Abuse Crisis," August 27, 2018, and "Why Remain Catholic? (With So Much Scandal)," August 29, 2018, both on Bishop Robert Barron's YouTube channel.

46. Carlo Maria Viganò, "Testimony," https://www.documentcloud.org/documents/4786599-Testimony -by-Archbishop-Carlo-Maria-Vigan%C3%B2.html. He claimed that in making reference to the John Jay College of Criminal Justice reports of 2004 and 2011, Cardinal Blase Cupich of Chicago "candidly ignored" its findings that 80 percent of victims were male. But Viganò in turn candidly ignored the same study's findings that being gay is not a risk factor in abuse. Despite the preponderance of male victims, the Australian Royal Commission into Institutional Responses to Child Sexual Abuse said it was "a misconception that all perpetrators who sexually abuse children of the same gender as them are same-sex attracted," 68.

47. Archbishop Eamon Martin of Armagh, "Irish Primate Says Viganò 'Hijacked' World Meeting of Families," *Crux*, October 22, 2018.

48. See Ivereigh, *The Great Reformer*, ch. 4. The literature on Bergoglio's discreet assistance to dozens of people is growing: to Nello Scavo, *La lista de Bergoglio: Los salvados por Francisco durante la dictadura* (Madrid: Ed. Claretiana, 2013) can be added Aldo Duzdevich, *Salvados por Francisco: Cómo un joven sacerdote se arriesgó para ayudar a perseguidos por la dictadura* (Buenos Aires: Ediciones B, 2019).

49. Bergoglio, "Silencio y Palabra," in *Reflexiones en Esperanza* (Buenos Aires: Ediciones Universidad del Salvador, 1992), quotes here translated by the author. The article is analyzed by Diego Fares, SJ, "Against the Spirit of Fierceness," *La Civiltà Cattolica*, September 1, 2018. See also Austen Ivereigh, "A Time to Keep Silence," *Thinking Faith*, August 30, 2018. On Francis's silence in the face of attacks, see Diego Fares, SJ, and Austen Ivereigh, "How to Communicate in a Polarized Society," *La Civiltà Cattolica* (English edition), Issue 1903, March 11, 2019.

50. The most comprehensive account and background to Operation Viganò is Andrea Tornielli and Gianni Valente, *Il giorno del giudizio* (Milan: Edizioni Piemme, 2018). Francis told Alazraki in May 2019 that he had "no idea" about the (pre-2018) McCarrick allegations, and had no recollection of Viganò telling him in July 2013, as the former nuncio claimed. See transcript of interview: "En Primicia el Papa en Televisa," *Vatican News*, May 28, 2019.

51. Michael Sean Winters, "Has the 'EWTN Schism' Begun?," *National Catholic Reporter*, August 31, 2018; and Massimo Faggioli, "Flirting with Schism," *La Croix International*, September 15, 2018.

52. Christopher White, "Wealthy Catholics to Target Cardinals with 'Red Hat Report,'" *Crux*, October 1, 2018; Heidi Schlumpf, "At 'Authentic Reform,' Conservative Catholics Rally to 'Fix' Church Failures," *National Catholic Reporter*, October 5, 2018; John Paul II, apostolic constitution, *Universi Domini Gregis* (on the vacancy of the apostolic see and the election of the Roman pontiff), February 22, 1996, no. 80.

53. Cindy Wooden, "Former Nuncio Now Says Sanctions Against McCarrick Were Private," Catholic News Service, September 1, 2018; and "Cardinal Ouellet Responds to Archbishop Vigano on McCarrick Case," Catholic News Service, October 7, 2018; Edward Pentin, "Archbishop Viganò Responds to Cardinal Ouellet's Letter with New Testimony," *National Catholic Register*, October 19, 2018.

54. Interview with Father Frédéric Fornos by Andrés Beltramo Álvarez, "Abusos, ataques y lucha de poder. 'Contra el demonio sólo basta la oración,'" *Vatican Insider*, October 5, 2018.

55. Nicole Winfield, "Vatican Letter Undermines U.S. Cardinal on Abuse," Associated Press, January 1, 2019, which quotes sections of the letter. I have seen the whole letter from Cardinal Ouellet to Cardinal DiNardo, dated November 11 and marked "Personal and Strictly Confidential." Ouellet refers in it as follows to his earlier correspondence: "Therefore, after having studied carefully the contents of the proposed documents and after having consulted with the Secretariat of State, I must insist on the request I made to Your Eminence in my November 6 letter, that at this time the USCCB not vote or reach any definitive decision concerning the proposals outlined in the documents."

56. Julie Zauzmer and Michelle Boorstein, "Vatican Tells Bishops Not to Vote on Proposals to Tackle Sexual Abuse, Spurns Lay Investigations," *Washington Post*, November 12, 2018.

57. Address of H. E. Archbishop Christophe Pierre, apostolic nuncio, to the USCCB, November 12, 2018; Pope Francis, "In-flight press conference from Rabat," March 31, 2019.

58. Francis, "Letter sent by the Holy Father to the Bishops of the United States Conference of Catholic Bishops," January 1, 2019.

six

1. On the experience of the Jesuits' parish mission, see Ivereigh, *The Great Reformer*, ch. 5; Father Rafael Velasco, SJ, interview with the author, July 27, 2018.

2. This recollection comes from an interview with Father Spadaro, in Spadaro, ed., *En tus ojos está mi palabra*, 21–22.

3. Jorge Mario Bergoglio, Prólogo, in Bergoglio et al., *Dios en la ciudad: Primer Congreso Pastoral Urbana Región Buenos Aires* (Buenos Aires: San Pablo, 2012), 5.

4. Francis, Foreword, *Discovering Pope Francis: The Roots of Jorge Mario Bergoglio's Thinking*, Brian Y. Lee and Rev. Thomas L. Knoebel, eds. (Collegeville, Minn.: Liturgical Press, 2019), xiii.

5. Quoted in Borghesi, *The Mind of Pope Francis*, 163. Monsignor Claude Dagens distinguishes between *la stratégie de l'accommodement*, in which he includes various forms of coping and resistance, and *la stratégie du dépassement* to which he sees Pope Francis calling the Church. "L'indifférence peut nous réveiller. Entretien avec Claude Dagens," *Le Débat*, no. 181 (September–October 2014). On the "strategies of resistance," see Rod Dreher, *The Benedict Option: A Strategy for Christians in a Post-Christian Nation* (New York: Sentinel, 2017); and a critique by Andreas Gonçalves Lind, "Qual è il compito dei cristiani nella società di oggi? 'Opzione Benedetto' ed eresia donatista," *La Civiltà Cattolica*, January 20, 2018, 105–15. See Rod Dreher's critique of Francis's vision, which he sees as "total dissolution of Christianity in liquid modernity," in "The 'Francis Option' Fantasy," *American Conservative*, October 29, 2018, in response to Austen Ivereigh, "To Discern and Reform: The 'Francis Option' for Evangelizing a World in Flux," *Thinking Faith*, October 24, 2018.

6. *Evangelii Gaudium*, nos. 71–75. The PUBA papers are in two books: Jorge Mario Bergoglio et al., *Dios en la ciudad*; and PUBA, *Aportes para una reflexión pastoral de las parroquias urbanas* (Buenos Aires: 2013). I am grateful to Virginia Bonard for access to the latter, which is also available at Scribd .com.

7. Francis, "Address to the Leadership of the Episcopal Conferences of Latin America During the General Coordination Meeting," Rio de Janeiro, July 28, 2013.

8. Bishop Juan Carlos Ares, interview with the author, Buenos Aires, August 1, 2018; Jorge Mario Bergoglio, "Palabras iniciales en el Primer Congreso," in *Dios en la ciudad*, 9–22.

9. The term *"charisme des sourciers"* is from Christoph Théobald, SJ, *Urgences pastorales du moment présent* (Paris: Bayard, 2017), 317.

10. Francis, "Address for the Meeting with the Executive Committee of CELAM," Apostolic Nunciature, Bogotá, Colombia, September 7, 2017.

11. Archbishop Edmundo Abastoflor, interview with the author, La Paz, Bolivia, April 21, 2016.

12. Borghesi, *The Mind of Pope Francis*, 300; Bergoglio/Francis reflections on Aparecida in interview with Stefania Felasca, "Lo que hubiera dicho en el consistorio,"*30 Días*, November 2007; and Francis, "Address to the Leadership of the Episcopal Conferences of Latin America During the General Coordination Meeting." On Aparecida as an "authentically synodal" process, see Diego Fares, "A 10 anni da Aparecida: Alle fonti del pontificato di Francesco," *La Civiltà Cattolica*, May 20, 2017.

13. Bergoglio "Homily," shrine of Aparecida, May 16, 2007; and "Letter to Catechists," August 21, 2007, both in A. Spadaro, ed., *En tus ojos está mi palabra*, 673–74, 692. On the pre-conclave address, see Ivereigh, *The Great Reformer*, ch. 9.

14. Ivereigh, "To Discern and Reform," 9–24.

15. The Latin American group was reported on by John Allen, "Synod Notebook: Catechists and 'Pastoral Conversion,'" *National Catholic Reporter*, October 23, 2012.

16. Bergoglio, "Religiosidad popular como inculturación de la fe en el espíritu de Aparecida," January 19, 2008, in Spadaro, ed., *En tus ojos está mi palabra*, 705.

17. Bergoglio, "Ponencia en la 5a conferencia," in Spadaro, ed., *En tus ojos está mi palabra*, 660–71; Documento de Aparecida, nos. 367, 370; Francis, "Homily, Holy Mass at Campo Grande," Ñu Guazú, Asunción, Paraguay, July 12, 2015; Bergoglio, address to urban pastoral meeting (PUBA), September 2, 2013, quoted in Diego Fares, *Papa Francisco: La cultura del encuentro* (Buenos Aires: Edhasa, 2014), 53; Francis, "'I Believe the Lord Wants a Change in the Church': A Private Dialogue with the Jesuits in the Baltics," *La Civiltà Cattolica*, October 17, 2018.

18. What he told the Latin American bishops was reported to me by Archbishop Abastoflor, interview with the author, La Paz, Bolivia, April 21, 2016. The synods of October 2018 and October 2019 have been on the topic of young people and vocation discernment (Documento de Aparecida, no. 446) and the Amazon (Documento de Aparecida, nos. 83–860).

19. Bergoglio, *Nosotros como ciudadanos, nosotros como pueblo. Hacia un bientenario en justicia y solidaridad, 2010–2016* (Buenos Aires: Ed. Claretiana, 2014), 42.

20. On the emergence of the "culture of encounter" in Bergoglio's thinking around 1999, see Fares, *Papa Francisco: La cultura del encuentro*, 45–49.

21. Borghesi, *Mind of Pope Francis*, 228–29 ; *Deus Caritas Est*, encyclical, Benedict XVI, December 25, 2005, no. 1; Documento de Aparecida, no. 243; Francis, *Evangelii Gaudium*, no. 7.

22. Professor Rodrigo Guerra López, interview with the author, Milwaukee, October 13, 2018. This chapter is indebted to his paper for a symposium at Sacred Heart Seminary, Milwaukee, at which we both spoke in October 2018. Rodrigo Guerra, "An Encounter That Becomes Method: The Influence of Hans Urs von Balthasar and Luigi Giussani in the Theology of the post–Vatican II Popes," in Brian Y. Lee and Rev. Thomas L. Knoebel, eds., *Discovering Pope Francis: The Roots of Jorge Mario Bergoglio's Thinking* (Collegeville, Minn.: Liturgical Press, 2019).

23. Cardinal (then archbishop) Carlos Aguiar Retes, interview with the author, Tlalneplantla, Mexico, January 28, 2016.

24. On the 2012 retreat, see Ivereigh, *The Great Reformer* ch. 8. His 2001 speech is quoted in Alberto Savorana, *Luigi Giussani: Su vida* (Madrid: Ediciones Encuentro, 2015), 1126.

25. Stefania Falasca, "Intervista con il cardenale Jorge Mario Bergoglio," *30 Giorni*, November 2007; Cardinal Donald Wuerl, interview with the author, Rome, September 19, 2017.

26. This story was told by Francis's sister, María Elena Bergoglio, in Deborah Castellano Lubov, *The Other Francis: 14 Interviews with Those Closest to Him* (Leominster, UK: Gracewing, 2018), 6. Benedict said he didn't anticipate Bergoglio's election but had foreseen it would be a Latin American pope, in Benedict XVI, with Peter Seewald, *Last Testament: In His Own Words* (London: Bloomsbury, 2016). Cardinal (then archbishop) Carlos Aguiar Retes, interview with the author, Tlalneplantla, Mexico, January 28, 2016.

27. See www.charis.international. On the pope's "renewal of the Renewal" see Austen Ivereigh, "Is Francis Our First Charismatic Pope?," *America*, June 14, 2019.

28. *Evangelii Gaudium*, no. 280.

29. "Pope Francis: Friday Mass in Santa Marta," Vatican Radio, February 21, 2014.

30. Karl Rahner, "Ideology and Christianity," in *Theological Investigations, Volume 6: Concerning Vatican Council II* (London: Darton, Longman and Todd, 1969), 43–58. Bergoglio, "Enseñemos a no tener miedo a buscar la verdad," in Spadaro, ed., *En tus ojos está mi palabra*, 759.

31. *Evangelii Gaudium*, nos. 34–36, 38–40, 94–95.

32. *Evangelii Gaudium*, nos. 165, 268–74.

33. Francis, "Address . . . to the Italian Episcopal Conference," May 16, 2016.

34. Darío López Capera, "Después que fue electo papa, es otro ser humano," *Nuestra Voz*, February 26, 2018. Paredes discussed the transformation with me in an interview in New York, February 8, 2019.

35. Spadaro, ed., *En tus ojos está mi palabra*, 23.

36. Francis made the remarks to Father Prado, *La fuerza de la vocación*, 81–82, author's translation. Cindy Wooden, "For Vocations, One Must Go Out, Listen, Call, Pope Says," Catholic News Service, October 21, 2016; Andrea Tornielli, "The Pope's Words on Celibacy and the 'Salus Animarum' Criteria," *Vatican Insider*, March 9, 2017; Salvatore Cernuzio, "Il Papa: 'Se c'è il dubbio di omosessualità, meglio non far entrare in seminario,'" *Vatican Insider*, May 25, 2018. The Vatican's guidelines on priestly formation revised in December 2016 repeated earlier 2005 stipulations that the Church should refuse "those who practise homosexuality, present deeply rooted homosexual tendencies, or are part of the so-called gay culture" (*Ratio Fundamentalis*, no. 199). On the "double life" of promiscuously homosexual yet rigidly homophobic prelates, see Martel, *In the Closet of the Vatican*.

37. For a critical response, see Kevin Clarke, "Understanding Pope Francis' Controversial Remarks on Homosexuality in the Priesthood," *America*, December 5, 2018. On the "ecclesiastical closet," a place of denial and doublethink tied up with clericalism, see James Alison, "Homosexuality Among the Clergy: Caught in a Trap of Dishonesty," *The Tablet* (August 1, 2018); and Andrew Sullivan, "The Gay Church," *Intelligencer*, January 21, 2019.

38. Antonio Spadaro, SJ, "'Wake Up the World! Conversation with Pope Francis About the Religious Life," *La Civiltà Cattolica*, January 3, 2014; Antonio Spadaro, "At the Crossroads of History: Pope Francis' Conversations with the Jesuits in Myanmar and Bangladesh," *La Civiltà Cattolica*, December 14, 2017; Francis, "Address to the Newly Appointed Bishops," September 16, 2016.

39. Congregation for the Clergy, *Ratio Fundamentalis Institutionis Sacerdotalis* (The Gift of the Priestly Vocation), December 8, 2016.

40. Francis, "Address to the General Assembly of the Italian Bishops Conference," May 21, 2018; *Die Zeit* interview reported by Inés San Martín, "Pope Francis: 'I do not see Cardinal Burke as an enemy,'" *Crux*, March 8, 2017. Despite the worldwide Catholic population doubling between 1970 and 2014 from 654 million to 1.23 billion, the number of priests declined from 420,000 to 414,000. The collapse was especially dramatic in Western countries: while the number of Catholics in the United States connected to a parish has risen over the past half-century from 46 million to 67 million, its number of priests has fallen from 59,000 to 38,000. In France, where levels of clergy have fallen from 29,000 in 1995 to about 15,000, about 800 priests die every year, while 100 are ordained. The place with the most dramatic gap between priests and faithful, however, remains the developing world: in Brazil, the world's largest country, just 18,000 priests serve 140 million Catholics. See Erasmus, "Fewer and Lonelier: Why the Celibate Priesthood Is in Crisis," *Economist*, January 22, 2017.

41. Francis, "Press Conference on the Return Flight from Panama to Rome," January 27, 2019.

42. *Die Zeit* interview reported by Inés San Martín, "Pope Francis: 'I do not see Cardinal Burke as an enemy'"; Christa Pongratz-Lippitt interview with Xingú's bishop Erwin Kräutler: "Pope Says Married Men Could Be Ordained, if World's Bishops Agree," *The Tablet*, April 10, 2014; Rafael Marcoccia interview with Cardinal Claudio Hummes, "Amazonas: Un laboratorio para decisiones audaces," *Tierras de América*, December 3, 2016; Cindy Wooden, "Serving Isolated Parishes May Mean Ordaining Married Men, Cardinal Says," Catholic News Service, January 22, 2018. For a systematic treatment of the question, see Antonio José de Almeida, *Procuram-se Padres: Centralidade da Eucaristia e escassez de clero* (São Paulo: Paulinas, 2018).

43. Francis, letter to young people on the occasion of the presentation of preparatory document for Synod 2018, January 13, 2017.

44. Synod on Young People, the Faith, and Vocational Discernment, October 3–28, 2018: "Preparatory Document" and "Final Document."

45. *Evangelii Gaudium*, nos. 20, 26, 30, 36, 40, 43, 44.

46. *Evangelii Gaudium*, nos. 169–173. Francis called for Jesuits to undertake this teaching in his meeting with them in Kraków, Poland, July 30, 2016. See Antonio Spadaro, SJ, transcript, *La Civiltà Cattolica*, September 10, 2016. He repeated his call a few months later in Rome. "Dialogue of Pope Francis with the Jesuits Gathered in the 36th General Congregation," October 24, 2016, published by *La Civiltà Cattolica*.

47. Christa Pongratz-Lippitt, "Missionary Bishop in Peru Says Pope Francis Has Caused Sea Change in Church," *La Croix International*, December 19, 2017.

48. Francis, "Address to a Meeting of the Congregation for Bishops," February 27, 2014; "Audiencia a los participantes en un encuentro de Representantes Pontificios," September 27, 2016.

49. John Paul II, "To the bishops of the United States of America," Chicago, October 5, 1979; Francis, "Meeting with the Bishops of the United States of America," St. Matthew's Cathedral, Washington, D.C., September 23, 2015; Francis, "Meeting with the Bishops of Mexico," Mexico City, February 13, 2016; Francis, "Address to the Meeting with the Colombian Bishops," Cardinal's Palace, Bogotá, September 7, 2017.

50. Donald Wuerl, interview with Joshua McElwee, "Cardinal Wuerl: Amoris Laetitia Is 'Consensus Document,' Rooted in Tradition," *National Catholic Reporter*, October 4, 2016; Francis, "Discurso a los participantes en las Jornadas dedicadas a los Representantes Pontificios," June 21, 2013.

51. Francis, "Audiencia a los participantes en el congreso para los obispos de nuevo nombramiento," September 19, 2013.

52. Francis, "Address to a Meeting of the Congregation of Bishops," February 27, 2014; "Pope Francis Warns Prelates Not to Be 'Airport Bishops,'" Agence France-Presse, September 23, 2013.

53. Francis, "Address to a Meeting with the Executive Committee of CELAM," Bogotá, Colombia, September 7, 2017.

54. John Allen, "Pope's Move in Milan Confirms That a 'Francis Bishop' Doesn't Have to Mean Rupture," *Crux*, July 7, 2017.

55. Rouco speech: "Resumen intervención Sínodo Nueva Evangelización cardenal Antonio María Rouco Varela, arzobispo de Madrid y presidente de la CEE," Revistaecclesia.com, October 15, 2012.

56. Juan G. Bedoya, "El papa Francisco está armando la que había que armar," El País, December 29, 2014.

57. Austen Ivereigh, profile of Cardinal Omella, "Barcelona's New Cardinal Is a Non-peripheral Pastor to the Poor," Crux, June 28, 2017.

58. José Lorenzo, "Conversión de los obispos españoles," Vida Nueva, March 18, 2016; Iglesia en misión al servicio de nuestro pueblo, Plan Pastoral 2016–2020, CVI Asamblea Plenaria de la Conferencia Episcopal Española, November 16–20, 2015; Simposio Homenaje a Pablo VI, October 14–15, 2016, both at www.conferenciaepiscopal.es.

59. Archbishop of Paris's letter to priests on archdiocesan website: "Lettre de rentrée de Mgr Michel Aupetit aux prêtres, diacres, salariés et bénévoles du diocèse de Paris," September 3, 2018.

60. Mensaje del Cardinal Carlos Aguiar Retes a la Arquidiócesis de México, Tlalnepantla de Corpus Christi, December 11, 2017; Conferencia del Episcopado Mexicano (CEM), Hacia el encuentro de Jesucristo Redentor, bajo la mirada amorosa de Santa María de Guadalupe (May 2018).

61. The fact that in 2007 Cipriani and José Antonio Eguren, then archbishop of Piura, Peru, did not vote for Aparecida was an open secret at the time (there was also one abstention). According to one Argentine participant at Aparecida, Cipriani exclaimed: "Enough of this 'option for the poor!' Are we going to go out of here and create popular kitchens everywhere?" See "El Obispo Caído: Falla Y Cruz," Caretas, September 26, 2013, and "La gira del papa verde," Caretas, July 2015.

62. "Cipriani: Nombramiento de Castillo Mattasoglio tiene una dimensión más profunda," America TV Noticias, January 25, 2019; Francis McDonagh, "New Archbishop of Lima Calls Diocese to Journey to Poor," The Tablet, March 4, 2019; Alfredo Quintanilla, "Por una Iglesia cercana y amiga," Noticias SER.PE, March 6, 2019.

63. Fernando Altmeyer, "Situação numérica da Igreja Católico-Romana e o Papa Francisco," www.leonardoboff.wordpress.com, March 2, 2019.

64. Spadaro, "At the Crossroads of History: Pope Francis' Conversations with the Jesuits in Myanmar and Bangladesh." On Podetti's influence on Bergoglio, see Borghesi, The Mind of Pope Francis, 28–36.

65. Interviews with Cardinals Lacunza and Nzapalaigna in Fabio Marchese Ragona, Los hombres de Francisco. Los nuevos cardenales se confiesan (Madrid: San Pablo, 2018), 223–34, 342–52. See also "Haiti's First Cardinal: 'I Hadn't Expected It at All," BBC News, February 22, 2014; "Thai Archbishop Got No Formal Notification He Had Been Named Cardinal," Catholic News Service, February 12, 2015; Peter Tran, "Laotian Bishop Surprised to Be Named Cardinal," National Catholic Reporter, June 24, 2017.

66. Antonio Spadaro, Interview with the author, Rome, September 17, 2017.

67. Francis, "Homily, Holy Mass with the New Cardinals," February 23, 2014; Francis, "Homily, Consistory for the Creation of 5 New Cardinals," June 28, 2017.

68. Austen Ivereigh, "The Messages Francis Wants to Send with His Cardinal Choices," Crux, October 11, 2016.

69. John Allen, "With Pope's Cardinal Picks, Bernardin's 'Seamless Garment' Is Back," Crux, October 9, 2016; David Gibson, "New Jersey's First Cardinal Evokes Pope Francis as He Takes Helm in Newark," Religion News Service, January 6, 2017. On the culture-war bishops appointed by Viganò, see George Weigel, "The End of the Bernardin Era," First Things, February 2011.

70. Bergoglio, "Formación permanente y reconciliación," in his Meditaciones para religiosos, 80–92. See also Diego Fares, "Quién es el mal pastor?" in Congregación para los Obispos, Papa Francisco a los Obispos (Vatican City: LEV, 2017), 305–18.

71. Cindy Wooden, "Pope Francis Calls on Jesuits to Teach Discernment," Catholic News Service, August 25, 2016; "To Have Courage and Prophetic Audacity," dialogue of Pope Francis with the Jesuits gathered in the 36th General Congregation, October 14, 2016.

72. Francis, "Meeting with the Clergy, Address of Pope Francis," Royal Palace of Caserta, July 26, 2014; Francis, "Address to a Meeting with the Clergy, Men and Women Religious and Permanent Deacons Gathered in the Cathedral," Naples, March 21, 2015; Tercer Retiro Mundial de Sacerdotes, June 12, 2015 (YouTube).

73. Francis, "Homily, Holy Mass," Enrique Olaya Herrera Airport, Medellín, Colombia, September 9, 2017.

seven

1. Nicole Winfield, "Pope Calls Space, Takes Small Step for Vatican-Russian Ties," Associated Press, October 26, 2017; Frank White, *The Overview Effect: Space Exploration and Human Evolution*, 2d ed. (Reston, Va.: American Institute of Aeronautics and Astronautics, 1998).

2. Thomas Berry, foreword to Thomas Merton, *When the Trees Say Nothing: Writings on Nature*, ed. Kathleen Deignan (Notre Dame: Sorin, 2003).

3. *Laudato Si'*, 106.

4. Michael Kirwan, SJ, "'Between Politics and Apocalypse': René Girard's Reading of Global Crisis," *Thinking Faith*, November 12, 2015; Damian Howard, SJ, "Laudato si': A Seismic Event in Dialogue Between the Catholic Church and Ecology," *Thinking Faith*, June 18, 2015.

5. The following section depends mainly on (then archbishop, now cardinal) Barreto's interview with the author, Huancayo, Peru, April 16, 2016, plus Barbara Fraser, "Climate Encyclical Expected to Send Strong Moral Message to the World," Catholic News Service, June 8, 2015; and "Peru's Cardinal-Designate Received Death Threats for Opposing Smelter," Catholic News Service, May 28, 2018.

6. Comisión Episcopal de Pastoral Social, Conferencia Episcopal Argentina, report, *Una tierra para todos*, June 2005. See also updated version of this report following Laudato Si' in book form by Mons Jorge Lugones, SJ, *Una tierra habitable para todos. La mirada ecológica de la Iglesia argentina* (Buenos Aires: Ed. Claretiana, 2015).

7. For a comprehensive account, see Verónica Toller, *Daños colaterales: Papeleras, contaminación y resistencia en el río Uruguay* (Buenos Aires: Ed. Marea, 2009).

8. See letter from Argentine and Chilean bishops to the U.N., "Clamor de la Patagonia: Carta de los Obispos de la Patagonia Chilena y Argentina al Secretario General de Naciones Unidas," at Iglesia .cl, November 24, 2009; "No Había Lugar Para Ellos: Mensaje de Navidad de los obispos de la región Patagonia-Comahue," December 2009, quoted in *Laudato Si'*, no. 51.

9. Grupo de Trabajo sobre la Ecología, *Sanar un Mundo Herido*, published by the Conferencia de Provinciales de América Latina, Lima, Peru, 2013.

10. Giuseppe Rusconi, "Laudato Si': Alcune considerazioni di Monsignor Mario Toso," June 19, 2015, www.rossoporpora.org.

11. A famous example is George Weigel, "Caritas in Veritate in Gold and Red," *National Review*, July 7, 2009. In March 2019, it was announced that Francis had named Professor Zamagni the next head of the Pontifical Academy of the Social Sciences.

12. Francis, interview with Leonardo Boff, "O Papa Francisco é um dos nossos," January 9, 2017, www.leonardoboff.wordpress.com.

13. The sizes of all the social encyclicals is compared in Luis González-Carvajal Santabárbara, "Laudato Si' en el marco de la doctrina social de la Iglesia," *Razón y Fe*, no. 1404, October 2015, 270.

14. Maureen Mullarkey, "Francis and Political Illusion," *First Things*, January 5, 2015. (The journal's editor, Rusty Reno, later apologized for publishing it.) Cardinal Rodríguez de Maradiaga quoted in Nicole Winfield, "Pope Says to Care for the Earth," Associated Press, May 12, 2015; Robert P. George, "Four Things to Remember About the Pope's Environment Letter," *First Things*, January 3, 2015; Anthony Annett, "The Fall of the House of Neuhaus," *La Croix International*, March 23, 2016.

15. Denise Robbins, "How Fox News Covered Pope Francis' Action on Climate Change," Media Matters, January 2, 2015; Coral Davenport, "Pope's Views on Climate Change Add Pressure to Catholic Candidates," *New York Times*, June 16, 2015.

16. Bishop Marcelo Sánchez Sorondo, "Paul VI's Prophecy: For a 'Civilization of Love' of Sustainable Development and Social Inclusion," Cafod lecture, London, November 7, 2014.

17. See the excellent paper by David Cloutier, "Working with the Grammar of Creation: Benedict XVI, Wendell Berry, and the Unity of the Catholic Moral Vision," *Communio* 37 (Winter 2010): 607–33. Benedict's address to the Bundestag in 2011 is quoted in *Laudato Si'*, no. 155.

18. Francis, "Address to Participants in the International Colloquium on the Complementarity of Man and Woman," sponsored by the Congregation for the Doctrine of the Faith and Pontifical Councils for Interreligious Dialogue and Christian Unity, November 17, 2014; Austen Ivereigh, "Humanum Conference Explores Divine Plan for Male-Female Complementarity," *Our Sunday Visitor*, November 20, 2014.

19. Bruce Wallace, "Most Americans See Combating Climate Change as a Moral Duty," Reuters, February 27, 2015; Robb Willer, "Is the Environment a Moral Cause?," *New York Times*, February 27, 2015.

20. The three references in *Laudato Si'* to the Second Vatican Council are all to *Gaudium et Spes*, which has undergone a remarkable rehabilitation under Francis.

21. Bergoglio, "Necesidad de una antropología política," in *Reflexiones en esperanza* (Madrid: Romana, 2013), 257–88.

22. Sixty-six years after Guardini's prophecy, during the Jubilee of Mercy called by Pope Francis in 2016, a bestselling book by an Israeli historian favorably painted precisely such a future in which technology emancipates humankind from moral restraints. Yuval Noah Harari, *Homo Deus: A Brief History of Tomorrow* (London: Harvill Secker, 2016). See also Romano Guardini, *The End of the Modern World* (Wilmington, Del.: ISI Books, 1998), 73–74.

23. Guardini, *The End of the Modern World*, 108–9. His prediction, based on his reading of the eschaton in Matthew 23:12 and 24:34, was more tentative and speculative than described here, but given the extraordinary accuracy of how it has turned out, there is little point in retaining his caveats.

24. *Laudato Si'*, no. 139.

25. In Philadelphia in August 2015, shortly before Pope Francis was due to arrive there, I was told by an angry senior adviser to Archbishop Charles Chaput that because it misunderstood the magic of free markets making the world richer, *Laudato Si'* was "the worst encyclical ever written."

26. Francis, "Meeting with Finance Ministers from Various Nations," May 27, 2019; Jeffrey Sachs, "Pope Francis and *Laudato Si'*," speech at Villanova University, April 23, 2018. See also Christopher White, "Economist Sachs Acts as Pope's Cheerleader on 'Laudato Si'," *Crux*, June 30, 2018.

27. "The Appeal to COP21 Negotiating Parties," www.catholicecology.net.

28. Tomás Insua, interview with the author, Skype, October 24, 2017.

29. Alessandro Gisotti, "Al Gore: Pope Francis a 'Moral Force' for Solving Climate Crisis," *Vatican News*, July 4, 2018; Megan Cornwell, "Lord Stern: Pope's Encyclical 'Perfectly Timed' for UN Climate Summit," *The Tablet*, March 11, 2016; Sachs, "Pope Francis and *Laudato Si'*"; Tony Annett, Skype interview with the author, November 9, 2017; recollections of Philippine delegate Renato Redentor Constantino at https://catholicclimatemovement.global/1-5c-victory/.

30. Sachs, "Pope Francis and *Laudato Si'*."

31. Edward Maibach et al., "The Francis Effect: How Pope Francis Changed the Conversation About Global Warming," Yale Program on Climate Change Communication, November 5, 2015; Brian Roewe, "On Climate, Polls Begin to Show Hints of 'Francis Effect,'" *National Catholic Reporter*, November 7, 2015; J. P. Schuldt et al., "Brief Exposure to Pope Francis Heightens Moral Beliefs About Climate Change," *Climatic Change*, December 30, 2017; David Siders, "Jerry Brown's Holy War on Donald Trump," *Politico*, November 5, 2017; Christopher White, "California's Bishops Call for Ecological Conversion on *Laudato Si'* Milestone," *Crux*, June 18, 2019.

32. Francis, "Address to Participants at the Meeting for Executives of the Main Companies in the Oil and Natural Gas Sectors, and Other Energy Related Businesses," June 9, 2018; Nicole Winfield and Frank Jordans, "Major Oil Companies Commit to Carbon Pricing at the Vatican," Associated Press, June 14, 2019. Francis, "Address to Teachers and Students of the Alphonsian Academy Higher Institute of Theology," Rome, February 9, 2019; Brian Roewe, "Nearly 600 Institutions Back Catholic Climate Declaration," *National Catholic Reporter*, June 18, 2018 (the figure has since increased: see "U.S. Catholic Climate Declaration," www.catholicclimate.covenant.org); "U.S. Bishops Chairman Regrets the President's Withdrawal from the Paris Agreement," USCCB statement, June 1, 2017.

eight

1. Archbishop Edmundo Abastoflor, interview with the author, La Paz, Bolivia, April 21, 2016.

2. All quotes in this chapter from Francis's addresses in Latin America between 2015 and 2019 can be found on the Vatican's website (www.vatican.va) under "Travels." I have taken the liberty in some cases of adjusting the English translations.

3. Francis, "'Where Have Our People Been Creative?'"

4. Archbishop Fausto Trávez, interview with the author, Quito, Ecuador, September 27, 2016.

5. Padre Francisco ("Paquito") Cortés, interview with the author, Guayaquil, Ecuador, September 26, 2016.

6. On background to the Romero canonization: Paul Elie, 'What Óscar Romero's Canonization Says About Pope Francis," *Atlantic*, November 2018.

7. This romantic view of the missions received support from a major study by Felipe Valencia Caicedo, who concluded from a study of the raw data that even 250 years after the expulsion of the Jesuits in 1767 the people living near their former missions had noticeably higher levels of income and literacy (Felipe Valencia Caicedo, "Missionaries, Human Capital Transmission, and Economic Persistence in South America," *Quarterly Journal of Economics* 134, no. 1 [February 2019]: 507–56). See Andrew Van Dam, "It Ended in 1767, Yet This Experiment Is Still Linked to Higher Incomes and Education Levels Today," *Washingon Post*, November 9, 2018.

8. Archbishop Valenzuela, interview with the author, Asunción, Paraguay, November 19, 2016.

9. Papa Francisco, *Latinoamérica: Conversaciones con Hernán Reyes Alcaide* (Buenos Aires: Ed. Planeta, 2017). The Pope's remarks to Peru's bishops were made in the course of the Q&A following his address to them in Lima.

10. Austen Ivereigh, "The Pope and the Patria Grande: How Francis Is Promoting Latin America's Continental Destiny," in *The Search for God in America*, eds. Peter Casarella and Maria Clara Bingemer (Washington, D.C.: Catholic University of America Press, 2019); Alberto Methol Ferré, "El resurgimiento católico latinoamericano," in *Religión y cultura. Perspectivas de la evangelización de la cultura desde Puebla. Encuentro del equipo de reflexión del Celam y otros pensadores sobre el tema «Religión y cultura»* (Bogotá: Ed. CELAM, 1980). See also Consejo Episcopal Latinoamericano, *Promoviendo la colegialidad episcopal y la integración latinoamericana* (Bogotá: Ed. CELAM, 2016); Alberto Methol Ferré, *Los estados continentales y el Mercosur* (Montevideo: Ed. HUM, 2013).

11. Amelia Podetti, *La irrupción de América en la historia* (Buenos Aires: Centro de Investigaciones Culturales, 1981).

12. Bergoglio, "Religiosidad popular como inculturación de la fe en el espíritu de Aparecida," January 19, 2008, in Spadaro, ed., *En tus ojos está mi palabra*, 703–32.

13. Francis, "Discurso a un grupo de la Pontificia Comisión por América Latina," March 4, 2019.

14. Loris Zanatta, "Un papa populista," *Criterio*, no. 2424 (2016), originally published in Italian as "Sul populismo di Bergoglio: storia, non teologia," *Il Mulino*, June 10, 2016.

15. Bergoglio, *Nosotros como ciudadanos, nosotros como pueblo*; and "Texto completo de la homilía completa del arzobispo Bergoglio en el Tedéum," *La Nación*, May 25, 2002.

16. On the meaning of *el pueblo* in Francis's thinking, see three essential texts: Juan Carlos Scannone, *La teología del Pueblo: Raíces teológicas del papa Francisco* (Maliaño, Spain: Ed. Sal Terrae, 2017); Emilce Cuda, *Para leer a Francisco. Teología, etica y política* (Buenos Aires: Manantial, 2016); and Rafael Luciani, *El papa Francisco y la teología del pueblo* (Madrid: PPC-Ed., 2016).

17. "Cardinal Dolan Reveals the Joke He Shared with Pope Francis," NBC *Today* show, September 29, 2015. The pope's question was overheard by more than one person.

18. The story is told by Andrea Riccardi, "Il sociologo. Bauman a papa Francesco: 'Sei la luce in fondo al tunnel,'" *Avvenire*, February 8, 2018.

19. Didier Fassin, *The Will to Punish*, The Berkeley Tanner Lectures, ed. Christopher Kutz (New York: Oxford University Press, 2018), 30.

nine

1. Cardinal John Dew, interview with the author over Skype, October 11, 2016.

2. This paragraph is the result of various conversations with Buenos Aires priests who went to the cardinal with complex situations, as well as an interview with Bishop Oscar Ojea of San Isidro (Buenos Aires), November 21, 2016; Documento de Aparecida, no. 437.

3. A thorough study of the 1980 synod is James Provost, "Intolerable Marriage Situations: A Second Decade," *The Jurist* 50 (1990): 573–612.

4. On the 1917 Code, see Greg Daly, "Excommunication of Remarried: Was It Ever a Reality?," *Irish Catholic*, February 22, 2018; and Andrea Tornielli, interview with Rocco Buttiglione, "*Amoris Laetitia* Takes a Step in the Direction Marked by Wojtyla," *Vatican Insider*, May 30, 2016.

5. *Ipse Namque* has no provenance in the councils (Trent, Vatican I, Vatican II) nor in the two papal encyclicals on marriage: neither *Casti Connubii* of 1930 nor *Humanae Vitae* of 1968. Clifford Longley, "Is a Pope Bound by Every Letter of Previous Catholic Teaching?," *The Tablet*, December 8, 2016. On

Familiaris 84, see Stephen Walford, *Pope Francis, the Family and Divorce: In Defense of Truth and Mercy* (New York: Paulist Press, 2018), ch. 1.

6. On Cardinal Ratzinger's position in the 1990s, see Antonio Spadaro, SJ, "Conversazione con il cardinale Christoph Schönborn sull' 'Amoris Laetitia,'" *La Civiltà Cattolica*, July 23, 2016; Congregation for the Doctrine of the Faith, "Letter to the bishops of the Catholic Church concerning the reception of Holy Communion by the divorced and remarried members of the faithful," September 14, 1994; Sandro Magister, "No Communion for Outlaws. But the Pope Is Studying Two Exceptions," *Chiesa*, December 5, 2011; Benedict XVI, "Address to 7th World Meeting of Families," Milan, June 2, 2012.

7. Cardinal Donald Wuerl, interview with the author, Rome, September 19, 2017; Carlo-Maria Martini, "L'Ultima Intervista al cardinal Martini: Un record su BBC e 'Le Monde,'" Cronache, *Corriere della Sera*, September 2, 2012; summary with quotes of Cardinal Martini's "I have three dreams" speech by his spokesman, Father Gianna Zappa, "L'arcivescovo al sinodo dei vescovi europei," October 7, 1999, www.chiesadimilano.it. Although the speech was widely reported as calling for a "Third Vatican Council," Martini was agnostic about exactly what kind of instrument of discernment was needed. See O'Connell, *The Election of Pope Francis*, 122.

8. Francis, interviews with *Corriere della Sera* (Ferruccio de Bortoli, "Benedetto XVI non è una statua," March 5, 2014); and *La Nación* (Joaquín Morales Solá, "Poder, política y reforma: A solas con Francisco," October 5, 2014).

9. Robert Dodaro, OSA, ed., *Remaining in the Truth of Christ: Marriage and Communion in the Catholic Church* (San Francisco: Ignatius Press, 2014) included essays by three cardinals who would later sign the *dubia* protest (Walter Brandmüller, Raymond Burke, and Carlo Caffarra) as well as the then CDF prefect, Cardinal Müller. Cardinal Pell wrote the foreword to J. J. Pérez-Soba and S. Kampowski, *The Gospel of the Family: Going Beyond Cardinal Kasper's Proposal* (San Francisco: Ignatius Press, 2014).

10. John Allen, "NY Cardinal Predicts No Change on Communion Ban," *Crux*, September 6, 2014; Christopher Lamb, "Church Must Rediscover Mercy, Says Cardinal Nichols," *The Tablet*, September 23, 2014.

11. Bishop Óscar Ojea of San Isidro, interview with the author, Buenos Aires, November 21, 2016; Alver Metalli interview with María Inés Narvaja, "Mi tío Jorge y yo," *Tierras de América*, August 12, 2014.

12. Terrence McCoy, "Did Pope Francis Just Call and Say Divorced Catholics Can Take Communion?," *Washington Post*, April 24, 2014.

13. Francis, "Address during the Meeting on the Family," St. Peter's Square, October 4, 2014.

14. Francis, "Address at the Meeting with the Clergy," Palatine Chapel, Caserta, July 26, 2014; Francis, "Greeting to the Synod Fathers during the First General Congregation," October 6, 2014.

15. Cardinal Vincent Nichols, interview with the author, London, November 27, 2017.

16. Transcript of Televisa interview: "Los primeros dos años de la 'Era Francisco' en entrevista a Televisa," March 12, 2015.

17. Austen Ivereigh, "True Reform Comes from the Margins," *Irish Catholic*, October 9, 2014; Thomas Reese, SJ, "How the Synod Process Is Different Under Pope Francis," *National Catholic Reporter*, October 17, 2014.

18. Archbishop Fausto Trávez, interview with the author, Quito, Ecuador, September 27, 2016.

19. This anecdote was told to me by more than one synod delegate.

20. Austen Ivereigh, "Two Words That Stand for More Than They Mean," *OSV Daily Take*, October 10, 2014; John Allen, "The Synod's Key Twist: The Sudden Return of Gradualism," *Crux*, October 8, 2014.

21. John Thavis quoted in Philip Pullella, "Vatican Document Challenges Church to Change Attitude to Gays," Reuters, October 13, 2014; John Allen, "Catholic Bishops Soften Tone on Same-Sex Unions," *Boston Globe*, October 14, 2014.

22. The claim was made by Edward Pentin in *The Rigging of a Vatican Synod: An Investigation into Alleged Manipulation at the Extraordinary Synod on the Family* (San Francisco: Ignatius Press, 2015). At a press conference in March 2018, Cardinal Baldisseri said: "I can say, as clearly as possible, that there was no maneuvering. . . . Unfortunately, there's a group of people who say that, but there's nothing to it." John Allen and Claire Giangravé, "Cardinal on Charges of Rigged Synods: 'There Was No Maneuvering!'" *Crux*, March 3, 2018.

23. Elisabetta Povoledo and Laurie Goodstein, "At the Vatican, a Shift in Tone Toward Gays and Divorce," *New York Times*, October 13, 2014; Nicole Winfield, "Vatican Mystery: Where Did Gay Welcome Originate?," Associated Press, October 15, 2014. "Erdő publicly blamed Forte, but it wasn't the bishop," according to one of Forte's collaborators in the 2014 synod, the Mexican philosopher Rodrigo Guerra López. Apart from anything else, says Guerra, Forte was too sophisticated to have come up with those crude formulations.

24. On conservative hysteria over the midterm report, see Pentin, *The Rigging of a Vatican Synod*, 22–23; George Weigel, "Between Two Synods," *First Things*, January 2015.

25. Cardinal Nichols, interview with the author, December 7, 2017; Austen Ivereigh, "From the Synod (5): A Snapshot at the End of the First Week," CV Comment, *Catholic Voices*, October 12, 2014; Bernd Hagenkord, SJ, quoted in Christa Pongratz-Lippitt, "Synod Attendee: Divorced and Remarried Catholics Most Frequent Topic at Debates," *National Catholic Reporter*, October 13, 2014.

26. Austen Ivereigh, "No Setback for Pope Francis: The Synod of Bishops Has Changed the Face of the Church," *ABC Religion & Ethics*, October 20, 2014; the "conservatives to the rescue" narrative is George Weigel's in "Between Two Synods"; John Allen, "Divided Bishops Water Down Welcome to Gays and the Divorced," *Crux*, October 18, 2014.

27. Francis, "Address for the Conclusion of the Third Extraordinary General Assembly of the Synod of Bishops," October 18, 2014.

28. Cindy Wooden, "Back to the Synod: Year Given for Discernment Also Brought Debate," Catholic News Service, October 3, 2015; "Communion for Divorced and Remarried? Africa's Bishops Have Other Concerns, Cardinal Says," Catholic News Agency, February 19, 2015.

29. See, e.g., Bishop Barthélemy Adoukonou's essay in Cardinal Robert Sarah, ed., *Christ's New Homeland—Africa* (Ignatius Press, 2015); and Davide Maggiore, "Homosexuality: The Difficult Balance in the African Church," *Vatican Insider*, October 5, 2015. See also Christa Pongratz-Lippitt, "Austrian, German Cardinals Stress Need for New Look at Teachings on Marriage, Family," *National Catholic Reporter*, October 10, 2014; John Dick, interview with Bishop Johan Bonny of Antwerp: "Belgian Bishop Advocates Recognition of Gay Relationships," *National Catholic Reporter*, December 30, 2014.

30. Francis, "In-Flight Press Conference of His Holiness Pope Francis from the Philippines to Rome," January 19, 2015.

31. Interview with Elisabetta Piqué, "El sínodo sobre la familia: 'Los divorciados vueltos a casar parecen excomulgados,'" *La Nación*, December 7, 2014; Francis Rocca, "Pope Calls for More Integration of Divorced Catholics, Gays," Catholic News Service, December 8, 2014; Aura Miguel, "Entrevista completa de Rádio Renascença al Papa Francisco," September 14, 2015.

32. Cindy Wooden, "Pope Shares Anecdotes, Talks to Priests About Mercy, Hearing Confession," Catholic News Service, March 6, 2014.

33. "Indianapolis, San Diego, and Alexandria, Virginia, for example, received 70 percent and higher increases in the number of new requests in 2016 over 2015, even while having to set aside time to retool tribunal procedures in response to the reforms." Dan Morris-Young, "Annulment Reform Seems to Cultivate Change in Culture," *National Catholic Reporter*, June 5, 2017.

34. Archbishop Ricardo Centellas, interview with the author, Potosí, Bolivia, April 19, 2016.

35. Francis, "Homily, Holy Mass for the Opening of the Ordinary General Assembly of the Synod of Bishops," Vatican Basilica, October 4, 2015.

36. John Thavis, "A Ploy That Will Boomerang," www.johnthavis.com, October 13, 2015; David Gibson, "Are Conservatives at High-Stakes Vatican Summit Overplaying Their Hand?," Religion News Service, October 16, 2015; Joshua McElwee, "Cardinal Napier: No More Concerns About Synod Process, Optimistic About Outcome," *National Catholic Reporter*, October 20, 2015; Cardinal Dew, interview with the author over Skype, October 11, 2016.

37. Bergoglio, "Sobre la acusación de sí mismo," in *Reflexiones espirituales sobre la vida apostólica* (Buenos Aires: Ed. Diego de Torres, 1987; Bilbao: Ed. Mensajero, 2013), author's translation. He was using Spiritual Exercises 315, 332, and 326. Francis's quote was tweeted by Antonio Spadaro, SJ, on October 7, 2015, as reported by Gerard O'Connell, "Pope to Synod Fathers: Don't Give in to the Conspiracy Theory," *America*, October 7, 2015.

38. Joshua McElwee, "Australian Archbishop: Synod Should Propose 'Less Negative' Reading of Reality," *National Catholic Reporter*, October 14, 2015; Archbishop Mark Coleridge, "On the Road Together—The Soil of Real Experience," *Synod on the Family* blog, www.brisbanecatholic.org.au, October 21, 2015.

39. Cardinal Nichols, interview with the author, London, December 7, 2017.

40. Austen Ivereigh, "From the Synod (8): An Interview with Archbishop Blase Cupich of Chicago," CV Comment, Catholic Voices, October 17, 2015; Cardinal Dew, interview with the author over Skype, October 11, 2016.

41. Andrés Beltramo Álvarez, interview with Bishop Alonso Garza Treviño of Piedras Negras, "México: 'Sínodo: Consenso sobre más apertura para los divorciados vueltos a casar,'" Vatican Insider, October 26, 2015. Synod speech by Archbishop of San Juan, Roberto González Nieves, OFM, published on diocesan website, n/d, http://www.arqsj.org.

42. Austen Ivereigh, "Synod Ends with New Pastoral Tone, Direction," OSV Newsweekly, October 27, 2015.

43. Thomas Reese, "Synod on Remarried Catholics, Consensus in Ambiguity," National Catholic Reporter, October 24, 2015.

44. Juan Vicente Boo, "El Sínodo de la Familia ultima un documento de consenso," ABC, October 23, 2015; Cardinal Nichols, interview with the author, London, December 7, 2017.

45. Final synod briefing, Holy See Press Office, October 24, 2015.

46. Mark Coleridge, "On the Road Together—Wonderment, Gratitude, Relief, Weariness," Synod on the family blog, www.brisbane.catholic.au.

47. Francis, "Address at the Conclusion of the Synod of Bishops," October 24, 2015.

48. Andrés Beltramo, interview with Bishop Alfonso Miranda Guardiola of Monterrey, Mexico, "Divorciados: Discernimiento y la sorpresa de la 'vía mexicana,'" Vatican Insider, October 24, 2015.

49. Press conference, Venerable English College, Rome, October 25, 2015.

50. Spadaro tweeted: "Col #Synod15 il #Giubileo passa dalla logica binaria della PORTA (aperta/chiusa) a quella del VOLTO (che muta vitalmente davanti a un altro)."

ten

1. Andrew Brown, "The War Against Pope Francis," Guardian, October 27, 2017. See, e.g., Matthew Schmitz, "How I Changed My Mind About Pope Francis," First Things, August 12, 2016; Carl E. Olson, "The Off-the-Cuff and Out-of-Focus Papacy," Catholic World Report, December 1, 2015; Steve Skojec, "The Dictator of the Vatican," April 8, 2016, foreignpolicy.com.

2. Heidi Schlumpf, "Cupich: Catholics Are Not Scandalized by Pope Francis," National Catholic Reporter, November 10, 2017.

3. Francis, Morning Meditation, "Justice and Mercy," February 24, 2017, also in L'Osservatore Romano, weekly edition in English, n. 10, March 10, 2017. Lawler's shock is recounted in the introduction to Philip F. Lawler, Lost Shepherd: How Pope Francis Is Misleading His Flock (Washington, D.C.: Gateway, 2018).

4. John Paul II, Dives in Misericordia (1980), no. 14. For an articulate expression of this "hermeneutic of suspicion" that Francis has a plan to change church doctrine, see one of his most prominent critics, the New York Times columnist Ross Douthat, To Change the Church: Pope Francis and the Future of Catholicism (New York: Simon and Schuster, 2018). On the invidia of the Pharisees, see José A. Pagola, Jesus: An Historical Approximation (London: Convivium, 2014), ch. 12. On Christianity as a "secularizing religion," because it destroys the boundaries religion erects, see Gianni Vattimo and René Girard, Christianity, Truth, and Weakening Faith: A Dialogue (New York: Columbia University Press, 2010).

5. On the background to the Livieres removal, see the detailed eight-part investigation by Grant Gallicho, "The Curious Case of Carlos Urrutigoity," Commonweal, August 14–December 31, 2014. The story of Livieres told here was shared by senior sources in Opus Dei. See also Francis, "Address to the Meeting with the Young People," Kasarani Stadium, Nairobi, November 27, 2015. Cindy Wooden, "Pope Shares Anecdotes, Talks to Priests About Mercy, Hearing Confession."

6. Stefania Felasca, "Quello che avrei detto al consistoro: Intervista con il cardenale Jorge Mario Bergoglio," 30Giorni, November 2007.

7. Pope Francis, "Homily," with announcement of Year of Mercy, March 13, 2015.

8. Rodney Stark, The Triumph of Christianity: How the Jesus Movement Became the World's Largest Religion (New York: HarperOne, 2011), 112. Stark used social science methodology to show that this growth was primarily due to their taking seriously Jesus's injunction to feed the hungry and visit the sick. He explains how the compassion shown to strangers by people who had experienced a God of

mercy astonished pagans because charity in the ancient world was a duty to kith and kin, not a divine command, and disconnected from religious observance, which centered on obligation and sacrifice.

9. Francis, *Misericordiae Vultus,* 11; John Paul II, *Dives in Misericordia,* November 30, 1980, 2, 5, 13, 14.

10. Francis, interview with Andrea Tornielli: *Pope Francis, The Name of God Is Mercy* (New York: Random House, 2016). In a review of the book I quoted a letter writer to *The Tablet* who argued that "this should be a year of 'love and compassion' or of 'showing loving kindness,' not a year of receiving God's forgiveness for sins with which some in the Church seem to think we are all obsessed." Austen Ivereigh, "Making Mercy Real," MercatorNet, January 20, 2016.

11. Francis, "Message for Lent 2016," October 4, 2015.

12. Manuela Tulli, "Benigni-show per il libro di Papa Francesco," ANSA Giubileo, January 13, 2016.

13. At times the first two stages were expressed as one, as in the heading of chapter 8 of *Amoris Laetitia*: "Accompanying, discerning and integrating weakness." But speaking about *Amoris* Francis told Dominique Wolton: "When I talk about families in difficulty, I say we must welcome them, accompany them, discern with them, and integrate them into the Church." Francis with Wolton, *The Path to Change,* 57. Francis's four "mileposts for action" to help migrants and refugees find the peace they need were articulated in January 2018 as "welcoming, protecting, promoting and integrating." Francis, "Message of His Holiness Francis for the Celebration of the 51st World Day of Peace: 'Migrants and Refugees: Men and Women in Search of Peace,'" January 1, 2018.

14. *Misericordiae Vultus,* 9. Bergoglio, "Criterios de acción apostólica," in *Reflexiones espirituales sobre la vida apostólica,* 264–89.

15. Francis, "Address for the Meeting with Young People," sports field of Santo Tomás University, Manila, Philippines, January 18, 2015.

16. Daniel Burke, "Seeing the Pope Help Strangers Made Me Tear Up. Later I Learned Why," CNN .com, April 6, 2018; Julie Zauzmer, "The World Saw Pope Francis Bless a Boy with Cerebral Palsy. Here's What We Didn't See," *Washington Post,* October 12, 2015.

17. Francis, morning meditation, "The Christian Way," March 6, 2014, and January 7, 2016. Antonio Caño and Pablo Ordaz , "El peligro en tiempos de crisis es buscar un salvador que nos devuelva la identidad y nos defienda con muros," *El País,* January 22, 2017.

18. Dave Yoder, "Pope Francis's Christmas Gift to a Grieving Photographer," *National Geographic,* December 14, 2018.

19. Eva Fernández, *El Papa de la Ternura* (Madrid: Planeta, 2019), 126.

20. Anecdotes from twenty people who have received calls from the pope are collected in Rosario Carello, *Gli abracci di Francesco: Quando il papa chiama al telefono* (Milan: San Paolo, 2016).

21. Francis, "Homily, Holy Mass," Ciudad Juárez fairgrounds, February 17, 2016; John Allen, "Pope Tells Immigrants, 'I Want to Carry Your Eyes in Mine, Your Hearts in Mine,'" *Crux,* October 1, 2017.

22. Francis gave a comprehensive answer on this question on the flight returning from Sweden in October 2016, in which he praised the country's welcoming policies but pointed out that it had to restrict numbers in order to prevent the danger of non-integration. "Those who govern need prudence. They must be very open to receiving refugees, but they also have to calculate how best to settle them, because refugees must not only be accepted, but also integrated. Consequently, if a country has, say, the ability to integrate twenty persons, they should do this. Another country that has greater capacity should do more." Francis, "In-Flight Press Conference of His Holiness Pope Francis from Sweden to Rome," November 1, 2016.

23. "Rights Groups, Rohingya Disappointed in Pope," Associated Press, November 28, 2017.

24. Francis, "Press Conference on the Return Flight from Bangladesh," December 2, 2017.

25. "Sant'Egidio: 'Pope's Support to Humanitarian Corridors Offers New Impetus,'" *Vatican Insider,* March 6, 2016.

26. See Jason Horowitz, "Steve Bannon Carries Battles to Another Influential Hub: The Vatican," *New York Times,* February 7, 2017; James Politi, "Pope Francis' Reforms Spark Revolt of the Hard-right," *Financial Times,* March 7, 2017. On Sant'Egidio's involvement with the Lesbos refugees: Mario Marazziti, interview with the author, February 25, 2019.

27. Cindy Wooden, "Mercy Fridays Give Pope a Year of Stories, Tears, Hugs," Catholic News Service, November 11, 2016.

28. Francis interview to TV2000 and InBlu Radio reflecting on the Jubilee, November 20, 2016.

29. Francis, "Letter of His Holiness Pope Francis According to Which an Indulgence Is Granted to the Faithful on the Occasion of the Extraordinary Jubilee of Mercy," September 1, 2015.

30. Francis with Wolton, *The Path to Change*, 50.

31. Marina Herrman, "La Hermana Mónica: 'Le dije al Papa que la que está haciendo lío soy yo,'" *La Nación*, September 4, 2015; profile of Sister Mónica by María Laura Favarel, *Hermana Mónica: En la periferia transexual* (Spain: Freshbook, Ed. San Pablo, 2019); Inés San Martín, "Nun Ministering to Transgender Women Gets Thumbs-up from Pope," *Crux*, July 25, 2017.

32. David Vigario, "El papa, a un transexual español: ¡Claro que eres hijo de la Iglesia!," *El Mundo*, January 28, 2015; Cameron Doody, "Diego Neria: 'El Papa me dijo que 'si alguien te intenta apartar, el problema está en el que te aparta,'" *Religión Digital*, April 20, 2017; Diego Neria, *El despiste de Dios: Cuadernos de viaje de un hombre que nació mujer* (Madrid: Tropo Editores, 2016).

33. Francis, "In-Flight Press Conference of His Holiness Pope Francis from Azerbaijan to Rome," October 2, 2016. Background: Eloise Blondiau, "The Catholic Church Is Still Silent on Gender Identity Issues. It's Left Trans Catholics in Limbo," *Vox*, March 11, 2019; and "The Many Faces of Pope Francis: A Five-Year Timeline of His LGBT Record," www.newwaysministry.org.

34. John-Henry Westen, "Pope Francis Calls Woman with Sex-Change Operation a Man," *Lifesite News*, October 3, 2016. Westen insists in the article on calling Neria "she." Also Christian Spaemann, "Note sulle affermazioni di Papa Francesco sui transessuali," in Sandro Magister's blog, *Settimo Cielo*, October 12, 2016.

35. Francis, general audience, January 27, 2016.

36. Francis, "Meeting with the Catholic Community," church of St. Michael the Archangel, Rakovski, Bulgaria, May 6, 2019.

37. *Amoris Laetitia*, no. 37.

38. When *Amoris* uses the term "irregular," it does so to point out the inadequacy of the category: "It can no longer simply be said that all those in 'irregular' situations are living in a state of mortal sin and are deprived of sanctifying grace." *Amoris Laetitia* 301.

39. Cardinal Schönborn, press conference, Press Office of the Holy See, April 8, 2016. He recalled his comments to Benedict XVI during an academic seminar at Mary Immaculate College in Limerick, Ireland, on July 13, 2017. See Austen Ivereigh, "Cardinal Schönborn: Moral Theology Needs Both Principles and Prudence," *Crux*, July 15, 2017.

40. Philippe Bordeyne, *Divorcés Remariés: Ce qui change avec François* (Paris: Salvator, 2017), 22–25. "Conscience needs to be better incorporated into the Church's praxis in situations which do not embody objectively our understanding of marriage. Conscience can do more than recognize that a given situation does not correspond objectively to demands of Gospel: it can recognize what God is asking within limits, while not yet the ideal." *Amoris Laetitia* 303. See also Austen Ivereigh, "Conscience," in Cindy Wooden and Joshua J. McElwee, eds., *A Pope Francis Lexicon* (Collegeville, Minn.: Liturgical Press, 2018).

41. Francis, morning homily ("La ninnananna di Dio"), December 11, 2014. The "liberal" lobbying was confirmed both by Archbishop Victor Fernández, who helped draft *Amoris*, as well as by Cardinal Schönborn. "I was so relieved and glad that Pope Francis stood clear on this," Schönborn said in Limerick. "The canonical dispositions are clear and need no supplement." Academic seminar at Mary Immaculate College in Limerick, Ireland, on July 13, 2017, reported in Ivereigh, "Cardinal Schönborn: Moral Theology Needs Both Principles and Prudence."

42. At his lecture at the academic seminar at Mary Immaculate College in Limerick, Ireland, in July 2017, Schönborn said he was moved to discover that the questions asked in *Amoris* 300 were "very similar" to the pastoral plan he had been using in Vienna for more than twenty years.

43. *Veritatis Splendor* 68; Víctor Manuel Fernández, "Vida trinitaria, normas éticas y fragilidad humana. Algunas breves precisiones," *Universitas* 6 (2011), available at http://bibliotecadigital.uca.edu .ar. Giertych's involvement in drafting chapter 8 was confirmed by a Francis collaborator.

44. Víctor Manuel Fernández, "El capítulo VIII de *Amoris Laetitia*: Lo que queda después de la tormenta," *Revista Medellín* (CELAM), no. 168 (May–August 2017): 459, 467; *Amoris Laetitia* 305, footnote 351. Francis, "'Where Have Our People Been Creative?'"

45. In his letter to Stephen Walford of August 1, 2017, Pope Francis said of the family synod: "There were of course temptations during this journey but the Good Spirit prevailed. Witnessing this brought

spiritual joy." Letter published as preface to Stephen Walford, *Pope Francis, the Family and Divorce: In Defense of Truth and Mercy* (New York: Paulist Press, 2018).

46. Austen Ivereigh, "Pope Francis in Epic Bid to Save the Family, Convert the Church," *Crux*, April 8, 2016; Jean-Marie Guénois, "Le pape François ouvre la porte de la communion à certains divorcés remariés," *Figaro*, April 8, 2016; Jim Yardley and Laurie Goodstein, "Pope Francis, Urging Less Judgment, Signals Path for Divorced on Communion," *New York Times*, April 8, 2016; Phil Lawler, "The Pope's Confused Message Undermines His Own Pastoral Program," CatholicCulture.org, April 8, 2016.

47. Mark de Vries, "An 'Existential Document'—Cardinal Eijk Presents *Amoris Laetitia*," www.incaelo.wordpress.com, April 8, 2016; Archdiocese of Philadelphia, "Pastoral Guidelines for Implementing *Amoris Laetitia*," July 1, 2016; "Pastoral Message from Bishop Philip About the Apostolic Exhortation '*Amoris Laetitia*,'" April 24, 2016, Catholic Diocese of Portsmouth, UK; Dan Hitchens, "Bishop Egan: Pray for the Church Because There Is a 'Growing Problem,'" *Catholic Herald*, February 8, 2017; Cardinal Raymond Burke, "'*Amoris Laetitia*' and the Constant Teaching and Practice of the Church," *National Catholic Register*, April 12, 2016.

48. Antonio Spadaro, SJ, "Conversazione con il Cardinale Schönborn sull' Amoris Laetitia," *La Civiltà Cattolica*, July 26, 2016.

49. Richard R. Gaillardetz, "Doctrinal Authority in the Francis Era," *Commonweal*, December 19, 2016; Rocco Buttiglione, "La gioia dell'amore e lo sconcerto dei teologi," *L'Osservatore Romano*, July 20, 2016. See also Buttiglione (with Ennio Antonelli), *Terapia dell'amore ferito in "Amoris Laetitia"* (Milan: Ares, 2017); and Buttiglione, *Risposte amichevoli ai critici di Amoris laetitia* (Milan: Ares, 2017). Bordeyne, *Divorcés Remariés*; Cardinal Lluís Martínez Sistach, *Cómo Aplicar Amoris Laetitia* (Barcelona: Claret, 2017); Rodrigo Guerra López, "Para comprender *Amoris Laetitia*. Premisas y argumentos, respuesta a dudas y objeciones, camino y esperanza," *Revista Medellín* (CELAM), no. 168 (May–August 2017): 409–47; and Walford, *Pope Francis, the Family, and Divorce*.

50. Die deutschen Bischöfe, "Die Freude der Liebe, die in den Familien gelebt wird, ist auch die Freude der Kirche," Einladung zu einer erneuerten Ehe-und Familienpastoral im Licht von *Amoris laetitia*, February 1, 2017. On bishops' responses generally in 2016, see Inés San Martín, "As recent Guidelines Show, 'Amoris' Argument Is Far from Over," *Crux*, January 18, 2017.

51. While attending an academic seminar at Mary Immaculate College in Limerick, Ireland, in July 2017, Schönborn said that Francis had asked him if the document was orthodox. "I said, 'Holy Father, it is fully orthodox,'" Schönborn replied. A few days later he received from Francis a little note that said: "Thank you for that word. That gave me comfort." See Ivereigh, "Cardinal Schönborn: Moral Theology Needs Both Principles and Prudence." On the sidelining of Müller, see Sandro Magister, "Müller Out, Schönborn In. The Pope Has Changed Doctrine Teachers," *Chiesa* blog, May 30, 2016; Müller's address to the seminary of Oviedo, "Qué podemos esperar de la familia?," May 4, 2016, published on the *Chiesa* blog.

52. Bishop Oscar Ojea of San Isidro, interview with the author, Buenos Aires, November 21, 2016. Text of the Buenos Aires guidelines and pope letter in José Manuel Vidal, "Los Obispos de la Región de Buenos Aires dan orientaciones, con el aval del Papa, sobre los 'divorciados en nueva unión,'" *Religión Digital*, September 11, 2016.

53. Regarding Josef Seifert's 2016 article, see statement by Archbishop of Granada: "Nota del Arzobispado de Granada," August 31, 2017; and Josef Seifert, "The Persecution of Orthodoxy," *First Things*, May 10, 2017. On Weinandy, see Thomas Reese, SJ, "Papal Loyalists Become Dissidents," Religion News Service, November 8, 2017. See also Edward Pentin, "Catholic Scholars Appeal to Pope Francis to Repudiate 'Errors' in Amoris Laetitia," *National Catholic Register*, July 11, 2016; Joshua McElwee, "Signers of Document Critiquing 'Amoris Laetitia' Revealed," *National Catholic Reporter*, July 22, 2016.

54. Dan Hitchens, "Ignore the Misleading Headlines: The Remarried Cannot 'Now Receive Communion,'" *Catholic Herald*, September 19, 2016; and Hitchens, "A Distinction Without Discipline," *First Things*, September 30, 2016, in which he speaks of "the beautiful teaching of the Church" that "no matter how much of a mess you are in, with God's grace you can always get out of it." The "Letter of the 45" similarly asks the pope to clarify that he does not mean "that a justified person has not the strength with God's grace to carry out the objective demands of the divine law, as though any of the commandments of God are impossible for the justified." This was to render grace all but meaningless; if people had all the resources they needed to obey all God's commands, what did grace really mean? On Saint Augustine versus Pelagius, see Alister McGrath, *Heresy: A History of Defending the Truth* (London: SPCK, 2009), 164–70.

55. He made the comparison in an interview on Raymond Arroyo's EWTN show *The World Over*, December 16, 2016.

56. The others were the archbishop emeritus of Bologna, Carlo Caffarra; Joachim Meisner, the archbishop emeritus of Cologne; and the former president of a Vatican history committee, Cardinal Walter Brandmüller. Cardinal Ratzinger, later Benedict XVI, told theologians not to use the media to whip up indignation at the magisterial teaching, because "it is not by seeking to exert the pressure of public opinion that one contributes to the clarification of doctrinal issues and renders service to the truth." Congregation on the Doctrine of the Faith Instruction, *Donum Veritatis*, May 24, 1990, 30.

57. Francis, "'Where Have Our People Been Creative?'"

58. Michael J. O'Loughlin, "Cardinal Nichols: Pope Francis' 'Toughness' Will See the Catholic Church Through Reforms," *America*, March 8, 2017; Napier tweet, December 6, 2016; Monsignor Vito Pinto, head of the Roman Rota, "Eminenz, warum haben Sie das gemacht?," Katholisch.de, December 1, 2016.

59. Edward Pentin, "Are Polish Bishops Leaning Towards Allowing Some Remarried Divorcees Holy Communion?" *National Catholic Register*, March 16, 2018; Grant Gallicho and James F. Keenan, eds., *Amoris Laetitia: A New Momentum for Moral Formation and Pastoral Practice* (Mahwah, NJ: Paulist Press, 2018).

60. John L. Allen and Inés San Martín, "Key Papal Ally Says 'Amoris' Means Tougher Line on Divorce in the West," *Crux*, June 1, 2017.

61. Fathers Bruno Nobre, SJ, and Miguel Almeida, SJ, interview with the author, Braga, Portugal, March 11, 2019. The process is outlined in Dom Jorge Ortiga, "Construir a Casa sobre a Rocha," Carta Pastoral, Arquidiocese de Braga, 2017; available in English as "Building the House Upon the Rock," at www.diocese-braga.pt.

62. Monsignor Philippe Bordeyne, "The Newness That Priests and People Face When They Receive Amoris Laetitia: An Overview in France," in Gallico and Keenan, eds., *Amoris Laetitia: A New Momentum*, 70–76.

63. Congregation for the Doctrine of the Faith, letter, *Placuit Deo*, On Certain Aspects of Christian Salvation, February 22, 2018.

64. *Gaudete et Exsultate* 34; Bergoglio, prologue, *Reflexiones espirituales sobre la vida apostólica*.

65. See Rita Ferrone, "There Are Also Women There," *Commonweal*, April 10, 2018.

66. A traditionalist convert who is editor of the U.S. edition of the *Catholic Herald* tweeted: "Imagine falling madly in love with the Church and her traditions, only to have the Holy Father call you a punctilious neo-Pelagian. What part of filial loyalty means we have to stand by and cop that abuse? #GaudateEtExsultate." Dan Hitchens of the UK *Catholic Herald* claimed the passages on grace, morality, and discernment were "worryingly ambiguous." Emily McFarlan Miller, "'Rejoice and Be Glad': Catholics Respond to Pope's Letter," Religion News Service, April 9, 2018.

Epilogue

1. Francis, "Good Politics Is at the Service of Peace," message for World Day of Peace, January 1, 2019, and "Address to the Members of the Diplomatic Corps Accredited to the Holy See," January 7, 2019. See also Massimo Faggioli, "The Catholic Church and Nationalism: The Shadow of the 'Long 19th Century,'" *La Croix International*, May 7, 2019.

2. Francis, "*Christus Vivit*. Post-Synodal Apostolic Exhortation of the Holy Father Francis to Young People and to the Entire People of God," March 25, 2019, nos. 230–238.

3. Bergoglio, presentation on May 12, 2012, of book by Enrique Ciro Bianchi, *Pobres en Este Mundo, Ricos en la Fe* (Buenos Aires: Agape, 2012), and reproduced in Ciro Bianchi, *La teología de la pastoral popular de Rafael Tello: Para entender las raíces teológicas del Papa Francisco* (self-published, 2016), which quotes Tello's letter to Bergoglio, dated January 20, 2002. Tello was informally given permission to say Mass privately by Bergoglio's predecessor, Cardinal Quarracino, but Bergoglio's move publicly restored to him his full faculties.

4. Francis, Homily, Palm Sunday, St. Peter's Square, April 14, 2019.

5. Austen Ivereigh, "New Paths: What to Expect from the Amazon Synod," *Commonweal*, June 18, 2019.

6. "Incontro del Santo Padre con i Parroci e i Sacerdoti della Diocesi di Roma," papal bulletin, March 7, 2019.

7. Gianni Valente, "The Summit on Abuse and the Donatist Trap," *Vatican Insider*, April 2, 2019. This is the English translation of Valente's original article ("Il Summit Sugli Abusi e L'insidia 'Donatista'") of February 22, 2019. On the risk of "evasion," see Austen Ivereigh, "From Evasion to Conversion: How Pope Francis Sees the Sex-Abuse Crisis," *Commonweal*, January 30, 2019; and Rita Ferrone, "The Abuse Crisis as Prophecy and Pascha," *Commonweal*, April 6, 2019.

8. On Donatism, see Yves Congar, OP, *True and False Reform in the Church*, trans. Paul Philibert, OP (Collegeville, Minn.: Liturgical Press, 2011), 76. The term "zero tolerance" is understood by the Vatican as meaning no priest guilty of abuse can remain in ministry, whereas for victims' groups it means the strictest possible penalties, a matter that for canonists necessarily depends on the nature of the crime and situation of the offender. On why "zero tolerance" is good rhetoric but legal fiction, see Yago de la Cierva, "¿Qué significa 'tolerancia cero'?," *Alfa y Omega*, February 28, 2019. On the *viganista* take, see Chico Harlan, "'Gay Priests Are in the Crosshairs': As Vatican Abuse Summit Begins, Debate over Homosexuality Is Divisive Undercurrent," *Washington Post*, February 20, 2019; see also Cardinal Robert Sarah interview, "As a Bishop, It Is My Duty to Warn the West," *Catholic Herald*, April 5, 2019.

9. Martel, *In the Closet of the Vatican*, 41; Andrew Sullivan, "The Corruption of the Vatican's Gay Elite Has Been Exposed," *New York*, February 22, 2019.

10. Martel writes that López Trujillo "exiled himself" to the Vatican in 1990 when he took up his appointment as president of the Council of the Family (*In the Closet of the Vatican*, 287). This isn't quite accurate. A senior Latin American cardinal who had received many complaints about the then archbishop of Medellín's behavior communicated them directly to John Paul II in a private audience in 1989, following which he named López Trujillo as president of the Council for the Family. The cardinal who had reported López Trujillo to the pope added, however, that the complaints made to him at that time did not include "denunciations of homosexuality."

11. Francis speaking on October 20, 2017, and in October 2018, quoted by Martel, *In the Closet of the Vatican*, 68.

12. "La pregunta de Jordi Évole al papa Francisco sobre los abusos," laSexta.com, March 31, 2019. The interview is summarized by Jesús Bastante, "Francisco: 'El Miedo es el Material sobre el cual Se Construyen las Dictaduras,'" *Religión Digital*, March 31, 2019.

13. Francis, introduction to meeting, "The Protection of Minors in the Church," February 21, 2019.

14. Jason Horowitz, "For the Vatican, Solving Clergy Sex Abuse Is 'Not So Simple,'" *New York Times*, February 20, 2019; Céline Hoyeau, interview with Archbishop Hollerich, "Nous, évêques, voulons rendre des comptes," *La Croix*, February 23, 2019.

15. Hans Zollner, speaking at Vatican abuse summit press conference, February 24, 2019; "Desgarrador testimonio de una víctima ante el Papa," and "Solemne mea culpa del Papa," *Religión Digital*, February 23, 2019.

16. Michael J. O'Loughlin, "Despite External Pressure, Little Talk of Homosexuality at Vatican Abuse Summit," *America*, February 24, 2019; Robert Royal, "After the Summit," *Catholic Thing*, February 26, 2019; Rachel Donadio, "Survivors of Church Abuse Want Zero Tolerance. The Pope Offers Context," *Atlantic*, February 24, 2019; Joshua McElwee, "Francis Ends Vatican Summit with Promise Church Will 'Decisively Confront' Abuse," *National Catholic Reporter*, February 24, 2019.

17. Francis, *Las cartas de la tribulación*, 47; Francis, "Address . . . at the End of the Eucharistic Concelebration", at meeting for "The Protection of Minors in the Church," February 24, 2019.

18. Two contrasting views: Frank Brennan, SJ, "Truth and Justice After the Pell Verdict," *Eureka Street*, February 26, 2019, and Peter Murnane, OP, "To Those Who Think George Pell's Verdict Was Wrong," FindingTheTreasure.Wordpress.com, March 11, 2019; George Weigel, "The Unfair, Anti-Catholic Conviction of Cardinal George Pell," *New York Post*, December 31, 2018. Pell's life and the accusations against him are researched in depth by Louise Milligan, *Cardinal: The Rise and Fall of George Pell*, 2nd ed. (Melbourne: Melbourne University Press, 2018).

19. Francis, "Apostolic Letter in the Form of 'Motu Propio' of the Supreme Pontiff: *Vos Estis Lux Mundi*," May 7, 2019.

20. Maike Hickson, "Cardinal Müller: Pope Benedict's Letter 'More Intelligent Than All' Contributions at Rome Abuse Summit," *Lifesite News*, April 17, 2019; Massimo Faggioli, "Benedict's Untimely Meditation," *Commonweal*, April 12, 2019; Michael Sean Winters, "Benedict's Letter About Sex Abuse Crisis Is a Regrettable Text," *National Catholic Reporter*, April 11, 2019.

21. Austen Ivereigh, "Pope Benedict's Letter on Sex Abuse Is Not an Attack on Francis (or Vatican II),"

America, April 11, 2019; Andrea Tornielli, "Benedict XVI's Birthday and That 'Penitential' Approach That Unites Two Pontificates," *Vatican News*, April 15, 2019.

22. On the "Regensburg Network," see Martel, *In the Closet of the Vatican*, 436; Robert Mickens, "Opposition to Reform Has Coalesced Around Former Pope Joseph Ratzinger," *La Croix International*, May 20, 2016. On the construction of the "emeritus papacy," see Massimo Faggioli, "The Fiction Behind the Idea of the 'Pope Emeritus,'" *La Croix International*, May 23, 2019; Elise Harris, "The Request of a Retired Pope—Simply Call Me 'Father Benedict,'" Catholic News Agency, December 9, 2014.

23. Francis, "In-Flight Press Conference . . . from Armenia to Rome," June 26, 2016.

24. Paul Elie, "The Pope in the Attic: Benedict in the Time of Francis," *Atlantic*, April 16, 2014; Jason Horowitz, "In Private Letters, Benedict Rebukes Critics of Pope Francis," *New York Times*, September 20, 2018.

25. Austen Ivereigh, "Benedict's Runaway Court: Is There One Pope Too Many?," *The Tablet*, May 30, 2019.

26. Joseph Ratzinger made the prediction in a famous 1969 radio broadcast. See Tod Worner, "When Father Joseph Ratzinger Predicted the Future of the Church," *Aleteia*, June 13, 2016.

27. Inés San Martín, Claire Giangravé, and Christopher White, "Assessing Francis's Successes and Unfinished Business at 5-Year Mark," *Crux*, March 13, 2018.

28. Chimamanda Ngozi Adichie, "How Pope Francis Brought Me Back to the Catholic Church," *Atlantic*, October 14, 2015.

29. "Divine Intervention: Vatican Aide Defies Police to Restore Power to Homeless Shelter," *Guardian*, May 13, 2019.

30. Austen Ivereigh, "Evangelization First: A New Vatican Constitution Will Embody New Priorities," *Commonweal*, April 23, 2019.

31. Francis, "Address to the Catholic Community," Church of Saint Michael Archangel in Rakovski, Bulgaria, May 6, 2019; "Gay Comedian Stephen K. Amos Was Prepared to Challenge Pope over Homosexuality," Press Association, April 19, 2019.

32. Michael O'Loughlin, "One Key to Understanding Pope Francis? His Approach to Judgment," *America*, February 27, 2018; Francis, Homily, Holy Chrism Mass, Vatican Basilica, March 29, 2018.

33. Perhaps the best contemporary Catholic take on the rise of nationalism is Archbishop Jean-Claude Hollerich, SJ, "Toward the European Elections," *La Civiltà Cattolica*, April 21, 2019. See also Austen Ivereigh, "Is the Pope the Anti-Trump?," *New York Times*, March 4, 2017.

34. Bannon's anti-Francis activities are documented in Leigh Baldwin, "The Heretic in the Vatican: How Pope Francis Became a Hate Figure for the Far Right," SourceMaterial, April 13, 2019, and Jason Horowitz, "Steve Bannon Is Done Wrecking the American Establishment. Now He Wants to Destroy Europe's," *New York Times*, March 9, 2018. See also Elise Harris and John Allen, "Challenging Pope on Multiple Fronts, Bannon Wants to Train Gladiators," *Crux*, April 1, 2019. In June 2019, Burke suddenly resigned from the Dignitatis Humanae Institute after Bannon—whom he had worked with for four years and openly admired—met Frédéric Martel to suggest making a film of Martel's book on Vatican homosexuality.

35. José M. Vidal, "Francisco, a los jóvenes," *Religión Digital*, May 7, 2019; Pope Francis and the Grand Imam of al-Azhar, Ahmed el-Tayeb: "A Document on Human Fraternity for World Peace and Living Together," Abu Dhabi, February 4, 2019.

36. Francis, address to Interreligious Meeting, Founder's Memorial, Abu Dhabi, February 4, 2019.

37. Francis, "Meeting with Migrants," Diocesan Caritas of Rabat, March 30, 2019; "Meeting with Priests, Religious, Consecrated Persons and the Ecumenical Council of Churches," cathedral of Rabat, March 31, 2019.

Note on Sources

As is clear from the notes, *Wounded Shepherd* draws heavily on Pope Francis's own homilies, addresses, and in-flight press conferences, mostly available on the Vatican website. The second source is my collection of interviews, around forty in total, with key players and thinkers in the Francis pontificate in Europe, Latin America, and the United States, conducted during reporting and travels in 2016 to 2018. The third source consists of reports and commentary by the *vaticanisti*, the full-time Rome reporters, as well as theologians and pundits whose essays and articles have helped shape my understanding.

What follows is a select bibliography of books that I have found particularly useful and noteworthy, divided into various sections:

On Francis's pre-papal life and thought

Since the publication of various biographies mentioned in my book *The Great Reformer: Francis and the Making of a Radical Pope* (New York: Henry Holt, 2014), new books on the life and thought of Jorge Mario Bergoglio have helped fill out his backstory. Mark Shriver, *Pilgrimage: My Search for the Real Pope Francis* (New York: Random House, 2016) is a great place to start, especially on his Jesuit years. Javier Cámara and Sebastián Pfaffen, *Aquel Francisco* (Córdoba: Ed. Raíz de Dos, 2015) is especially good on his exile years in Córdoba. On his assistance to people fleeing the repression of the 1970s, see Nello Scavo's *La lista de Bergoglio: Los salvados por Francisco durante la dictadura* (Madrid: Ed. Claretiana, 2013) and now Aldo Duzdevich, *Salvados por Francisco: Cómo un joven sacerdote se arriesgó para ayudar a perseguidos por la dictadura* (Buenos Aires: Ediciones B, 2019).

On Francis's intellectual and theological origins, an essential, brilliant overview is Massimo Borghesi's *The Mind of Pope Francis: Jorge Mario Bergoglio's Intellectual Journey* (Collegeville, Minn.: Liturgical Press, 2018), which complements an earlier book of essays, Emmanuel Falque and Laure Solignac, eds., *François, Philosophe* (Paris: Salvator, 2017). Another good introduction is Thomas R. Rourke, *The Roots of Pope Francis's Social and Political Thought: From Argentina to the Vatican* (London: Rowman & Littlefield, 2016). On the influence of the "pueblo" theologians, see Juan Carlos Scannone, *La teología del Pueblo: Raíces teológicas del papa Francisco* (Maliaño, Spain: Ed. Sal Terrae, 2017); Emilce Cuda, *Para leer a Francisco. Teología, etica y política* (Buenos Aires: Manantial, 2016); Rafael Luciani, *El papa Francisco y la teología del pueblo* (Madrid: PPC-Ed., 2016); and Enrique Ciro Bianchi, *La teología de la pastoral popular de Rafael Tello: Para entender las raíces teológicas del Papa Francisco* (self-published, 2016).

See also the recent book of essays by key interpreters of Bergoglio's thinking such as Borghesi, Guzmán Carriquiry, Rocco Buttiglione, and Rodrigo Guerra López in: Brian Y. Lee and Rev. Thomas L. Knoebel, eds., *Discovering Pope Francis: The Roots of Jorge Mario Bergoglio's Thinking* (Collegeville, Minn.: Liturgical Press, 2019).

Alexandre Awi de Mello, *Maria é Minha Mãe: Encontros do Papa Francisco com Nossa Senhora* (Parede, Portugal: Lucerna, 2015) is a beautiful exploration of Francis's Marian spirituality linked to his pueblo theology.

Gerard O'Connell, *The Election of Pope Francis* (New York: Orbis Books, 2019) offers a definitive, fly-on-the-wall account of how Jorge Mario Bergoglio became pope.

Books by Bergoglio/Francis, including book-length interviews with him

The three collections of Jorge Mario Bergoglio's Jesuit writings from the 1980s and 1990s have come out in new Spanish and Vatican editions but are still (amazingly) untranslated into English. They are *Meditaciones para religiosos* (Loyola, Spain: Mensajero, 2014), *Reflexiones espirituales sobre la vida apostólica* (Loyola, Spain: Mensajero, 2013), and *Reflexiones en espe-*

ranza (Madrid: Romana, 2013). Another key text from the late 1980s has been republished with extra material: Jorge Mario Bergoglio/Francisco, *Las cartas de la tribulación*, ed. Antonio Spadaro and Diego Fares (Barcelona: Herder, 2019).

His speeches and homilies as cardinal archbishop of Buenos Aires (1998–2013) are collected in the invaluable Antonio Spadaro, SJ, ed., *En tus ojos está mi palabra. Homilías y discursos de Buenos Aires, 1999–2013* (Madrid: Ed. Claretianas, 2018). Other key texts include: *Corrupción y pecado: Algunas reflexiones en torno al tema de la corrupción* (Buenos Aires: Ed. Claretianas, 2005, 2013), *Nosotros como ciudadanos, nosotros como pueblo. Hacia un bientenario en justicia y solidaridad, 2010–2016* (Buenos Aires: Ed. Claretianas, 2014), and Bergoglio et al., *Dios en la ciudad: Primer Congreso Pastoral Urbana Región Buenos Aires* (Buenos Aires: San Pablo, 2012).

The only book-length interview with Cardinal Bergoglio was republished after his election: Sergio Rubin and Francesca Ambrogetti, *Pope Francis: Conversations with Jorge Bergoglio*, trans. Laura Dail Literary Agency (London: Hodder & Stoughton, 2013). There have been three seminal interview books with Francis: Antonio Spadaro, SJ, *A Big Heart Open to God: A Conversation with Pope Francis* (New York: HarperCollins, 2013); *The Name of God Is Mercy: A Conversation with Andrea Tornielli*, trans. Oonagh Stransky (New York: Penguin Random House, 2016); and Pope Francis with Dominique Wolton, *The Path to Change: Thoughts on Politics and Society*, trans. Shaun Whiteside (London: Bluebird, 2018). Papa Francisco, *Latinoamérica: Conversaciones con Hernán Reyes Alcaide* (Buenos Aires: Ed. Planeta, 2017) is interesting on Latin America, while *La fuerza de la vocación. La vida consagrada hoy. Una conversación con Fernando Prado, CMF* (Madrid: Pub. Claretianas, 2018) has the pope's thoughts on vocations and the religious life.

Books on Francis and his pontificate

The choice here is vast and this selection necessarily brief, beginning with a trio of books by Spanish Vatican reporters packed with beautiful anecdotes and stories whose titles capture the pope's mercy, joy, and tenderness: Javier Martínez Brocal, *El Papa de la Misericordia* (Barcelona: Planeta, 2015); Juan Vincente Boo, *El Papa de la Alegría* (Madrid: Espasa, 2016); and Eva Fernández, *El Papa de la Ternura* (Barcelona: Planeta, 2019).

For the theological resources of the reform, Yves Congar's *Power and*

Poverty in the Church: The Renewal and Understanding of Service (New York: Paulist Press, 2016) and *True and False Reform in the Church* (Collegeville, Minn.: Liturgical Press, 2011) are indispensable. So, too, indirectly, is John J. Navone, *Triumph Through Failure: A Theology of the Cross* (1984; repr., Eugene, Ore.: Wipf & Stock, 2014), originally published as *La teologia del fallimento* (Italy: Paoline, 1978).

On the thinking behind the reform, see the essays in Antonio Spadaro and Carlos Galli, eds., *La riforma e le riforme nella Chiesa* (Brescia: Ed. Queriniana, 2016). Despite the title, Massimo Faggioli's *Catholicism and Citizenship: Political Cultures of the Church in the Twenty-First Century* (Collegeville, Minn.: Liturgical Press, 2017) is really about the ecclesiological shifts of the pontificate. Antonio Spadaro, SJ, *Il nuovo mondo di Francesco. Come il Vaticano sta cambiando il mondo* (Venice: Ed. Marsilio, 2018) is a key text for understanding the thinking behind Francis's diplomacy. On women: Maria Teresa Compte Grau, *Diez cosas que el Papa Francisco propone a las mujeres* (Madrid: Claretianas, 2018) is an excellent guide.

Gerald Posner, *God's Bankers: A History of Money and Power at the Vatican* (New York: Simon & Schuster, 2015) gives a good background on Vatican finances. Francesca Immacolata Chaouqui, *Nel nome di Pietro: Ricchezze, affari, intrighi e scandali delle carte segrete della commissione del Papa* (Milan: Sperling & Kupfer, 2017) and Guanluigi Nuzzi, *Merchants in the Temple* (New York: Henry Holt, 2015) are insider accounts of the COSEA financial reform.

To understand *Amoris Laetitia*, three essential texts are: Philippe Bordeyne, *Divorcés Remariés: Ce qui change avec François* (Paris: Salvator, 2017); Stephen Walford, *Pope Francis, the Family and Divorce: In Defense of Truth and Mercy* (New York: Paulist Press, 2018); and James F. Keenan, ed., *Amoris Laetitia: A New Momentum for Moral Formation and Pastoral Practice* (Mahwah, N.J.: Paulist Press, 2018). Rocco Buttiglione has written two defenses of *Amoris* against its critics: (with Ennio Antonelli), *Terapia dell'amore ferito in "Amoris Laetitia"* (Milan: Ares, 2017); and *Risposte amichevoli ai critici di Amoris laetitia* (Milan: Ares, 2017). An excellent Argentine text is Carlos Avellaneda et al., *Para leer Amoris Laetitia: Hablemos de amor* (Buenos Aires: Agape, 2016).

On the "Viganò Operation," see the definitive account by Andrea Tornielli and Gianni Valente, *Il giorno del giudizio* (Milan: Edizioni Piemme, 2018). Frédéric Martel, *In the Closet of the Vatican: Power, Homosexuality,*

Hypocrisy, trans. Shaun Whiteside (London: Bloomsbury, 2019) is indescribable but unmissable.

Cindy Wooden and Joshua J. McElwee, eds., *A Pope Francis Lexicon* (Collegeville, Minn.: Liturgical Press, 2018) is full of gems, while *The Search for God in America*, eds. Peter Casarella and Maria Clara Bingemer (Washington, D.C.: Catholic University of America Press, 2019) has thoughtful essays on Francis's relationship with the New World.

Acknowledgments

A book as big and broad as *Wounded Shepherd* is only possible because of the generosity of many, many people who supported me in many different ways in many countries, and who in many cases have had to wait a long time to see any fruits. I need to thank especially:

- all who shared with me their knowledge and insights about Francis and the pontificate, both those who are named in the text—cardinals, bishops, priests, religious sisters and brothers, missionary disciples of many kinds—as well as many anonymous "collaborators" who prefer to stay under the radar. A special thanks to the many who agreed to be interviewed, and to those who facilitated the meetings.
- for their particular guidance and insights, a special thanks in Rome to Fathers Antonio Spadaro, SJ, and Diego Fares, SJ, of *La Civiltà Cattolica*, who have helped me untie many Bergoglio knots, to Father Michael Czerny, SJ, and Tomás Insua for help with *Laudato Si'*, and to Professor Guzmán Carriquiry, who until his retirement in 2019 was the indispensable secretary of the Pontifical Commission for Latin America and a key Francis interpreter. For their insights and friendship, thank you also to Massimo Borghesi, Rocco Buttiglione, and Rodrigo Guerra López.

- all who gave me hospitality in Latin America, where a personal introduction goes a very long way. There is no way of remembering and thanking everyone, but a special thanks for their hospitality to the Jesuit communities of Guayaquil, Quito, Bogotá, Lima, and Buenos Aires; and for their kindness Marilú Esponda (Mexico City), Gustavo Andújar (Havana), Andrés Eichmann (La Paz), Juan Pablo Cannata, Federico Wals, Roberto Bosca, Rafael Velasco, SJ, and Virginia Bonard (Buenos Aires), Mauricio López (Quito), Rosana Kcomt (Lima), Cardinal Pedro Barreto (Huancayo), and Maria Paz Lagos and Sergio Carrasco (Santiago de Chile).
- former and current communications officials in Rome for their support and kindness, then (Father Federico Lombardi, SJ, Greg Burke, Paloma García Ovejero) and now (Andrea Tornielli, Alessandro Gisotti). In Milan, a big *grazie* to Lucia Capuzzi for brokering the world of Rosa.
- in North America: Zachary Karabell, David Gibson, Christopher White, and Father James Martin, SJ, in New York; the apostolic nuncio, Archbishop Christophe Pierre, and Kim Daniels, in Washington, D.C.; Father Manuel Dorantes in Chicago; and professors Massimo Faggioli (Villanova), Peter Casarella (Notre Dame), Bill Clark (Holy Cross), and James Keenan (Boston). In Canada, thank you to Father Tom Rosica and Sebastian Gomes of Salt & Light.
- transcribers of my interviews: in Spanish, Mariana Rolón Salazar and José Antonio Michelena; in Italian, Daniele Palmer; and in English, Isabel Errington.
- the Fellows of Campion Hall, Oxford, for their friendship and support, with a special thanks to the former Master, Father James Hanvey, SJ, for helping me lift the big spiritual and theological stuff, and the current Master, Father Nick Austin, SJ, for his encouragement and kindness. Also to Father Ian Tomlinson, SJ, for his wise guidance of my inner life; and elsewhere in the British Jesuit province, to Fathers Tim Byron, SJ, and Damian Howard, SJ, for various kinds of help and support.
- editor in chief Serena Jones and her team at Henry Holt in New York for their encouragement, patience, and professionalism; and my industrious agent, Bill Barry.

- colleagues at Catholic Voices across the globe, especially Jack Valero and Yago de la Cierva, for challenging me to communicate with mercy.
- my wife, Linda, and our dogs (Wellington, Harriet, Ben, and Lily) for the love, with apologies for being grumpy and snippy when the burden of the deadlines was overwhelming.
- J, to whom this book is dedicated, for helping me "see" Francis.
- and finally Francis, for showing forth Jesus Christ in our time.

Index

About the Author

AUSTEN IVEREIGH is a British writer, journalist, and commentator specializing in the Catholic Church and the papacy of Francis, and is a Fellow in Contemporary Church History at Campion Hall, University of Oxford, from where he has a doctorate in history and politics. He writes regularly for publications in the UK and the US, including *The Tablet*, *Commonweal*, *Crux*, and *America*, and is a popular speaker and lecturer who speaks fluent Spanish, as well as Italian, French, and Portuguese. He lives in England but travels regularly to Rome, the United States, and Latin America. For more on the author, his books and articles, and his responses to reactions to *Wounded Shepherd*, visit his website austeni.org and follow him on Twitter @austeni.